Urdu Language and Literature

A Bibliography of Sources in European Languages

Urdu Language and Literature

A Bibliography of Sources in European Languages

Shabana Mahmud

MANSELL

First published 1992 by
Mansell Publishing Limited. *A Cassell Imprint*
Villiers House, 41/47 Strand, London WC2N 5JE, England
387 Park Avenue South, New York, NY 10016-8810, USA

British Library Cataloguing in Publication Data.
A catalogue record for this book
is available from the British Library.

Library of Congress Cataloging-in-Publication Data applied for.

ISBN 0-7201-2143-4

Printed and bound in Great Britain by
Biddles Ltd., Guildford and King's Lynn

To Roomana

CONTENTS

CONTENTS

FOREWORD

Over the years a number of bibliographies have appeared, listing translations from, and articles about, Urdu authors, but nothing so comprehensive as the present work has ever been produced. It covers all genres of poetry and prose, literary movements, and materials for the study of the language and its literature, and lists not only works in English but books and articles in other European languages. It is a most valuable addition to the stock of materials on Urdu.

Ralph Russell
Emeritus Reader in Urdu
University of London
April 1992

INTRODUCTION

URDU LANGUAGE AND LITERATURE

The present bibliography aims at covering the whole range of European language sources on Urdu language and literature. It includes monographs and articles from journals, Festschriften, symposiums, proceedings of conferences, and encyclopaedias. The bibliography, it is hoped, will serve as a guide to those seeking information on any aspect of the Urdu language and its literature.

Knowledge of the Urdu language in the West has come a long way from the time when the first Europeans settled in India and accorded it a number of names such as 'Hindostan' or the 'Moors'. The British called it Hindustani, a Persian word for 'Indian', and adopted the language for semi-official purposes, and then established a chair in the subject at Fort William College in Calcutta in 1800. It was probably not until the nineteenth century that the name Urdu was generally adopted for the language, a name by which it is now universally known.

Urdu - the word is of Turkish origin, meaning 'army camp'- developed in the Delhi region out of the interaction between the local population and the conquering Muslims from Central Asia in the twelfth and thirteenth centuries. It was based upon the widely spoken dialect of the area, known as 'khari boli' or 'established speech', and while retaining its Indian grammatical structure, it soon absorbed a substantial amount of vocabulary from Persian and through Persian from Arabic. The language of the Delhi court and of culture generally was Persian, and it remained so well into the eighteenth century. Urdu was given little serious attention at first. It was not until the decline of the Moghuls and the consolidation of British power over northern India as a whole that Urdu replaced Persian as the official language.

The literature produced in Urdu until the start of the nineteenth century consisted almost entirely of poetry based on Persian models. Although Urdu prose had emerged early, it was used mainly for religious and mystic writings. Later, with the establishment of Fort William College, adaptations or translations of traditional Persian and Arabic tales were produced, thus giving some impetus to prose writing. Some of the most important works on the Urdu language were produced at Fort William in the nineteenth century. In the late nineteenth and early twentieth centuries British scholars continued to make important contributions in this field, some of which are even now regarded as indispensable for students of Urdu. The present bibliography is particularly strong in its coverage of the early publications.

By the late nineteenth century far-reaching changes began to take place in the attitudes of writers and Muslims generally. With the suppression of the 1857 revolt and the decline of the role long played by Delhi and Lucknow as the great centres of Urdu, a multitude of changes and modernizations were introduced. Muslim thinkers were forced to re-evaluate old ideas and values and face the new political and social realities of British rule. One of the most important figures to emerge was Sir Syed Ahmad Khan (1817-1898). Sir Syed almost single-handedly started a reform movement (later known as the Aligarh Movement) in the Muslim community which gave birth to a didactic and reformist trend in literature, introducing political and social themes into both poetry and prose. This trend, expressed in simple and direct language, marked a radical change.

From around the turn of the century Muhammad Iqbal (1873-1938) further changed the form and content of Urdu poetry. He used both Urdu and Persian poetry as vehicles for the expression of his pan-Islamic philosophy.

The period following the First World War, right up to the late 1930's, was one of increasing political, economic and social upheaval in India. Mass politics were emerging through the Indian freedom movements. In the 1930's, writers organized themselves in the Progressive Writers Movement, the most significant literary movement of the twentieth century, which made important and fresh contributions to the form and content of Urdu literature. Urdu writing emerged violently and defiantly and writers began to experiment with new styles to meet the changing reality that faced them. One of the important developments was the emergence of women writers, which has added a new dimension and has significantly enriched Urdu literature.

Altogether, the twentieth century has seen a remarkable development in all aspects of the Urdu language and its literature. Urdu today is the official language of Pakistan, where it is increasingly used at most administrative and educational levels. In India, it is one of the country's official languages, and has a large number of speakers in the northern states of Uttar Pradesh and Bihar. It is also the state language of Jammu and Kashmir. A significant phenomenon of the twentieth century has also been the large scale emigration of Urdu speakers to other countries. As a result Urdu has taken root in all the areas of immigration - in East Africa, Fiji, the Caribbean, Mauritius, and on the western coast of Canada and the USA. Later in the century Pakistanis began to settle in Britain and to a lesser extent in Scandinavia, other European countries, and North America, and later still began to go as temporary workers to the Arab countries.

In Europe, North America, and the former Soviet Union, chairs of Urdu studies were established in major universities, and important works of research and translations are being produced in the West. In contemporary Britain, Urdu is one of the most widely spoken languages, other than English, and is taught in many schools.

THE BIBLIOGRAPHY

A number of bibliographic sources have been used in the compilation of this work. Most important among these are; *Bibliography of South Asian studies* (Michigan: Association for Asian Studies, 1941-); *Linguistic bibliography/Bibliographie linguistique* (Utrecht-Brussels, 1939-); *Library of Congress Accessions list: South Asia* (Washington 1962-); Frances Pritchett's *Urdu literature: a bibliography of English language sources on Urdu literature* (New Delhi: Manohar, 1979), and the automated version of the *British Library general catalogue*. Entries were also collected from journals in European languages serving the disciplines of linguistics, philology and literature. Much information has been obtained by correspondence with librarians and custodians of collections and through personal visits to research libraries. Although a great number of relevant post-graduate dissertations have been submitted in this field, most of these are unpublished, and only a few have been listed. In principle every publication that was available has been included. Numerous works on Iqbal are included, though completeness has not been attempted in view of the enormous amount of publication in this area which would seem to warrant a separate bibliography of its own.

A few titles not, strictly speaking, directly related to Urdu have been included when these seemed to be of use to Urdu scholars.

The bibliography is arranged by subjects. The classification has evolved through the attempt to find the most practically convenient divisions into which the subject matter falls, rather than being built up from preconceived ideas of what was proper and logical. It was, however, quite impossible to read every one of the more than three thousand items listed in the book, and one can not be completely certain that every item has been assigned to its correct subject designation. No claim can therefore be made for complete accuracy or consistency of treatment in this respect. Where it seemed useful to do so, cross-references have been given, but these have been kept to the minimum. It has been seen as convenient to subdivide chronologically the contents of some of the subject categories, that is, to separate twentieth century publications from those of the nineteenth century and earlier.

A few words may be said about some of the subject divisions themselves. The rubric 'Works of Reference' includes general bibliography and catalogues relating to all aspects of the Urdu language and its literature; more specific bibliographies are entered under the relevant subjects. Under the rubric 'Language', the subdivision on language history includes works on philology and linguistics, and reports on language policy and the relationship between Urdu and Hindi. The section on 'Literature' includes literary histories and criticism further subdivided by genre and movement. In the section on 'Poetry', the entries for anthologies provide the names of authors whose poems are included, but not the titles of the poems themselves. However, in the section on 'Prose', the entries for anthologies provide not only the names of authors represented but also, wherever possible, the titles of stories included. Lastly, in the genre of 'Dastan' (often an adaptation or translation from Persian), entries are given under the names of the original authors, with cross-references to the Urdu translators whose names are more commonly known.

Within each division all entries are entered alphabetically under the name of the author or compiler, followed by the title. In the case of anonymous works, the entry is under the title. Bold type is used for the names of the authors and italics for the titles. For journal articles, the names of the authors are also in bold letters, the title of the article in quotation marks and the title of the journal in italics. Information following the title includes the volume and issue number, the date in parentheses and then pagination. It has also been decided to include items even when some standard detail in the bibliographic entry was missing, such as the place or date of publication, or the volume, date, or pagination of articles. The appended 'Index of Authors' provides names of authors, joint authors, editors and translators, and short titles in the case of anonymous works. The index does not include the names of the literary authors treated in the 'Poetry', 'Prose', 'Drama' and 'Dastan' sections of the bibliography; they are listed separately after this introduction.

ACKNOWLEDGEMENTS

I wish to acknowledge all the help that has been generously offered to me during the compilation of this book. The names of individual libraries and members of library staff who have given me assistance are far too many to be mentioned individually, but there are certain persons who have provided specialised information, encouragement and useful advice.

INTRODUCTION

Dr Christina Oesterheld of the South Asia Institute, University of Heidelberg, Professor Rahim Raza of the Istituto Universitario Orientale, Napoli, and Dr Ludmilla Vasilyeva of the Institute of Oriental Studies, Moscow, have been extremely generous in providing information on current research in Germany, Italy and the (former) Soviet Union. I am particularly indebted to Qazi Mahmudul Haq of the Oriental and India Office Collections (OIOC), The British Library, for this bibliography was his original idea, and it was with his initial encouragement and help that I embarked upon the project. Together with Professor Christopher Shackle of SOAS, he also assisted in the initial arrangement of the bibliography. Brad Sabin Hill and Catherine Pickett of OIOC helped me with additions and suggestions, and most generously aided me in the laborious task of correction and proof reading, making many corrections and improvements. My thanks are also due to Iftikhar Arif, Director General of the Pakistan Academy of Letters, Islamabad, who with his world-wide contacts introduced me to individuals and institutions in Europe and Pakistan and eased my task enormously. Finally I must thank Joan Francis for preparing the camera-ready copy with such speed and accuracy.

August 1992   Shabana Mahmud

LITERARY AUTHORS TREATED IN THE BIBLIOGRAPHY

WORKS OF REFERENCE

Bibliographies

This section includes only General Bibliographies. Bibliographies of individual authors are cited under relevant sections.

1 Ali, R. Mohammad
"Bibliographical control in Pakistan". *International Library Review* 18, 1 (January 1986), pp. 33-56.
Examines the major instruments available for the bibliographical control of what is published in Pakistan, notably the *Pakistan National Bibliography* and the Library of Congress's *Accession list for Pakistan, South Asia.*

2 Ali, S. Amjad
Book world of Pakistan. Karachi: National Book Centre of Pakistan, 1967. 48p.

3 Anwar, Mumtaz A. and Tiwana, Bashir Ali
Pakistan: a bibliography of books and articles published in the United Kingdom from 1947-64. Lahore: Research Society of Pakistan, University of the Punjab, 1969. 102p.

4 Besterman, Theodore
A world bibliography of oriental bibliographies ... London, 1939-1940. 2 vols.

2nd ed. 1947-1949. 3 vols.

4th ed. Revised and enlarged. With Supplement. Lausanne: Societa Bibliographica, 1965- .
7 vols.

[Another ed.] Revised by J D Pearson. Oxford: Blackwell, 1975. 727 cols.

5 *Bibliography of Asian Studies.* Ann Arbor, Michigan: Association of Asian Studies, 1941. Annual.
Before 1956 it was called *Far Eastern Quarterly*, and until 1967 published as a special issue of the *Journal of Asian Studies*. Two complete versions of the earlier bibliographies, arranged both by author and subject, have been published (Boston: G.K. Hall), covering 1941-65 and 1966-70 respectively. South Asia was covered in the scope of the bibliography from 1955.

6 *Books from Pakistan published during the decade of reforms, 1958-1968.* Karachi: National Book Centre of Pakistan, 1968. 159p.
A guidelist.

7 Case, Margaret H.
South Asian history, 1750-1950: a guide to periodicals, dissertations and newspapers. Princeton, New Jersey: Princeton University Press, 1968. 561p.
"Language and Literature - Urdu": pp. 339-347.
Nearly all of the 7,000 entries have brief annotations.

8   Cheema, Pervaiz Iqbal
A select bibliography of periodical literature on India and Pakistan, 1947-70. Islamabad:
National Commission on Historical and Cultural Research, 1976, 1979, 1984. 3 vols.
Over 5,000 entries from 575 journals covering a wide range of topics. All sources are in
English. The first volume deals with Pakistan, the second with India, and the third with both.

9   Coppola, Carlo
"Addendum to A bibliography of English sources for the Urdu language and literature".
Mahfil 1, 1, pp. 1-12.

10   Flemming, Leslie and Narang, Gopi Chand
"An additional bibliography of English sources for the Urdu language and literature".
Literature East and West 15, 1 (1972), pp. 17-37.

11   Kesavan, B.S.
The national bibliography of Indian literature 1901-1953. New Delhi, 1974. 799p.
Urdu titles are listed in the fourth volume.

12   Mohanty, Jatindra Mohan
Indian literature in English translation: a bibliography. Mysore: Central Institute of Indian
.Languages, 1984. 187p.

13   Naim, C.M.
"A bibliography of English sources for the Urdu language and literature". *Literature East
and West 7* (Spring 1963), pp. 17-18.

14   Patterson, Maureen, L.P. and Alspaugh, William J.
South Asian civilizations: a bibliographical synthesis. Chicago; London: University of
Chicago Press, 1981. 853p.
"Literature of Pakistan in Urdu and English": p. 480.

15   Pearson, J.D.
South Asian bibliography: a handbook and guide. Hassocks, England: Harvester Press;
Atlantic Highlands, New Jersey: Humanities Press, 1979. 381p.
Contains detailed descriptive articles, arranged both by country and by subject, on the
bibliographical resources available for study on South Asian topics. Includes a section on
notable books on Urdu language and literature: pp. 199-201.

16   Pritchett, Frances W.
Urdu literature: a bibliography of English language sources. New Delhi: Manohar, 1979.
162p.

17   Shaw, Graham and Quraishi, Salimuddin
*The bibliography of South Asian periodicals: a union list of periodicals in South Asian
languages.* Sussex: John Spiers, 1982. 135p.
Urdu titles are listed on pp. 111-134.

18 Sher Singh and Sadhu, S.N.
Indian books in print, 1972: a bibliography of Indian books published up to Deceumber 1971, in English language. Delhi: Indian Bureau of Bibliographies, 1972. 3 vols.

19 Zenker, J.T.
Bibliotheca Orientalis: manuel de bibliographie orientale. Leipzig: Chez Guillaume Engelman, 1861. 2 vols.
Hindustani titles are listed in the second volume.

WORKS OF REFERENCE

Catalogues

20   **Abdul Aziz**
The Imperial library of the Mughuls. Ed. Shakoor Ahsan. Lahore: Panjab University Press,
1967. 62p.

21   **Abdul Moid**
Urdu language collections in American libraries. Ph.D. diss. University of Illinois, Urbana,
1964. 287p.
"Union list of authors whose Urdu works are available in American libaries": pp. 173-275.

22   **Agra College Library**
*Catalogue of English, Oriental, and translated works in the library of the Agra College at the
close of 1854.* Agra: Printed at the Secundra Orphan Press, 1855.
Contains list of works on poetry, grammar, education and drama.

23   **Allahabad Public Library**
Alphabetical catalogue of Arabic, Persian and Urdu books in the Allahabad Public Library.
Allahabad, 1911. 2 pts.

24   **Asiatic Society Library, Calcutta**
Author-catalogue of the Haidarabad collection of manuscripts and printed books. Calcutta:
Printed for the Asiatic Society of Bengal at the Baptist Mission Press, 1913. 62p.
"Collection of Urdu, Arabic, and Persian works ... presented in 1907 by Nawab Azizjang
Bahadur of Haidarabad to the Society's Library".

25   **Barrois, Théophile**
*Catalogue des livres Persans, Hindoustanis, Malabars, Sanskrits, Chinois, Tartares-
Mantchous, Japonais, Malais, Géorgiens, Kurdes, Wolofes, Esquimaux, Éthiopiens... qui se
trouvent à la librairie étrangère de T. Barrois fils...* Paris, 1832. 22p.

26   **Bibliothèque Nationale, Paris**
Catalogue sommaire des manuscrits indiens, indo-chinois et malayo-polynesiens. Comp.
A. Cabaton. Paris: Bibliothèque Nationale, 1912. 319p.

27   **Board of Examiners Library, Calcutta**
*Catalogue of books in Oriental languages in the Library of the Board of Examiners, late
College of Fort William.* Prepared under the superintendence of G.S.A. Ranking. Calcutta:
Govt. Press, 1903-05.
Vol. 1: Catalogue ...
Vol. 2: Index - arranged alphabetically according to the names of work.
Vol. 3. Index - arranged alphabetically according to the names of authors.

28   **Bodleian Library, Oxford**
*Catalogue of the Persian, Turkish, Hindustani and Pashtu mansucripts in the Bodleian
Library, Oxford.* Comp. Hermann Ethé and Eduard Sachau. Oxford: Bodleian Library,
1889-1930. 1766 cols.

29 **Bombay University Library**
A descriptive catalogue of the Arabic, Persian and Urdu manuscripts in the Library of the University of Bombay. Comp. Abdul Qadir-i Sarfaraz Khan Bahadur Shaikh. Bombay, 1935. 430p.

30 **British Library. Oriental and India Office Collections**
Catalogue of the Hindi, Panjabi and Hindustani manuscripts in the Library of the British Museum. Comp. James Fuller Blumhardt. London: British Museum, 1899. 458p.

31 — • *Catalogue of the Hindustani manuscripts in the Library of the India Office.* Comp. James Fuller Blumhardt. London: India Office Library, 1926. 171p.

32 — • *Catalogue of Hindustani printed books in the Library of the British Museum.* Comp. James Fuller Blumhardt. London: British Museum, 1889. 458 cols.

33 — • *Catalogue of the Library of the India Office.* Vol II, pt. 2. Hindustani books. Comp. James Fuller Blumhardt. London: India Office Library, 1900. 380p.

34 — • *Catalogue of Urdu books in the India Office Library, 1800-1920.* Comp. Salimuddin Quraishi. London: India Office Library, 1982. 280p. Supplementary to James Fuller Blumhardt's catalogue of 1900.
Catalogue of Urdu tracts.

35 — • *A descriptive catalogue of the uncatalogued Arabic, Persian and Urdu manuscripts, relevant to the history and culture of the Muslims in India, acquired by the British Museum since the publication of its last printed catalogues ...* Comp. Qazi Mahmudul Haq. London [in preparation].

36 — • *Publications proscribed by the Government of India. A catalogue of the collections in the India Office Library and Records and the Department of Oriental Manuscripts and Printed Books, British Library Reference Division.* Eds. Graham Shaw and Mary Lloyd. London: The British Library Board, 1985. 203p.
The Urdu section includes largely nationalistic poetry and religious and political tracts. pp. 140-169.

37 — • *A supplementary catalogue of Hindustani books in the Library of the British Museum acquired during the years 1889-1908.* Comp. James Fuller Blumhardt. London: British Museum, 1909. 678 cols.

38 **Calcutta University Library**
Catalogue of books in the Calcutta University Library: Sanskrit, Pali, Arabic, Persian, Bengali, Urdu, Philology. Calcutta: Calcutta University, 1931. 288p.

39 **Cambridge University Library**
A handlist of the Muhammadan manuscripts, including all those written in the Arabic character, preserved in the Library of the University of Cambridge. Comp. Edward G. Browne. Cambridge: University Press, 1900. 440p.

40 — • *A supplementary handlist of the Muhammadan manuscripts in the libraries of the University and Colleges of Cambridge.* Cambridge: University Press, 1922. 348p.

41   **Dacca University Library**
Descriptive catalogue of the Persian, Urdu and Arabic manuscripts in the Dacca University Library. Comp. Abul Barkat Muhammad Habibullah. Dacca: University Library Publication, 1966-68. 2 vols.
Includes a note on the history of the manuscript collection by M. Siddiq Khan.

42   **Deccan College Research Institute, Poona**
A descriptive handlist of Arabic, Persian and Hindustani mss. belonging to the Satara Historical Museum at present held at the Deccan College Research Institute, Poona. Comp. C.H. Shaikh. Satara: Historical Museum, 1943.
Reprinted from the Bulletin of the Deccan College Research, vol. 4, no. 3.

43   **Deloncle, François**
Catalogue des livres orientaux et autres composant la bibliothèque de feu M. Garcin de Tassy; suivi du catalogue des manuscrits hindustanis, persans, arabes, turcs. Paris, 1879.

44   **Desgranges, A., Woepcke, F., Bianchi, Th.**
Catalogue des livres en langues européennes et des ouvrages en langues orientales provenant des bibliothèques de feu MM. Alix Desgranges, Woepcke et Bianchi, membres de la Société asiatique. Paris, 1865.

45   **Durgah Library, Bahawalpur**
A descriptive catalogue of the oriental manuscripts in the Durgah Library, Uch harif Gilani. Comp. Ghulam Sarwar. Bahawalpur: Urdu Academy, 1961. 219p.

46   **Eton College Library**
Catalogue of the oriental manuscripts in the library of Eton College. Oxford, 1940.

47   **Forbes, Duncan**
Catalogue of a valuable collection of oriental manuscripts, Persian, Arabic, Pali, Urdu, and Turkish, chiefly from the library of the late Dr Duncan Forbes... London, 1879.

48   **Fort William College**
Catalogue of books in oriental languages in the library of the Board of Examiners, late College of Fort William. Calcutta, 1903-05.

49   **Government Oriental Manuscripts Library, Madras**
Alphabetical index of manuscripts in the ... Library ... Sanskrit, Telugu, Tamil, Kanarese, Malayalam, Mahráthi, Uriya, Arabic, Persian and Hindustani. Madras: Govt. Press, 1893. 9 pts.
Includes works on Urdu readers, grammars, literature, poetry and fiction.

50   — • *An alphabetical index of Urdu manuscripts in the Government Oriental Manuscripts Library, Madras.* Comp. S. Kuppuswami Sastri. Madras: Government Press, 1931. p. 4 [35].

51   — • *An alphabetical index of Urdu, Arabic and Persian manuscripts in the Government Oriental Manuscripts Library.* Comp. T. Cantiracekaran, et al. Madras: Government Oriental Manuscripts Library, 1963. 77p.

52 — • *A descriptive catalogue of the Islamic manuscripts in the Government Oriental Manuscripts Library, Madras.* Comp. P.P. Subrahmanya Sastri and T. Chandrasekharan. Madras: Government Press, 1939. 3 vols.

53 **Government Oriental Manuscripts Library and Research Institute, Hyderabad**
An alphabetical subject wise index of Urdu... manuscripts, available in the Andhra Pradesh Government Oriental Manuscripts Library and Research Institute... Comp. Mir Karamath Ali. Hyderabad: The Institute, 1985. 106p.

54 **Husain, Agha Iftikhar**
A catalogue of manuscripts in Paris: Urdu and Punjabi and Sindhi. Karachi: Urdu Development Board, 1967. 35, 30p.
English and Urdu.

55 **Hyderabad Museum**
Catalogue of the Arabic, Persian and Urdu manuscripts in the Hyderabad Museum. Comp. Muhammad Ghaus. Hyderabad: Director, Archaeological Dept., Govt. of Hyderabad, 1953. 131p.

56 **Kaul, Hari Krishen**
Urdu manuscripts: a descriptive bibliography of manuscripts in Delhi libraries. Assisted by Salahud-Din Khan. New Delhi: Heritage Publishers, 1977. 228p.

57 **Khalsa College. Sikh History Research Department**
A catalogue of Punjabi and Urdu manuscripts in the Sikh History Research Department uptil 31 March 1963. Comp. Kirpal Singh. Amritsar: Khalsa College, 1963. 251p.

58 **King's College, Cambridge**
Catalogue of the oriental manuscripts in the Library of King's College, Cambridge. Comp. E.H. Palmer. London, 1867.

59 **Karachi University Library**
Catalogue of rare books. Karachi: Karachi University Library, 1974. 2 vols. (v. 2: Karachi University Library publications; no. 4).
Includes works on language, fine arts, literature, history, biography, travel.

60 **Lucknow University Library**
Catalogue of oriental maunscripts in the Lucknow University Library... Comp. Kali Prasad. Lucknow: The Library, 1951. 75p.

61 **Mahmud, Shabana**
Catalogue of the political publications in Urdu (1900-1947) in the British Library. London. [in preparation 1992].

62 **Mehren, August Ferdinand Michael**
Codices Persici, Turcici, Hindustanici variique alii Bibliothecae Regiae Hafniensis. Hafniae (Copenhagen): Ex officina J.H. Schultzii, 1857. pp. 73-74. (Codices Orientales Bibliothecae Regiae Hafniensis, pt.3.)

63   **Mulla Firuz Library, Bombay**
Catalogue raisonné of the Arabic, Hindostani, Persian and Turkish mss. in the Mulla Firuz Library. Comp. E. Rehatsek. Bombay, 1873.

64   **Musharaf-ul-Hukk, Mahommed**
Katalog der Bibliothek der Deutschen Morgenländischen Gesellschaft. Zweiter Band. Handschriften. Teil B: Persische und hindustanische Handschriften. Leipzig, 1911. 76p. Hindustani: 2.

65   — • *Verzeichnis der persischen und hindustanischen Handschriften der Bibliothek der Deutschen Morgenländischen Gesellschaft zu Halle a.S.* Inaugural-Dissertation. Leipzig: Deutsche Morgenländische Gesellshaft, 1911.

66   **National Library of Wales**
Catalogue of Oriental manuscripts: Persian, Arabic and Hindustani. Comp. Hermann Ethé. Aberystwyth: The National Library of Wales, 1916. 30p.

67   **New College of the Free Church of Scotland, Edinburgh**
A handlist of the Arabic, Persian and Hindustani mss. of New College, Edinburgh. Comp. R.B. Serjeant. London: Luzac and Co., 1942. 15p.

68   **Ouseley, William**
Catalogue of several hundred manuscript works in various Oriental languages. London: A.J. Valpy, 1831. pp. 20-22.

69   **Paulinus, a Sancto Bartholomaeo**
Musei Borgiani Velitris codices manuscripti Avenses, Peguani, Siamici, Malabarici, Indostani. Romae, 1793. 266p.
"Die Handschriften früher im Collegio de Propaganda Fide in Rom, befinden sich seit 1902 in der Biblioteca Vaticana".

70   **Pearson, J.D.**
Oriental manuscripts in Europe and North America: a survey. Zug: Inter Documentation, 1971. 515p.
Indic languages: pp. 347-390.

71   **Pertsch, Wilhelm**
Die orientalischen Handschriften der Herzoglichen Bibliothek zu Gotha. Gotha: Friedrich Andreas Perthes, 1893.

72   **Poleman, I.H.**
A census of Indic manuscripts in the United States and Canada. New Haven, Conn., 1938. (America Oriental Series, vol. 12).

73   **Preussische Staatsbibliothek, Berlin**
Katalog der Handbibliothek der orientalischen Abteilung. Leipzig: Harrassowitz, 1929. 573p.

74   **Pritchett, Frances W.**
South Asian popular literature (Hindi and Urdu) collection. Chicago: Center for Research Libraries, 1983. 75p.

75   **Reference Library of the Provincial Museum, N.W.P and Oudh**
Catalogue of the Reference Library of the Provincial Museum, N.W.P. and Oudh. Corrected to 1st December 1891. Comp. G.D. Ganguli. Allahabad: Govt. Press, 1892. 169p. Appendix II: Classified List of Arabic, Persian, and Urdu Manuscripts in the Reference Library of the Provincial Museum ... Comp. Munshi Chhote Lal.

76   **Royal Asiatic Society, London**
Catalogue of Arabic, Persian, Hindustani, and Turkish mss. in the Library of the Royal Asiatic Society. Comp. O. Codrington. London, 1892.

77   — • *A descriptive catalogue of the uncatalogued Oriental manuscripts, relevant to the history and culture of the Muslims in India, acquired by the Royal Asiatic Society since the publication of its last printed catalogue ...* Comp. Qazi Mahmudul Haq. London. [in preparation].

78   **Siddiqui, Sarwar Ahmad**
Catalogue of Arabic, Persian and Urdoo manuscripts presented for the Dacca University by Khan Bahadur ... Ahmad Siddiqui. Dacca, [1929]. 24p.

79   **Sprenger, Aloys**
A catalogue of the Arabic, Persian and Hindustany manuscripts of the libraries of the King of Oudh. Calcutta: Govt. of India, 1854. 2 vols.
Vol 1. Includes Persian and Hindustani poetry.

80   **Stewart, Charles**
A descriptive catalogue of the Oriental Library of the late Tippo Sultan of Mysore. To which are prefixed memoirs of Hyder Ali Khan, and his son Tipoo Sultan. Cambridge: University Press, 1809.

81   **Thwaytes, Edmund Charles**
Dakani manuscripts. Containing 50 specimens of Hindustani hand-writing, produced in facsimile, accompanied by Hindustani printed transcriptions, and English translations. Madras: Addison and Co., 1892.

82   **United Provinces Congress Committee. Committee on Adult Literacy**
Annotated Urdu bibliography. Comp. M.H. Langley. Landaur printed, 1944. 385p.

83   **Uttar Pradesh State Archives**
An alphabetical index of Persian, Arabic, and Urdu manuscripts in the State Archives of Uttar Pradesh. Allahabad, [1968].

84   **Victoria Memorial**
Manuscripts in Arabic, Persian, and Urdu: a descriptive catalogue. Calcutta: Victoria Memorial, 1973. 51p.

85   **Weitbrecht, H.U.**
A descriptive catalogue and review of Urdu Christian literature, 1902-1907. Lahore, 1908.

86   **Zaidi, Mujahid Husain**
"Aloys Sprengers Beitrag zum Urdu-Studium". In: *18. Deutscher Orientalistentag 1972 in Lübeck. Vorträge.* Ed. Wolfgang Voigt. Wiesbaden: Steiner, 1974, pp. 259-265.

87   — • "Hindustani-Handschriften in Deutschland".   *Zeitschrift der Deutschen Morgenländischen Gesellschaft.* (Stuttgart), Suppl. 1-2, pp. 546-556.

88   — • *Urdu-Handschriften.*   (*Verzeichnis der orientalischen Handschriften in Deutschland*, Band XXV). Wiesbaden: Franz Steiner Verlag, 1973. 104p.
With a note on Benjamin Schultz's *Grammatica Indostanica*, 1745.

LANGUAGE

Dictionaries

BIBLIOGRAPHY

89   **Calcutta National Library**
A bibliography of dictionaries and encyclopaedias in Indian languages. Calcutta, 1964.
165p.

90   **Navlani, K. and Gidwani, N.N.**
Dictionaries in Indian languages: a bibliography. Jaipur: Sarawah Publications, 1972. 370p.

91   **Pattanayak, D.P.**
Indian languages: bibliography of grammars, dictionaries and teaching materials. 2nd ed.
New Delhi: Education Resources Center, 1973. 91p.

NINTEENTH CENTURY AND EARLIER

92   **Abdool Wadud**
New romanized dictionary, English and Urdu. Calcutta: Thacker, Spink and Co., 1876.

93   *An Anglo-Roman Urdu dictionary in the English Roman and Persian characters.*
Lucknow: "Newul Kishore" Press, 1898. 1120p.

94   **Blochmann, Heinrich Ferdinand**
English and Urdu school dictionary. Romanized. 8th ed. Calcutta: Calcutta School Book
Society, 1877.

95   — • *Romanized school dictionary, English and Urdu.* 7th ed. Calcutta: Calcutta
School Book Society's Press, 1867. 180p.

96   **Brice, Nathanie**
Dictionary, Hindustani and English. Romanized. 3rd ed. Revised by E.J. Lazarus.
Calcutta, 1847.

[Another ed.] Benares, 1880.

97   — • *A romanized Hindustani and English dictionary; designed for the use of schools,
and for vernacular students of the language.* London: Trübner and Co., 1864. 357p.

3rd ed. Benares: Medical Hall Press, 1880.

98   **Carmichael-Smyth, William**
A dictionary, Hindoostanee and English; abridged from the 4th edition of J. Taylor... Ed.
W.H. Hunter. London, 1820.

99   Craven, Thomas
The gem dictionary, in English and Hindustani. Lucknow: Methodist Episcopal Church Press, 1881. 106p.

100   — • *The people's dictionary in English and Roman-Urdu: an etymological, idiomatic and illustrated dictionary.* Lucknow: American Methodist Mission Press, 1880. 200p.

101   — • *The popular dictionary in English-Hindustani and Hindustani-English, with a number of useful tables.* London and Lucknow: Methodist Episcopal Church Press, 1881. 200, 200p.

[Another ed.] Revised and enlarged by B.H. Badley. Lucknow, 1889.

102   — • *The royal dictionary, English-Hindustani.* London: Bell and Sons, 1895.

103   — • *The royal school dictionary in English and Roman-Urdu, etymological, pronouncing and idiomatic.* Lucknow, 1880. 274p.

104   — • *The royal school dictionary in English and Roman Urdu: a pronouncing, derivative, idiomatic and illustrated dictionary.* Lucknow: Methodist Episcopal Church Press, 1881. 384p.

105   — • *The royal school dictionary. In two parts, English and Hindustani, and Hindustani and English.* Lucknow: Methodist Publishing House, 1893. 457, 600p.

106   Deloncle, François
Dictionnaire hindoustani-français et français-hindoustani, suivi d'un vocabulaire mythologique, historique et géographique de l'Inde, publié sous la direction de M. Garcin de Tassy. Paris, 1875.

107   Dobbie, Robert Sheddon
A pocket dictionary of English and Hindoostani. London, 1846-1847. 222p.

108   D'Rozario, P.S.
A dictionary of the principal languages spoken in the Bengal Presidency, viz English, Bangali, and Hindustani, in the Roman character ... Calcutta, 1837.

109   Durga Prasad, Munshi
The student's practical dictionary: containing English words with English and Urdu meanings in Persian character. Allahabad: Ram Narain Lal, 1897. 764p.

110   *English and Hindustani dictionary: a romanised English and Hindustani dictionary, designed for the use of schools ... and for English students.* Revised and enlarged by Henry Fanthome... Lucknow: Nawal Kishore Press, 1872. 183p.

111   Fallon, S.W., et al.
A new Hindustani-English dictionary, with illustrations from Hindustani literature and folklore. Benaras: E.J. Lazarus and Co.; London: Trübner and Co., 1879. 1216p.

[Another ed.] Assisted by Lala Faqir Chand and others. Benaras and London, 1883.

112 **Fergusson, John**
A dictionary of the Hindostan language, in two parts. *I. English and Hindostani*
II. Hindostani and English ... To which is prefixed a grammar of the Hindostan language.
London, 1773.

113 **Forbes, Duncan**
A dictionary, Hindustani and English to which is added a reversed part English and
Hindustani. 2nd ed. enlarged. London: Wm. H. Allen and Co., 1848. 2 vols.(in 1).

[Another ed.] London, 1859.

114 — • *Dictionary, Urdu and English.* Lahore: Ali Kamran, 1986. 802p.
Reprint of the first part of: *A Dictionary, Hindustani and English*, 2nd ed., published in
London, 1857.

115 — • *English and Hindustani dictionary.* 2nd ed. London: Wm. H. Allen and Co.,
1866.
Hindustani in Persian and Roman characters.

116 — • *A smaller Hindustani and English dictionary: printed entirely in the Roman*
character. London, 1862.

117 **Gilchrist, John Borthwick**
A dictionary, English and Hindoostanee, in which the words are marked with their
distinguishing initials; as Hinduwee, Arabic and Persian, whence the Hindoostanee ... is
evidently formed. Calcutta: Stuart and Cooper, 1787-1790. 2 vols.
Hindustani in Roman characters.

118 — • *A dictionary, English and Hindoostanee. To which is prefixed a grammar of the*
Hindustani language. Calcutta: Part I: Stuart and Cooper, 1786. Part II: Cooper and
Upjohn, 1790.
Hindustani in Persian and Roman characters.

119 — • *Hindoostani philology: comprising a dictionary, English and Hindoostanee, also*
Hindoostanee and English; with a grammatical introduction ... 2nd ed. with many additions
and improvements by Thomas Roebuck. 1825.
A reprint of the 1810 edition. Hindustani in Roman characters.

120 **Gladwin, Francis**
A dictionary, Persian, Hindoostanee, and English: including synonyma. Calcutta:
T. Hubbard, 1809. 2 vols.

121 **Harris, Henry**
Dictionary, English and Hindoostany: to which is annexed a copious and useful alphabetical
list of proper names of men, women, towns... a great majority of which appear to be of
Persian, Arabic or Indian original. Madras: the author, 1790.

122   *Hindustani school dictionary. English and Urdu.* Calcutta, 1854.
Hindustani in Roman characters.

123   **Hunter, William**
Dictionary, Hindoostanee and English. Calcutta: Hindustani Press, 1808. 2 vols.

124   **Mahdee, Mohamed**
A dictionary, English, Hindoostanee and Persian. Madras, 1851. 576p.

125   **Misra, Mathuraprasada**
A trilingual dictionary, being a comprehensive lexicon, in English, Urdu, and Hindi, exhibiting the syllabi, pronunciation, and etymology of English words. With explanation in English, Urdu and Hindi in the Roman character. Benares: E.J. Lazarus, 1865.

126   **Platts, John Thompson**
A dictionary of Urdu, classical Hindi and English. London: Sampson Low, Marston and Co., 1884. 1259p.

127   *The pocket dictionary with Hindustani meanings.* Allahabad: Ram Narain Lal, 1896.
134p.

128   *Practical dictionary, English-Urdu.* Allahabad, 1897.

129   **Ramacharana**
School dictionary, English and Urdu. Meerut, 1876. 224p.

130   *Royal school dictionary in English and Roman Urdu.* Lucknow, 1880.

131   **Sadasukh Lal**
An Anglo-Urdu dictionary. Allahabad, 1873.

132   **Sangaji, S.**
A handy Urdu-English dictionary; based on Shakespear and the best modern authorities. Madras: S.P.C.K. Press, 1899. 938p.

133   **Shakespear, John**
A dictionary, Hindustani and English. London: the author, 1817. 837p.

2nd ed. London: Cox and Baylis, 1820.

134   — • *Dictionary, Hindustani and English; with a copious index, fitting the work to serve also as a dictionary English and Hindustani.* London: Printed for the author, 1834.

135   — • *A dictionary, Hindustani and English, and English and Hindustani, the latter being entirely new.* 4th. ed. London, 1849.

136   *The student's practical dictionary, containing English words, with English and Urdu meanings in Persian character.* Allahabad, 1897.

137   **Taylor, Joseph**
*A dictionary, Hindoostanee and English originally compiled for his own private use by
Joseph Taylor*. Revised and prepared for the press, with the assistance of staff of the Fort
William College, by William Hunter. Calcutta, 1808. 2 vols.

138   — • *A dictionary, Hindoostanee and English, abridged from the quarto edition of ...
Joseph Taylor, as edited by William Hunter*. By William Carmichael-Smyth. London, 1820.

139   **Thompson, Joseph T.**
A dictionary in Oordoo and English, arranged according to the order of the English alphabet.
Serampore, 1838.

140   — • *An English and Oordoo school dictionary in Roman characters, with the
accentuation of the Oordoo words calculated to facilitate their pronunciation*.   2nd ed.
Serampore, 1834.

3rd ed. with... additions and improvements. Calcutta, 1841.

141   — • *An English and Oordoo dictionary in Roman characters. An Oordoo and English
dictionary abridged from the larger work*. Calcutta: the author, 1852.   332p.

142   **Yates, Williams**
A dictionary, Hindustani and English. London and Calcutta: J.Madden, 1847. 589p.

TWENTIETH CENTURY

143 Abdul Haq
Advance twentieth century dictionary: English into Urdu... 6th ed. Revised and enlarged by Abdul Haq. Delhi: Educational Publishing House, 1979. 800p.

144 *Anjuman's Urdu-English dictionary. Anjuman ki Urdu-Angrezi lughat.* Karachi: Anjuman-i Taraqqi-yi Urdu, 1977. 1028p.

145 — • *The English-Urdu pocket dictionary.* Karachi: Anjuman-i Taraqqi-yi Urdu, 1971.

146 — • *The popular English-Urdu dictionary.* Karachi: Anjuman-i Taraqqi-yi Urdu, 1970. 746p.

147 — • *The standard English-Urdu dictionary.* Aurangabad: Anjuman-i Urdu Press, 1937. 1513p.

4th ed. Karachi: Anjuman-i Taraqqi-yi Urdu, 1985.
Introduction in Urdu.

148 — • *The student's standard English-Urdu dictionary.* Karachi: Anjuman-i Taraqqi-yi Urdu, 1965. 1462p.

149 Ahmad, S. Nasir
Urdu-English dictionary. Lahore, 1964. 716p.

150 — • *The student's Urdu-English dictionary.* Lahore, n.d. 716p.

151 Ali, H. Saiyid
The concise dictionary of Urdu words, phrases, idioms and proverbs explained and rendered into English. Calcutta: S.C. Auddy and Co., 1937. 1620p.

152 Anandarama T. Shahani
The pocket English-Hindustani dictionary. Karachi: Educational Publishing Co., 1940. 377p.

153 Anjum, A.R. and Fareed, M.S.
Franc-Urdu lughat, matalaffuzat. French-Urdu dictionary, with pronunciation. Lahore: Maktaba al-Quraish, 1977.

154 Ansari, Zoe
Urdu-Russkĭ slovar'. Moscow, 1904. 890p.

155 Barannikov, A.P.
Slovar' urdu-russko-angliiskĭ k obraztsam sovremennoĭ prozy khindustani. Leningrad, 1930. 280p.

156   Barker, M.A.R., Hamdani H.J., K.M.S. Dihlavi.
Urdu-English vocabulary: students pronouncing dictionary.   Ithaca, New York: Spoken Language Services, 1980. 341p.

157   Becker, Donald A.
A reverse dictionary of Urdu. New Delhi: Manohar Publications, 1980. 261p.
Arranged alphabetically according to their final rather than their initial letters; of great use to linguists and poets.

158   Beskrovnyi, V.M. and Krasnodemskii, V.E.
Urdu-russkii slovar´. Moscow: Izdatel´stvo Akademiia Nauk SSSR, 1951. 844p.

159   Biriulev, S.V., et al.
Urdu-russkii slovar´, 30,000 slov. Ed. Zoe Ansari. Moscow: Sov. entsiklopediia, 1964. 860p.

160   *A comprehensive Hindustani-English dictionary.* Allahabad, 1914. 1024p.

161   Craven, Thomas
The royal dictionary: in two parts, English and Hindustani and Hindustani and English. Lucknow: Methodist Publishing House, 1904. 608p.

[Another ed.] Lucknow: Methodist Publishing House, 1911. 342p.

[Another ed.] Revised by Bishop J.R. Chitambar. Lucknow: Methodist Publishing House, 1932.

162   Deva, A.T.
Jewel dictionary of English, Bengali and Hindustani. Calcutta, 1930. 1195p.

163   Durga Prasad, Munshi
The student's practical dictionary ... Together with a list of Latin and Greek words and phrases with their equivalents both in English and Urdu in Persian character. 2nd ed. revised and improved. Allahabad: Ram Narain Lal, 1903. 811, 15p.
First published 1897.

164   Fallon, S.W.
English-Urdu dictionary. Revised and enlarged and recast by the editorial staff, Mohammad Ikram Chaghtai, Fazale Qadir Fazli, Ashfaq Anwar. Lahore: Central Urdu Board, 1976. 1106p.
Originally published as: *A new English-Hindustani dictionary*, 1927.

165   — • *A new English-Hindustani dictionary: with illustrations from English literature and colloquial English.* Completed by J.D. Bate et al. Lahore, 1941. 703p.

166   — • *Urdu-English dictionary.* Lahore: Central Urdu Board, [1976]. 1216p.
Originally published as: *A New Hindustani-English dictionary with illustrations from Hindustani literature and folklore*, 1879.

167   *Ferozson's concise dictionary: English to Urdu.* Chief ed. A. Hameed Khan. Lahore: Ferozsons, 1978. 647p.

168   *Ferozsons English to English and Urdu dictionary.* Lahore: Ferozsons, 1977.

169   *Ferozsons English-Urdu dictionary.* Students edition. English words with their equivalents in Urdu. Lahore: Ferozsons, 1952. 835p.

4th ed. Lahore: Ferozson's 1964.

170   *Ferozsons Urdu-English dictionary: Urdu words, phrases and idioms with English meanings and synonyms.* 2nd ed. Lahore: Ferozsons, 1962. 831p.

171   *Ferozsons Urdu-English dictionary: a comprehensive dictionary of current vocabulary.* Lahore: Ferozsons, [1975]. 831p.

172   **Forbes, Duncan**
A dictionary, Hindustani and English. Lucknow: Uttar Pradesh Urdu Academy, 1987. 2 vols. (in 1).

173   *Gem Oxford pocket dictionary. English into English, Hindi and Urdu.* Delhi: Sant Singh, 1979.

174   **Hussain, Ali Syed**
Concise dictionary (Anglo-Urdu). Calcutta: Auddy, 1969. 212p.

175   **Kibirkshtis, L. and Pomerantsev, L.M.**
Karmannyĭ urdu-russkiĭ slovar´. Moscow, 1958. 552p.

176   **Majid, A.**
A new Urdu dictionary. Lahore: Jami-ul-Lughat Press, 1935. 4 vols.

177   — • *The modern concise dictionary containing (1) English words with the English and Urdu meanings. (2) Idiomatic Urdu translation of English idioms, phrases and proverbs ...* Allahabad: Ram Narain Lal, 1930. 1036p.

178   **Marek, N.M.**
English aro Hindusthani kusiko Altui agangrikani. Tura, 1927. 52p.

179   **Martirosi, Giuseppe**
Nuovo dizionario tascabile delle lingue italiana-indostana-inglese con brevi accenni grammaticali. Dehra Dun; Bombay printed, 1944. 200p.

180   **Morris, J.**
The classified dictionary of English and Hindustani terms. Lahore, 1911.

181   *Mumtaz practical dictionary. Urdu to English.* Lahore: Ashraf Brothers, 1960. 583p.

182   **Nasri, M.H., Husain, S.Z., Muqbil Dehlvi**
The royal practical Urdu-English dictionary, with pronunciation and English-Urdu proverbs and idioms in Urdu clear nastaliq. 3rd ed. Lahore: Malik House, 1950. 955p.

183   *The new popular dictionary: English into Roman Urdu and Roman Urdu into English.* Aligarh: P.C. Dwadash Shreni, [1944?]. 319p.

184   *Pak triplet dictionary: English to English, Sindhi and Urdu.* Hyderabad: R.H. Ahmed, 1959. 816p.

185   **Parnwell, Eric Charles and Faruqi, Khwaja Ahmad**
Oxford picture dictionary: English-Urdu: Aksfard ba tasvir dikshanari: Angrezi-Urdu. Delhi; [Oxford]: Oxford University Press, [1977] (1985 printing). 90p.
Parallel English and Urdu introduction.

186   **Paul, Stephen C.**
Persian, English and Urdu dictionary. New Delhi: Deep and Deep Publication, 1989. 904p.
Caption title: *Dictionary of Persian into English and Urdu.*

187   — • *The twentieth century Persian, English and Urdu dictionary.* Allahabad: G.A. Asghar and Co., 1930. 904p.

188   **Phillott, Douglas Craven**
An Eng[ish]-Hind[ustani] vocabulary ... 2nd ed. enlarged. 1917.
This copy contains the author's corrections and additions for a third edition.

189   *The pioneer's practical dictionary: Urdu to English.* Revised by R.L. Bhatia and S.K. Sachdeva. Delhi: J.S. Sant Singh, [1962]. 368p.
"Containing Urdu with Roman words to English with standard pronunciation, grammar and explanations".

190   **Platts, John Thompson**
A dictionary of Urdu, classical Hindi and English. 5th ed. London, New York: Oxford University Press, 1974. 1260p.
First published 1884.

[First Indian ed.]. New Delhi: Oriental Books Reprint Corporation, 1977. 1259p.
Reprint of the 1884 London edition.

191   — • *The student's practical dictionary: containing Hindustani words with English meanings.* 12th ed. Allahabad: Ram Narain Lal, 1956. 667p.

192   — • *The student's romanised practical dictionary, Hindustani-English, English-Hindustani.* Allahabad: Ram Narain Lal, 1946. 363, 536p.

193   *Popular Oxford practical dictionary: containing Urdu words with English meanings in Persian character.* Lahore: Oriental Book Society, [1977]. 560p.

194   **Puri, K.C.**
The new royal Urdu-English dictionary. Allahabad: City Press, 1925. 530p.

195   **Qureshi, Bashir Ahmad.**
Kitabistan's 20th-century standard dictionary: Urdu into English, for modern readers and foreign learners of Pakistan's cultural-cum-national language: first-ever lexicon giving modern English renderings of over 50,000 words, phrases and proverbs used in spoken and literary Urdu today, with copious graphic illustration. Lahore: Kitabistan Publishing Co., [1971?]. 688p.

196   — • *Standard twentieth century dictionary: Urdu into English: over 50,000 words, phrases and proverbs used in spoken and literary Urdu with copious graphic illustrations.* Revised and enlarged by Abdul Haq. Delhi: Educational Pub. House, [1983?]. 688p.

197   **Ramaswami, Natarajan**
Brokskat-Urdu-Hindi-English dictionary. Mysore: Central Institute of Indian Languages, 1989. 139p.

198   **Ranking, George Spiers Alexander**
An English-Hindustani dictionary. Calcutta: Thacker, Spink and Co., 1905. 758p.

199   *Russko-urdu slovar'.* Sostavili: B.I. Kliuev, et al. Pod redaktsiei Zoe Ansari i L.M. Pomerantseva. Moscow: Izd. inostrannykh i natsional'nykh slovarei, 1959. 1135p.
Russian-Urdu dictionary with an outline of Urdu grammar.

200   **Razi, F.D.**
Farhang nama-i-jadid: the modern Persian dictionary, Persian-Urdu-English. Lahore: Ripon Press, 1952.
Miscellaneous vocabulary of special terms: pp. 216-237.

201   **Sabri, Makhdoom**
Home dictionary. Urdu into English. Lahore: al Hamd, [198-?].

202   **Sangaji, S.**
Dictionary Urdu-English based on Shakespear and the best authority. New Delhi: Asian Educational Services, 1983.
Originally published as: *A handy Urdu-English dictionary,* 1899.

203   **Sant-Ram**
The student's modern dictionary, containing English words with English and Urdu meanings together with a list of words, phrases and sayings with their English and Urdu meanings. Lahore: Sat Dev and Co., 1933. 674p.

204   **Shakespear, John**
Dictionary: Urdu-English and English-Urdu. 3rd ed. Lahore: Sang-e-Meel Publications, 1980. 2052 cols, 2053-2209p.
Reprint. Originally published as: *Dictionary, Hindustani and English,* 1834.

205   *The student's home dictionary, containing Urdu words with their meanings in English.* 2nd ed. Allahabad: Ram Narain Lal, 1937. 980p.

206   *The student's latest practical dictionary: containing English words with English and Urdu meanings and Roman pronunciations.* 16th ed. Delhi: J.S. Sant Singh, [197?]. 625p.

207   *The student's new model practical dictionary. English-Urdu and Hindi.* Lahore, 1938. 904p.

208   *The student's new model practical dictionary: Urdu to English.* Delhi: J.S. Sant Singh, 892p.

209   *Student's pocket dictionary: Urdu-English.* Lahore: Punjab Kitab Ghar, 892p.

210   *The student's romanized practical dictionary, Hindustani-English and English-Hindustani.* 3rd ed., 4th reprint. Allahabad: Ram Narain Lal, 1923. 536p.

211   *Urdu-Angrezi dictionary: Anglo Urdu dictionary.* Amritsar, 1913. 200p.

212   *Urdu-English dictionary: an Urdu-English dictionary with Urdu words, phrases and idioms and their English equivalents.* Lahore, 1964. 831p.

213   *Urdu-English dictionary.* Lahore: Shaikh Ghulam Hussain and Sons, 1965. 1000p.

214   *Urdu-English dictionary.* New York: Saphrograph Corp., 1969. 831p.

215   **Whyte, R.R.**
New century English Urdu dictionary. Allahabad: Ram Narain Lal, 1097p.

216   — • *The new century English-Urdu dictionary, pronouncing and literary.* Madras: S.P.C.K. Press, 1905. 943p.
Urdu in Roman characters.

217   **Yatindranath Sena**
Twentieth century Roman-English   (i.e. Hindustani-English, with Hindustani words transliterated in the Roman character) pocket dictionary. Allahabad: G.A. Ashgar, 1912. 814p.

DICTIONARIES AND GLOSSARIES OF TECHNICAL AND LITERARY TERMS

BIBLIOGRAPHY

218   **Ghani, A.R and Siddiqi**, A.
Guide to English Urdu dictionaries and glossaries of technical terms. Lahore, 1955. 23p.

GENERAL

219   **Abd al-Rashid, Munshi**
The probationer's handy help to language, containing a complete vocabulary of only those words as are likely to meet the eye of the average students for lower and higher standards, Hindustani and Persian. Lucknow, 1895. 78p.

220   *A dictionary of technical terms: economics, commerce, banking, English-Urdu.* Karachi: Bureau of Composition, Compilation and Translation, University of Karachi, 1972. 12, 370p.

221   *Dictionary of official terms and phrases: Daftari istilahat o muhavarat ki lughat: Angrezi-Urdu.* Lahore: Majalis Zabani Daftari, 1976. 571p.

222   *Glossary of Indian terms, for the use of officers of revenue.* Madras, 1877.

223   *Glossary of technical terms, English-Urdu, economics.* New Delhi: Bureau of Promotion of Urdu, Ministry of Education and Culture, 1983. 141p.

224   *A glossary of technical terms. (English-Urdu)* Part II. (a) Sociology (b) Economics (c) History and politics. Delhi: Anjuman-Taraqqi-yi Urdu, 1940. 3 pts.

225   *Khizanat al-lughat. A dictionary of select terms in Hindustani, Persian, Arabic, Sanskrit, English, and Turkish.* Compiled by order of Shahjahan Begam. Bhopal, 1886. 87p. 2 vols.

226   **Latif, Muhammad and Hasan, Ahmad**
A dictionary of technical terms: sociology, English-Urdu. Revised by Sabihuddin Baqal and Arshad Rizvi. Karachi: Bureau of Composition and Translation, University of Karachi, 1970. 149p.

227   **Nusrat, Saiyid Ali**
Mufid-i amm. An English-Urdu vocabulary of useful and technical words. Shahjahanpur, 1882. 24p.

228   **Pieterse, Liberius**
English-Urdu dictionary of Christian terminology. Ed. Jan Slomp. Rawalpindi: Christian Study Centre, 1976. 108p.

229   **Raverty, Henry George**
Thesaurus of English and Hindustani technical terms used in building and other useful arts; and scientific manual of words and phrases in the higher branches of knowledge. Hertford and London, 1859. 106p.

230   **Yule, Henry and Burnell, A.C.**
Hobson-Jobson; a glossary of colloquial Anglo-Indian words and phrases and of kindred terms, etymological, historical, geographical and discursive. 2nd ed. Ed. William Crooke. Delhi: Munshiram Manoharlal, 1968. 1021p.

ANTHROPOLOGY

231   *Glossary of technical terms (English-Urdu): Anthropology Farhang-i istilahat insaniyat.* New Delhi: Bureau of Promotion of Urdu, Ministry of Education and Culture, 1981.

CIVIL ENGINEERING

232   *Technical dialogues in English and Urdu: prepared for the use of the students of the Thomason Civil Engineering College, Roorkee.* 4th ed.   Roorkee: Thomason Civil Engineering College Press, 1877. 144p.

ECONOMICS

233   *Glossary of technical terms, English-Urdu, Economics-Farhanag-i istilahat, mashiyat.* New Delhi: Bureau for Promotion of Urdu Ministry of Education & Culture, 1983.

LAW AND COMMERCIAL

234   **Ahmad, Husain Khan**
Law technicalities ... or, a collection of law terms in vernaculars [ie. Hindustani] *with their equivalent in English.* [Lahore, 1898.] 32p.

235   **Brown, Charles Philip**
The zillah dictionary in the Roman character: explaining the various words used in business in India. Madras, 1852. 132p.

236   *The concise law dictionary and translator's guide.* 2nd ed. Allahabad: Ram Narain Lal, 1906. 490p.
In English and Hindustani.

237   **Durga Prasad, Munshi**
Guide to legal translations; or a collection of words and phrases used in the translation of legal papers from Urdu into English. Benares: E.J. Lazarus and Co.; London: Trübner and Co., 1869. 177p.

2nd ed. Benares, 1974.

238   **Fallon, S.W.**
An English-Hindustani law and commercial dictionary of words and phrases used in civil criminal, revenue, and mercantile affairs; designed especially to assist translators of law papers. Calcutta, 1858.

239   — • *A Hindustani-English law and commercial dictionary, comprising many law phrases and notes in addition to the law phrases given to the general dictionary.* Benaras, 1879.

240   — • *A romanized English-Hindustani law and commercial dictionary of words and phrases used in civil, criminal, revenue and mercantile affairs.* Ed. and revised by Lala Faqir Chand. Benares, 1888. 85p.

241   **Farani, M.**
The law dictionary, English and Urdu. Lahore: Lahore Law Times Publications, [1972?].

242   **Hassan, Masudul**
Manual of consolidation of holdings laws instructions in Urdu with redemption and restitution of mortgaged lands act, 1964, with rules, 1969. Lahore: Eastern Law House, 1983.

243   **Hutchinson, Robert Fame**
Glossary of medical and medico-legal terms including those most frequently met with in the law courts. 2nd ed. Calcutta, 1881.

244   **Jvalanatha, Munshi**
Commercial Hindustani: a collection of practical commercial phrases with a vocabulary of useful terms in English and Hindustani ... 2nd ed. Calcutta: Thacker, Spink and Co., 1902. 125p.

245   **Kshetramohana Vandyopadhyaya**
The translator's friend; or, a dictionary of law terms ... Pt. 1. Bengali-English-Roman Urdu. Revised by Purna Chandra Dutta. Calcutta: Bose Bros., 1898. 94,8,32,19p.

246   **Ramaji Dasa Bhatiya**
The law dictionary: both from English into Urdu and Urdu into English. Lahore: Punjab Economical Press, 1907. 126p.

247   **Rousseau, Samuel**
A dictionary of words used in the East Indies... to which is added, Mohammedan law and Bengal revenue terms. 2nd ed. London, 1805. 287p.

[Another ed.] *A dictionary of Mohammedan law, Bengal revenue terms ... used in the East Indies.* London, 1841.

248   Wilson, Horace Hayman
A glossary of judicial and revenue terms, and of useful words occurring in official documents relating to the administration of the Government of British India, from the Arabic, Persian, Hindustani... London: Wm. H. Allen and Co., 1855. 728p.

[Another ed.] Delhi: Munshiram Manoharlal, [1868].

MEDICAL

249   Chittenden, John Franks
Medical phrase book in Hindustani, English, French and Spanish... Port-of-Spain: Govt. Printing Office, [1893]. 74p.

250   Cox, Edward Thomas
The regimental moonshi: being a course of reading in Hindustani, designed to assist officers and assistant surgeons on the Madras establishment preparing for the examination ordered by Government. London: Wm. H. Allen and Co., 1847. 3 pts.

251   Hutchinson, Robert Fame
A glossary of medical and medico-legal terms [English and Roman Urdu], *including those most frequently met with in the law Courts.* 2nd ed. Calcutta: Thacker, Spink and Co., 1881. 164p.

252   Khan, Muhammad Sharif
The Taleef Shereef, or Indian materia medica. Trans. G. Playfair. Calcutta, 1833. 189p.

253   Mouat, Frederic John
An atlas of anatomical plates of the human body, with descriptive letterpress in English and Hindustani ... Calcutta: Published by order of Government, 1849.

254   *The public medical services: the Army, Navy and Indian medical services, what they are and what they are not, being hints to candidates for commissions on the choice of a service ... to which is added a vocabulary of Hindustani medical terms...* London, 1878.

255   Small, George
Anglo-Urdu medical handbook, or Hindustani guide for the use of medical practitioners ... in Northern India. Assisted by C.R. Francis and Mrs Fraser Nash. Calcutta: Thacker and Co., 1895. 199p.

MILITARY AND NAVAL

256   Abdullah, Saiyid Risaldar
Military vocabulary. Jhansi, [1918.] 30p.
English and Hindustani.

257   **Ballantyne, James Robert**
Hindustani letters lithographed in the nuskh-tu'leek and shikustu-amez character. With translations. Preparation for the use of the Scottish Naval and Military Academy. London: Madden and Co.; Edinburgh: C. Smith; Military Academy, 1840. 9, 12p.

258   — • *Hindustani selections in the Naskhi and Devanagari character. With a vocabulary of the words. Prepared for the use of Scottish Naval and Military Academy.* London: Madden and Co., C. Smith; Edinburgh: Military Academy, 1840. 10, 39, 20p.

259   **Blumhardt, James Fuller**
Military vocabularies - 1. English Hindustani: compiled for the use of gentlemen studying at 12 and 14 Earl's Court Square. London, 1892. 23p.

260   **Borradaile, G.E.**
A vocabulary, English and Hindustani, for the use of military students in the Madras Presidency. Madras: Graves, Cookson and Co., 1868. 246p.

261   **Campbell, William Rose**
Hindoostanee, Persian, Teloogoo, and Tamil examinations. English extracts suitable for civil and military officers for practice in the "viva voce" and "written exercises". Madras: Gantz Bros., 1864.

262   **Chandra, Sena**
A soldier's practical guide to Hindustani. Adapted for the lower standard examination. Shahjahanpur: Arya Darpan Press, 1882. 26p.

263   **Chapman, Francis Robert Henry**
Urdu Reader graduated for military students... London: C. Lockwood and Son, 1920. 2 pts.

264   **Dayarama T. Shahanni and Anandarama T. Shahani, Munshi**
Hindustani military colloquial. One month's course. Karachi: Educational Publishing Co.; London: Crosby Lockwood and Son, 1919. 2 pts.

265   — • *Guide to military Urdu and the elementary examination.* Revised by W. Turner. Karachi: Educational Publishing Co., 1942. 262p.

266   **Harrison, Norwood**
Manual of Lascari-Hindustani with technical terms and phrases. 3rd ed. London: Imray, Laurie, Norie and Wilson, 1911. 133p.

267   **Husain, Muhammad Imdad**
A hand-book of exercises for officers preparing for Urdu colloquial examinations ... with a vocabulary of military terms. Calcutta: Habib-un-Naby Khan 'Saulat', [1918?].

268   **Hutchinson, Henry Doveton**
Military training in English and Hindustani. 1890. 129p. (Gale and Polden's Military Series. Vol. 48.)

269   Isvari Dasa
The soldier's Hindoostanee companion or a guide to the most widely spoken language of the country. 2nd ed. Benares, 1861.

270   Kadir, Saiyad
An easy guide to Hindustani, for the use of the military officers and others preparing for the lower standard examination. Madras: S.P.C.K. Press, 1888. 60p.

271   Khan Haidari, Mohammed Akbar
The army Urdu teacher official text-book for the British service Urdu test (for other ranks). Delhi: Haidari's Oriental Book Depot, 1944.

272   Mascarenhas, C.
A pocket glossary of English and Hindustani naval terms, with Indian days, months and numerals. London: the author, 1888. 23p.

273   Parry, Shedden Chalmers St. George Cole
Lascar Hindustani for ship-surgeons. London: W.J. Clark and Co., [1930.] 48p.

274   Philips, H.L.
Urdu military vocabulary with reading exercises. London: Oxford University Press; Madras printed, 1943. 77p.

275   Ranking, George Spiers Alexander
A pocket-book of colloquial Urdu for military reconnaissance, for use of officers and men, for examination, reference, and on service. Calcutta: Thacker, Spink and Co., 1895. 63p.

276   — • *Talim-i-zaban-i urdu: a guide to Hindustani ... for the use of officers and men serving in India...* Calcutta: Thacker, Spink and Co., 1889. 130p.

277   Roebuck, Thomas
An English and Hindoostanee naval dictionary of technical terms and sea phrases ... to which is prefixed a short grammar of the Hindoostanee language... 4th ed. Revised by W. Carmichael-Smyth. Calcutta, 1811. 180p.
Hindustani in Roman characters.

278   — • *A Laskari dictionary or Anglo-Indian vocabulary of nautical terms and phrases in English and Hindustani. Chiefly in the corrupt jargon in use among the Laskars ...* Revised by W. Carmichael Smyth ... and now ... re-edited and enlarged by G. Small. London: Wm. H. Allen and Co., 1882. 85p.

279   Vaz, Anthony
The marine officer's Hindustan interpreter, containing a vocabulary of nautical terms... Bombay, 1879. 50p.

PHILOSOPHY, PSYCHOLOGY AND EDUCATION

280   *Glossary of technical terms (English-Urdu), philosophy, psychology and education: Farhang-i istilahat (Angrezi-Urdu) falsafah, nafsiyat, aur talim.* New Delhi: Bureau for Promotion of Urdu, Dept. of Education, 1988.

PLANTS AND DRUGS

281   **Fleming, John M.A.**
A catalogue of Indian medicinal plants and drugs, with their names in the Hindustani and Sanscrit languages. Calcutta, [1810]. 44p.

POETRY

282   *Glossary of difficult Urdu words usually found in popular ghazals, songs, qawallies and radio programmes with meaning in Urdu and English with couplets.* Hyderabad: H.E.H. The Nizam's Urdu Trust Publication, 1987. 321p.
Cover title: *Glossary of words towards understanding Urdu poetry.*

283   **Kalimuddin, Ahmad**
Dictionary of literary terms, English-Urdu Farhang-i adabi istilahat. New Delhi: Bureau for Promotion of Urdu, Ministry of Human Resource Development, 1986.

284   **Nathani, Sultan**
Urdu for pleasure for ghazal lovers: 3500 words English-Hindi. Bombay: Nathani Trust, 1986. 210p.

285   **Painter, T.A.**
1500 words towards understanding Urdu poetry. Bombay: Nathani Trust, 1974. 240p.
Urdu words in Roman characters, followed by an English glossary, a Devanagari version, and a Hindi glossary.

PROVERBS AND IDIOMS

286   **Ali, Mir Gholam**
English and Hindustani phraseology or exercises in idioms, English and Dakhini Hindustani. Prepared under the directions of C.P. Brown. Madras, 1855. 235p.

287   *The Anglo-vernacular idiomatic sentences and phrases... in English and Hindustani.* Lahore: Shams-ul Hind Press, 1898. 152p.

288   **Brown, Charles Philip**
English and Hindustani phraseology, or exercises in idioms. Madras, 1855.

289   **Dossabhaee Sorabjee**
Idiomatical sentences in the English, Hindustani, Goozratee and Persian Languages, in six parts ... Bombay, 1843.

290   — • *A new self-instructing work entitled idiomatic sentences in the English, Gujarati, Hindustani, and Persian language ... in seven parts (enlarged from the first edition of D. Sohrabi's Idiomatic sentences). With notes explanatory and illustrative, to which are added copious vocabularies ...* by Bahmanji Dosabhai... Bombay, 1873. 427, 290p.

291   **Eardley-Wilmot, H.**
One thousand Hindustani idiomatic sentences. Madras: Addison and Co., 1887. 96p.

292   **Fallon, S.W.**
A dictionary of the Hindustani proverbs, including many Marwari, Panjabi, Maggah, Bhojpuri and Tirhuti proverbs. ... Ed. and revised by R.C. Temple, assisted by Lala Faqir Chand. Benares: E.J. Lazarus; London: [printed], 1886. 320p.

293   **Ghulam Rasul, Muhammad**
Azad-i muhawarat. Idiomatic sentences in English and Hindustani. Jalandhar, 1887. 65p.

294   **Gupta, Chhanu Lal**
Bunch of proverbs. (Guldastah-i amsal o muhawarat): a magazine containing about 1,100 English proverbs, idioms, idiomatic sentences and aphorisms, with their equivalents in Urdu, some in Hindi and Persian. Delhi: Imperial Medical Hall Press, 1892. 60p.

295   **Haleem, A.**
Idiomatic sentences in English, Hindustanee and Guzeratee. Bombay, 1873. 199p.

296   **Hashmat Ali, M.**
A manual of English idiomatic phrases with Urdu equivalents. Lucknow: the author, 1889. 149p.

297   **Hoosain, Ghoolam**
A collection of idiomatic sentences in English and Hindoostanee. Madras, 1858.

298   **Kunwar Bahadur**
Treasury of proverbs. Part II. Containing many English proverbs, idioms, and idiomatic sentences, with their equivalents in Urdu. [Ganjinah-i muhawarat o amsal]. Delhi, 1898. 32p.

299   **Lal, Chiranji**
A collection of moral precepts and reflections, gathered from various sources, in English and Hindustani, and translated for the instruction of youth. Lucknow, 1833. 169p.

300   **Lal, Dhunna**
The hand-book of idiomatic phrases, containing explanations in English, Urdu and Roman, with illustrative sentences selected from the works of the best modern English writers ... 3rd ed. Benares: Medical Hall Press, 1901. 76p.

301   **Madhava Narayana**
Makhzan al-muhauwarat. A collection of English idiomatic sentences and proverbs, with their Hindustani equivalents. Delhi, 1885. 56p.

[Another ed.]   — • *Makhzan-ul-mahawrat ... Containing English proverbs, idioms, idiomatic sentences with their equivalents in vernacular* [ie. Hindustani]. Delhi: Imperial Book Depot Press, 1903. 48p.

302   **Mitra, S.C**
The student's constant companion: a dictionary of phrases, idioms and proverbs. Calcutta: the author, 1908. 1456p.

303   **Morris, J.**
The dictionary of dictionaries, or A dictionary of: 1. words; 2. phrases and idioms... 3. Maxims, sayings, proverbs... with parallels from English, and other ... languages... with a general index for the subject matter. Lahore, 1898. 64p.

304   — • *English proverbs, with Hindustani parallels.* 3rd ed. Lahore: Shams-ul Hind Press, [1896]. 123p.

305   **Phillips, Arthur Noel**
Hindustani idioms with vocabulary and explanatory notes... London: Kegan Paul and Co., 1892. 228p.

306   **Phillot, Dougas Craven**
Khazina-i muhavarat or Urdu idioms. Calcutta: Baptist Mission Press, 1912. 125p.

307   **Prabhudasa Dasa**
Proverbs, Hindi, Urdu and Persian, collected and alphabetically arranged. Allahabad, 1870.

308   **Prasad, M.**
A treasury of Hindustani idioms, colloquial and proverbs, with their equivalents. Aligarh, [1914]. 192p.

309   **Roebuck, Thomas**
A collection of proverbs, and proverbial phrases in the Persian and Hindoostanee languages. Commenced by W. Hunter. Compiled and translated by T.R. Roebuck. Ed. with additions, by H.H. Wilson. Calcutta, 1824. 397p.
Persian, Hindustani and English.

310   **Shamsher Singh**
A book of proverbs Urdu-English. Lahore, 1924. 65p.

311   **Sukhadevaprasada**
A manual of English proverbs, containing for each proverb, a full explanation in English; its corresponding English proverbs; and its equivalents in Persian, Urdu, and Hindi... Agra: Moon Press, 1896. 31p.

312   Tagliabue, Camillo
Proverbi, detti e leggende indostani.   Rome: Tipografia della Casa Edit. Italiana, 1899.
254p. (Pubblicazioni scientifiche del R. Istituto orientale in Napoli, vol. 4).

313   Wazir, Ahmad
Knowledge of English idioms and choice expressions. With their English explanations and Urdu equivalents. Pt. 2.   Agra: Anwari Press, 1889.

314   — • *One thousand proverbs, with Urdu equivalents.*   Bareilly, 1892.   52p.

TECHNICAL AND SCIENTIFIC TERMS

315   *List of technical and scientific terms, English and Urdu.* [Madras: Printed by the Supt., Govt. Press, 1947].

LANGUAGE

Grammar

316   **Amanatullah, Maulavi**
Surf-e Urdu, or short grammar of the Hindoostanee language written in Hindee verse.
Calcutta, 1810.

317   **Andrew, W.**
A comprehensive synopsis of the elements of the Hindoostani grammar. London, [183-?].

318   **Arnot, Sandford**
A new self-instructing grammar of the Hindystani tongue, the most useful and general language of British India, in the Oriental and Roman character ... with an appendix of reading exercises and a vocabulary. London, 1831. 132p.

319   — • *A grammar of the Hindustani tongue in the Oriental and Roman character, with ... illustrations of the Sanscrit, Arabic, and Persian systems of alphabetic writing ...   To which is added, a selection of easy extracts for reading in the Persi-Arabic and Devanagari characters; with a copious vocabulary and explanatory notes, by Duncan Forbes ...* London: Wm. H. Allen and Co., 1844. 132p.

320   **Bagchi, S.C.**
The complete manual of Hindustani grammar. Revised by H.T.H Wrightwick and K.M. Maitre. Lahore, 1917. 70p.

321   **Bakhsh, S. Karim**
Urdu made easy: a simplified Urdu grammar specially prepared for elementary B.O.R.'s test, army special colloquial examinations in Urdu. Lucknow: Printed by R.S. Bhargava, 1941. 241p.

322   **Balfour, F.**
"A table containing examples of all different species of infinitives and participles that are derived from tri-literal verbs, in the form in which they are used in the Persian, and in the language of Hindustan". *Asiatick Researches* 2 (1790), pp. 205-206.

323   **Ballantyne, James Robert**
Appendix and key to the Hindustany grammar of J.R. Ballantyne. London, [1842?].

324   — • *A grammar of the Hindustani language: followed by a series of grammatical exercises.* 2nd ed. London: Cox and Co.; Edinburgh: Ballantyne and Co., 1838. 78p.

[Another ed.] London: Madden and Co., 1842. 76p.

325   — • *A grammar of the Hindustani language with notices of the Braj and Dakhani dialect.* London, 1839.

326   **Beg, Mirza Khalil Ahmad**
Urdu grammar: history and structure. New Delhi: Bahri Publications, 1988. 228p.

327   Bender, Ernest
Urdu; grammar and reader. Philadelphia: University of Pennsylvania Press, 1967. 487p.

328   Bhargava, S.L. and Morris, H.E.A.
Hindustani grammar. For the use of officers, non-commissioned officers and men preparing for the lower, higher, and colloquial examinations. Lahore, 1918.

329   Carmichael-Smyth, William
The Hindoostanee interpreter, containing the rudiments of Hindoostanee grammar, an extensive vocabulary... London, 1824.

330   Deva, Dina-Natha
Hindustani grammar. Calcutta: Bharata Mitra Press, 1886. 225p.

331   — • *Hindustani and Persian grammar with pleasing thoughts: containing grammatical rules...* Calcutta, 1904. 274p.

332   Devi-Prasad
Devipresad's polyglott grammar and exercises in Persian, English, Arabic, Hindee, Oordoo and Bengali. With an analysis of Arabic and synonymous words; and of logical argument. For the use of students. Calcutta, 1854.

333   Dowson, John
A grammar of the Urdu or Hindustani language. London, Hertford [printed], 1872.
Reviewed by J. Beames in *Indian Antiquary* 11, p. 56.

334   Duncan, John
A grammar of the Hindustani language ... Madras, 1863.

335   Eastwick, Edward Backhouse
A concise grammar of the Hindustani language, to which are added selections for reading, with a vocabulary, dialogues ... London: James Madden, 1847.

2nd. ed. London: G. Small, 1858.

336   *Elements of Hindoostanee grammar. Prepared for the Thomson Civil Engineering College, Roorkee.* Roorkee, 1872.

337   *English and Hindustani: exercises of the irregular verbs.* Madras, 1842.

338   Faulkner, Alexander
The Orientalist's grammatical vade-mecum: being an easy introduction to the rules and principles of the Hindustani, Persian, and Gujarati languages. Bombay: American Mission Press, 1853. 3 pts.

339   Forbes, Duncan
A grammar of the Hindustani languages in the oriental and Roman character ... to which is added a copious selection of easy extracts for reading in the Persi-Arabic and Devanagari characters. London: Wm. H. Allen and Co., 1846. 148p.

[Another ed.] London: Allen, 1862. 148p.

340 — • *The Hindustani Manual... Pt. 1: A compendious grammar of the language...* Revised by John T. Platts. London: Crosby Lockwood, 1912. 188p.

341 **Garcin de Tassy, Joseph Héliodore Sagesse Vertu**
"Analyse des Grammaires hindoustanis originales intitulées, sarf-i Urdu et Qawaid-i Zaban-Urdu". *Journal Asiatique* 3, 5 (1838), pp. 66-.

342 **Gilchrist, John Borthwick**
A grammar of the Hindoostanee language; or, part third of volume first, of a system of Hindoostanee philology. Calcutta: Chronicle Press, 1796.

343 — • *A grammar of the Hindustani language.* 1796 ... Facsimile. Menston, Yorks: Scolar Press, 1970. 336p. (English linguistics, 1500-1800, no. 225.)
Made from copies in the British Library.

344 *Gramatica Indostana a mais vulgar que se practica no Imperio do gram Mogol offerecida aos muitos reverendos Padres Missionarios do ditto Imperio.* Roma: Na Estamperia da Sagrada Congregaçao de Propaganda Fide, 1778.

2nd ed. Lisboa, 1805.

345 **Green, Arthur Octavius**
A practical Hindustani grammar. Oxford: Clarendon Press, 1895. 2 vols.

346 **Hadley, George**
A compendious grammar of the current corrupt dialect of the jargon of Hindostan. 7th ed. London, 1809. 17-184, 103p.

347 — • *Grammatical remarks on the practical and vulgar dialect of the Indostan language commonly called Moors, with a vocabulary, English and Moors ...* London: T. Cadell, 1772.

Facsimile. Menston, Yorks: Scolar Press, 1967. 133p.

348 — • *A short grammar and vocabulary of the Moors language.* London, 1771.

349 *Hindoostanee grammar simplified and adapted to the use of students in the Presidency of Madras.* 2nd ed. Madras, 1851. 56p.

350 **Iman Bakhsh**
Grammar of the Urdu language. Delhi, 1849.

351 *Introduction to the Hindoostanee grammar, adapted to the use of students in the Presidency of Madras.* Madras, 1842.

352 **Kashi Natha, Munshi**
Hindustani grammar. Ambala: Station Press, 1909. 127p.

353   **Keegan, William**
Grammatica linguae Indostanae. Sardhanae, 1883. 87p.

354   **Kellog, Samuel Henry**
A grammar of the Hindi language ... with copious philological notes. New Delhi: Oriental Books Reprint Corp., 1972. 584p.
Includes pronunciation notes by T. Grahame Bailey.

355   **Khan Haidari, Mohammad Akbar**
The Munshi: a standard Hindustani grammar with exercises and full vocabulary officially recommended for examinations in Urdu. 2nd ed. Calcutta: Baptist Mission Press, 1917 [1918]. 2 pts.

356   — • *The Munshi: a standard Hindustani grammar with exercises and full vocabulary officially recommended for examinations in Urdu.* Delhi: Haidari's Oriental Book Depot, 1945. 182p.

18th ed. Karachi: [s.n.], 1961. 262p.

357   **Khan, M.A.**
A complete Hindustani grammar with military vocabulary and exercises. Simla, 1939. 115p.

358   **Khubchandani, Lachman Mulchand**
"Toward a selection grammar: fluidity in modes of address and reference in Hindi-Urdu". *Indian Linguistics* 39, 1-4 (1978), pp. 1-24.

359   — • *Toward a selection grammar fluidity in modes of address and reference in Hindi-Urdu.* Pune: Centre for Communication Studies, 1981.
"Study conducted during 1971-72 at the University College, London and at Delhi".

360 **Lebedev, G.S.**
A grammar of the pure and mixed East Indian dialects with dialogues affixed. London, 1801. 86p.

[Another ed.] With notes, biographical sketch... of Lebedev by M.P. Saha. Calcutta, 1963. 40, 118p.

361   **MacCarthy, Laurent**
Grammaire hindoustani-française. Verviers, [1895.] 244p.

362   **Makbah, Muhammad Ibrahim**
Lessons in Hindustani grammar, letter-writing, arithmetic... (Ta'lim Nama). Bombay, 1847.

[Another ed.] Madras, 1850.

363   — • *Tuhfa-e-Elphinstone; or A grammar of the Hindustani language...* Revised by V. Kennedy. Bombay, 1832. 112p.

364   *Memorandum on a point of Dakhni grammar.* London, 1878.

365   **Monier-Williams, Monier**
Hindustani primer: containing a first grammar suited to beginners, and a vocabulary of common words on various subjects. Together with useful phrases and short stories. London, 1860.

366   — • *A practical Hindustani grammar; containing the accidence in Roman type, a chapter on the use of Arabic words and a full syntax ... also Hindustani selections ... with a vocabulary ... by Cotton Mather ...* London, Hertford [printed], 1862.

2nd ed. London: Longmans, Green and Co., 1868 [1870]. 161, 33p.

367   — • *Rudiments of Hindustani grammar for the use of Cheltenham College.* Cheltenham, 1858. 72p.

368   **Muhammad Salih, Mirza and Price, William**
A grammar of the three principal languages, Hindoostanee, Persian, and Arabic, on a plan entirely new, and perfectly easy; to which is added a set of Persian dialogues. London, Worcester [printed], 1823. 3 pts.
Reviewed by Silvestre de Sacy in the *Journal des Savants* for January 1824.

369   **Palmer, Edward Henry**
Simplified grammar of Hindustani, Persian and Arabic. 2nd ed. London: Trübner and Co., 1882. 104p. (Trübner's collection of simplified grammars, no. 1).

370   **Pelikan, Heike**
Die Sprachforschungen des Missionars Benjamin Schultze unter besonderer Berücksichtigung der "Grammatica hindostanica". Historisch-linguistische Untersuchungen. Halle, 1898. Ph.D. thesis.

371   **Pershad, R.**
A modified compilation on elements of Hindustani grammar. Ajmer, 1916. 57p.

372   **Pezzoni,** *Monsignore*
Grammatica italiana e indostana. Sardhana, 1874. 462p.

373   **Platts, John Thompson**
Grammar of the Hindustani or Urdu language. London: Wm. H. Allen, 1874. 400p.

2nd ed. New Delhi: Munshiram Manoharlal, 1990. 400p.

374   *Polyglot grammars and dialogues.* Delhi, 1885.

375   **Pray, Bruce Raymond**
Topics in Hindi-Urdu grammar. Berkeley: Center for South and Southeast Asia Studies, University of California, 1970.

376   **Price, William**
A new grammar of the Hindoostanee language. To which are added, familiar phrases and dialogues in the proper character. London, Worcester [printed], 1828.

377 Prochnow, J.D.
Anfangsgründe einer Grammatik der hindustanischen Sprache. Berlin, 1852.

378 Saihgal, Moolchand and Mitchel, D
Hindustani grammar. 2nd. ed. Subathu, Simla Hills: M.C. Saihgal, 1918. 180p.

11th. ed. Subathu, 1943. 2 vols. (in 1).

379 Saihgal, Moolchand and Saihgal, P.C
Hindustani grammar. In three simultaneous but separate scripts, Urdu, Nagri, and Roman-Urdu. With English into Urdu and Urdu into English vocabulary, by Rev. Fr. Albert. 11th ed. Subathu, 1945. 304p.

380 — • *Saihgal's Hindustani grammar, assisted by P.C. Saihgal. Officially recommended for the lower and higher standard examinations in Urdu and Nagri by the Government of India.* Subathu: M.C. Saihgal, [1944?]. 2 vols. (in 1) 262p.

381 — • *Saihgal's Hindustani grammar.* Subhathu: M.C. Saihgal and Son, 1974. 218p. In Roman characters.

382 — • *Key to Saihgal's Hindustani grammar and manual.* Subathu: M.C. Saihgal, 1945. 114p.

383 Saint-Quentin, René de
Abrégé de grammaire hindoustânie. Essai d'étude phonétique de la langue hindoustânie à l'aide de caractères romains, suivi d'un choix de phrases les plus usuelles et d'un vocabulaire. Rouen, 1890. 109p.

384 Schultze, Martin
Grammatik der hindustanischen Sprache. Hindî und Urdû, in indischer, arabischer und lateinischer Schrift. Leipzig: Verlag von Karl Schultze, 1894. 56p.

385 Schultz, Benjamin
Grammatica Hindostanica. Halae Saxonum, 1745.

386 Seidel, A.
Theoretisch-praktische Grammatik der Hindustani-Sprache, mit Übungsstücken in arabischer Schrift, und ein deutsch-hindustani Wörterbuch. Wien, Pest, Leipzig, 1893.

387 Shakespear, John
A grammar of the Hindustani language. London, 1813.

6th ed. To which is added, a short grammar of the Dakhani. London: Wm. H. Allen, 1895. 192p.

388 Simpson, J.
Urdu grammar in Roman characters for the use of European schools in India. Pt. 1. London: Longmans and Co., 1918. 38p.

389   Small, George
A grammar of the Urdu or Hindustani language in its romanized character. Calcutta: Thacker and Co., 1895. 205p.

390   Smith, Robert Percy
Urdu grammar, for the higher and lower standard examinations. Assisted by Mohideen Beg. Calcutta, 1890. 309p.

391   Tagliabue, Camillo
Grammatica della lingua indostana o urdu. Naples, 1898. 288p. (Università degli studi, Istituto superiore orientale. Collezione scolastica, vol. 2.).

392   Thimm, Carl Albert
Hindustani grammar self-taught. Ed. Sayyid Ali Bilgrami. London: E. Marlborough and Co., 1908. 118p.

3rd ed. 1916, 120p.

393   Tisdall, William St. Clair
A conversation-grammar of the Hindustani language: method Gaspey-Otto-Sauer. London: David Nutt; Heidelberg: Julius Groos, 1911. 2 vols.
Vol. 2 has title *Key to the Hindustani conversation-grammar.*

394   Vaughan-Arbuckle, Benjamin
Urdu grammar. London: Longmans and Co., Allahabad [printed], 1911. 164p.

395   Vinson, Élie Honoré Julien
Éléments de la grammaire hindoustanie. Paris, Orléans [printed], 1883. 82p.

396   Vogel, Jean Philippe
De eerste 'Grammatica' van het Hindoestansch. Amsterdam: N.V. Noord-Hollandsche Uitgevers Maatschappij, 1941. 32p. (Mededeelingen der Nederlandsche Akademie van Wetenschappen. Afd. Letterkunde. Nieuwe reeks, dl. 4. no. 15.)
On J.J. Ketelaar's "Instructie off onderwijsinge der Hindoustanse, en Persiaanse talen", 1698.

397   Weston, S.
A short grammar and vocabulary of the Moors language. London: W. Flexney, 1771. 51p.
Includes Ms. notes and additions.

LANGUAGE

History

BIBLIOGRAPHY

398 Acharya, K.P.
Classified bibliography of articles in Indian linguistics. Mysore: Central Institute of Indian Languages, 1978. 106p.

399 Dil, Anwar S.
A directory of Pakistani linguists and language scholars. Lahore: Linguistic Research Group of Pakistan, 1962. 60p.

400 Grierson, George Abraham
"A bibliography of western Hindi, including Hindustani". *Indian Antiquary* 32 (Bombay, January, February, April, June 1903), pp. 16-25, 59-76, 160-179, 262-265.
Detailed history of the study of Hindi and Urdu, with bibliography of books about these languages (including a complete bibliography of Garcin de Tassy's works), and of translations from them.
Less complete than his *Linguistic Survey of India* bibliography.

401   — • "Bibliography of western Hindi and Hindostani". In his *Linguistic Survey of India* vol. 9 pt 1. Delhi: Motilal Banarsidass, 1968, pp. 13-41.
Reprint of original 1916 edition.
Contains much early material, including many grammars and dictionaries.

---

402 Abbi, Anvita
"The conjunctive participle in Hindi-Urdu". *International Journal of Dravidian Linguistics* (Trivandrum, June 1984), 13, 2, pp. 252-263.

403 Afzal, Omar
The subjunctive in Hindi-Urdu: semantic correlates and theoretical implications. Ph.D. thesis, Cornell University, Ithaca, 1986. 250p.

404 Afzal, Qaisar
"New trends in Urdu". *Pakistan Review* 8 (September 1960), pp. 7-8.

405 Ahmad, Aziz
"Cultural orientations: Urdu and Hindi". In his *Studies in Islamic culture in the Indian environment.* London: Oxford University Press, 1964, pp. 239-262.

406   — • "Urdu". In his *An intellectual history of Islam in India.* Edinburgh: Edinburgh University Press, 1969, pp. 91-111.

407   Ahmad, M.G. Zubaid
The contribution of Indo-Pak's to Arabic literature: from ancient times to 1857. Lahore, 1968. 539p.
Reprint of the 1946 ed.
Originally presented as the author's Ph.D. thesis, London University, 1929.

408   Alam, Qaiser Zoha
"An aspect of the impact of English on Urdu". *Indian Linguistics* 49, 1-4 (March-December 1988), pp. 25-33.

409   — • "Commands and requests in English and Urdu". *Indian Linguistics* 41, 3-4 (September-December 1980), pp. 129-132.

410   Ali, Ahmad
"The rise of Urdu". *Pakistan Quarterly* 4, 3 (1954), pp. 44-54.

411   Ali, Muhammad
"Urdu: the lingua franca of India". In: *Select writings and speeches of Maulana Muhammed Ali.* Ed. Afzal Iqbal. Lahore, 1963, pp. 29-51.

412   Anand, Som
"Urdu: death by strangulation". *Times of India Magazine* 8 (1 March 1970), pp. 1-8.

413   Anjuman Taraqqi-e-Urdu Pakistan, Karachi
Pre-eminence of Urdu as appraised by several distinguished publicmen [sic] *of East Bengal.* Karachi, 1952. 69p.

414   Ansari, M.A.
Chrestomathie der Urdu-Prosa des 19. und 20. Jahrhunderts. Leipzig: Verlag Enzyklopädie, 1977. 186p.
First published 1965.
Introduction (bibliographical) in German, text in Urdu.

415   Ansari, Zoe
"Should Urdu be allowed to live: the case for Urdu". *Illustrated Weekly of India* 95, 10 (5 May 1974), pp. 31-32.

416   Apte, Mahadev L.
"Linguistic diversity in India: its nature and implications". *Journal of Asian Pacific and World Perspectives* (Honolulu) 5, 2 (Winter 1981-82), pp. 19-26.

417   — • "Pidiginization of a lingua franca: a linguistic analysis of Hindi-Urdu spoken in Bombay". *International Journal of Dravidian Linguistics* (Trivandrum, India) 3, 1974, pp. 21-41.

418   Arnot, Sandford and Forbes, Duncan
An essay on the origin and structure of the Hindoostanee tongue, or general language of British India, with an account of the principle elementary works on the subject... London, 1828. 24p.

419   — • *Clavis Orientalis, or lecture card of the London Oriental Institute, containing an easy introduction to the principles of oriental writing ... Includes brief sketch of the elements of Hindoostanee grammar.* London, 1827. 2 pts.
Pt. 1 lithographed; pt. 2, consisting of letterpress and 14 engraved plates of oriental characters.

420   **Askari, Muhammad Hasan**
"Urdu language and literature". *Pakistan Pictorial* 6 (November-December 1973), pp. 129-131.

421   **Azeem, Anwar**
"Urdu: a victim of cultural genocide?" In: *Muslims in India.* Ed. Zafar Iman. New Delhi, 1975, pp. 260.

422   — • "Urdu: a light at the end of tunnel". *Indian Literature* 21, 6, (1978), pp. 107-121.

423   **Bahadur Singh**
The dialect of Delhi. New Delhi: University of Heidelberg South Asia Institute, 1966. 68p.

424   **Bailey, T. Grahame**
Studies in north Indian languages. London: Lund Humphries and Co., 1938.
Includes articles on Urdu language and poetics.

425   **Barannikov, P.A.**
"Khindi i urdu: ikh vozniknovenie, razvitie i vzaimodeistvie". In: *Voprosy social'noĭ lingvistiki.* Eds. A.V. Desnitskaia, V.M. Zhirmunskii, L.S. Kovtun. Leningrad: Nauka, 1969, pp. 157-182.

426   — • "Problem suchasnykh khindi i urdu v svitli leksychnoĭ synonimiï movy". *Movoznavstvo* (1963), pp. 79-90.
On the interrelations between modern Hindi and Urdu in the light of lexical synonymy.

427   **Barker, Muhammad Abdur Rahman**
"A script for Pakistan". *Pakistan Review* 10 (July 1962), pp. 9-13.

428   **Barz, Richard Keith**
An introduction to Hindi and Urdu. Canberra: Australian National University, Faculty of Asian Studies, 1986. 232p.

429   **Bawa, Jagdish**
"Urdu language and literature". In: *The languages of India.* Ed. V.K. Narasimhan. Madras: Our Indian Directories and Publications Pvt. Ltd., 1958, pp. 79-84.

430   **Beames, J.**
"Outlines of a plea for the Arabic element in official Hindustani". *Journal of the Asiatic Society of Bengal* 35 (1866), Pt. 1, p. 1.

431   — • "On the Arabic element in official Hindustani". *Journal of the Asiatic Society of Bengal* 36, 1 (1867), p. 145.

432   **Becker, Donald A. and Narang, Gopi Chand**
"Aspiration and nasalization in the generative phonology of Hindi-Urdu". *Language* 47, 3 (1971), pp. 646-667.

433   — • "Generative phonology of the retroflex flaps of Hindu-Urdu". *General Linguistics* 14, 3 (1974), pp. 129-155.

434   **Bedar, Abid Raza**
"Urdu: search for validity". *Indian Literature* 11, 4 (October 1968), pp. 103-108.

435   *Bengali-Urdu common words.* Karachi: Dept. of Films and Publications, 1968. 41p.

436   **Benson, Robson**
A few words on the Arabic derivatives in Hindustani... Being an easy method of acquiring a vast number of useful Hindustani words. London: James Madden, 1852. 34p.

437   **Bhargava, Prem Sugar**
Linguistic interference from Hindi, Urdu and Panjabi and internal analogy in the grammar of Indian English. Ph.D. diss., Cornell University, Ithaca, 1968. 223p.

438   **Bhatia, Tej K.**
"In search of the oldest grammar of Hindustani". *South Asian Review* (Jacksonville), *FL 6-3,* (1982), pp. 214-227. 2 facsim.
On a grammar written in Dutch by Joshua J. Ketelaar, 1698.

439   **Bhatti, Muhammad Ismail**
"Our multi-lingual heritage and English". *Journal of Research (Humanities)* 18, 1 (January 1983), pp. 1-13.

440   **Boyle, O., et al.**
"Sound-meaning relationships in speakers of Urdu and English: evidence for a cross-cultural phonetic symbolism". *Journal of Psycholinguistic Research* 16-3 (New York, 1987), pp. 273-288.

441   **Brass, Paul**
Language, religion and politics in north India. Cambridge: Cambridge University Press, 1974.

442   **Broadbent, John, et al.**
Assessment in a multicultural society: community languages at 16+: a discussion document. Yorkshire: Longman for Schools Council, 1983. 121p.

443   **Bruecke, Ernst Wilhelm**
Über die Aussprache der Aspiraten im Hindustani... Wien, 1859. 8p.
Reprinted from the "Sitzungsberichte der phil.-hist. Classe der k. Akademie der Wissenschaften".

444   **Buddruss, Georg**
"Kritische Randnotizen zu Übersetzungen aus der Hindi- und Urdu-Literatur". In: *Studien zur Indologie und Iranistik* 3 (1977), pp. 23-24.

445   **Bukhari, Suhail**
Phonology of Urdu language. Karachi: Royal Book Co., 1985. 84p.

446   **Chalmurzaev, T. Ch.**
"O peredace v urdu terminologiĭ otnosiasceisia k oblasti kosmonavtiki ´ (po dannym indiiskich gazet)". In: *Issledovaniia po vostocnym iazykam*. Eds. A.G. Belova and L.I. Skarban. Moscow: Nauka, Glavnaia red. vostochnoĭ literatury, 1973, pp. 219-229.

447   — • "Vzaimootnoseniia iazykov urdu i khindi v svete indussko-musul´manskoĭ problemy v kolonial'noĭ Indii". In: *Problemy iezykow Azii i Afryki: materialy II Miedzynarodowego Symopozjum, Warszawa-Krakow 10-15 listopada 1980*. Eds. Stanislaw Pilaszewicz; Jerzy Tulisow. Warsaw: Panstwowe Wyd. Naukowe (Komitet Nauk Orientalistycznych PAN), 1987, pp. 169-174.

448   **Chatterji, Nandalal**
"The East India Company's military staff and instruction in the Hindustani language". *Uttar Pradesh Historical Society Journal* 4 (Lucknow 1956), pp. 1-10.
A debate in 1826 on whether to teach Hindustani to soldiers before going to India.

449   — • "The government's attitude to Hindi-Urdu-Hindustani in the post-mutiny period". *Journal of the U.P. Historical Society* (Lucknow) 3, (1955), pp. 10-34.

450   — • "Bengal and the Hindi-Urdu Question in 1875". *Bengal Past and Present* [Calcutta, (June 1907)] 138, pt. 1 (1955), pp. 5-21.
A controversy among administrators as to the language to be used in Oudh courts. Correspondence is reproduced here.

451   — • "A nineteenth century controversy on the teaching of Hindustani". *Journal of Indian History* 42, 124 (Trivandrum April 1964), pp. 77-87.

452   — • "The problem of Court language in British India". *Journal of Indian History* 31 (Trivandrum, December 1953), pp. 213-16.
Arguments of the Hindi-Urdu controversy of 1875-76 in Lucknow.

453   **Chatterji, Suniti Kumar**
India, a polyglot nation and its linguistic problems vis-a-vis national integration. Bombay: Mahatma Gandhi Memorial Research Centre, Hindustani Prachar Sabha, 1973. 80p.

454   — • *Indo-Aryan and Hindi*. Calcutta: K.L. Mukhopadhyay, [1960]. 329p.

455   — • "The oldest grammar of Hindustan". *Indian Linguistics* 5, 4 (1935), pp. 68-83. (Grierson Commemoration Volume).
Also in a reprint edition of volumes 1-15 of *Indian Linguistics* in 2 vols., Linguistic Society of India, 1964.

456   — • "Sumiti Kumar Chatterji on Urdu". *Illustrated Weekly of India* 95, 10 (5 May 1974), p. 35.

457   **Chattopadhyaya, N.**
"Hindustani as the national language of India". *Hindustan Review* 21, 19. pp. 361-371; 21, 20, pp. 463-472.

458   **Chaudhry, Nazir Ahmad**
Development of Urdu as official language in the Panjab, 1849-1974. Lahore: Punjab Government Record Office, 1977. 444p.

459   **Clark, T.W.**
"The language of Calcutta, 1760-1840". *Bulletin of the School of Oriental and African Studies* (London University), 18 (1956), pp. 453-74.
History of Arabic, Bengali, English, Hindustani, Persian, Portuguese, Sanskrit in the light of British policies, missionary activities, and the history of education.

460   **Contractor, Minocher K.**
Our language problem and unity of India: an approach. Surat: Contractor, 1982. 198p.

461   "Controversy over Urdu". *Link* 7, 47 (4 July 1965), 19p.

462   **Coppola, Carlo**
"Urdu possibilities". *Books Abroad* 41 (Winter 1967), p. 44.

463   **Cummings, Thomas Fulton**
An Urdu manual of the phonetic, inductive or direct method based on the Gospel of John. With a progressive introduction to the constructions of the Urdu language.
2nd rev. ed. Gujranwala: Sialkot Mission of the United Presbyterian Church of North America, 1916. 156p.

464   **Danecki, Janusz**
"Fonologiczna asymilacja slownictwa arabskiego w jezyku urdu". *Acta Philologica* 3 (Warsaw, 1971), pp. 89-95.

465   **Dar, M.I.**
"Gujarat's contribution to Gujarati and Urdu". *Islamic Culture* 28 (1953), pp. 18-36.

466   **Daschenko, G.M.**
"Iz sintaksisa urdu". *Narody Azii i Afriki. Istoriia, ekonomika, kul´tura* 4 (Moscow, 1974), pp. 112-118.

467   — • "O raspolozhenii zavisimykh komponentov slozhnoi atributivnoi sintagmy v iazyke urdu". In: *Voprosy indiiskoi filologii.* Eds. A.T. Aksenova i N.M. Sazanovoi. Moscow: Izd. MGU, 1974, pp. 22-36.

468   **Dasgupta, Jyotirindra**
Language conflict and national development: group politics and national language policy in India. Berkeley: University of California Press, 1970. 293p.

469   **Dass, Dayal**
"Language controversy a century ago". *Indian Historical Records Commission Proceedings*. 32 (New Delhi, 1956), pp. 103-106.
Persian versus Hindustani.

470   **Daudi, M.A.**
"Case for Urdu type-script". *Pakistan Review* 6, 1 (January 1958), pp. 15-16.

471   **Davidovoĭ, A.A.**
"Nekotorye voprosy frazeologii urdu i khindi". In: *Indiiskaia i iranskaia filologiia*. Sbornik statei. otv. red.: N.A. Dvoriankov. Moscow: Nauka, 1964, pp. 234-246.
Philology. A collection of 22 papers.

472   — • "Nekotorye voprosy glagol´nogo slovoobrazovaniia v iazyke Khindustani". In: *Uchenye zapiski instituta vostokovedeniia, Akademiia Nauk SSSR*. 13 (Moscow, 1958), pp. 213-232.

473   **Davison, Alice**
"Case and control in Hindi-Urdu". *Studies in the Linguistic Sciences* 15-2, (Urbana, 1985), pp. 9-23.

474   — • "Wh-movement in Hindi-Urdu relative clauses". *Studies in the Linguistic Sciences* 17-1, (Urbana, 1987), pp. 25-33.

475   — • "Experiencers and patients as subjects in Hindi-Urdu". In: *Proceedings of the conference on participant roles: South Asia and adjacent areas: an ancillary meeting to the CLS regional meeting, April 25th, 1984, University of Chicago*. Eds. Arlene R.K. Zide, David Magier, Eric Schiller. Bloomington: Indiana University Linguistics Club, 1985, pp. 160-178.

476   *A defence of the Urdu language and character. Being a reply to the pamphlet called "Court character and primary education in N.W.P. and Oudh"*. Allahabad: Liddell's N.W.P. Printing Works, 1900. 77, 18p.

477   **Deshmukh, Sir Chintaman Dwarkanath**
Hindustani: rashtrabhasha or lingua franca. Bombay: Mahatma Gandhi Memorial Research Centre, 1972. 73p.

478   **Dil, Afia**
"A comparative study of Bengali and Urdu noun phrase types". *Pakistani Linguistics* 174 (1963), pp. 153-168.

479   **Dil, Anwar S.**
An outline of Urdu sentence structure. Lahore: Linguistic Research Group of Pakistan, 1964. 64p.
First published in *Pakistani Linguistics* (1963), pp. 197-246.

480   — • *Pakistan Conference of Linguists, 1st, Lahore, 1962. Pakistani linguistics*. Lahore: Linguistic Research Group of Pakistan, 1963. 210p.

481 — • *Pakistan Conference of Linguists. 2nd, Lahore, 1964. Pakistani linguistics*
Lahore: Linguistic Research Group of Pakistan, 1964. 316p.

482 — • *Readings in modern linguistics.* Lahore: Linguistic Research Group of Pakistan, 1964. 140p.

483 — • *Studies in Pakistani linguistics.* Lahore: Linguistic Research Group of Pakistan, 1965. 231p.

484 **Dittmer, Kerrin**
Die indischen Muslime und die Hindi-Urdu-Kontroverse in den United Provinces. Wiesbaden: O. Harrassowitz, 1972. 272p. (Schriftenreihe des Südasien-Instituts der Universität Heidelberg).

485 **Doi, Kyuya**
"The influence of Urdu pronunciation on the Hindi language". In: *Onsei no Kenkyū* 12 (Tokyo, 1966), pp. 510-51.
In Japanese with English summary.

486 **Dolcini, Donatella**
"Il significato di khari nella denominazione khari boli". *Annali della Facoltà di lingue e letterature straniere di Ca' Foscari* (Università degli studi di Venezia) 10-3 (1971) (Serie Orientale 2), pp. 51-57.

487 **D'Souza, Jenn**
"Schwa syncope and vowel nasalization in Hindi-Urdu: a non-linear approach". *Studies in the Linguistic Sciences* 15-1 (Urbana, 1985), pp. 11-30.

488 **Dua, Hans Raj**
Language use, attitudes, and identity among linguistic minorities: a case study of Dakhini Urdu speakers in Mysore. Mysore: Central Institute of Indian Languages, 1986. 129p.

489 **Dymshits, Zalman Movshevich**
Iazyk urdu. Moscow: Izd. vostochnoĭ lit., 1962. 144p.

490 **Elizarenkova, T. Ia.**
"K voprosu o nelichnykh imennykh formakh glagola Khindi i Urdu Ksiega Stuszkiewicza". In: *Ksiega pamiatkowa ku czci Eugeniussza Stuszkiewicza.* Ed. Komitet pod przewodnictwem Jana Reychmana. Warsaw: Panstwowe Wyd. Naukowe, 1974, pp. 277-287.
On the non-finite form of the verb in Hindi and Urdu.

491 **Elzafar, Aslam G.**
"The script problem". *Pakistan Review* 12 (February 1964), pp. 30-31.

492 **Evelyn D. Vardy**
"Bazm-e-Urdu, Lucknow: a women's response to the decline of Urdu". *Annual of Urdu Studies* 1 (1986), pp. 89-97.

493 *The evils of the Urdu characters.* Comp. by a member of the Deva-nagri Pracharni Sabha, Meerut. Shahjahanpur: Agra Darpan Press, 1883. 22p.

494   **Faridah, Hafiz**
The women of Islamabad and our national language survey report. Trans. Jamil Azar.
Islamabad: National Language Society, 1988.

495   **Farman Fatihpuri, Dildar Ali**
Pakistan Movement and Hindi-Urdu conflict. Lahore: Sang-e-Meel Publications, 1987.
394p.

496   **Farrukhi, Asif Aslam**
"Images in a broken mirror: the Urdu scene in Bangladesh". *Annual of Urdu Studies* 7
(1990), pp. 83-87.

497   **Faruqi, Khwaja Ahmad**
"Some observations on the Urdu script". *Indian P.E.N.* 36 (April 1970), pp. 91-94.

498   — • "Urdu". In: *Indian Literature.* Ed. Dr Nagendra. Agra: Lakshmi Narain
Agarwal, 1959, pp. 566-591.

499   **Faruqi, Shamsur Rahman**
"Some aspects of the theory of translation". *Urdu Canada* 1, 3 (1987), pp. 5-11.

500   **Feroze, S.**
"The evolution of Urdu press". *Pakistan Quarterly* 4, 4 (1954), pp. 18-23.

501   **Gait, Edward Albert**
The Indian linguistic survey and the vernaculars. London, 1928. 16p.
Reprinted from the *Journal of the East India Association*, New Series.

502   **Gandhi, Mohandas Karamchand**
"Our language problem". Ed. Anand T. Hingorani. Bombay: Bharatiya Vidya Bhavan,
1965. 133p.

503   **Ganguli, Symacharan**
"Hindi, Hindustani and the Behar dialects". *Calcutta Review* 75, 149 (1882), pp. 24-40.

504   — • "In self-defence". *Calcutta Review* 75, 150 (1882), pp. 256-263.

505   **Gankovskiĭ, Iu. V.**
"Natsional'no-iazykovaia situatsiia v Pakistane". In: *Iazyki Indii, Pakistana, Nepala i
Tseilon.* Materialy nauchnoi konferentsii 18-20 ianvaria 1965 goda. V.M. Beskrovnyi,
E.M. Bykova, V.P. Liperovskiĭ. Moscow: Nauka, 1968, pp. 89-95.

506   **Garcin de Tassy, Joseph Héliodore Sagesse Vertu**
Chrestomathie Hindoustani. Urdu et Dakhni. Intikhab-i tasanif-i Hindustani. Prepared
under Garcin de Tassy's direction by T. Pavie. Vocabulary by l'abbé Bertrand, et al. Paris:
École spéciale des langues orientales vivantes, 1847. 128, 104p.

507 — • *Rudiments de la langue Hindoustanie, à l'usage des élèves de l'École royale et spéciale des langues Orientales vivantes ... Appendix ... contenant, outre quelques additions à la Grammaire, des lettres hindoustanis originales, accompagnées d'une traduction et de facsimile.* Paris, 1829-1833. 99, 68p.

Deuxième édition, adaptée aux dialectes Urdu et Dakhni. Paris, 1863.

508 — • *Mémoire sur le système metrique des Arabes, adapté à la langue Hindoustani.* Paris, 1832.

509 — • *Origine et diffusion de l'Hindoustani appelée langue générale ou nationale de l'Inde.* Caen, 1871. (Memoire de l'Académie de Caen).

510 **Ghani, Muhammad Abdul**
A history of Persian language and literature at the Mughal court, with a brief survey of the growth of Urdu language (Babur to Akbar). Allahabad: Indian Press, 1929-1930.

511 **Gilani, Ijaz and Muttaqeen-ur-Rahman**
The language question: public attitudes on language of education and employment. Islamabad: Gallup Pakistan and National Language Authority, [1986?]. 36p.
"Finding of a nation-wide survey"--Cover.

512 **Gilchrist, John Borthwick**
The Hindee-Arabic mirror: or improved Arabic practical tables of such Arabic words which are intimately connected with a due knowledge of the Hindoostanee language. Calcutta, 1802.

513 — • *The oriental linguist; an easy and familiar introduction to the Hindoostanee or grand popular language of Hindoostan.* 2nd ed. Calcutta: Ferris and Greenway, 1802. 163p.
First published 1798.

514 "Give Urdu due place: CIP Executive Resolution". *New Age* 15, 41 (8 October 1967), p. 7.

515 **Grierson, George Abraham**
The languages of India. A reprint of the chapter on languages contributed to the *Report on the Census of India, 1910,* together with the Census statistics of language. 1903.

516 — • "Hindostani". In: *Encylopaedia Britannica* 13 (11th ed.), Cambridge, 1910.

517 — • "Hindostani". In his *Linguistic survey of India* 9, 1. Delhi: Motilal Banarsidass, 1968, pp. 42-65.
Reprint of original 1916 ed.

518 — • *Linguistic survey of India.* Calcutta: Govt. of India, Central Publications Branch, 1903-28. 11 vols (some in multiple parts).
Altogether 179 languages and 544 dialects are covered. Hindustani is mainly covered in volumes 8, 9 and 10.

519 — • "On certain suffixes in the modern Indo-Aryan vernaculars". In: *Zeitschrift für Vergleichende Sprachforschung auf dem Gebiete der indogermanischen Sprachen.* Vol. 38 (18) (1903), p. 473.
Reviewed by A.F.R. Hoernle in the *Journal of the Royal Asiatic Society* 1903, pp. 611-.

520 — • "On the early study of Indian vernaculars in Europe". *Journal of the Asiatic Society of Bengal* 62, 1 (1893), p. 41.

523 — • "The phonology of the modern Indo-Aryan vernaculars". In: *Zeitschrift der Deutschen Morgenlandischen Gesellschaft.* Vol. 49 (1895), p. 393; Vol. 50 (1986), p. i. Reprinted, Leipzig, 1895-96.

524 Griguard, A.
"Our romanized Hindustani-English dictionaries; their partial ineffeciency and its remedies". *Journal of the Asiatic Society of Bengal,* New series, 20 (1924), pp. 85-98.

525 Growse, Frederic Salmon
"Common Hindustan". *Bengal Magazine* 2 (1874), pp. 239-245.
Advocates Hindi as against Urdu, as the language of the courts and missionaries.

526 — • "Some objections to the modern style of official Hindustani". *Journal of the Asiatic Society of Bengal* 35 (1866), pt. 1, p. 172.

527 Gulhamid Begum
The Urdu language in Mauritius. Port Louis, Mauritius, [1967?]

528 Hamidullah, M.
"Brief notes on 'Nirali Urdu of Delhi'". *Indian Linguistics: Journal of the Linguistic Society of India* 7 (Pune, 1939), pp. 167-179.
Also in reprint edition of volumes 1-15 of *Indian Linguistics* in 2 vols., Linguistic Society of India, 1964, pp. 341-351.

529 Hanitchak, John J.
"An Urdu word study". *Pakistani Linguistics* 174 (1963), pp. 143-152.

530 Hans, Surjit Singh
"Urdu: its future". *Century* 1, 27 (23 November 1963), p. 3.

531 Harley, Alexander Hamilton
Colloquial Hindustani. London: Kegan Paul, Trench, Trübner and Co., 1944. 147p.

532 Hasan, Aftab
"Urdu translation of technical terms and text books". *Jamia Educational Quarterly* 5 (July 1964), pp. 50-65.

533 Hasan, Mohammad
"Urdu". *Book Chronicle* (January 1, 16, 1978), pp. 56-60.
Mainly on the issue of cultural identity in Pakistan.

534 — • "Urdu: awaiting its moment of truth". *Indian Literature* 14, 1 (1971), pp. 61-68.

535   **Hasan, Nazir**
"Garcin de Tassy: a French devotee of Urdu". *Pakistan Review* 10 (April 1962), pp. 21-22.

536   **Hasan, Ruqaiya**
"The verb "be" in Urdu. The verb "be" and its synonyms". In: *Philosophical and grammatical studies. (5) Urdu/Turkish/ Bengali/Amharic/Indonesian/ Telugu/Estonian.* Ed. John W.M. Verhaar.   Dordrecht, The Netherlands: Reidel, 1972, pp. 1-63.
(Folia Linguistica, Supplementary Series 14).

537   **Hashmi, Bilal and Gardezi, Hasan Nawaz**
"Urdu: the structural and cultural context of intellectuals". In: *South Asian Intellectuals and Social Change.* Ed. Yogendra K. Malik.   New Delhi: Heritage Publishers, 1982, pp. 202-234.

538   **Hoenigswald, Henry M.**
"Declension and nasalization in Hindustani". *Journal of the American Oriental Society* 78 (New Haven, 1948), pp. 139-144.

539   **Holle, Stuart R.**
"Hindi, Urdu and Hindustani: an analysis". *Quest* 66 (July-September 1970), pp. 22-23.

540   **Hook, Peter, et al.**
"Differential S-marking in Marathi, Hindi-Urdu and Kashmiri". *CLS ...Papers from the ... Annual Regional Meeting of the Chicago Linguistic Society* 23-1 (Chicago, 1987), pp. 148-165.

541   **Husain, Mahmud**
"Problems of translation in Pakistani languages: an introduction". *Jamia Educational Quarterly* 5 (July 1964), pp. 1-6.

542   **Husain, Masud**
A phonetic and phonological study of the word in Urdu. Aligarh, [195-?].   47p.   (Aligarh Muslim University. Department of Urdu. Studies, no. 1)

543   **Husain, Syed L.**
"Urdu in India, 1972-73". *Indian Literature* 17, 4 (October 1974), pp. 60-68.

544   — • "Urdu: a precious heritage". *Indian Literature* 19, 1 (1976), pp. 82-89.

545   **Huttar, G.L. and Eslick, Judith A.**
"Distinctive features in Sarnami Hindustani". *Phonetica* 25, (1972), pp. 108-118, 5 tab. German and French summaries.

546   *Introduction to the study of the Hindostany language as spoken in the Carnatic.* Calcutta, 1808.

547   "Insafi - Sir George Campbell on vernacular education". *The Oriental* 4 (1875), p. 83.
On the value of the Urdu language compared with that of Hindi.

548   Iqbal, Muzaffar
"Urdu's tacit lover: a conversation with Donald A. Becker". *Annual of Urdu Studies* 6 (1987), pp. 116-119.
Professor Becker's pioneering work on the development of a word processor which will allow computer generated Urdu text.

549   Kachru, Yamuna
"Conjunct verbs in Hindi-Urdu and Persian". *South Asian Review* (1892), pp. 117-126.

550   — • "Ergativity, subjecthood and topicality in Hindi-Urdu". *Lingua* 71, 1-4, (1987), pp. 223-238.

551   — • "Hindi-Urdu". In: *The world's major languages.* Ed. Bernard Comrie. London: Croom Helm, 1987, pp. 470-489.

552   — • "On relative clause formation in Hindi-Urdu". *Linguistics* 207 (1978), pp. 5-26.

553   — • "On the semantics of the causative construction in Hindi-Urdu". *Syntax and Semantics* 6 (New York, 1976), pp. 353-369.

554   — • "On the syntax, semantics and pragmatics of the conjunctive participle in Hindi-Urdu". *Studies in the Linguistic Sciences* 11 (Urbana, 1981-1982), pp. 35-49.

555   — • "Pragmatics and verb serialization in Hindi-Urdu". *Studies in the Linguistic Sciences* 9-2 (Urbana, 1979-1980), pp. 157-169.

556   — • "Some aspects of pronominalization and relative clause construction in Hindi-Urdu". *Studies in the Linguistic Sciences* 3, 2 (Urbana, 1973), pp. 87-103.

557   — • "The syntax of ko-sentences in Hindi-Urdu". *Papers in Linguistics* 2, (Edmonton, 1970), pp. 299-31.

558   — • "Transivity and volitionality in Hindi-Urdu". *Studies in the Linguistic Sciences* 11 Urbana, (1981-1982), pp. 181-193.

559   Kachru, Yamuna and Bhatia, Tej K.
"On reflexivization in Hindi-Urdu and its theoretical implications". *Indian Linguistics Journal of the Linguistic Society of India* 38, (Pune, 1977), pp. 21-38.

560   — • "Evidence for global constraints: the case of reflexivization in Hindi-Urdu". *Studies in the Linguistic Sciences* 5 (Urbana, 1975), pp. 42-73.

561   — • "Notes on participant roles and grammatical categories in Hindi-Urdu sentences". In: *Linguistic and literary studies in honor of Archibald A. Hill.* Ed. Mohammad Ali Jazayery, Edgar C. Polomé, Werner Winter. 4: *Linguistics and literature/sociolinguistics and applied linguistics - trends in linguistics.* (Studies and Monographs 10). The Hague: Mouton, 1979. 392p.

562   **Kay, W.**
"On the connection of the dative and accusative cases in Bengali and Hindustani". *Journal of the Asiatic Society of Bengal* 21 (1852), p. 105.

563   **Kazimi, Syed Shabbir Ali**
Common words of Urdu/Bengali: a glossary. Karachi: Guild Publishing House, 1965, 201p.

564   **Kelkar, Ashok R.**
Studies in Hindi-Urdu. 1. Introduction and word phonology. Poona: Deccan College, 1968. (Building Centenary and Silver Jubilee Series 35)

565   — • *Studies in Hindi-Urdu. Introduction and word phonology.* Poona: Deccan College, 1968.

566   — • "Reply to Srivstava's review of Studies in Hindi - Urdu I". *Indian Linguistics* 31, 3 (July-September 1970), pp. 103-108.
Comments on review published in *Language Journal of the Linguistic Society of America* (Baltimore) 45, pp. 913-927. Rejoinder by R.N. Srivastava in *Indian Linguistics* 31 (1970), pp. 186-196.

567   **Khader Mohiddin, S.**
Dakhani Urdu. Annamalainagar, 1980. 212p. (Annamalai University, Department of Linguistics, Publications 71).

568   **Khalil ur Rahman**
Advertisements for the posts and the national language survey report Khalil-ur-Rahman and Syed Muttaqeen-ur-Rehman under the guidance of Ijaz Shafi Gilani. Trans.
Jamil Azar. Islamabad: National Language Authority, 1988.

569   **Khalmurzaev, T.**
Status urdu v sovremennoĭ Indiĭ i tendentsiĭ ego razvitiia. Tashkent: Fan, 1979.

570   **Khan, Baber S.A.**
"The ergative case in Hindi-Urdu". *Studies in the Linguistic Sciences* 17-1 (Urbana, 1987), pp. 91-101.

571   **Khan, Hamid Ali**
The vernacular controversy: an account and criticism of the equalisation of Nagri and Urdu, as the character for the Court of the North-West Provinces and Oudh, under the Resolution. no. 585/111343-C 68 ... dated 18th April 1900. [Lucknow 1900]. 123p.

572   **Khan, Iqbal**
"Urdu and the partition: the course not taken". *Viewpoint* 13, 5 (September 1987), pp. 27-30.

573   **Khan, Iqtidar H. and Mustafa, Khateeb S.**
"Simple finite verbs in Dakkhni". *Indian Linguistics* 45, 1-4 (March-December 1984), pp. 49-54.

574   **Khan, Yusuf Husain**
"The origin and growth of the Urdu language in medieval times".   *Islamic Culture* 30, 4
(October 1956), pp. 351-364.

575   **Khawaja, Sarfraz**
"Sikh revivalism and Panjabi-Hindi-Urdu language controversy in the Punjab (India) 1908-
1911".   *Journal of the University of Baluchistan* 11, 2 (Autumn 1982),   pp. 45-58.

576   *Khindi i Urdu: voprosy leksikologii i slovoobrazovaniia*.   Ed. V.M. Beskrovnyi.
Moscow: Izd. vostochnoi literatury, 1960. 247p.

577   **Khubchandani, Lachman Mulchand**
"Towards a selection grammar: fluidity in modes of address and reference in Hindi-Urdu".
Indian Linguistics. Journal of the Linguistics Society of India. 39 (1978), pp. 1-24.

578   **Kidwai, Sadiqur Rahman**
Gilchrist and the language of Hindustan. New Delhi: Rachna Prakashan, 1972. 160p.
A revision of the author's thesis, University of Delhi, entitled: *Critical study of the works of
John Borthwick Gilchrist.*
"Gilchrist's works in chronological order": (151)-153p.

579   **King, Christopher**
"The Hindi-Urdu controversy of the North-Western Provinces and Oudh and communal
consciousness". *Journal of South Asian Literature* 13, 1-4 (1977-78), pp. 111-120.

580   **Kirkpatrick, William**
"A comparative vocabulary of the language of European Gypsies, or Romnichal, and
colloquial Hindustani". *Journal of the Asiatic Society of Bengal,* New series (1913), pp. 93-
105.

581   — • *A vocabulary, Persian, Arabic, and English; containing such words as have been
adopted from the two former of those languages, and incorporated into the Hindvi: together
with some hundreds of compound verbs formed from Persian or Arabic nouns, and in
universal use: being the seventh part of the new Hindvi grammar and dictionary.* Printed by
Joseph Cooper, 1785. 196, 4p.

582   **Kliuev, B.I.**
"Nekotorye voprosy razvitiia urdu v Pakistane". *Sovremennoi literatury iazyki Stran Azii*
326, pp. 82-115, 9 tab.

583   **Komal, Balraj**
"Urdu: being and not being". *Indian Literature* 23, 5 (1980), pp. 24-31.

584   **Kripa Shanker Singh**
Readings in Hindi-Urdu linguistics. New Delhi: National, 1978. 298p.

585   **Kumaranangalarn, S. Mohan**
India's language crisis, an introductory study. Madras: New Century Book House, 1965.
122p.

586   Lall, Inder Jit
"Patriotic Urdu". *Century* 1, 10 (27 July 1963), p. 21.

587   — • "Urdu: a language of composite culture". *Indian Literature* 19, 4 (1976), pp. 48-53.

588   Lea, C.H.
Hindustani vs English. Allahabad: The Indian Press, 1911. 68p.

589   Liperovskiĭ, V.P.
"Voprosy iazyka urdu v publikatsiiach gruppy lingvisticeskikh issledovaniĭ Pakistana". *Narody Aziĭ i Afriki. Istoriia, ėkonomika, kul'tura.* 4 (Moscow, 1967), pp. 164-172.

590   Masood, Husain Khan
"Urdu: a progressive language". *Radiance* (11 February 1968), pp. 5-12.

591   Matthews, David J.
"Urdu and Hindustani". In: *South Asian languages: a handbook.* Ed. Christopher Shackle. London: School of Oriental and African Studies, External Services Division, 1985, pp. 21-26.

592   M.C. Singh
Readings in Hindi-Urdu linguistics. New Delhi: National, 1978. 298p.

593   Mehdi, Baqar
"Urdu: the 'relay race'". *Indian Literature* 24, 6 (November-December 1981), pp. 34-41.

594   Meile, P.
"Hindoustani" and "Langues modernes de l'Inde". In: *Centcinquantenaire de l'École des Langues Orientales*, (Paris, 1830), pp. 113-127.

595   Minault, Gail
"Begamati zuban: women's language and culture in nineteenth century Delhi". *Indian International Centre Quarterly* 11, 2 (New Delhi, June 1984), pp. 155-70.

596   Mittal, Gopal
"Urdu without illusions". *Radiance* 8 (January 1967), pp. 8-10.

597   Mobbs, Michael C.
"Two languages or one? The significance of the language names 'Hindi' and 'Urdu'". *Journal of Multilingual and Multicultural Development* 2-3 (Clevedon, Avon, 1981), pp. 203-214.

598   Mohiddin, S. Khader
Dakhani Urdu. Annamalainagar: Annamalai University, 1980. 212p.

599   Mohyeddin, K.
"Language work in Urdu in the primary department". *Pakistan Review* 9, 3 (March 1961), pp. 23-24.

600   Moizuddin, Mohammad
Word forms in Urdu. Islamabad: National Language Authority, 1989.

601   Molholt, Garrett G.
"A generative discourse grammar of Hindi-Urdu nominal reference".   Ph.D. thesis, University of Wisconsin-Madison, 1976. 185p.

602   Molteno, Marion
Word forms in Urdu. Islamabad: National Language Authority, 1989. 108p.
Originally presented as the author's thesis (M. Phil.), University of London, 1967.

603   Morgenstierne, Georg
Report on a linguistic mission to north-western India. Oslo: H. Aschehoug, 1932. 76p. (Instituttet for Sammenlignende Kulturforskning, series C III-1).

604   Morisy, John
"Inquiry into the existence of a pure passive voice in Hindustani". *Proceedings of the Royal Irish Academy* 8, 2 (1862), p. 197.

605   — • "On Hindustani syntax". *Proceedings of the Royal Irish Academy* 9, 3 (1866), p. 263.

606   Muhammed, Sayed
The value of Dakhni language and literature. Mysore: Prasaranga, University of Mysore, 1968. 59p.

607   Mujeeb, Muhammad
"What is happening in Urdu". *Weekend Review* 1, 18 (8 April 1967), pp. 29-30.

608   Myers, Jill
"Urdu in Blackburn". *Pakistan Studies* 11, 3 (Winter 1983-84), pp. 43-52.

609   — • "A neglected language". *Eastern Economist* 30, (23 May, 1958), p. 968. Urdu's position in India.

610   Naim, C.M.
"The consequences of Indo-Pakistani war for Urdu language and literature". *Journal of Asian Studies* 28, 2 (February 1969), pp. 269-283.

611   — • "Urdu in the pre-modern period: synthesis or particularism?". *New Quest* 6 (February 1978), pp. 5-12.

612   Narang, Gopi Chand
Karkhandari dialect of Delhi Urdu. Delhi: Munshi Ram Manohar Lal, 1961. 80p.

613   Narang, Gopi Chand and Becker, Donald A.
"Aspiration and nasalization in the generative phonology of Hindi-Urdu". *Language* 47, 3 (1971), pp. 646-667.

614 — • "Development and use of writing system across culture: the case of Arabic-Persian Urdu orthographic model". *Journal of South Asian and Middle Eastern Studies* 10, 2 (Winter 1986), pp. 64-77.

615 — • "Generative phonology of the retroflex flaps of Hindu-Urdu". *General Linguistics* 14, 3 (1974), pp. 129-155.

616 — • *Handbook of Urdu sounds and scripts.* Madison: University of Wisconsin, Indian Language and Area Centre, 1964.

617   **Nespital, Helmut**
Das Futursystem im Hindi und Urdu: ein Beitrag zur semantischen Analyse der Kategorien Tempus, Aspekt und Modus und ihrer Grameme. Wiesbaden: Franz Steiner Verlag, 1981. 340p. (Schriftenreihe des Südasien-Instituts der Universität Heidelberg, 29).

618 — • "Zur Aufstellung eines Seminventars der Tempuskategorie im Hindi und Urdu und zu einer Charakteristik". In: *Zeitschrift der Deutschen Morgenländischen Gesellschaft* 130 (Stuttgart, 1980), pp. 490-521.

619 — • "Zur syntaktischen Verwendung der Verbalaspekte im Hindi und Urdu". *Wissenschaftliche Zeitschrift der Humboldt-Universität, Berlin.* In: (Gesellschaftswissenschaftliche Reihe.) 23 (1974), pp. 224-226.
Also in: *Zeitschrift für Phonetik, Sprachwissenschaft und Kommunikations Forschung* 28 (Berlin, 1975), pp. 398-431.

620   **Ohala, Manjari**
Topics in Hindi-Urdu phonology. Ph.D. diss., University of California, Los Angeles, 1972. 334p.

621   **Olphen, Herman Van**
"Religion and language varieties: the case of Hindi-Urdu". In: *Languages and Cultures: studies in honor of Edgar C. Polomé.* Ed. Mohammad Ali Jazayery; Werner Winter. TLSM 36; Berlin: Mouton de Gruyter, 1988. 791p.

622   *On language problem.* Calcutta: Socialist Unity Centre of India, 1981. 24p.
Marxist viewpoint on the official language of India, reprinted from an article originally published in *Socialist Unity* in 1965, entitled, "On the question of official language of India".

623   **Pakistan Conference of Linguists**
Pakistan linguistics; selected papers (Lahore, 1963-   ).
Annual.

624   **Pandharipande, Rajeshwari**
"On the semantics of Hindi-Urdu Calna". *Studies in the Linguistic Sciences* (University of Illinois) (Urbana, 1975), pp. 93-112.
Also in: *Indian Linguistics. Journal of the Linguistic Society of India* 36 (Pune, 1975), pp. 104-118.

625   Pandharipande, Rajeshwari and Kachru, Yamuna
"Relational grammar, ergativity, and Hindi-Urdu". *Studies in the Linguistic Sciences* 6 (University of Illinois, Urbana, 1976/1), pp. 82-99.

626   — • "Relational grammar, ergativity, and Hindi-Urdu". *Lingua* 41, (1977), pp. 217-238, tab.

627   Peer, Mohammad
"Urdu language and the Indian Muslims". *Guru Nanak Journal of Sociology* 4, 2 (October 1983), pp. 138-149.

628   Pelikan, Heike
"Arabische und persische elemente in Dakhini (anhand von materialien des Missionars Benjamin Schultz)". In: *Wissenschaftliche Zeitschrift der Universität Halle* 36 (1987), H. 4, pp. 125-129.

629   Pertold, O.
Učebnice Hindustání pro školy i samouky se zvláštním zřetelem k protřebám obchodniků a turistů: Jazykové příručky orientálního ustavu I. Praha: Orientálni Ústav, 1939. 377, 31p.

630   Pickthall, Marmaduke
"The advance of Urdu". *Islamic Culture* 2, 3 (1928). pp. 464-471.

631   Pořízka, Vincenc
"Hindi-Russian and Urdu-Russian dictionaries". *Archiv Orientální. Journal of the Czechoslovak Oriental Institute* 47 (Praha, 1979), pp. 185-192.
Lexicographical work linked to linguistic research. On the work of V.M. Beskrovnyi (1908-78).

632   Prasad, Nawal Kishore
The language issue in India. Delhi: Leeladevi, 1979. 126p.

633   Pray, Bruce Raymond
Agreement in Hindi-Urdu and its phonological implications. Ph.D diss., University of Michigan, 1969. 202p.

634   — • "Evidence of grammatical covergence in Dakhini Urdu and Telugu". *Proceedings of the ... Annual Meeting of the Berkeley Linguistics Society, Berkeley, Ca.* 6, 1980. pp. 90-99.

635   — • *Topics in Hindi-Urdu grammar.* Berkeley, 1970. 195p. (Center for South and South East Asian Studies, University of California, Research Monograph 1).

636   Pybus and Captain G.D.
A text-book of Urdu prosody and rhetoric. Lahore: Rama Krishna and Sons, 1924. 151p.

637   Qadir, A.
"The importance of translations in the languages of Pakistan". *Jamia Educational Quarterly* 5 (July 1964), pp. 24-34.

638   —• *Urdu language and literature*. Allahabad: University of Allahabad, 1942.

639   **Rai, Amrit**
A house divided: the origin and development of Hindi/Hindavi. Delhi; New York: Oxford University Press, 1984. 322p.

640   **Rajendra Lal Mitra**
"On the origin of the Hindvi language and its relation to the Urdu dialect". *Journal of the Asiatic Society of Bengal* 33 (1864), pp. 469, 489.

641   **Ramakrishnan, Ayikudi**
"Should Urdu be allowed to live: the case against Urdu". *Illustrated Weekly of India* 95, 10 (5 May 1974), p. 30.

642   **Rau, S.K.**
"Urdu and Hindi". *Swarajya* 9, 37 (13 March 1965), p. 16.

643   **Ray, Punya Sloka**
"Hindi-Urdu stress". *Indian Linguistics. Journal of the Linguistic Society of India* 27 (Pune, 1966), pp. 95-101.

644   **Raza, Rahim**
"Problemi di politica linguistica in India: la controversia hindi-urdu e i nazionalismi linguistici in Punjab e Bihar." *Lingua e Politica* (1976), pp. 114-142.

645   —• "L'insegnamento della lingua urdu agli stranieri: gli strumenti didattici e le difficoltà incontrate dai principianti". In: Didattica delle lingue del Medio e dell'Estremo Oriente: metodologie ed esperienze. *Atti del Convegno nazionale* (Napoli-Sorrento, 17-20 April 1985), (1988), pp. 161-169.

646   **Rifat, Taufiq**
"Towards a Pakistani idiom". *Venture* 6 (1969), pp. 60-73.

647   **Rizvi, S.A.A.**
"A farewell address in Urdu presented to John Panton Gubbins by the citizens of Delhi in 1852". *Bulletin of School of Oriental and African Studies* 27 (1964), pp. 297-407.
"The earliest known farewell address written in Urdu". (Gubbins, 27 years in India, the last 7 as Sessions Judge at Delhi; Syed Ahmad Khan was his subordinate. Plates and translation).

648   **Rudin, S.G.**
"Nekotorye voprosy fonetiki iazyka khindustani". *Uchennye zapiski Instituta vostokovedeniia*. Moscow: Akademiia Nauk SSSR, 159p.

649   **Russell, Ralph**
"Aziz Ahmad, South Asia, Islam and Urdu". In: *Islamic Society and Culture: essays in honour of Professor Aziz Ahmad*. Eds. Milton Israel and N.K. Wagle. New Delhi: Manohar Publications, 1983, pp. 59-68.

650 — • "The British contribution to Urdu studies". *Oriental College Magazine* (Lahore), Centenary Number;
Translated and republished in *Afkar as "Angrezon ki Urdu-dosti"* 133 (Karachi, 1981), pp. 422-430.

651 — • *Ethnic minority languages and the schools (with special reference to Urdu)*. London: Runnymede Trust, 1980.

652 — • *The last four years of Urdu in Britain: a personal statement*. Urdu translation by Inamul Haq Javed. Islamabad: National Language Authority, 1986. 22p.

653 — • *Oriental despotism: a report on the School of Oriental and African Studies, University of London*. London: Council for Academic Freedom and Democracy, [1973]. 10p.

654 — • "Urdu in Britain: a note". *Pakistan Studies* 1, 2 (Spring 1982), pp. 61-63.

655 — • *Urdu in Britain: a report on the first and second national Urdu Conference 1979 and 1981*. London: Urdu Markaz; Karachi: Golden Block Works, 1982. 167p.
Selected papers, tracing the development of Urdu language instruction in British schools.

656 **Sabzawari, S.A.**
"A phonetic tendency of Urdu". *Journal of the Asiatic Society of Pakistan* 1 (1956), pp. 78-86.

657 **Saksena, Ram Babu**
Gandhiji's solution of the language problem of India. Bombay: Mahatma Gandhi Memorial Research Centre, Hindustani Prachan Sabha, 1972. 58p.

658 **Saroor, Aley Ahmad**
"Urdu: a wind of change: a view of Urdu writing in 1966". *Indian Literature* 10, 4 (October 1967), pp. 90-105.

659 **Sayyid, Muhammad Abdul-Wahid**
"Contemporary Urdu: a language within limited ergativity". *Journal of the College of Arts, King Saud University* (Saudi Arabia), 10 (1983), pp. 127-146.

660 **Schmidt, Ruth Laila**
Dakhini Urdu, history and structure. New Delhi: Bahri Publications, 1981. 110p.

661 — • *Structural analysis of Hyderabadi Dakhini Urdu*. Ph.D. thesis. University of Pennsylvania, 1969. 157p.

662 **Semeen, Anwar Quddus**
The national language and the habits of study among the women. A survey report. Trans. Jamil Azar. Islamabad: National Language Authority, 1988.

663 **Seshadri, T.K.**
The language question: a historical analysis. Bangalore: Varada, 1965. 12p.

664   **Seton-Karr, W.S.**
"The Urdu language and literature". *Calcutta Review* 4, 8 (1845).

665   **Shackle, Christopher and Snell, Rupert**
Hindi and Urdu since 1800: a common reader. London: School of Oriental and African Studies, University of London, 1990. 222p.

666   **Shah, Sayid Ghulam Mustafa**
"Urdu: failure of a language and mayhem of a nation". *Sind Quest* 13, 1 (1985) pp. 3-20.

667   — • "Urdu: thirty years accountability, a sociological study and analysis. Urdu as a national language and medium of instruction". *Sind Quarterly* 9, 2 (1981), pp. 1-15.

668   **Shahidullah, Mohammad**
"The influence of Urdu-Hindi on the Bengali language and literature". *Journal of the Asiatic Society of Pakistan* 7 (June 1962), pp. 1-16.

669   — • "Common origin of Urdu and Bengali". *Pakistan Quarterly* 9, 3 (Autumn 1959), pp. 52-53.

670   **Sharma, Ran Singh**
Linguistic studies in modern India. New Delhi: Arya Book Depot, 1981. 92p.

671   **Sharma, Swami Nath**
Lingua Indiana. Bombay: Nalanda Publications, [1947]. 57p.

672   **Shrivastava, Gopinath**
The language controversy and the minorities. Delhi: Atma Ram, 1970. 160p.

673   **Siddiqui, Abu Lais**
"Common elements in the structure of Turkish and Urdu". *University Studies* (Karachi) 3, 3 (August 1966), pp. 1-22.

674   — • The importance of translation in Pakistani languages". *Jamia Educational Quarterly* 5 (July 1964), pp. 16-23.

675   — • "The language problem in Pakistani literature". *Pakistani Linguistics* 174 (1963), pp. 91-96.

676   — • "Urdu language and literature". *Pakistan Quarterly* 8, 3 (Winter 1958), pp. 44-49.

677   **Siddiqui, Ahmad H.**
"Notes on queclaratives and tag questions in Hindi-Urdu". *Studies in the Linguistic Sciences* (University of Illinois, Urbana) 3, 1973, pp. 134-148.

678   — • *The syntax and semantics of questions in English, Hindi and Urdu: a study in applied linguistics*. Ph.D. thesis, Ohio State University, 1977. 243p.

679   **Siddiqi, M.A**
"The progress of Urdu in Pakistan". *Pakistan Quarterly* 3, 3-4 (August-September 1977), pp. 31-32.

680   **Siddiqui, S.A.**
Urdu script and orthography. Delhi: Idarah-i Adabiyat-i Delhi, 1976. 102p.

681   **Siegel, Jeffrey**
"Fiji Hindustani". In: *Working papers in linguistics.* (Department of Linguistics, University of Hawaii, Honolulu) 7, 1975/3, pp. 127-144.

682   **Sinha, R.M.**
"An old document dealing with Hindi-Urdu controversy". *Indian Historical Records Commission Proceedings* 34 (New Delhi, 1958), pp. 91-93.
Summary of proceedings of a meeting in 1871 at Jabalpur.

683   **Smekal, Odolen**
Aplikovaná mluvnice hindštiny 1; 2. Praha: Státní pedag. naklad, 1986. 298, 312p.

684   — • *Hindština. Učební text.* Cast 1 & 2. Praha: Státní pedag. naklad., 1955 (1956), pp. 109-113.

685   **Southworth, Franklin C.**
The student's Hindi-Urdu reference manual. Tucson: University of Arizona Press, 1971. 238p.

686   **Spies, Otto**
"Türkisches Sprachgut im Hindustani". In: *Studia Indologica ...* Bonn, 1955. pp. 321-343.

687   **Spies, Otto and Bannerth, E.**
Lehrbuch der Hindustani-Sprache. Leipzig: Harrassowitz, 1945. 203p.

688   **Stewart, Charles**
An introduction to the study of the Hindostany language as spoken in the Carnatic. Compiled for the use of the Company of Gentlemen Cadets on the Madras Establishment at New Town Cuddalore, 1808. Madras, 1843.

689   **Subbarao, K.V. and Arora, Harbir**
"On extreme convergence: the case of Dakkhini Hindi-Urdu". *Indian Linguistics* 49, 1-4 (March-December 1988), pp. 92-108.

690   **Sukhochev, A.S.**
"Nachal´nyi etap formirovaniia realisticheskogo romana na Urdu". *Kultura slova.* Bratislava 8 (1965), pp. 53-61.

691   **Sundara Reddi, G.**
The language problem in India. Delhi: National Publishing House, 1973. 90p.
Comprises articles by eminent Indian scholars.

692   **Suraj Bhan Singh**
"Concepts of semantic field and collocation in Hindi/Urdu lexicography". *Studia et Acta Orientalia* 10 (Bucharest, 1980), pp. 129-145.

693   **Swarajya Lakshmi, V.**
Influence of Urdu on Telugu: a study of bilingualism. Hyderabad, India: V. Swarajya Lakshmi, 1984.
Prefatory matter in English and Telugu.

694   **Tamannai, A.Z.**
"Urdu typography: a problem?". *Vision* 13, 6 (July 1964), pp. 9-13.

695   **Temple, R.T.**
"Hindustani in the XVIIth century". *Indian Antiquary* 32 (1903), p. 239.

696   **Thwates, Edmund Charles**
Dakani manuscripts. Containing 50 specimens of Hindustani hand-writing, produced in facsimile, accompanied by Hindustani printed transcriptions, and English translations. Madras: Addison and Co., 1892.

697   *"Un-ne"-nama; or, the Urdu pronominal expressions "Un-ne", "In-ne", "Jin-ne" and "Kinne", are they of plural or singular number?* 2nd ed. London, 1869.

698   "Urdu as medium of instruction". *Pakistan Review* 10 (April 1962), p. 5.

699   *Urdu: a symposium in the shadow of a linguistic genocide.* New Delhi: Seminar, 1987. 40p.

700   **Usmanov, Akpar Rakhmatovich**
Voprosy sintaksicheskoi klasifikatsii glagolov urdu. Moscow: Nauka, Glavnaia redaktsiia vostochnoi literatury, 1980. 47p.

701   **Vallancey, Charles**
Prospectus of a dictionary of the language of the Aire Coti, or Ancient Irish, compared with the language of the Cuti, or Ancient Persians, with the Hindoostanee, the Arabic, and Chaldean languages ... Dublin, 1802. 39p.

702   **Vinson, Élie Honoré Julien**
Manuel de la langue hindoustani (Urdu et Hindi). New Delhi: Asian Education Services, 1987. 268p.

703   **Wahab, A.M. Fazul**
"The Hindustani language: its history, literature and how to study it". *Hindustan Review* 11 (January-June 1905), pp. 363-372.

704   **Waheed, A.**
"Problem of script for Urdu". *Pakistan Review* 9, 5 (May 1961), pp. 13-14.

705   **Weitbrecht, H.U.**
The Urdu New Testament: a history of its language and its versions. London: British and Foreign Bible Society, 1900.

706   **Yadav, Ram Kanwar**
The Indian language problem, a comparative study. Delhi: National Publishing House, 1966. 181p.

707   **Zahur-ud-Din**
Development of Urdu language and literature in the Jammu Region. Srinagar, Kashmir: Gulshan Publishers, 1985. 481p.

708   **Zaidi, Ali Jawad**
"Urdu in post-Independence era". *Indian and Foreign Reviews* 7, 10 (1 March 1970), pp. 16-19.

709   **Zaidi, Mujahid Husain**
Language reform: history and future. La reforme des langues ... Sprachreform ... Eds. Istvàn Fodor and Claude Hagège. Vol. III. Hamburg: Burke, 1984. 586p.

710   — • "Word-borrowing and word-making in modern South Asian languages: Urdu" In: *Word-borrowing and word-making in modern South Asian languages.* Ed. Ayyadurai Dhamotharan. Heidelberg, 1975, pp. 98-121.

711   — • "Word-borrowing and word-making in Urdu". In: *South Asia Digest of Regional Writing* 4 (Heidelberg: South Asia Institute, 1975), pp. 98-122.

712   **Zakir, Mohammad**
"Urdu: between survival and reform: the Indian situation". In: *Language reform: history and future. La réforme des langues ... Sprachre form ...* Eds. Istvàn Fodor and Claude Hagège. Vol. III. Hamburg: Burke, 1984, pp. 423-429.

713   **Zaman, Mukhtar**
The language policy of India: problems of its implementation and their solution. Islamabad: National Language Authority, 1984. 246p.

714   — • *Thoughts on national language policy.* Islamabad: National Language Authority, 1985. 21, 26p.

715   **Zmotova, O.D.**
"Sintaksicheskie funktsii infinitiva khindi i urdu". In: *Voprosy indiiskoi filologii.* Eds. A.T. Aksenova and N.M. Sazanovoi. Moscow: Izd. MGU, 1974.

716   **Zograf, G.A.**
"Khindi, urdu i khindustani (ob upotreblenii terminov)". *Kratkie soobshcheniia Instituta vostokovedeniia, Akademiia Nauk SSSR 18* (Moscow, 1956), pp. 49-55

717   — • "Iranskie i arabskie elementy v urdu". In: *Khindi i urdu. Voprosy leksikologii i slovoobrazovaniia.* Ed. V.M. Beskrovnyi. Moscow: Izd. vostochnoi literatury, 1960, pp. 152-244.

718 — • *Iazyki Indiĭ, Pakistana, Tseilon i Nepala: iazyki zarubezhnogo vostoka i Afriki.* Moscow: Izd. literatury, 1960. 132p.

719 — • "Kal'kuttskii khindustani Kontsa XVIII osveshchenii G.A. Lebedeva". *Kratkie Soobshcheniia Instituta narodov Azii* 61 (Moscow, 1963), pp. 142-153.

720 — • *Languages of South Asia: a guide.* Trans. G.L. Campbell. London: Routledge and Kegan Paul, 1982. 231p. (Languages of Asia and Africa, vol. 3).
Based initially on Grierson's *Linguistic Survey of India.* Other languages covered are Pashtu, Baluchi, Brahui and the Dardic group. The book was originally published in Russian in 1960 as *Iazyki Indii, Pakistan, Tseilona i Nepala.*

721 — • "Otritsaniia pri glagole v Khindustani". *Kratkie soobshcheniia Instituta vostokovedeniia, Akademiia Nauk SSSR* 18 (Moscow, 1956), pp. 74-78.

722 — • "Voprosy formirovaniia Urdu". *Uchenye Zapiski Instituta vostokovedeniia, Akademiia Nauk SSSR* 13 (Moscow, 1958), pp. 287-311.

LANGUAGE

Study and Teaching

NINETEENTH CENTURY AND EARLIER

723 Abdul Fattah, Saiyid
Ashraf al-lughat. A vocabulary of nouns in Hindustani, Persian, Arabic, and English. Pt. 1 Masadir al afal. Pt. 2 Majami al-asma. Bombay, 1871. 96p.

724 — • *Masadir al-afal... Amadan namah, or the collection of verbs in Hindustani, Persian, Arabic and English...* Bombay, 1870. 96p.

725 — • *Tohfatul makal: Hindustani, Persian, Arabic, and English sentences and proverbs.* Bombay, 1872. 208p.

726 Abdul Ghafur
Talim-i Angrezi: an English-Hindustani vocabulary. Arrah, 1878. 22p.

727 Abdul Karim
Takallum al-madrasah: school dialogues in English and Hindustani. Bombay, 1871. 134p.

3rd ed. Lucknow, 1874. 68p.

728 Abul Rashid
The probationer's handy help to language, containing a complete vocabulary of only those words as are likely to meet the eye of the average students for lower and higher standards, Hindustani and Persian. Lucknow, 1895. 78p.

729 Ali, Saiyid Ahmad
A useful manual, comprising different meanings and derivations of important words, important explanations, notes on English composition, idiomatic translations (into Hindustani) ... and choice quotations from standard authors ... Revised by A.S. Phillips. Patna, 1890. 134p.

730 Ali, Saiyid Muhammad Nusrat
Mufid-i amm. English and Hindustani vocabulary. Dialogues and letters. Delhi, 1873. 132p.

731 Ali, Saiyid Shah
A spelling book, in which not only the meaning of every word is explained, but the correct pronunciation of every word is shown in the Hindoostanee language and characters according to John Walker's pronouncing dictionary. Madras, 1852. 94p.

732 Ali, Waris
Young man's conductor. Urdu-English vocabulary and dialogues. Agra, 1871. 36p.

733 Ali, William E.
Anglo-Urdu first book. Allahabad, 1869. 72p.

734   *Anglo Hindustanee handbook; or stranger's self-interpreter and guide to colloquial and general intercourse with the natives of India.* Calcutta and London, 1850.

735   **Aurillac, H.**
Petit manuel Français-Hindoustani avec vocabulaire et dialogues. Calcutta: T. Black and Co., 1876. 117p.

736   **Ballantyne, James Robert**
Hindustani selections in the Naskhi and Devanagari character. With a vocabulary of the words. Prepared for the use of the Scottish Naval and Military Academy. London: Madden and Co., C. Smith; Edinburgh: Military Academy, 1840. 10, 39, 20p.

737   — • *Hindustani letters in the nuskh-taleek and shikustu-amez character, with translations.* London, 1840.

738   — • *Pocket guide to Hindoostanee conversation.* London, 1839.

739   — • *The practical oriental interpreter, or Hints on the art of translating readily from English into Hindustani and Persian.* London, 1843. 54p.

740   **Baness, J. Frederick**
Manual of Hindustani; or The stranger's Indian interpreter: a practical and easy guide to Hindustani conversation. Calcutta: W. Newman and Co., 1886. 145p.

741   **Barrow, C.M.**
Fourth reader. Anglo-Hindustani. Madras, 1881. 310p.

742   **Begbie, William Henry and Joseph, Abraham**
A vocabulary, English, Burmese, Hindustani and Tamil. In English characters with the Burmese also in native letters. Rangoon: Albion Press, 1877. 153p.

743   **Besant, Thomas Henry Gatehouse**
The Persian and Urdu letter-writer, with an English translation and vocabulary ... with the assistance of Namat Khan and Munshi Akbarabadi. Calcutta, 1843. 175, 191p.

744   — • *Farsi aur Urdu ki insha. The Persian and Urdu letter-writer, with an English translation and vocabulary.* 2nd. ed. Assisted by Namat Khan and Munshi Akbarabadi. Calcutta: Ostell and Lepage, 1845. 175, 191p.

745   **Bradshaw, J.**
Fifth reader. Anglo-Hindustani. 3rd ed. Madras, 1883. 10, 398p.

746   **Brown, Charles Philip and Ali, G.**
English and Hindustani phraseology, or exercises in idioms. English and Dakhini Hindustani. Madras, 1855. 235p.

747   **Chandra Sena**
A soldier's practical guide to Hindustani. Adapted for the lower standard examination. Shahjahanpur, 1882. 26p.

748   **Chapman, Francis Robert Henry**
Urdu reader for beginners. Delhi: Delhi Press, 1876. 148p.

749   **Chowdhury, A.K.**
Urdu reader in Anglo-Urdu for the use of Europeans studying Urdu. Calcutta, 1879. 41p.

750   **Courtois, Atwill**
Hints to candidates for examination by the higher standard in Hindustani, with specimen translations ... Madras: S.P.C.K. Press, 1888. 48, 17p.

751   — • *A manual of the Hindustani language as spoken in Southern India.* Madras: Higginbotham and Co., 1887. 146p.

752   **Dasa, Dharama**
Maani-i alfaz: vocabulary of difficult words in the first English reader. Lahore, 1879. 8p.

753   **Devi-Prasada, Raya**
Polyglot munshi or vocabulary, exercises ... in English, Persian, Hindi, Hindustani and Bengali. 1841.

754   **Dias, D.F.X.**
A vocabulary in English, Portuguese, Goa, Marathi and Hindustani languages. [1878]. 196p.

755   **Dias, S.S. de Jesus**
Manual de tres mil vocabulos em Portuguez, Concani, Inglez e Industani. Bombay, 1892. 137p.

756   **Dowson, John**
A Hindustani exercise book: containing a series of passages and extracts adapted for translation into Hindustani. London: Trübner and Co., Hertford [printed], 1872. 96p.

757   **Durga Prasad, Munshi**
The English-Urdu translator's companion, in the Roman character. Benares, 1884-1890. 2 pts.

758   *The English and Hindustani student's assistant; or idiomatical exercises in these languages...* Calcutta, 1834. 4 pts. 229p.

759   *English and Hindustani exercises of the irregular verbs.* Madras, 1842.

760   *The English and Hindustani student's assistant: or idiomatical exercises in those languages ...* Calcutta, 1837. 151p.
Adapted from Dr J. Wilson's *Idiomatical exercises in English and Marathi.*

761   *English and Hindustani vocabulary.* Madras, 1854. 42p.

762   **Forbes, Duncan**
The Hindustani manual; a pocket companion for those who visit India ... Revised by J.T. Platts. London, 1848. 2 vols.

763   —• *The Hindustani manual intended to facilitate the essential attainments of conversing with fluency, and composing with accuracy.* London: Crosby Lockwood and Son, 1874.

764   **Furrell, J.W.**
Hindustani synonyms: a collection of proximately synonymous words in daily use in the Hindustani language. Calcutta, 1873. 66p.

765   **Garcin de Tassy, Joseph Héliodore Sagesse Vertu**
Chrestomathie hindoustani, urdu et dakhni. Paris, 1847.

766   —• *Corrigé des thèmes du Manuel du cours d'Hindoustani.* Paris, 1837.

767   —• *Cours d'hindoustani à l'École impériale ... des langues orientales vivantes ... Discours à l'ouverture du cours.* Paris, [1861-1864]. 8p.

768   —• *Discours à l'ouverture de son cours d'hindoustani à l'École spéciale des langues orientales vivantes.* Paris: Moniteur Universel, 1850-1869.

2nd ed. of preceding, entitled *La langue et la littérature hindoustanies de 1850 à 1869.* Paris, 1874.

769   —• *Manuel de l'auditeur du cours d'hindoustani, ou thèmes gradués pour exercer à la conversation et au style épistolaire, accompagnés d'un vocabulaire français-hindoustani.* Paris, 1836. 89p.

770   **Ghoolam Muhammad, Munshi**
Colloquial dialogues in Hindustani. To which is annexed a short grammar of the language and a vocabulary. London, Hertford [printed], 1859 [1858].
2nd ed. Bombay, 1863.

771   —• *The Urdu instructor. An easy medium for the study, revision, and perusal of Hindustani.* Bombay, 1882. 2 vols.

772   **Gilbertson, G.W.**
A literal translation into English of the lower standard Urdu text book with vocabulary. Benares, 1899. 352p.

773   **Gilchrist, John Borthwick**
The antijargonist, or a short introduction to the Hindoostanee language ... with an extensive vocabulary, English Hindoostanee, and Hindoostanee and English ... Calcutta, 1800.
Partly an abridgement of *The Oriental linguist.*

774   —• *The British Indian monitor, or the antijargonist, stranger's guide, Oriental linguist, and various other works, compressed into a series of portable volumes on the Hindoostanee language ...* 2 vols. Edinburgh, 1806-1808.
Hindustani in Roman characters.

775 — • *A collection of dialogues, English and Hindoostanee on the most familiar and useful subjects.* Calcutta, 1804. 243p.
Hindustani in Roman characters.

776 — • *Dialogues, English and Hindoostanee. Calculated to promote the colloquial intercourse of Europeans on the most useful and familiar subjects ...* Calcutta, 1804.
Hindustani in Roman characters.

2nd ed. Edinburgh, 1809. 253p.

3rd ed. London, 1820.

777 — • *Hindee-Arabic mirror; or improved practical table of such Arabic words as are ultimately connected with a due knowledge of the Hindoostanee language.* Calcutta, 1804.

778 — • *The Hindee Roman orthoepigraphical ultimatum or a systematic, descriminative view of oriental and occidental visible sounds, on fixed and practical principles, for the languages of the east exemplified in the popular story of Sukoontula Natuk.* Calcutta, 1804.

779 — • *The Hindee Roman orthoepigraphical ultimatum ... exemplified in 100 anecdotes, tales, jests of Hindustani story teller.* London, 1820.

780 — • *The Hindee story teller or aqliat-e-Hindee; entertaining expositor of Roman, Persian, and Nagree characters simple and compound in their applications to the Hindoostanee language.* Calcutta, 1803-1806. 2 vols.

781 — • *The Hindoostanee principles.* Calcutta, 1802.

782 — • *The oriental linguist or easy and familiar introduction to the popular language of Hindoostan comprising the rudiments of the tongue, with an extensive vocabulary, English and Hindoostanee, and Hindoostanee and English; ... with practical notes and observations.* Calcutta: Ferris and Greenway, 1798.

783 — • *Practical outlines, or sketch of Hindoostanee orthoepy in the Roman characters.* Calcutta, 1802.

784 **Gokhale, V.**
Hindustani without a master. Bombay, 1892.

785 **Grant, F.W.**
The pocket Hindoostanee vocabulary, by an officer of the Bengal Staff Corps. Calcutta, 1869. 293p.

786 **Grant, Henry N.**
An Anglo-Hindustanee vocabulary, adapted for European sojourners in India. Calcutta, 1850.

787 **Habersack, A.**
Conversational Hindustani phrases ... Hindustani by Nasiruddin Ahmed. London, 1861.
Hindustani in Roman characters.

788   **Haidari Jang, Bahadur**
Key to Hindustani, or an easy method of acquiring Hindustani in the original character.
London, Hertford [printed], 1861. 196p.

789   **Haig, Thomas Wolseley**
Hints on the study of Urdu, for the use of candidates for the lower and higher standard examinations in that language. Allahabad: Pioneer Press, 1898. 40p.

790   *Handbook to Hindustanee conversation.* Calcutta: Barada Prasad Majumdar, 1886. 56p.

791   *The handbook to Hindoostanee conversation, with familiar phrases and an easy vocabulary, English and Hindoostanee.* Calcutta: People's Press, 1890. 56p.

792   **Harichand Lund**
Hari's Hindustani manual of useful words and sentences for the candidates for the higher and lower standard examinations. Shahjahanpur: Arya Darpan Press, 1899. 64p.

793   **Hazelgrove, G.P.**
A vocabulary English and Hindoostanee.   Bombay: Education Society Press, Byculla [printed], 1865. 3 pts.

794   *Handbook to Hindustani conversation...* Calcutta: Barada Prasad Majumdar, 1866. 56p.

795   *The Handbook to Hindoostanee conversation, with familiar phrases and an easy vocabulary, English and Hindoostanee.* Serampore: Tomshur Press, 1886. 63p.

796   *Hindoostanee and English students assistant; or idiomatical exercises.* Calcutta, 1826.

797   *Hindustani manual for beginners.* Bombay, 1886.

798   *Hindustani spelling book in the Roman character.* 4th ed. Allahabad, 1850.

799   *Hindustani without a master.* Bombay: Education Society Press, Byculla, 1892.

800   **Holroyd, William Rice Morland**
Scheme for transliterating Urdu in Roman characters. Amritsar, 1878.

801   — • *Tashil al-Kalam. Hindustani-English dialogues.* Delhi, 1867. pt. 1

[Another ed.] Lahore, 1870.

802   — • *Tashil al-Kalam or, Hindustani made easy.* London: Wm. H. Allen and Co., 1873. 267p.

803   — • *The Urdu-English primer.* 3rd ed. Lahore, 1907. 59p.

804   Homem, Paulo Maria
Novo vocabulario em Portugues, Concanim, Inglez e Hindustani co-ordenado para o uso dos seus patricios que percorrem a India Ingleza. Assagao, Bombay (printed), 1874.

805   Howard, Edward Irving
The English primer. With translation and pronunciation into Marathi, Hindustani and Persian. Trans. Ganpat Mahadew Airkar. Bombay, 1868. 45p.

806   *Javab o su'al. Dialogues, English and Hindustani.* [Calcutta?], 1853. 30p.

807   Jawahir Singh
The Urdu teacher ...   Amballa: Empress Press, 1898. 206, 12, 28p.

808   Keegan, William
A vocabulary in Urdu, Latin and English, with pronunciation in Roman characters. Sardhana: Roman Catholic Orphan Press, 1882. 320p.

809   Kempson, Simon Matthews Edwin
Key to the translation exercises of Kempson's syntax and idioms of Hindustani. London: Wm. H. Allen and Co., 1890. 74p.

810   — • *The syntax and idioms of Hindustani or progressive exercises in translation, with notes and directions and vocabularies.* London: Wm. H. Allen and Co., 1890 [1889]. 278p.

811   Khadurbuksh, Henry T.
Hindustani made easy. Conversing without a master... Gloucester, 1876.

812   Khan, Adalat
A vocabulary of one thousand words ... in Hindustani, Persian and Bengali ... 5th ed. Calcutta: Baptist Mission Press, 1890. 67p.

813   Khan, Muhammad Nusrat Ali
Self-educator: exercises in English and Hindustani. Delhi, 1884. 3 vols.

814   Laik, Ahmad
The Urdu self-instructor, or Ataliq-i Urdu. Delhi: Ansari Press, 1899. 240p.

815   Loyal, C.J.
Anglo-vernacular Bol-Chal in English and Urdu for the use of students in the High and Middle classes. Lahore: Shams-al-Hind Press, 1897. 137p.

816   Lyall, Sir Charles James
A sketch of the Hindustani language. Edinburgh: A. and C. Black, 1880. 55p.

817   Madhusudana Sila
A manual of English and Hindustani terms, phrases... in the Roman character. Calcutta, 1860.

818   Misra, Mathuraprasada
English-Urdu primer. 3rd ed. Benares, 1871. 12p.

819   **Monier-Williams, Monier**
An easy introduction to the study of Hindustani, in which the English alphabet is adapted to the expression of Hindustani words, with a full syntax. Also ... selections in Hindustani, with a vocabulary and dialogues, by Cotton Mather. London, 1858.

820   — • *Hindustani primer: containing a first grammar suited to beginners, and a vocabulary...* London, 1860. 72p.

821   **Mookerji, M.M.**
Key to P.C. Sircar's first book of reading. Revised by G. Lethbridge. Patna, 1877. 76p. English and Hindustani. With transliteration in Devanagri characters.

822   — • *Key to P.C. Sircar's second book of reading.* Calcutta, 1871. 27p. English and Hindustani in Roman characters.

823   **Muhammad Abdulghani, Saiyid,**
Zinat al-iskul. An Urdu-English vocabulary. Cawnpur, 1881. 34p.

824   **Muhammad Ali**
The Hindustani teacher. 3rd ed. Bangalore, 1870.

825   **Muhammad Asad Ali**
The muallim-i English. A classified vocabulary of useful words, phrases and dialogues, in Hindustani and English. 1898. 194p.
With transliterations in Persian and Devanagari characters.

826   **Muhammad, Hasan Ibn Mushtati Husain**
Danishafza: a vocabulary and short sentences in Hindustani and English. [Delhi,] 1884. 2 pts.
Pt. 1 is lithographed.

827   **Muhammaduddin**
Guide to transliteration in Roman characters. Lahore, 1877. 36p.

828   **Mukhopadhyaya, Gangadhara**
Child's companion: an Anglo-Urdu vocabulary. Calcutta, 1878. 66p.

829   **Mulvihill, P.**
A vocabulary for the lower standard in Hindustani, containing the meanings of every word and idiomatic expression in Jarrett's Hindu period, and in the selections from the Bagh-o-Bahar. London: Wm. H. Allen and Co., 1884. 99p.

830   **Narayana Dasa, Munshi**
A help to candidates for lower and higher standard examinations in Hindustani. 3rd ed. Shahjahanpur: Arya Darpan Press, 1897. 148, 32p.

831   **Pavie, Théodore Marie**
Chrestomathie hindoustani (urdu et dakhni). Begun by T. Pavie and continued by F.M. Bertrand. Ed. J.H. Garcin de Tassy. Paris: Impr. Dondey-Duprè, 1847. 2pts.

832 **Plunkett, George Tindall**
The conversation manual, a collection of ... useful phrases in English, Hindustani, Persian and Pashtu, with summaries of the grammars of these languages, and a vocabulary ... London: Richardson and Co., 1875. 130p.

833 *Pocket Hindoostanee vocabulary.* Calcutta, 1869.

834 *A practical method of learning the Hindustani language.* Madras: S.P.C.K. Press, Vepery, 1897. 96p.

835 **Rajagopala Setti, B.**
Telugu, Canarees, Tamil, English and Hindustani vocabulary in Canarees character. Pt. 3. Bellary: C.L.S. Press, 1887. 62p.

836 **Rajarama (R.R. Bail)**
A manual of English and Hindustani terms, phrases... or Bolchal Angrazy Urdu, in the Roman character. Lahore: Empress Press, 1889. 101p.

837 **Rama Narayana, Mahabani**
The best instructor of Hindustani without the aid of a Munshi ... Agra: Ornamental Job Press, 1898. 159p.

838 **Ranking, George Spiers Alexander**
A guide to Hindustani ... Including colloquial phrases in Persian and Roman characters, and a collection of arzis, with transliteration ... and English translations. 3rd ed. Calcutta: Thacker, Spink and Co., 1895. 246p.

839 — • *Introductory exercise in Urdu prose composition. A collection of 50 exercises with idiomatic phrases and grammatical notes, accompanied by a full vocabulary and translation of each passage.* Calcutta, 1896.

840 — • *Specimen papers for the lower and higher standard examinations in Hindustani...* 2 pts. Calcutta: Thacker, Spink and Co., 1899.

841 — • *Talim-i-zaban-i urdu: a guide to Hindustani ... for the use of officers and men serving in India...* Calcutta: Thacker, Spink and Co., 1889. 130p.

842 — • *Urdu-English Primer, for the use of the Colonial Artillery.* London, 1899. 136p.

843 **Reid, Henry Stewart**
Urdu-Hindi English vocabulary. Agra, 1854. 2 vols.

844 — • *Urdu-Hindi-English vocabulary, compiled for the use of beginners ...* 2nd ed. Assisted by Chiranji Lal and ... Bunsi Dhar. Allahabad, 1860. 2 pts.

845 **Reynold, M.C.**
Household Hindustani. A manual for new-comers. Calcutta, 1886.

846 **Roberts, T.T.**
An Indian glossary: words and terms commonly used in the East Indies. London, 1800.

847   **Robertson, Elphinstone Pourtales**
Vocabulary, English and Hindustani ... Revised and enlarged. Bombay, 1858.

848   **Roebuck, Thomas**
The Hindustani interpreter, containing the rudiment of grammar, an extensive vocabulary, and a useful collection of dialogues ... 2nd ed. Revised by W. Carmichael-Smyth. London, 1841.

849   **Rogers, E. H.**
How to speak Hindustani: being an easy guide to conversation in that language designed for the use of soldiers... London: Crosby Lockwood and Son., 1861. 84p.

850   *Romanized Hindustanee manual.* Madras, 1869.

851   **Rowlandson, W.**
English and Hindoostani: a vocabulary of words and phrases likely to occur in the extracts given by the examiners at Madras for translation into Hindoostani. Madras, 1864.
Lithographed.

852   *Sabaq-i Salis. Introductory exercises for translation from Hindustani into English.*
Madras, 1846. 78p.
Compiled for Bishop Corries Grammar School.

853   **Sambhunatha**
The student's friend, or a vocabulary of Hindustani and English words in verse. Agra: Secundra Orphanage Press, 1877. 125p.
Hindustani in Persian and Devanagari characters.

854   **Shakespear, John**
An introduction to the Hindustani language. Comprising a grammar and a vocabulary, English and Hindustan, also short sentencs in Persian and Nagari characters ... Hindustani composition ... and military words of command Nagari and English. London, 1845.

855   **Shoukut, Ali**
A Hindustani and Persian guide. Calcutta: Baptist Mission Press, 1895. 37p.

856   **Stewart, Charles**
An introduction to the study of the Hindostany language as spoken in the Carnatic. Compiled for the use of the Company of Gentlemen Cadets on the Madras Establishment at New Town Cuddalore. [Cuddalore,] 1808.

[Another ed.] Madras, 1843.

857   **Syamapad Vandyopadhyaya**
Manual of translation from Urdu into English ... Agra, 1893. 120p.

858   **Tagliabue, Camillo**
Manuale e glossario della lingua indostana o urdu. Naples, 1898. 288p. (Università degli studi, Istituto superiore orientale. Collezione scolastica, vol. 2.)

859   **Thompson, Joseph T.**
An English and Hindoostanee spelling guide. Serampore, 1832.

860   *Translator's assistant; Hindustani and English.* Bangalore, 1869.

861   **Tweedie, John**
Hindustani as it ought to be spoken. ... 2nd ed. Calcutta: Thacker, Spink and Co., 1893. 350p.

862   — • *Hindustani as it ought to be spoken. Supplement. Being translations of all the exercises and of "The Reader", contained in that book.* Calcutta: Thacker, Spink and Co., 1893. 39p.

863   *The Urdu instructor. Published monthly. An easy medium for the study, revision, and perusal of Hindustani.* Ed. Munshi Ghoolam Muhammad. Bombay, 1882-1883. 2 vols.

864   *Urdu-English vocabulary.* Benares, 1860.

865   *Useful sentences. English and Urdu.* Lucknow, 1888.

866   **Venimadhava Gangopadhyaya and Visvesvara Chakravarti**
A manual of translation from Urdu into English. 2nd ed. Calcutta: S.A. Auddy, 1894. 360p.

867   **Venkatrava Pantulu D.**
A vocabulary in Hindustani, English and Telugu. Madras, 1873. 68p.

868   **Vinson, Élie Honoré Julien**
Manuel de la langue hindoustani, (urdu et hindi), grammaire, textes, vocabulaires. Paris: Maisonneuve, 1899. 232p.

869   *A vocabulary, English and Hindoostanee. For the use of schools.* Madras: Madras School Book Society, 1854. 320p.

870   *Vocabulary, Hindustani and English.* Madras, 1853. 73p.

871   *Vocabulary in English and Urdu.* Rurki, 1854. 149p. (Rurki College Papers, no. 8).

872   **Wazir Singh**
Mufid al-atfal. A vocabulary of English and Hindustani words, in verse. Delhi, 1870. 58p.

873   **Williams, Henry Richard**
Explanations in Urdu and English of the difficult words and phrases in the first 48 pages of the Urdu middle course for European and Anglo-Vernacular schools. Shahjahanpur: Arya Darpan Press, 1898. 32p.

874   **Yates, William**
Introduction to the Hindoostanee language in three parts, viz, Grammar with vocabulary and reading lessons. Calcutta, 1827.

5th ed. Calcutta, 1843.

875   **Yusuf, Saiyid, Munshi**
Taleem-i-Hindustani, or Hindustani lessons for beginners, with complete vocabularies. Madras: S.P.C.K. Press, 1895. 156p.

876   **Ziaullah, Shaikh**
Angrezi bol chal. Lahore: Victoria Press, 1888. 73p.
In English and Hindustani.

TWENTIETH CENTURY

877   **Abd al-Karim Nashtar**
Hindustani colloquial manual. Calcutta: the author, 1918. 69p.

878   **Abdul Hakim, J.R**
Modern colloquial Hindustani. Allahabad: Pioneer Press, 1914. 165p.

879   **Ahmad, Mumtaz**
Urdu newspaper reader. Kensington, Md: Dunwoody Press, 1985. 322p.
Fifty selections from three Pakistani Urdu newspapers, serial glossaries and translations.
Reviewed by C.M. Naim in *Annual of Urdu Studies* 5 (1985), pp. 137-138.

880   **Ajitsaria, Aruna**
The tiger and the woodpecker. Urdu translation by Qamar Zamani and Ralph Russell. London: Middlesex Polytechnic, Multicultural Study Centre, [1984?].

881   **Akhtar, Pervez**
Learn Urdu the easy way: step by step Urdu. Bradford: Book Centre, 1986. 40p.

882   **Ali, Mahreen and Mann, Elizabeth**
Mahreen's secret. Maharin ka raz. A story in English and Urdu. Urdu version by Shaukat Khan. London: Borough of Waltham Forest English Language Centre, 1982.

883   **Ali, Mir Sahib**
Hints on study of Hindustani colloquial. Benares: Medical Hall Press, 1901. 28p.

884   **Ali, William E.**
Basic Urdu and English wordbook. Washington, D.C.: the author, 1975. 135p.

885   **Ashraf, Mohammad**
French Urdu reader: Frenc Urdu reader. Revised by Zahur Husain Chohan. Lahore: Polymer Publications, [1975?].

886   Azizi, Khalil
Spoken Urdu. Karachi: Azizi's Oriental Book Depot, 1960. 106p.

887   Azizur Rahman
English translation of Urdu conversational exercises. Ed. Khalil Azizi. Karachi: Azizi's Oriental Book Depot, 1970. 158p.
First published 1925. "17th revised printing".
Sequel to *Urdu conversational exercises in Roman characters.*

888   — • *Teach yourself Urdu in two months.* Ed. Khalil Azizi. Karachi, 1965. 253p.

889   — • *Urdu conversational exercises in Roman characters.* Ed. Khalil Azizi.
Karachi: Azizi's Oriental Book Depot, 1964. 161p.
First published 1923.
"Also available in Urdu script as well as in English translation".

890   — • *Urdu made easy; being an easy guide to conversation adapted for the use of foreigners.* Ed. Khalil Azizi. Karachi: Azizi's Oriental Book Depot, 1969. 113p.
First published 1915.

891   Bailey, T. Grahame
Teach yourself Urdu. Eds. J.R. First and A.H. Harley. London: English University Press, 1956. 40, 314p.
Includes English-Urdu and Urdu-English glossaries.
First published 1950 under title: *Teach yourself Hindustani.*

892   Balamukunda Chaturvedi
The English popular book of instruction in Hindustani. Agra, 1905. 234p.

893   Baldeo Prasad Labanniya
Sure success in Hindustani intended to do away with the difficulties of Europeans... Revised by Munshi Gour Dhan Dass. Agra: the author, [1917]. 175p.

894   Barker, Muhammad Abdur Rahman, et al.
A course in Urdu. Montreal: Institute of Islamic Studies, McGill University, 1967. 3 vols.

895   — • *An Urdu newspaper reader.* Ithaca, New York: Spoken Language Services, 1974. 453p.

896   — • *An Urdu newspaper reader.* Montreal: McGill University, Institute of Islamic Studies, 1968. 404p.

897   — • *An Urdu newspaper reader: key.* Montreal: McGill University, Institute of Islamic Studies, 1968. 47p.

898   — • *An Urdu newspaper word count.* Montreal: McGill University, Institute of Islamic Studies, 1969. 453p.

899   **BBC**
Hindi Urdu bol chaal: a beginner's course in spoken Hindi and Urdu on BBC Television.
London: BBC Books, 1989.

900   **Bellew, J.S.**
Pitman's phonography made easy, with explanations, in Urdu ... specially intended for students in India. Lahore: Civil and Military Gazette Press, 1901. 80p.

901   **Bright, William and Khan, Saeed A.**
The Urdu writing system. New York: American Council of Learned Societies, Program in Oriental Languages, 1958. 48p.

902   — • *The Urdu writing system.* Ithaca, New York: Spoken Language Services, 1976. 48p.

903   **Busher, R.C.**
A complete Urdu course, consisting of the essentials of grammar, progressive exercises, reading lessons and vocabularies: designed for the use of European middle and high schools, and of Europeans beginning to learn the language. Bombay: Longmans Green, 1910. 142p., 16 leaves.

904   **Catchpole, H.**
Elementary Urdu, general and military. Ipswich: W.S. Cowell, 1946. 146p.
Urdu in Roman characters.

905   **Chandola, Anoop**
A systematic translation of Hindi-Urdu into English. Tucson: The University of Arizona Press, 1970. 365p.
Devanagari version.

906   **Chapman, Francis Robert Henry**
How to learn Hindustani: a guide to the lower and higher standard examinations. 2nd ed. London: C. Lockwood and Son, 1910. 364p.

907   — • *Urdu reader for beginners.* London: W. Thacker and Co., 1906. 82, 5, 137p.

908   — • *Urdu Reader [Graduated] for Military Students.* London: C. Lockwood and Sons, 1910. 102, 76p.

909   **Chatterjee, N.C**
A manual of colloquial Hindustani and Bengali in the Roman character. Calcutta: the author, 1914. 180p.

910   **Cummings, Thomas Fulton**
An Urdu manual of the phonetic, inductive or direct method based on the Gospel of John. 2nd ed. Sialkot, 1916. 156p.

911   **Daulat, Ram**
A golden book of progressive translation; English and Hindustani. 2nd ed. Lahore, 1929. 355p.

912   De, R.P.
Hindustani at a glance: being a manual on the most simple principles for universal self-tuition. With an accurate pronunciation of every word together with a concise grammar and a comprehensive vocabulary ... 5th ed. Calcutta: Dey Bros, 1913. 112p.

913   Dhillon, Harinder Johal
Thirty-two basic steps into Urdu vocabulary: a vocabulary/workbook. Pasadena, MD: H.J. Dhillon, 1986. 143p.

914   — • *Urdu newspaper articles for reading comprehension.* Student's ed. Pasadena, MD: H.J. Dhillon, 1987. 80p.

915   Dhunna Lal
The hand-book of idiomatic phrases, containing explanations in English, Urdu and Roman, with illustrative sentences selected from the works of the best modern English writers ... 3rd ed. Banares: Medical Hall Press, 1901. 76p.

916   *The elves and the shoemaker and other tales;* written, translated and produced by the Newham Women's Community Writing Group. Harpenden: Dove, 1983.

917   Gambhir, Surendra Kumar
Spoken Hindi-Urdu: with emphasis on intonation in natural conversation. [Madison]: South Asian Studies; University of Wisconsin, 1978. 151p.
Accompanied by a set of twenty tapes.

918   Glassman, Eugene H.
Spoken Urdu: a beginning course. Tehran: The Resource-Study Center, 1977. 335p.
Spoken language is emphasized; only a transliteration is used.

919   Gregory, Eve and Penman, Dorothy
The fisherman and his wife and other wishing tales. Machira aur us ki bivi aur dusri kahaniyan. Urdu version by Khalid Hasan Qadiri. London: Edward Arnold, 1985. 48p.

920   — • *Manu and the snake, a tale of courage. Manu aur sanp bahadri ki kahani.* Urdu version by Khalid Hasan Qadiri. London: Edward Arnold, 1987.

921   Gumperz, John Joseph and Naim, C.M.
Urdu reader. Berkeley: University of California, Committee on South Asian Studies, 1960. 226p.
Includes introduction to writing system; graded lesson in Urdu prose; Urdu-English glossary.

922   Gumperz, John Joseph, et al.
Conversational Hindi-Urdu. Berkeley: ASUC Store, 1962-1963. 2 vols. (in 3).

[Another ed.] *Conversational Hindi-Urdu.* Delhi: Radha Krishna, 1967. 270p.

923   Hamilton, N.J.
Hindustani for the tourist; a phonetic phrase book for every day use. Translations under the direction of M.K. Jetley. Bombay: the author, 1965. 239p.

924   **Harnam Das**
Guide to translation (into Hindustani) with grammar and hints on the method of teaching for the use of students and teachers. Allahabad: Ram Dayal Agarwala, 1906. 83p.

925   **Hassan, Nazir and Koul, Omkar, N.**
Urdu phonetic reader. Mysore: Central Institute of Indian Languages, 1980. 85p.

926   **Heaslip, Peter C.**
Birthdays. Salgra. London: Methuen, 1987.

927   — • *The hole in the road. Srk main grha.* London: Methuen, 1987.

928   — • *Jobs. Kam.* London: Methuen, 1987.

929   — • *The Launderette. Landret.* London: Methuen, 1987.

930   — • *Me. Main.* London: Methuen, 1987.

931   — • *My dad. Mere abu.* London: Methuen, 1987.

932   — • *My home. Mera ghr.* London: Methuen, 1987.

933   — • *My mum. Meri ami.* London: Methuen, 1987.

934   — • *My school. Mera askool.* London: Methuen, 1987.

935   — • *The supermarket. Spr market.* London: Methuen, 1987.

936   — • *School dinners. Askool diner.* London: Methuen, 1987.

937   — • *Our house. Hamara ghr.* London: Methuen, 1987.

938   — • *Which twin wins?* London: Methuen, 1987.

939   **Hoenigswald, Henry M.**
Spoken Hindustani. New York: Henry Holt, 1945-1955. 2 vols.
A spoken language course with accompanying phonograph records.

[Another ed.] Ithaca, New York: Spoken Language Services, 1976.

940   **Hoey, William**
Urdu praxis: a progressive course of the Urdu composition. Oxford: Parker and Son, 1907. 98p.

941   **Holroyd, William Rice Morland**
Hindustani for every day. Lahore: Rai Sahib M. Ghulab Singh and Sons; London: Crosby Lockwood and Son, 1906. 324p.

942   **Hooper, William**
Helps to the attainment of Hindustani idiom. Designed for the use of young foreign missionaries in India. London: Christian Literature Society for India, 1901. 166p.

943   **Hugo, Charles**
Hindustani simplified... London: Hugo's Language Institute, 1925. 160p.

944   **Hutchins, Pat**
Rosie's walk. Rosie tahlne ghi. London: Bodley Head, 1987.

945   **Ingham, Jennie**
Me shopping. Main shaping kar rah huin. London: Blackie, 1987. 24p.

946   — • *My school. Mera askool.* London: Blackie, 1987. 24p.

947   **Ingham, Jennie and Das, Prodeepta**
Me playing. Main khel rah huan. London: Blackie, 1987.

948   — • *My favourite things. Meri pasandeeda chezain.* London: Blackie, 1987.

949   **Jafari, Muhammad Yusuf**
Kalam-i Urdu: a reader. Trans. E.G.S. Trotter and Munshi Abdur Rahman. London: Lund, Humphries and Co., Nagpur printed [1939.] 2 pts.

950   **Jawahir Singh**
The Urdu teacher ... 2nd ed. Ed. Dera Singh. Amritsar: Wazir-i-Hind Gas Press, 1909. 206p.

951   **Jhabboo Lall**
How to speak Hindustani language. Lucknow, 1919. 70p.

952   **John, Edward**
The self Urdu teacher. Allahabad: Ram Narain Lal, 1940. 256p.

953   — • *Hindustani self taught through the medium of romanized Urdu and English.* Allahabad: Ramnarain Lal, 1943. 236p.

954   **Johnston, R.**
Pass that Urdu test! Bombay, 1944. 166p.

955   **Jotsing, Munshi and Anandarama, Munshi**
European's guide to Hindustani. London: Crosby Lockwood and Co.; Karachi: Oriental Publishing Co., 1919. 85p.

956   **Kasymova, K.T.**
"O prepodavanii jazykov khindi i urdu v skole". *Journal of Austronesian Studies* 1 (Victoria, B.C. 1962), pp. 47-51.

957   **Kaufman, Steve**
Running away. Ghar se firar. London: Side by Side, 1986.

958   **Kelley, Gerald B.**
The teaching of Hindi-Urdu in the United States: the state of the art. Washington: ERIC Clearinghouse for Linguistics, Centre for Applied Linguistics, [1968]. 22p.

959   **Khan Haidari, Mohammed Akbar**
The interpreter; or, the key to the Munshi; the English and Urdu translation of all the exercises used in The Munshi and in the military appendix. 3rd ed. Ambala: Haidari's Oriental Book Depot, [1918]. 90p.

960   **Khan, Siddiq-ul-Hasan**
The jadid Hindustani teacher: Hindustani by a new method. Allahabad: Printed at Modern Printing Works, 1942. 248p.

[Another ed.] *The new Urdu teacher.* Lahore: Qamar Bros., 1963. 228p.

961   **Khan, Sughra B. Choudry and Molteno, Marion**
Resource guides for teachers: Urdu. London: Centre for Information on Language Teaching and Research, 1985. 78p.

962   — • *Urdu.* London: CILT, 1991.

963   **Kliuev, B.**
Prakticheskii ucebnik iazyka urdu. Ed. A.A. Davidovoi. Moscow: Izd. lit. na in iaz., 1962. 432p.

964   *Language and cultural guide 27: Urdu.* London: Centre for Information on Language Teaching and Research, 1985. 78p.

965   **Masood, Husain Khan and Abdul Azim**
A second year Urdu reader. Berkeley: University of California, Center for South Asia Studies, 1962. 190p.

966   **Mavi, Baldev Singh**
Teach yourself Urdu: an audio visual course. Walsall: B.S. Mavi, 1988.

967   **Mirza, A. Jan**
The modern Urdu phrase book. Nowshera: Printed at the Northern Army Press, 1942. 98p.

968   **Missionary Language Board of West Pakistan**
Urdu course 1. Lahore: J.H. Hewitt for the Missionary Language Board of West Pakistan, 1959-63.
Vol. 1, "corrected reprint of the 1960 edition".
Vol. 2, with title *First year Urdu course*, published by Murree Language School Committee; First published 1952.

969   **Mohyeddin, K.**
"The teaching of Urdu". *Pakistan Review* 10 (April 1962), pp. 36-40.

970   **Molteno, Marion**
Teaching Britain's community languages: materials and methods with examples from teaching Urdu. London: Centre for Information on Language Teaching and Research, 1986. Includes bibliography, and information about other resources.

971   **Naim, C.M., et al.**
Introductory Urdu. Chicago, Ill.: Committee on Southern Asian Studies, University of Chicago, 1980. 2 vols.
First published 1975.

972   — • *Readings in Urdu prose and poetry.* Chicago: University of Chicago South Asian Languages Program, 1962. 229, 259p.
Includes selections from various types of Urdu prose; notes on grammatical and cultural features; comprehensive Urdu-English glossary.

973   **Naim, C. M.**
"How Bibi Ashraf learned to read and write". *Annual of Urdu Studies* 6 (1987), pp. 99-115.

974   **Najm, T.A.**
Thirty lessons in Hindustani, or Hindustani for beginners. Bombay: Bombay Education Society's Press, 1904 [1905]. 201p.

975   **Narang, Gopi Chand and Becker, Donald A.**
A serial glossary of Naim's Readings in Urdu. Madison: University of Wisconsin, Indian Language and Area Center, 1964.

976   — • *Urdu: Readings in literary Urdu prose.* Madison, London: Published for the Department of Indian Studies, University of Wisconsin Press, 1968. 381p.
Includes a biographical sketch of each contributor.

977   **Oakley, E. Sherman**
Manual of translation into English for Hindustani students ... 3rd ed. Allahabad: National Press, 1903. 175p.

978   **Pahwa, Thakardass**
Key to the Pucca Munshi. Peshawar: Faqir Chand Marwah, 1936. 100p.

979   — • *The modern Hindustani scholar, or, The pucca munshi. Specially adapted to the present-day requirements of the lower and higher standard examinations.* Calcutta: Printed at the Baptist Mission Press, 1919.

980   — • *The Pucca munshi specially adapted to the present-day requirements of lower, higher and interpretership examinations in Urdu.* Peshawar: Faqir Chand Marwah, 1936.

981   **Parks, Hedley Charles**
Hindustani simplified, for tourists and all military ranks ... with ... some personal views of India. London: Luzac and Co., 1937. 64p.

982   **Phillott, Douglas Craven**
Annotated English translation of Urdū rozmarra or "Every-day Urdu", the text-book for the Lower Standard Examination in Hindustani. Calcutta, 1911. 3pts. 68, 36, 18p.

983   — • *Domestic Hindustani* ... Calcutta: Baptist Mission Press, 1919. 115p.

2nd ed. *Domestic Hindustani.* Revised by W.G. Grey. London: Kegan Paul and Co., 1931. 115p.

984   — • *Hindustani exercises for the proficiency and high proficiency with notes and translations.* Calcutta: Wellington Printing Works, 1912. 63, 119p.

985   — • *Hindustani manual.* Calcutta: Art Union Printing Works, 1910. 25p.

4th ed. Revised by the author and by ... W.G. Grey. Calcutta: Thacker, Spink and Co., 1933.

986   — • *Hindustani stepping-stones.* Allahabad: Pioneer Press, 1908. 180p.

987   — • *Hindustani stumbling-blocks: being difficult points in the syntax and idiom of Hindustani explained and exemplified.* London: Crosby Lockwood and Son, 1909. 131p.

988   — • *Urdu rozmarra, or "Everyday Urdu". Official text book for the examination of military officers and others.* Calcutta, 1911. 3 pts. 98, 74, 30p.

989   **Pollock, W. and Hosain, M.**
Pollock's pocket Hindustani. Calcutta, 1900. 71p.

990   **Pořizka, Vincenc**
Hindština Hindī language course. Praha: Státní Pedagogické Nakladatelství, 1972. 747p. First published 1963.

991   **Prasad, Kashi**
"Some problems of translation from Indian languages, with special reference to Premchand". *Indian Literature* 25, 5 (September-October 1982), pp. 86-98.

992   **Prithvi-Chand**
Everybody's vocabulary: English, Malay, Hindustani and Japanese ... Singapore, 1922. 95p.

993   **Ranking, G.S.A. and Jafari, M.J.**
Introductory exercises in Urdu prose composition, with notes and translations. 2nd ed. Calcutta: Thacker, Spink and Co., 1905. 151p.

994   **Raza, Ali Wahshat**
A word-for-word translation of the Urdu rozmarra. Pt 1. 2nd ed. Calcutta, 1931. 64p.

995   Russell, Ralph
A new course in Urdu and spoken Hindi for learners in Britain. 2nd ed. London: School of
Oriental and African Studies, External Services Division, 1986. 4 vols.
First published in 1980 as *A new course in Hindustani,* designed specifically as a Teach
Yourself course for adult learners in Britain.

996   Sabri, Makhdum
English-Urdu-Arabic conversation. Revised by Sameer Abdal Hameed Ibrahim. Lahore:
Sabri Bros., 1980. 208p.

997   — • *English Urdu conversation.* Lahore: Malik Book Depot, [1983?].

998   Sadruddin Bahuddin, Syed
Hindustani simplified. Bombay: British India Press, 1909. 223p.

[Another ed.] Bombay: Karim Mahomed Master, 1928. 262p.

999   — • *Hindustani without a master, a simple method of learning the Hindustani or Urdu
language in three weeks with a copious English-Hindustani vocabulary and Laskar's
Hindustani.* 12th ed. Bombay: D.D. Taraporeval Sons and Co., 1967. 251p.
Hindustani in Roman characters.

[Another ed]. Bombay: Taraporevala, 1981.

1000   Saiduzzafar Khan, Sahabzada
Urdu for adults; a phonetic method. Allahabad: Kitabistan, 1941. 33p.

1001   Scarsbrook, Ailsa and Scarsbrook, Alan
Skool main pahla din. First day of school. London: Blackie, 1987.

1002   Schomer, Karine and Reinhard, Geoffrey G.
Basic vocabulary for Hindi and Urdu. Berkeley, California: Centre for South and Southeast
Asia Studies, University of California, 1978. 177p.
Basic vocabulary for the first year, ca. 1000 words, arranged according to the Devanagari,
followed by the English glossaries and the Urdu version. Two appendices present words
grouped together according to grammatical and thematic categories.

2nd ed. Revised in collaboration with Usha R. Jain. Lanham: London University Press of
America, 1983.

1003   Sehmi, Parmjeet
Irfan's present. Irfan ka tuhfah: a story in English and Urdu. Urdu version Ghazala Bhatti.
London: London Borough of Waltham Forest English Language Centre, 1982.

1004   Shah, I.A.
The Briton in India: being a pocket interpreter and guide to India and its language.
London: Leopold B. Hill, 1918. 78p.

1005   Shahani, M.J.
American's guide to Hindustani. Karachi: K.T. Shahani, [1942]. 213p.

1006 Sharma, Elizabeth
The four friends. Retold by Elizabeth Sharma. Perivale, Middlesex: Tiger Books Ltd., 1985. 15p.

1007 — • *The mighty rabbit*. Retold by Elizabeth Sharma. Perivale, Middlesex: Tiger Books Ltd., 1986. 15p.

1008 — • *Moon lake*. Retold by Elizabeth Sharma. Perivale, Middlesex: Tiger Books Ltd., 1985. 15p.
Includes Urdu text.

1009 Shaw, Alison
Get by in Hindi and Urdu: a quick beginners course for those working with Hindi and Urdu speakers in Britain, with a section for travellers to India and Pakistan. London: BBC Books, 1989.

1010 — • *A new course in Urdu and spoken Hindi for learners in Britain*. Pt. 1. Teacher's guide. London: School of Oriental and African Studies, 1991.

1011 Siddhi-Natha Misra and Muhammad Abd al-Rabb
The matriculation translation from Urdu into English. 3rd ed. Benares, 1933. 308p.

1012 Southworth, Franklin C.
The student's Hindi-Urdu reference manual. Tucson: University of Arizona Press, 1971. 238p.

1013 Stanley, H.
Spoken Hindustani: a guide to beginners. Poona, 1929. 424p.

1014 Stone, Susheila
Nadeem makes samosas. Nadeem samose banata hai. Urdu version by Maherunissa Panwahr. London: Hamilton, 1987.

1015 — • *Where is Batool? Batool kaham hai?* Urdu version by Maherunissa Panwahr. London: Hamilton, 1987.

1016 *Talk English-Urdu*. Birmingham: Birmingham ILT Services, 1984. 46p.

1017 Tariq, A.R.
Urdu made easy. Lahore: M. Sirajuddin and Sons, 1966. 256p.

1018 Thimm, Carl Albert
Hindustani self-taught by the natural method, with phonetic pronunciation. 3rd ed. Revised by J.F. Blumhardt. London: E. Marlborough and Co., Ltd., 1908. 112p.
Urdu in Roman characters.
First published 1902.

1019 Tweedie, John
Hindustani as it ought to be spoken. 4th ed. Calcutta: Thacker, Spink and Co.; London: W. Thacker and Co., 1909. 134p.

1020   *Urdu.* London: Centre for Information on Language Teaching and Research, 1985. 78p. Language and Culture guide, 27.

1021   *Urdu, how to speak and write it; a practical handbook for the use of European travellers, military men and citizens of Pakistan; also adapted to the requirements of the students for the various proficiency examinations in Pakistan, by ten teachers.* Lahore: Indus Publishing House, 1966. 143p.

1022   *Urdu.* London East Anglian Group for GCSE. London: Hodder and Stoughton, 1991.

1023   **Vaidyanatha, Munshi**
Hindustani examination papers set at the various lower and higher standards. With copious notes by Munshi Baij Nath. Shahjahanpur: Arya Darpan Press, 1900. 68p.

1024   — • *A junior text-book of translation from Urdu into English.*   Assisted by Mahommad Mohsin. Calcutta: S.A. Auddy, 1903. 284p.

1025   **Vermeer, Hans Josef, et al.**
Urdu-Lautlehre und Schrift. Heidelberg: Julius Groos, 1966. 166p.

1026   — • *Urdu-Lesebuch (mit Kurzgrammatik).* Heidelberg: Julius Groos, 1967. 2 pts.

1027   — • *Übersetzung der Texte des Urdu-Lesebuches als Verständnishilfe und Schlüssel.* Heidelberg: Julius Groos, 1967. 63p.
Cover title: *Schlüssel zum Urdu-Lesebuch.*

1028   — • *Untersuchungen zum Bau zentral-süd-asiatischer Sprachen: ein Beitrag zur Sprachbundfrage.* Heidelberg: Julius Groos, 1969. 278p.

1029   **Walker, Brenda**
Naughty Imran. Sharir larka: a story in English and Urdu. Urdu version by Tasawwur Khan. London: English Language Centre, London Borough of Waltham Forest, 1984.

1030   **Wazir Chand, L.**
Urdu conversation: a practical handbook for the use of European travellers, also adapted to the requirements of the students. Lahore: Sheikh Mubarak Ali, 1975. 141p.
Previous edition: *Hindustani conversation.*

1031   **Willatt, John**
A textbook of Urdu in the Roman script. 4th ed. London: Oxford University Press, Madras printed, 1942. 188p.

1032   **Willson, C.T.**
The Malim sahib's Hindustani. For use ... in connection with ... low-caste natives of India who speak the bazaar "bat". Glasgow: J. Brown and Son, 1921.

[Another ed.] Glasgow, 1930.

1033   Zakir, Muhammad
Lessons in Urdu script. Delhi: Idara-e-Amini, 1973. 93p.

GENERAL LITERATURE

History and Criticism

1034 Abbas, Khwaja Ahmad
"Urdu literature". *Indian Literature* 3, 1 (October 1959-March 1960), pp. 111-115.

1035 — • "Urdu literature after the partition". *United Asia* 3, 2 (1950), pp. 115-118.

1036 Abbasi, R.M.I.
"Urdu literature in Pakistan". *Pakistan Review* 3 (June 1955), pp. 31-34.

1037 Abdul Haq
"Urdu literature". In: *Encyclopaedia of Islam* (1913), 4, 2. pp. 1023-1029.

1038 Abdullah, S.M.
"The spirit of Urdu literature". *Pakistan Review* 13, 11 (November 1965), pp. 21-23.

1039 — • "Aspects of Urdu criticism". *Pakistan Review* 14, 3 (March 1966), pp. 28-29.

1040 Afzal, Qaiser
"Eleven years of Urdu literature in Pakistan". *Pakistan Review* 6, 11 (November 1958), pp. 12-14.

1041 — • "The late Dr. Ram Babu Saksena". *Pakistan Review* 6 (April 1958), p. 43.

1042 Ahmad, Aijaz
"Some reflections on Urdu". *Seminar* (New Delhi) No. 359 (July 1989), pp. 23-29.
Contribution to a symposium on "Literature and society".

1043 Ahmad, Aziz
"Influence de la littérature française sur la littérature ourdoue". *Orient* (Paris), 11 (3 trimestre, 1959), pp. 125-135.

1044 — • "La littérature de langue ourdou". *Orient* (Paris) 7, (3 trimestre 1958), pp. 97-111.

1045 — • "Urdu literature 1945-1947". In: *Writers in free India*. Bombay: P.E.N.A.I. Center, 1950, 253p.

1046 Ahmad, Munir
Pakistanische Literatur: Übersetzungen aus den Sprachen Pakistans. Mayen: Deutsch-Pakistanisches Forum, 1986. 233p.

1047 Ahmad, Saleem
"The ghazal, a muffler, and India". Trans. John A. Hanson. *Annual of Urdu Studies* 2 (1982), pp. 53-83.
Taken from "Ghazal maflar aur Hindustan". In: *Nai nazm aur pura admi*. Karachi: Adabi Academy, 1962, pp. 82-112.

1048   Ahmad, Zamiruddin
"Literature or the art of public relations". *Outlook* (Karachi) 2 (November 1963), pp. 8-9.

1049   Ahmed, Sheikh
The problem of arts and literature in Pakistan. Karachi: Pakistan Institute of Arts and Design, [1965?] 8p.

1050   Ahsan, Syed Ali
Bengali and Urdu: a literary encounter. Dacca: Bengali Academy, 1964. 186p.

1051   Akhtar, Waheed
"Intellectual tradition in Urdu". In: *Modern thought and contemporary literary trends: papers presented at a Seminar in Hyderabad, 14th, 15th and 16th February 1981: a felicitation volume.* Eds. Narsing Rao and Kadir B. Zaman. Hyderabad: Committee on Modern Thought and Contemporary Literary Trends, 1982.

1052   — • "Traditions and trends in Urdu literature". In: *Profiles in Indian languages and literatures.* Ed. Arunkumar Biswas. Kanpur: Indian Languages Society, 1985, pp. 181-204.

1053   Aleem, A.
"Modern Urdu literature". In: *Literature in modern Indian languages.* Ed. V.K. Gokak. Delhi: Publications Division, Ministry of Information and Broadcasting, 1957, pp. 266-272.

1054   Anderson, David D.
"Contemporary Pakistani literature". *Pakistan Quarterly* 12, 2 (Winter 1964), pp. 13-18.

1055   — • "Pakistani literature today". *Literature East and West* 10, 3 (September 1966), pp. 235-244.

1056   Anis, Qari M.
An insight into Urdu literature. Lahore: Qasierul Adab, 1988.

1057   Anjum, A.R.
Conspectus: articles on Pakistani themes and some literary essays. Lahore: Arsalan Publications, 1979. 162p.

1058   Anwar, M.
"Crisis in literature of Pakistan". *U.N. World* 4, 2 (November 1950), pp. 58-59.

1059   Asiri, Fazl Mahmud
Studies in Urdu literature. Santiniketan: Visvabharati, [1952?].   146p.
On the origin and development of Urdu literature; also includes articles on Ghalib and Iqbal.

1060   Askari, Syed Hasan
"Mulla Daud's *Chandain* and Sadhain's *Maina Sat*; Manuscripts found in Urdu script".
Patna University Journal 15 (1960), pp. 61-83.

1061   Bailey, T. Grahame
A history of Urdu literature. Calcutta: Association Press; London: Oxford University Press, 1932. 120p.

1062 — • *A history of Urdu literature.* Lahore: al-Biruni, 1977. 119p.
Reprint of the 1932 ed.

1063 Barannikov, A.P.
Kratkiu ocherk literatury urdu. Leningrad: Oriental Institute, 1930.

1064 Bausani, Alessandro
Storia delle letterature del Pakistan: Urdu, Pangiâbi, Sindhi, Pasc'tô, Bengali Pakistana.
Milan: Nuova Accademia Editrice, 1958. 370p. (Storia delle letterature di tutto il mondo).

1065 Bokhari, A.S.
"The Urdu writer of our times". *Pakistan Quarterly* 1, 2 (1949), pp. 14-15, 36.
Also in: *Perspective* 1, 8 (February 1968), pp. 5-9.

1066 Bukhsh, Salauddin Khuda
"Hindustani literature of today". *Contemporary Indian Literature* 8, 1 (February 1967),
pp. 13-15.

1067 Chatterji, Suniti Kumar
"Urdu literature". In his *Languages and literatures of modern India.* Calcutta: Bengal
Publishers, 1963, pp. 142-155.

1068 Coppola, Carlo
"Urdu literary reaction to the 1943 Bengal famine". *Vagartha* (New Delhi) 18 (July 1977),
pp. 41-50.

1069 Dar, Bishan Naryan
"Lucknow in Hindustani literature". *Hindustani Review* 33.

1070 Dasgupta, Alokeranjan, et al.
*... Ganz unten, wie shesha, bin ich: Textproben zum Literatursymposium anlässlich des
Schwerpunktthemas "Indien, Wandel in Tradition" der 38. Frankfurter Buchmesse, 1986.*
Frankfurt a. M., 1986. 142p.
Includes a translation from Qurratulain Hyder.

1071 Dekhtiar, Anna Aronovna
Problemy poetiki dastanov urdu. Moscow: Nauka, 1979.

1072 Diwana, Mohan Singh
Handbook of Urdu literature. Lahore: Careers, [1938]. 166p.
Covering the syllabus of the I.C.S. (Urdu paper), and of the M.A. (Urdu) Examinations of
the various Indian Universities.

1073 Duggal, Kartar Singh
"Sex and violence in Punjabi and Urdu literature". In: *Sex and violence in literature and
arts.* Ed. Suresh Kohli. New Delhi: Sterling Publishers, 1973, pp. 80-93.

1074 Dymshits, Zalman Movshevich
Iazyk Urdu. Moskva: Izd-vo Vostochnoi lit-ry, 1962. 142p. (Iazyki zarubezhnogo Vostoka
i Afriki).

1075   **Faiz, Faiz Ahmad**
"Decolonising literature". *Viewpoint* (Lahore) 7, 2 (20 August 1981), pp. 15-16.

1076   — • "Unicorn and the dancing girl". *Viewpoint* (Lahore) 10, 28 (14 February 1985), pp. 9-10.

1077   **Faridi, S.N.**
Hindu history of Urdu literature. Agra: Ram Prasad and Sons, 1966. 129p.

1078   **Farquhar, John Nicol**
An outline of the religious literature of India. Delhi: Banarsidass, 1967. 451p.

1079   **Faruqi, Khwaja Ahmad**
"Modern Urdu literature". In: *Contemporary Indian Literature.* 2nd ed. New Delhi: Sahitya Akademi, 1959.

1080   **Faruqi, Muhammad Hamza**
"Socio-political aspects of Urdu literature during 1857 and its aftermaths". *Journal of the Research Society of Pakistan* 22, 1 (January 1985), pp. 23-35.

1081   **Faruqi, Shamsur Rahman**
"Images in a darkened mirror: issues and ideas in modern Urdu literature". *Annual of Urdu Studies* 6, (1987), pp. 43-54.

1082   — • "Is theoretical criticism possible?". Trans. the author. *Indian Literature* 30, 5 (September-October 1987), pp. 200-211.

1083   **Firaq Gorakhpuri**
"Symposium: rural themes in Indian literature (Urdu Section)". *Illustrated Weekly of India* (8 September 1963), p. 49.

1084   — • "Urdu literature: a link between India and Afro-Asia". *United Asia* 16, 4 (July 1964), pp. 269-271.

1085   **Flemming, Lesley A.**
"The splendour of the rose: recent publications in Urdu literature". *Journal of Asian Studies* 33, 4 (August 1974), pp. 673-677.

1086   **Garcin de Tassy, Joseph Héliodore Sagesse Vertu**
Histoire de la littérature hindoue et hindoustanie. 2ième. ed. rev., corr., et considérablement augm., 1870.
Reprint. New York: B. Franklin, 1968. 3 vols.

1087   — • *Les auteurs hindoustanis et leurs ouvrages d'après biographies originales.* Paris, 1855. 47p.

1088   — • "Prefaces to Garcin de Tassy's history". Trans. Gita Krishnankutty. *Indian Literature* 27, 3 (May-June 1984), p. 97.

1089   **Gardezi, Hassan N.**
"Literature and politics: the tradition of Faiz I".   *Viewpoint* (Lahore) 4, 18 (10 December 1978), pp. 23-24, 26.

1090   — • "Literature and politics: the tradition of Faiz II".   *Viewpoint* (Lahore) 4, 19 (17 December 1978), pp. 21-22.

1091   **George, K.M.**
Comparative Indian literature.   Madras: Macmillan, with the cooperation of Kerala Sahitya Akademi, Trichar, 1985.

1092   **Glebov, N. and Sukhochev, A.S.**
Literatura Urdu.   Moscow: Nauka, 1967.

1093   **Gorekar, N.S.**
Glimpses of Urdu literature.   Bombay: Jaico Publishing House, 1961.   88p.
Historical survey of Urdu language and literature; coverage includes post-independence India.

1094   **Gorekar, N.S. and Naim, A.A.**
"Modern trends in Urdu literature".   *Indian P.E.N.* 28 (September 1962), pp. 269-277.

1095   **Grierson, G.A.**
The modern vernacular literature of Hindustan.   Calcutta, 1889.

1096   **Gulati, Azad**
"Poetry and short story dominate: the Urdu scene".   *Indian Literature* 28, 6 (November-December 1985), pp. 167-174.

1097   **Gulhamid Begum**
A glimpse of Urdu.   Port Louis, Mauritius: Librarie Plaine Verte, 1971.   68p.

1098   **Hasan, Mohammad**
"Communalism in Indian literature".   In: *Communalism in India.*   Eds. Engineer Asghar Ali and Shakir Moin.   Delhi: Ajanta Publications, 1985, pp. 194-200.

1099   — • "Literary criticism in India: Urdu".   In: *Literary criticism in India.*   Ed. Dr Nagendra.   Meerut: Sarita Prakashan, 1976, pp. 266-288.

1100   — • "A review of current Indian writing: Urdu literature".   *Indian Literature* 7, 2 (1964), pp. 113-117.

1101   — • "Thought patterns of Urdu literature".   In: *Problems of modern Indian literature.*   Calcutta: Statistical Publishing Society, pp. 122-127.

1102   — • "Urdu".   In: *Indian literature since independence: a symposium.*   Ed. K.R. Srinivasa Ivengar.   New Delhi: Sahitya Academy, 1973, pp. 346-358.

1103   **Hasan, Sibte**
"The battle of ideas in modern Urdu literature - I".   *Viewpoint* (Lahore) 2, 8 (October 1985), pp. 27-30.

1104 — • "Battle of ideas in Urdu literature - II: from Iqbal to the Progressive Writer's Movement". *Viewpoint* (Lahore) 2, 9 (October 1985), pp. 27-28.

1105 — • "Battle of ideas in Urdu literature - III: this stained light, this night-bitten dawn". *Viewpoint* (Lahore) 2, 10 (1985), pp. 28-30.

1106 — • "Battle of ideas in Urdu literature - IV: the years of an unequal fight". *Viewpoint* (Lahore) 2, 11 (1985), pp. 27-29.

1107 **Hasan, S.M.**
"Some Urdu manuscripts of the Asiatic Society of Bengal". *Journal of Asiatic Society of Calcutta* 10, 1-4 (1968), pp. 18-31.

1108 **Hashmi, Alamgir**
"The historiography of Urdu literature: a rejoinder to Ralph Russell". *The Muslim Magazine* (31 August 1989).

1109 — • "Dr Sadiq and historiography of Urdu literature". *Viewpoint* (Lahore) 10, 27 (February 1985), pp. 27-29.

1110 — • "Muhammad Sadiq and Urdu literature historiography". *The Pakistan Times: Midweek Edition* (6 June 1989), pp. B.C.

1111 — • "The year that was: Pakistan". *Kunapipi* 6, 1 (1984), pp. 91-94.
Survey of important Urdu publications from Pakistan.

1112 **Horrwitz, Ernest Philip**
A short history of Indian literature. London: T.F. Unwin, 1907.
Reprint, Delhi: Rare Books, 1973. 188p.

1113 **Husain, S. Ehtesham**
"The history of Urdu literature". In: *Literature in modern Indian languages.* Ed. V.K. Gokak. Delhi: Publciations Division, Ministry of Information and Broadcasting, 1957, pp. 152-160.

1114 — • "A review of current Indian writing: Urdu". *Indian Literature* 2, 1 (October 1958 - March 1959), pp. 158-163.

1115 — • "Urdu literature 1962". *Indian Literature* 6, 2 (1963), pp. 142-147.

1116 — • "Urdu literature 1971". *Indian Literature* 15, 4 (October-December 1972), pp. 142-149.

1117 — • "Urdu literature and the revolt". In: *Rebellion 1857: a symposium.* Ed. P.C. Joshi. New Delhi: People's Publishing House, 1957, pp. 236-241.

1118 **Husain, S. Sajjad**
"The literature of Pakistan". In: *The commonwealth pen.* Ed. Alan McLeod. Ithaca, New York: Cornell University Press, (1961), pp. 142-166.

1119   **Ikram Azam**
Literary Pakistan. Rawalpindi: Nairang-e-Khayal Publications; Islamabad: Margalla Voices, 1989. 192p.
Literary and political articles.

1120   **Innaiah, N. and Khundmiri, Alam**
Tradition and modernity in Telugu and Urdu literature. [Hyderabad]: Indian Committee for Cultural Freedom, Hyderabad Chapter, 1967. 38p.

1121   **Insha, Ibne**
Literature for children in Urdu. Karachi: National Book Centre of Pakistan, 1967.

1122   — • "Literature for children in Urdu". *Pakistan Quarterly* 12, 2 (1964), pp. 52-58.

1123   *Istoriia literatury urdu.* Moscow: Izd-vo vostochnoi literatury, 1961. 258p.

1124   **Italiaander, Rolf**
In der Palmweinschenke. Pakistan in Erzählungen seiner besten zeitgenössischen Autoren. Mit iner Einführung in die pakistanischen Literaturen von Annemarie Schimmel. Herrenalb-Schwarzwald: Horst Erdmann Verlag, 1966. 347p. (Reihe Geistige Begegnung, Band 14).

1125   **Jain, M.S.**
"Historical biography in Urdu literature". *Quest* 92 (November-December 1974), pp. 19-26.

1126   **Jamil, Maya**
A squint at the truth: a collection of papers, articles and reviews. [Pakistan?], 1979. 220p.
On English, American and Urdu literature.

1127   **Kalim, M. Siddiq**
Pakistan: a cultural spectrum. Lahore: Arsalan Publications, 1973. 235p.

1128   **Khan, Hyder Ali**
"National trends in Urdu literature". In: *Annals of Oriental Research* 19, 2 (1964), pp. 1-21.

1129   — • "Urdu literature in India". *Sameeksha* 67, pp. 39-42.

1130   **Khan, Inayat and Westbrook, Jessie Duncan**
Hindustani lyrics. London: Sufi Publishing Society, 1919. 59p.

1131   — • *Songs of India.* London, 1915. 48p.

1132   **Khan, Masud Husain**
"The new approach criticism". *Indian Literature* 30, 5 (September-October 1987), pp. 197-198.
Review of S.R. Faruqi's *Tanqidi afkar,* which won the Sahitya Akademi award for Urdu in 1986. Includes a short biographical sketch of Shamsur Rahman Faruqi.

1133   **Khan, Nuzrat Yar**
Urdu literature in Canada: a preliminary survey. Ed. Michael S. Batts. [Ottawa]: Dept of the Secretary of State of Canada, 1988. 45p.

1134   **Khan, Zubaida Yaseen Ali**
"History in Urdu literature". In: *History in modern Indian literature*. Ed. S.P. Sen. Calcutta: Institute of Historical Studies, 1975, pp. 95-109.

1135   **Khullar, K.K.**
"Post-independence trends in Urdu literature".   *Indian and Foreign Review* 12, 3 (15 November 1974), pp. 19-21.

1136   — • "Satire in Urdu - II". *Times of India Magazine* (5 July 1970), p. 8: 7-8.

1137   **Khundmiri, S. Alam**
"Recent Urdu writing". *Illustrated Weekly of India* 1, 1 (July-September 1967), pp. 78-85.

1138   — • "The situation of literary criticism in Urdu today". In: *Indian writing today* 2, 1 (January-March 1968), pp. 55-59.

1139   **Kliuev, B.I.**
"Nekotorye voprosy razvitiia Urdu v Pakistane". In: *Sovremennye literaturnye iazyki stran Azii*. Moscow: Akademiia nauk SSSR, Institut narodov Azii, 1965, pp. 82-115.

1140   **Kohli, Suresh**
Aspects of Indian literature: the changing pattern. Delhi: Vikas Publishing House, 1975. 179p.

1141   **Komal, Balraj**
"Urdu: a lean year, but promises ahead". *Indian Literature* 27, 6 (November-December 1984), pp. 172-179.
Survey of Urdu literature in India in 1983.

1142   — • "Urdu: literary criticism dominates".   *Indian Literature* 32, 6 (November-December 1989), pp. 207-215.
Survey of significant Urdu books published in 1988.

1143   **Kripalani, Krishna**
Literature of modern India: a panoramic glimpse. New Delhi: National Book Trust, India, 1982. 124p.

1144   **Lall, Inder Jit**
"Urdu: a bird's eye view". *Indian Literature* 26, 6 (November-December 1983), pp. 152-162.

1145   — • "Urdu: a kaleidoscope view". *Indian Literature* 25, 6 (November-December 1982), pp. 71-83.

1146   **Latif, Sayyid Abdul**
The influence of English literature on Urdu literature. London: Forster, Groom and Co., 1924. 141p.

1147   **Lehmann, Fritz**
"Urdu literature and the Mughal decline". *Mahfil* 6, 2-3 (1970), pp. 125-131.
Paper originally presented at the 82nd annual meeting of the American Historical Association, Toronto, 29 December, 1967.

1148   **Lyall, Charles James**
"Hindustani literature". In: *Encyclopaedia Britannica.* 9th ed. Edinburgh, 1880. Vol. 11, p. 843.

1149   — • "Hindustani literature: the modern period". In: *Encyclopaedia Britannica* 11th ed. Cambridge: Cambridge University Press, 1910. Vol. 13, pp. 489-491.

1150   **Machwe, Prabhakar**
"1857 and Indian literature". *Indian Literature* 1, 1 (October 1957), pp. 53-59.

1151   — • *Four decades of Indian literature: a critical evaluation.* New Delhi: Chetana Publications, 1976. 160p.
Study of the period 1930-70.

1152   **Makhdum Mohiuddin**
"Urdu literature in Andhra Pradesh". *Illustrated Weekly of India* 87, 37 (11 September 1966), p. 22.

1153   **Matthews, D.J., Shackle, C. and Husain, Shahrukh**
Urdu literature. London: Urdu Markaz, Third World Foundation for Social and Economic Studies, 1985. 139p.
Surveys the main phases in the development of Urdu literature, particularly poetry, over the last four centuries.

1154   **Memon, Muhammad Umar**
"Pakistani Urdu creative writing on national disintegration: the case of Bangladesh". *Journal of Asian Studies* 43, 1 (November 1983), pp. 105-127.

1155   **Mittal, Gopal**
"Contemporary Urdu literature." *Thought* (20 July 1957), pp. 14-16.
Review of K.A. Faruqi's article in *Contemporary Indian Literature.*

1156   **Mohyeddin, K.**
"A brief survey of the history of Urdu literature". *Illustrated Weekly of India* (26 May 1963), pp. 341-353.
Also in: *Pakistan Review* 2 (December 1954), pp. 28-35.

1157   **Mujeeb, Muhammad**
"Trends in regional literature, Urdu". *Illustrated Weekly of India* (26 May 1963), pp. 65-66.

1158   **Naim, C.M.**
"The consequences of Indo-Pakistani war for Urdu language and literature". *Journal of Asian Studies* 38, 2 (February 1969), pp. 269-83.
Includes poems by Ali Sardar Jafri, Jagan Nath Azad, Muhammad Safdar Mir, Ahmad Nadim Qasimi, Wazir Agha, Mustafa Zaidi.

1159   — • "Prize-winning adab: a study of five Urdu books written in response to the Allahabad Government Gazette notification". In: *Moral conduct and authority: the place of adab in South Asian Islam.* Ed. Barbara Daly Metcalf. Berkeley: University of California Press, 1984, pp. 290-314.

1160   **Naim, A.A. and Gorekar, N.S.**
"Modern trends in Urdu literature". *Indian P.E.N.* (28 September 1962), pp. 269-277.

1161   **Naqvi, S.A.**
A glimpse into the common literary heritage of Pakistan, Iran and Turkey. Karachi: National Museum of Pakistan, 1966. 65p.

1162   **Narang, Gopi Chand and Flemming, Leslie A.**
Modern Urdu literature. Wiesbaden: Otto Harrassowitz, 1983. *(A history of Indian literature,* ed. Jan Gonda, vol. 8, fasc. 4, pt. 1.)

1163   **Naz**
An outline of Urdu literature. Lahore: Ferozons, 1971. 98p.

1164   **Orainui, Syed Akhtar Ahmad**
"The impact of freedom movement on Urdu literature in Bihar". *Bihar Information* 18, 16 (16 September 1970), pp. 9-11.

1165   **Prem Chand**
"The nature and purpose of literature". *Indian Literature* 29, 6 (November-December 1986), pp. 184-191.

1166   **Prigarina, N.I.**
"Melody of joy and sorrow". In: *Problems of modern Indian literature.* Calcutta: Statistical Publishing Society, pp. 160-166.

1167   — • *Problems of modern Indian literature.* Ed. by N.I. Prigarina. Calcutta: Statistical Pub. Society, 1974. 202p.
Articles by Indian and Soviet scholars.

1168   **Pritchett, Frances W.**
South Asian popular literature [Hindi and Urdu] *collection.* Chicago: Center for Research Libraries, 1983. 75p.

1169   **Qadir, Shaikh Abdul**
Famous Urdu poets and writers. 2nd ed. New Delhi: Seemant Prakashan, 1977. 200p.
First published 1947.

1170   — • *The new school of Urdu literature; a critical study of Hali, Azad, Nazir Ahmad, Rattan Nath Sarshar, and Abdul Halim Sharar.* Lahore: Panjab Observer Press, 1898.
Introductory chapter on Urdu literature, by Shaikh Mubarak Ali.
Reprint Lahore: Shaikh Mubarak Ali, 1932. 79p.

3rd ed. (1941), published under the title: *Urdu literature of the nineteenth century.*

1171 — • *Urdu language and literature*. Allahabad: University of Allahabad, 1942. 159p.
Includes studies of Ghalib, Sayyid Ahmed Khan, Dagh, Akbar Allahabadi, Nazir Ahmed,
Hali, Azad, Zakaullah, Shibli, Sharar, Sarshar.

1172 **Rahbar, Daud**
"Urdu literature: a neglected field". *Muslim World* 54, 3 (July 1964), pp. 245-249.
A paper read on 8 April 1964, in the Islamic section of the 174th meeting of the American
Oriental Society held in New York.

1173 **Rashed, N.M.**
"Social influences on Urdu literature". *Asia* 9 (Autumn 1967), pp. 34-50.

1174 **Riaz, Fehmida**
Pakistan, literature and society. New Delhi: Patriot Publishers, 1986. 124p.
Reviewed by Asif Aslam Farrukhi in *Annual of Urdu Studies* 6 (1986), pp. 140-141.
Reprinted with some abridgement from *The Herald*, May 1986.

1175 **Rothen-Dubs, Ursula**
Allahs Indischer Garten: ein Lesebuch der Urdu-Literatur. Frauenfeld: Verlag im Waldgut,
1989. 605p.

1176 **Russell, Ralph**
"How not to write the history of Urdu literature". *Annual of Urdu Studies* 6 (1987), pp. 1-
10.

1177 — • *The pursuit of Urdu literature. A select history*. London: Zed Books, 1992.

1178 — • "Urdu literature". In: *Encyclopaedia Britannica*. Chicago: Encyclopaedia
Britannica, 1962. Vol. 11, pp. 572-574.
Also in *Encylopaedia Britannica* (revised version 1970), Vol. 22, pp. 789-792.

1179 **Sadiq, Muhammad**
A history of Urdu literature. 2nd ed. Delhi: Oxford University Press, 1984. 652p.
One of the most comprehensive works of its kind in English.
Reviewed by Ralph Russell in *Asia Major* 12, 1 (August 1966).

1180 — • "A key to modern Urdu literature". *Iqbal* 17, 1 (July 1968), pp. 52-74.

1181 — • *Twentieth century Urdu literature*. Karachi: Royal Book Co., 1983. 414p.

1182 — • *Twentieth century Urdu literature: a review*. Baroda: Padrnaja Publications,
1947. 95p.

1183 **Sahitya Akademi**
"Urdu". In: *Sahitya Akademi Awards: books and writers (1955-1978)*. New Delhi: Sahitya
Akademi, 1990, pp. 501-529.
Includes entries for Z.H. Khan, K.A. Faruqi, S. Abid Hussain, Jigar Moradabadi, Syed
Masud Hasan Rizvi, Firaq Gorakhpur, Imtiaz Ali 'Arshi', Akhtarul Iman, K.G. Saiyidain,
Anand Narain Mulla, Rajinder Singh Bedi, Qurratulain Hyder, Makhdum Mohiuddin,
Hayatullah Ansari, Rashid Ahmad Siddiqui, Aley Ahmed Saroor, Kaifi Azmi, Jan Nisar
Akhtar, Yusuf Husain Khan.

1184 — • *Contemporary Indian literature: a symposium.* 2nd ed. Delhi, 1959. 338p.
Essays on the growth of each literature and a survey of existing trends.

1185 **Saksena, Ram Babu**
History of Urdu literature. Allahabad, 1927. 379p.

1186 — • *A history of Urdu literature.* Lahore: Sind Sagar Academy, 1975. 379p.
On the development of Urdu literature from the earliest time to 1920's; includes biographical
sketches of eminent writers and critical appreciation of their work.

1187 **Salierno, Vito**
Pakistan: dal deserto alla vita. Milano: Ceschina, 1972. 179p.

1188 **Saroor, Aley Ahmad**
"Humour: modern Urdu". In: *Indian writers in conference: sixth P.E.N. conference Mysore
1962.* Ed. Nissim Ezekiel. Bombay: P.E.N. All India Centre, 1964.

1189 — • "Urdu literature since independence: some significant aspects". In: *Proceedings
of the XXV International Congress of Orientalists.* Moscow, 1963. Nendeln, Lichtenstein:
Kraus - Thomson, 1972, pp. 281-288.

1190 **Sarvari, Abdul Qadir.**
"The influence of the Ramayana on Urdu literature". In: *Proceedings of the All-India Writers
Conference,* Bombay, 1954, pp. 126-129.

1191 **Schimmel, Annemarie**
Classical Urdu literature from the beginning to Iqbal. Wiesbaden: Otto Harrassowitz, 1975.
(*A history of Indian literature,* ed. Jan Gonda, vol. 7, fasc. 5.).

1192 — • *Islamic literatures of India.* Wiesbaden: Otto Harrassowitz, 1973. 60p. (*A
history of Indian literature,* ed. Jan Gonda, vol. 7, fasc. 5.).

1193 **Schmidt, Ruth Laila**
Dakhini Urdu history and structure. New Delhi: Bahri, 1981. 110p.
Revision of the author's Ph.D. thesis entitled *A structural analysis of Haiderabadi Dakhini,*
University of Pennsylvania, 1969.

1194 **Schreiner, Kay-Michael, et al.**
*Lesebuch Dritte Welt: eine Auswahl von Texten aus afrikanischen, asiatischen und
lateinamerikanischen Entwicklungsländern für den Unterricht.* Wuppertal: Hammer, 1974.
354p.
Includes translations from Manto and Faiz.

1195 **Seton-Karr, W.S.**
"The Urdu language and literature". *Calcutta Review* 4, 8 (1845).

1196   **Shackle, Christopher**
Urdu and Muslim South Asia: studies in honour of Ralph Russell. London: School of Oriental and African Studies, University of London, 1989. 205p.
Includes articles on the study and teaching of Urdu in Britain; Urdu Mushaira; Urdu ghazal in performance; poetry of Quli Qutb Shah and Khavaja Ghulam Farid; Rashid-ul Khairi's novels and Urdu literary journalism for women; and Shi'te consciousness in *Basti*, a novel by Intizar Husain. Also includes a select bibliography of Ralph Russell's writings on Urdu language and literature, 1955-1986.

1197   **Shafi, Murtaza**
Modern Urdu critics. Karachi: Urdu Academy Sind, 1959. 80p.

1198   **Shaheen, Wali Alam, Nasim, Anwar and Mirza, Izhar**
Across continents: a review of Urdu language and literature in Canada. Ottawa: National Federation of Pakistani Canadians, 1988. 112p.
Five articles and two introductory notes dealing with the progress of Urdu language and literature in Canada providing information about Urdu writers, literary associations and journals active in Canada and instruction of Urdu in Schools.

1199   **Shinozani, S. Fazal Abbas**
"Freedom movement in Urdu literature". *Perspective* 4, 2-3 (August-September 1970), pp. 75-76.

1200   **Siddiqi, Abu Lais**
"Urdu language and literature". *Pakistan Quarterly* 8, 3 (Winter 1958).

1201   **Siddiqi, M. Atique**
Origins of modern Hindustani literature - source material: Gilchrist letters. Aligarh: Naya Kitab Ghar, 1963. 191p.
Includes bibliography of Gilchrist's works and other Fort William material.

1202   **Siddiqi, M.H.**
The growth of Indo-Persian literature in Gujarat. Baroda: Department of Persian, Arabic and Urdu, M.S. University of Baroda, 1985.

1203   **Siddiqi, Nazir**
"Urdu literature". *Urdu Canada* 1, 3 (1987), pp. 7-32.

1204   — • "The Urdu language and literature". *Calcutta Review* 4 (1945), pp. 318-354.

1205   **Siddiqi, R.A.**
"Urdu literature 1857-1947". In: *The Indian literature of today: a symposium.* Ed. Bhratan Kumarappa. Bombay: The International Book House Ltd., 1947.

1206   **Srinivasan, K.S.**
The ethos of Indian literature: a study of romantic tradition. Delhi: Chanakya Publications, 1985. 244p.

1207   **Subhan, A.**
"Hindu contributions to Urdu literature". *Indo-Asian Culture* 17, 1 (January 1968), pp. 47-56.

1208   **Sud, Kedar Nath**
"New trends in Urdu writing". *Indian Literature* 22, 6 (1979), pp. 120-124.

1209   **Sukhochev, A.S.**
"Avadh seredini XIX veka". In: *Vzaimodeistvie kul´tur vostoka i zapada*. Moscow: Nauka, 1991, pp. 121-132.

1210   — • "O kharaktere kontaktov mezhdu evropeiskimi literaturami i literaturoǐ urdu v XIX v". In: *The theoretical problems of Oriental literatures*. Moscow, 1969, pp. 189-196.

1211   **Taher, Mohamed and Pangal, Abdul Majeed**
"Bibliographical control of Islamic literature in India: perspectives". *Islamic Culture* (Hyderabad) 58, 2 (April 1984), pp. 161-169.

1212   **Talib, Gurbachan Singh**
"Modern Urdu literature". *Quest* 20 (January-March 1959), pp. 42-44.

1213   **Winternitz, Moritz**
A history of Indian literature. Trans. from German by S. Ketkar and revised by the author. Calcutta: University of Calcutta, 1954. 865p.

1214   **Yadav, R.S.**
"Urdu literature: decline and progress". *Thought* 25, 7 (17 February 1973), pp. 13-17.

1215   **Zahur-ud-Din**
Development of Urdu language and literature in the Jammu Region. Srinagar: Gulshan Publishers, 1985. 481p.

1216   **Zaidi, Ali Jawad**
"Urdu: balanced growth". *Indian Literature* 31, 6 (November-December 1988), pp. 149-160. Brief survey of significant books published in 1987.

1217   — • "Annual review of Indian writing in 1964: Urdu". *Indian Literature* 8, 2 (1965), pp. 133-143.

1218   **Zaidi, Mujahid Husain**
"Biography in modern Urdu literature". In: *Biography and autobiography in modern South Asian literatures*. Heidelberg: South Asia Institute, (1976), pp. 99-120.

1219   **Zaman, Mukhtar**
"Modern Urdu literature; some new trends". *Perspective* 5, 7 (January 1972), pp. 23-31.

1220   **Zenkor, Th.**
"Neueste Hindustani-Literatur". *Zeitschrift der Deutschen Morgenländischen Gesellschaft* 19 (1865), p. 599.

1221 **Zeno**
"Rejection of modernism". *Annual of Urdu Studies* 1 (1981), pp. 98-104.
Discussion based on Muhammad Hasan Askari's book *Jadiyat, ya Maghribi gumrahiyon ki tarikh ka khaka*. Reprinted from *The Muslim* (Islamabad) (September 2, 1979).

1222 **Zia-Islam**
Glimpses of modern Urdu literature. Allahabad, 1945.

1223 **Zore, M.Q.**
"Urdu literature after 1947". In: *Third All India Writers Conference*. Bombay, 1954, pp. 384-388.

LITERATURE ON WOMEN

1224 **Hashmi, Nasiruddin**
"Muslim women story writers of India and Pakistan". *Islamic Review* 39, 1 (1951), pp. 32-36.
Brief discussion of twenty-two female Muslim writers.

1225 **Husain, Saliha Abid**
"Women writers and Urdu literature". Trans. Muhammad Zakir. *Indian Horizons* (New Delhi), 23, 2-3 (1974), pp. 5-14.

1226 **Ikramullah, Begum Shaista Suhrawardy**
"The role of women in the life and literature of Pakistan". *Asian Review* 55, pp. 14-26.
Also in: *Islamic Review* 47, 4 (1959), pp. 15-19, 22.

1227 **Machwe, Prabhakar**
"Prominent women writers in Indian literature after independence". *Journal of South Asian Literature* 12, 3-4 (Spring-Summer 1977), pp. 145-149.
Writers include Qurratulain Hyder, Ismat Chughtai and Razia Sajjad Zahir.

1228 **Metcalf, Barbara Daly**
"Islam and custom in nineteenth-century India: the reformist standard of Maulana Thanawi's *Bihishti Zewar*". *Contributions to Asian Studies* 17 (1982), pp. 62-78.

1229 — • "Islamic reform and Islamic women: Maulana Thanawi's *Jewelry of paradise*".
In: *Moral conduct and authority: the place of adab in South Asian Islam*. Ed. Barbara Daly Metcalfe. Berkeley: University of California Press, 1984, pp. 184-185.

1230 — • "The making of a Muslim lady. Maulana Thanawi's *Bihishti Zewar*". In: *Islamic Society and culture: essays in honour of Professor Aziz Ahmad*. Eds. Milton Israel and N.K. Wagle. New Delhi: Manohar Publications, 1983, pp. 17-38.

1231 **Minault, Gail**
"Sayyid Mumtaz Ali and Huquq al-niswan: an advocate of women's right in Islam in the late 19th century". *Islamic Culture* 59, 4 (October 1985), pp. 295-322.

1232   **Ray, L.**
"Women writers". In: *Women of India*. Ed. T.A. Bagi. Delhi: Publications Division, 1958, pp. 181-196.

1233   **Sakala, Carol**
Women of South Asia: a guide to resources. New York: Kraus International, 1980.
Includes "Urdu literature: criticism and in translation", with 42 individual entries, pp. 267-270.

1234   **Zeno**
"Women and literature: the new revolution". *The Herald* (Karachi), 14, 1 (January 1983), pp. 62-66.

PROGRESSIVE WRITERS MOVEMENT

1235   **Ali, Ahmad**
"The Progressive Writer's Movement and creative writers in Urdu". In: *Marxist Influences and South Asian literature*. Michigan, 1974, Vol. 1, pp. 35-44.

1236   — • "The Progressive Writer's Movement and its historical perspective". *Journal of South Asian Literature* 13, 1-4 (1977-78), pp. 91-97.

1237   **Azad, Jagan Nath**
"Sajjad Zaheer: a beacon of light". Trans. Faruq Hassan. *Urdu Canada* 1, 3 (1987), pp. 49-56.

1238   **Coppola, Carlo**
"The All-India Progressive Writer's Association: the European phase". In: *Socialist realism and South Asian literature*. East Lansing: Asian Studies Center, Michigan State University, 1974, Vol. 1, pp. 1-34.

1239   — • "Indian and Pakistani Marxist literature: the case of Urdu, 1935-1970".   In: *Oakland symposium on socialist realism in literature*. Ed. Renate Gerulaitis. Rochester, Michigan: Oakland University, 1975, pp. 52-65.

1240   — • *Marxist influence and South Asian literature*. East Lansing, Michigan, 1974.
A collection of papers arising out of a 1972 conference of the All-India Progressive Writer's Association.
Discusses the work of a number of writers.

1241   **Iftikharuddim, Mian Muhammad**
Selected speeches and statements of Mian Iftikharuddin. Ed. Abdullah Malik.   Lahore: Nigarishat, 1971. 503p.

1242   **Khullar, K.K.**
"Influence of October revolution on Urdu literature". *Indian Literature* 24, 3 (May-June 1981), pp. 124-139.

1243 Kidwai, Sadiq-ur-Rahman
"Urdu: Progressivism is past." *Link* 16, 25 (26 January 1974), pp. 73-75.

1244 Makhmoor Jullundhari
"Impact of October revolution on Urdu literature". *Contemporary Indian Literature* 10, 3-4 (October-December 1970), pp. 39-41.

1245 Malik, Hafeez
"The Marxist literary movement in India and Pakistan". *Journal of Asian Studies* 26 (August 1967), pp. 649-664.

1246 "PWA jubilee Declaration". *Viewpoint* (Lahore) 11, 9 (10 October 1985), pp. 29-32.

1247 Rahman, Tariq
"Pakistan: introduction". In: *Frank: an International Journal of Contemporary Writing and Art* (France) 10 (Autumn 1988), pp. 105-165.

1248 Rais, Qamar
October Revolution: impact on Indian literature. New Delhi: Sterling, 1978. 136p. Contributed articles.

1249 Russell, Ralph
"Leadership in the All India Progressive Writer's Association". In: *Leadership in South Asia.* Ed. B.N. Pandey. Delhi: Vikas, 1977, pp. 108-128.

1250 Sahni, Bhisham
"A golden jubilee feature: The Progressive Writer's Movement". *Indian Literature* 24, 6 (November-December 1986), pp. 178-183.

1251 Zahir, Sajjad
"Thirty years of the Progressive Writer's Movement". *Contemporary Indian Literature* 6, 5 (May 1966), pp. 16-18; 6, 6-7 (June-July 1966), pp. 13-15.

1252 — • "The future of the PWA Movement". *Contemporary Indian Literature* 7, 1 (February 1967), pp. 17-19, 22.

QAVVALI

1253 Joshee, O.K. and Hyder, Qurratulain
"Qawwali then and now". *Illustrated Weekly of India* 90, 34 (24 August 1969), pp. 30-31.

POETRY

Individual Authors

AALI, JAMILUDDIN

1254   "Poems". *Pakistan Studies* 1, 3-4 (Autumn 1982), pp. 101-106.

AATISH, KHWAJA HAIDER ALI

TRANSLATIONS

1255   "A couplet". Trans. Carla R. Petievich. *Urdu Canada* 1, 1 (February 1986), p. 70.

1256   "From a ghazal". Trans. Carla R. Petievich. *Urdu Canada* 1, 3 (1987), p. 91.

ABBAS, AZRA

TRANSLATIONS

1257   "Six poems". Trans. C.M. Naim. *Annual of Urdu Studies* 7 (1990), pp. 45-48.
— • "Hands lying on a table."
— • "It's difficult to remove the dirt."
— • "It's difficult to write a poem".
— • "She asked me."
— • "Today was a holiday".
— • "When the entire day goes by."

ABDULWAHID, "GHAZI"

TRANSLATION

1258   *Selected poems of Navab Ghazi of Gewarda with their English translations and notes.*
Ed. Muhammad Zahirul Haq. Gorakhpur, [Lucknow printed], 1938.

ADIB, KRISHAN

TRANSLATIONS

1259   "Dead leaves". *Thought* 6, 16 (April 17, 1954), p. 10.

1260   "My dreams". Trans. Satindra Singh. *Thought* 12, 7 (13 February 1960), p. 11.

1261   "My estate". Trans. [Satindra Singh?] *Thought* 6, 17 (1954), p. 11.

1262   "Question". Trans. Satindra Singh. *Thought* 12, 31 (July 1960), p. 12.

AFSOS

STUDY

1263   **Blumhardt, J.F. and Inayatullah, S.H.**
"Afsus (Afsos)". In: *Encyclopaedia of Islam* 1 (1960), pp. 241-242.
In 1800 Afsos was appointed Head Munshi in Hindustani department, College of Fort William.

AGHA, WAZIR

TRANSLATIONS

1264   "Forecast". Trans. C.M. Naim. *Journal of Asian Studies* 27 (February 1969), pp. 282-283.

1265   "Wazir Agha: eleven poems". Trans. and Intro. C.M. Naim. *Annual of Urdu Studies* 6 (1987),
— • "Apprehension." p. 39.
— • "The calling mountain". p. 40.
— • "Down the slope." p. 34.
— • "An encounter." p. 36
— • "The grief of the soiled sky." p. 35.
— • "Lava." p. 37.
— • "A night in war". p. 40.
— • "Poet." p. 35.
— • "The second stage of the journey." p. 39.
— • "A strange man." p. 34
— • "The wind kept calling ..." p. 38.

1266   "Poem". Trans. C.M. Naim. *Translation* (New York), 9 (Fall 1982), 252p.

107

1267   "Poems by Wazir Agha". Trans. C.M. Naim. *Urdu Canada* 1, 3 (1987),
— • "Apprehension." p. 84.
— • "Lava". p. 85.
— • "A night in war". p. 84.
— • "The second stage of the journey." p. 82.
— • "The wind kept calling ..." p. 83.

1268   *Selected poems*. Eds. and Intro. Jamil Azar and Mushtaq Qamar. Sargodha: Maktaba Urdu Zaban, 1979. 91p.

1269   *Skylark* (Aligarh) 46 (1982). *Wazir Agha's poetry number.*
Twenty-one poems, two introductions, one review.

STUDY

1270   **Naim, C.M.**
"Selected poems". *Annual of Urdu Studies* 1 (1981), pp. 115-117.
A review

AHMAD, AIJAZ

TRANSLATIONS

1271   "The old catastrophes". Trans. the author. *Journal of South Asian Literature* 13, 1-4 (1977-78), pp. 311-316.

1272   "Two poems". Trans. the author. *Poetry India* 2, 2 (April-June 1967), p. 43.
— • "August, 66".
— • "Poem".

AHMED, AKBAR

TRANSLATIONS

1273   *More lines: selected poems*. Karachi: Royal Book Co, 1980. 92p.
"Published under arrangement with ...... Academy of Letters".

AKBAR ALLAHABADI, AKBAR HUSAIN

STUDIES

1274 Case, Margaret H.
"The social and political satire of Akbar Allahabadi" (1846-1921)". *Mahfil* 1, 4 (1964), pp. 11-20.

1275 Hoda, Najmul
"Nationalism and Urdu poet Akbar Allahabadi". *Annals of Oriental Research* 31, 2 (1983), pp. 1-9.

1276 Inayatulah, S.H.
"Akbar, Sayyid Husayn Allahabadi". In: *Encyclopaedia of Islam* 1 (1960), p. 317.

1277 Nath, Kidar
"Akbar Allahabadi". *Illustrated Weekly of India* (21 October 1962), p. 45.

1278 Rattan, H.R.
"Akbar Allahabadi's poetry". *The Hindustan Times Weekly Magazine* (1 May 1960), p. 5.

1279 Russell, Ralph and Islam, Khurshidul
"The satirical verse of Akbar Allahabadi (1846-1921)". *Modern Asian Studies* 8, 1 (1974), pp. 1-58.

1280 Sadiq, Muhammad
"Akbar Allahabadi: his outlook on life". *Iqbal* 13 (January 1965), pp. 87-99.

1281 — • "Akbar Allahabadi and politics". *Iqbal* 14, 1 (1965), pp. 20-38.

1282 — • "Understanding Akbar Allahabadi". *Iqbal* 16, 3 (January 1968), pp. 27-47.

1283 — • "Akbar Allahabadi". *Pakistan Review* 18, 6 (June 1970), pp. 29-33.

AKHTAR, JAN NISAR

STUDIES

1284 Bilgrami, Madhosh
"Jan Nisar Akhtar". *Illustrated Weekly of India* 95, 50 (14-20 December 1975), pp. 46-47.

1285 Engineer Asghar, Ali
"His poetry flows from life". *Times of India* (29 August 1976), pp. 13, 5-8.

AKHTAR SHIRANI, MUHAMMAD DAUD KHAN

STUDIES

1286 Lall, Inder Jit
"Akhtar Sheerani". *Thought* 13, 27 (8 July 1961), pp. 12-13.

1287 — • "Akhtar Sheerani: a noted poet of love". *Poetry India* 2, 2 (April-June 1967), pp. 57-60.

ALVI, MUHAMMAD

TRANSLATIONS

1288 "Moonlight". Trans. C.M. Naim. *Books Abroad* 43, 4 (Autumn 1969), p. 546.

AMIR MINAI, AMIR AHMAD

STUDY

1289 Beg, Abdullah Anwar
"Amir Minai of Lucknow". *Pakistan Review* 19, 2 (February 1971), pp. 16-19.

AMIR, S. JAVED

TRANSLATION

1290 "The black wilderness". *Pakistan Review* 16, 4 (April 1968), p. 55.
Includes Urdu text.

AMJAD, AMJAD ISLAM

TRANSLATION

1291 "Two poems". Trans. Dildar Parvez Bhatti. *Urdu Canada* 1, 3 (1987),
— • "A love poem". p. 87.
— • "Whatever is around". p. 86.

AMJAD, MAJEED

TRANSLATIONS

1292   "Autograph". Trans. M.H.K. Qureshi. *Urdu Canada* 1, 1 (February 1987), p. 67.

1293   "The beggar". Trans. Faruq Hassan and M. Salim-ur-Rahman. *Pakistani Literature* (Islamabad) 1, 1 (1992), p. 54.

1294   "A Harrappan inscription".   Trans. Faruq Hassan and M. Salim-ur-Rahman. *Pakistani Literature* (Islamabad) 1, 1   (1992), p. 56.

1295   "The scream". Trans. Faruq Hassan and M. Salim-ur-Rahman. *Pakistani Literature* (Islamabad) 1, 1   (1992), p. 55.

1296   "Spring". Trans. Faruq Hassan and M. Salim-ur-Rahman. *Pakistani Literature* (Islamabad) 1, 1   (1992), p. 57.

1297   "Sons of the mountains". Trans. Faruq Hassan and M. Salim-ur-Rahman. *Pakistani Literature* (Islamabad) 1, 1   (1992), p. 58.

1298   "Children". Trans. Faruq Hassan and M. Salim-ur-Rahman. *Pakistani Literature* (Islamabad) 1, 1   (1992), p. 59.

1299   "The individual".   Trans. Faruq Hassan and M. Salim-ur-Rahman.   *Pakistani Literature* (Islamabad) 1, 1   (1992), p. 60.

1300   "A prisoner of war on the radio". Trans. Faruq Hassan and M. Salim-ur-Rahman. *Pakistani Literature* (Islamabad) 1, 1   (1992), p. 61.

1301   "Now after a long spell of sunshine..." Trans. M. Salim-ur-Rahman. *Pakistani Literature* (Islamabad) 1, 1 (1992), pp. 62-63.

1302   "What days, indeed". Trans. Faruq Hassan and M. Salim-ur-Rahman. *Pakistani Literature* (Islamabad) 1, 1 (1992), p. 64.

STUDIES

1303   Amjad, Majeed
"Why do I write?" Trans. Muzaffar Iqbal. *Pakistani Literature* (Islamabad) 1, 1 (1992), p. 53.

1304   "Majeed Amjad". *Pakistani Literature* (Islamabad) 1, 1 (1992), pp. 51-52. Biographical sketch.

ANIS, MIR BABBAR ALI

STUDIES

1305   **Abbas, Syed Ghulam**
The immortal poetry and Mir Anis: with the versified translation of a marsia of Mir Anis.
Karachi: Majlis-e-Milli, 1983. 368p.

1306   **Hasan, Masood**
"Mir Anis and the elegy". *Indian Literature* 16, 3-4 (July-December 1973), pp. 26-30.

1307   — • "Mir Anis and his poetry". *Illustrated Weekly of India* 82, 50 (12 December 1971), pp. 35-37.

1308   **Imam, Syed Ghulam**
Anis and Shakespeare: a comparison. Karachi: Indus Publications, 1980. 344p.
Reprint of the 1950 ed.
Urdu quotations are not translated.

1309   **Inayatullah, Shaikh**
"Anis". In: *Encyclopaedia of Islam* 1, 8 (1957), pp. 508-509.

1310   **Jawaid, S.A.**
"Life and times of Mir Anis". *Perspective* 1, 8 (February 1968), pp. 43-48.

1311   **Zaidi, Ali Jawad**
Mir Anis. New Delhi: Sahitya Akademi, 1986. 109p.
Life and works of Mir Babbar Ali Anis.
Urdu text in Roman characters.

ARIF, IFTIKHAR

TRANSLATIONS

1312   "Five poems". Trans. Naomi Lazard. *Annual of Urdu Studies* 4 (1984),
— • "Balance sheet". p. 51.
— • "A moments distance" p. 51.
— • "On the shore of memory". p. 49.
— • "The twelfth man". p. 50.
— • "Waiting for the Messiah". p. 52.

1313   "Four poems". Trans. Ralph Russell and Richard Harris.   *Pakistan Studies* 1, 2 (Spring 1982), pp. 58-60.
— • "And the wind was silent".
— • "Ghazal".
— • "Twelfth player".
— • "Written in climate of fear".

1314   "Ghazal". Trans. Ralph Russell. *Urdu Canada* 1, 2 (1986), p. 77.

1315   "Ghazal". In: *The new British poetry*. Eds. Gillian Allnut, et al. London: Paladin, 1988, p. 8.

1316   "To a despondent evening". In: *The new British poetry*. Eds. Gillian Allnut, et al. p. 9.

1317   "Translations from *The twelfth man*". Trans. Brenda Walker. *Artrage International Magazine* (Summer 1989), pp. 32-33.
— • "A question".
— • "To a sad evening".
— • "How wrong I was".

1318   "The twelfth man". Trans. Mahmud Jamal. In: *Stories from Asia*. Ed. John Welch. London: Oxford University Press, 1988, p. 111.

1319   *The twelfth man. Poems by Iftikhar Arif.* Trans. Brenda Walker. London: Forest Books, 1989. 69p.
Includes Urdu text.

STUDIES

1320   **Ahmad, Jalaluddin**
["A review of *The twelfth man. Poems by Iftikhar Arif*"]. *New Horizon* (August 1989).

1321   **Farrukhi, Asif Aslam**
"Arif in English. *The twelfth man*". *Newsline* 1, 6 (December 1989), p. 90.
A review

1322   **Hashmi, Alamgir**
"A division of the sun". *Pakistan Times* (9 March 1990), p. 6.

1323   **Husain, Imdad**
"Iftikhar Arif's poetry". *Pakistan Times* (1 June 1984).

1324   **Mughal, Amin**
"Iftikhar: the odd man out". *Daily Jang* (London) (24-25 June 1989).
Review of *The twelfth man.*

1325   **Nadeem, Shahid**
["A review of *Mehri-i do neem.*"] *Herald* (Karachi) 1984.

1326   **Nasarullah, Nusrat**
"Urdu poet's 'New world'". *Mag* (November 1988), p. 23.

1327   "A poet of tragic times". *The Statesman* (New Delhi), (24 March 1983).

1328   Rahman, Tariq
"An interview with Iftikhar Arif". *Muslim* (17 May 1991).

1329 — • "Pioneering art". *Third World Quarterly* 11, 4 (October 1989), pp. 303-305.
Review of *The twelfth man.*
Also in: *World Literature Today* (Autumn 1989).

1330 — • "On oppression and injustice". *Dawn* (2 June 1989).
Review of *The twelfth man.*

1331   Tar, Mikhail
"Our guest from Pakistan". *Soviet Literature* (Moscow).

1332   Zeno
"A poet in a country of vacillations". *Dawn* (2 September 1983).
Also in: *Jang* (London), (24 September 1983).

ASAR LAKHNAVI, JAFAR ALI KHAN

STUDY

1333   Nath, Kidar
"Asar Luckhnavi's prose and poetry". *Thought* 17, 15 (10 April 1965), p. 13.

ASHK, BIMAL KRISHAN

TRANSLATION

1334   *And there was light ...* Trans. the author. Rohtak: Umesh Publications, 1980. 59p.

AZAAD, ALEXANDER HEATHERLEY

STUDY

1335   Zaidi, Nasir Hasan
"Alexander Heatherley Azzad [a European poet of Urdu]". *Pakistan Review* 15 (October 1967), pp. 35-39.

AZAD, MUHAMMAD HUSSAIN

STUDIES

1336   "Q.A. Muhammad Husain Azad: in prose - an unsurpassed style; in poetry - a new trend". *Pakistan Review* 8 (September 1960), pp. 37-39.

1337   **Afzal, Qaiser**
"Muhammed Hussain Azad: a pioneer of modern Urdu poetry". *Pakistan Review* 11 (June 1963), pp. 9-10.

1338   **Naqvi, S.A.H.**
"Muhammad Hussain Azad". *Pakistan Review* 16 (February 1968), pp. 34, 43.

1339   **Sadiq, Muhammad**
Muhammad Husain Azad. His life and works. Lahore: West Pak Publishing Co., 1965. 174p.

AZIMI, FAHIM

TRANSLATION

1340   "In memory of my birth place". Trans. Nuzhat Naqvi. *Urdu Canada* 1, 3 (1987), p. 90

AZIZ, IRFANA

STUDY

1341   "Spring's palms". *Urdu Canada* 1, 1 (February 1986), pp. 89-90.
Review of Irfana Aziz's *Kafe Bahar.*

AZIZ LAKHNAVI

STUDY

1342   **Nath, Kidar**
"Aziz Lakhnavi and his poetry". *Thought* 17, 1 (2 January 1965), pp. 12-13.

AZMI, KAIFI

TRANSLATIONS

1343   *The poetry of Kaifi Azmi*. Trans. Pritish Nandy. Calcutta: The Poet's Press, [1957?]. 32p.

STUDIES

1344   **Azmi, Shabana** [As told to Sailesh Kottary]
"My father Kaifi". *Illustrated Weekly of India* (20 November 1983), pp. 36-40.

1345   **Lall, Inder Jit**
"Kaifi: noted man of letters". *Indian P.E.N.* 33 (October 1967), pp. 286-287.

AZMI, KHALIL-UR RAHMAN

TRANSLATIONS

1346   "Four poems". Trans. C.M. Naim and Norman Zide. *Indian Writing Today* 4, 3 (1970), pp. 185-186.
— • "Distances".
— • "I and I".
— • "I fear dreams ..."
— • "The peddler".

1347   "The peddler". Trans. C.M. Naim. *Books Abroad* 43, 4 (Autumn 1969), 546p.

AZURDA, SADRUDDIN KHAN

STUDY

1348   **Ansari, A.S. Bazmee**
"Azurda, Sadruddin Khan b Lutf Allah". In: *Encyclopaedia of Islam* 1, 13 (1958), pp. 827-828.

BAHRI

STUDY

1349 Hafiz, S.M.
Muhammad Hafiz Syed, Quasi Mahmud Bahri - a mystic poet of the 12th century A.H., his times, life and work. Ph.D. thesis, University of London, 1932.

BEDIL, MIRZA ABDUL QADIR

STUDIES

1350 Abdul Ghani
The life and works of Abdul Qadir Bedil. Lahore: Publishers United, 1960. 326p.

1351 Bazmi, Syed Yaqub
"Mirza Abdul Qader 'Bedil': a revolutionary poet of India". *Indo-Iranica* 16 (December 1963), pp. 36-54.

BHOPALI, MOHSIN

TRANSLATIONS

1352 Two poems (Nazmanay). Trans. Syed Munir Wasti. *Urdu Canada* 1, 3 (1987),
— • "The last dialogue". p. 89.
— • "Tragedy". p. 89.

BUKHARI, FARIGH

TRANSLATIONS

1353 *Farigh's poems: song of love and struggle.* Trans. Yunus Ahmer. Lahore: Khalid Academy, 1982. 63p.

DAGH DIHLAVI, MIRZA KHAN

STUDY

1354   Nath, Kidar
"The muse of Dagh Dehlavi". *Illustrated Weekly of India* 85, 31 (2 August 1964), 47p.

DAR, ZAHID

TRANSLATIONS

1355   "To my betters". Trans. Aijaz Ahmad. *Poetry India* 2, 2 (April-June 1967), pp. 44-45.

STUDY

1356   Janus
"Zahid Dar's bombshell". *Viewpoint* (Lahore) 7, 48 (July 1982), p. 27.

DARD, KHWAJA MIR

STUDIES

1357   Ansari, A.S.Bazmee
"Dard". In: *Encyclopaedia of Islam* 2, (1965), pp. 137-138.

1358   Lall, Inder Jit
"Mir Dard: great Urdu poet of sufism". *Thought* 12, 38 (17 September 1960), pp. 17-18.

1359   Schimmel, Annemarie
"Khaja Mir Dard, poet and mystic". In: *German scholars on India.* vol. 1. Varanasi, 1973, pp. 279-293.

1360   — • "Khwaja Mir Dard, a sincere Muhammadan". In her *Mystical dimensions of Islam.* Chapel Hill: University of North Carolina Press, 1975, pp. 373-383.

1361   — • *Pain and grace: a study of two mystical writers of eighteenth-century Muslim India.* Leiden: E.J. Brill, 1976. 310p.
A study of Dard and Shah Abdul Latif.

DAYARAM, BULCHAND

STUDY

1362   "A modern Hindustani poet". *East and West* (Bombay) 4 (August 1905), pp. 884-891.

FAIZ, FAIZ AHMAD

TRANSLATIONS

1363   "Ask me not for that old fervour". Trans. Shiv K. Kumar. *Indian Literature* 31, 4 (July-August 1988), pp. 57-60.

1364   "The bitter fire". Trans. Daud Kamal. *Frontier Post* (Lahore) (6 February 1987).

1365   "Bouquet of a hundred colours". *Viewpoint* (Lahore) 10, 17 (November, 1984), pp. 18-20.
Translations of Faiz in English from *Selected poems of Faiz in English* rendered by Daud Kamal.

1366   "Chopin's music". Trans. Daud Kamal. *The Muslim* (Islamabad) (7 May 1982).

1367   "Come back, Africa". Trans. Daud Kamal. *Frontier Post* (Lahore) (3 June 1987).

1368   "The day death comes". Trans. Daud Kamal. *The Muslim* (Islamabad) (4 November 1983).

1369   "Dedication". Trans. Daud Kamal. *The Muslim* (Islamabad) (9 March 1984).

1370   "Dogs". Trans. Shiv K. Kumar. *Indian Literature* 31, 4 (July August 1988), pp. 57-60.

1371   "Do not ask me O love!". In: *Contemporary Urdu Verse*. Ed. and Trans. Rajinder Singh Verma. Delhi: Atma Ram, 1989, p. 1.

1372   "Do what you have to do". Trans. Daud Kamal. *The Muslim* (Islamabad) (28 May 1982).

1373   "Eight Panjabi and Urdu poems". Trans. Alamgir Hashmi. *Pacific Quarterly* 6, 2 (1981), pp. 190-193.
Includes poems of Faiz and four other poets.

1374   "Eight poems". Trans. Baidar Bakht and Kathleen Grant Jaeger. *The Toronto South Asian Review* 6, 1 (Summer 1987), pp. 24-28.
— • "An evening in prison".
— • "The cemetery of Leningrad".

— • "A few more days".
— • "The heart attack".
— • "The last letter".
— • "Loneliness".
— • "The mind still searches for a word".
— • "Travelogue".

1375 *"Eleven poems and an introduction"*. Trans. C.M. Naim and Carlo Coppola. Ed. Pritish Nandy. Calcutta: Dialogue Calcutta 19, 1972.
— • "The colour of my heart".
— • "This crop of hope o friend".
— • "Evening".
— • "The meetings".
— • "Memory".
— • "Solitude".
— • "Speak".
— • "There is no saviour of crystal".
— • "We who were killed in half lit streets".
— • "The window".
Introduction to *Dast-i sabah*.

1376 *An elusive dawn: selections from the poetry of Faiz Ahmad Faiz*. Trans. Mahbubul Haq. Islamabad: Pakistan National Commission for UNESCO, 1985. 87p.

1377 "Evening, be kind". Trans. Daud Kamal. *The Muslim* (Islamabad) (5 November 1982).

1378 *Faiz Ahmed Faiz poèmes*. Trans. into French by Laiq Babree. Paris: Seghers, 1979. 119p.

1379 "Faiz Ahmad Faiz - two poems". Trans. Shiv K. Kumar. *New Quest* 53 (September-October 1985), pp. 313-314.

1380 "Faiz's latest ghazal". *Viewpoint* (Lahore) 7, 1 (13 August 1981), p. 9.
Poem with an Urdu text in Faiz's own hand.

1381 "For the Palestinian martyrs". Trans. Daud Kamal. *Viewpoint* (Lahore) 7, 52 (5 August 1982), p. 9.

1382 "Four poems". In: *Only connect: literary perspective east and west*. Eds. Guy Amirthanayagam and S.C. Harrex. Adelaide and Honolulu: Center for Research in the New Literatures in English and East-West Center, 1981, pp. 209-210.

1383 "Four poems by Faiz". Trans. Shiv K. Kumar. *Indian Literature* 28, 2 (March-April 1985), pp. 35-38.

1384 "Ghazal". Trans. Begum Naz. *Pakistan Review* 14, 11 (November 1966).

1385 "Icy flames of dawn". Trans. Daud Kamal. *The Muslim* (Islamabad) (28 December 1984).

1386   "If I were certain". Trans. A. Ahmad. *Nation* (New York) 207 (November 1968), p. 474.

1387   "If you look at the city from here". Trans. Naomi Lazard. *Pakistani Literature* (Islamabad) 1, 1 (1992), p. 22.

1388   "Independence dawn". Trans. K.K. Khullar. *Indian Literature* 23, 1-2 (1980), pp. 530-531.

1389   "The last letter". Trans. Daud Kamal. *The Muslim* (Islamabad) (15 June 1984).

1390   "Legend of a tall tree". Trans. Daud Kamal. *The Muslim* (Islamabad) (27 May 1983).

1391   "The Leningrad cemetery". Trans. Daud Kamal. *Viewpoint* (Lahore) 8, 33 (24 March 1983), p. 13.

1392   "A lover to his beloved". Trans. Daud Kamal. *Viewpoint* (Lahore) 7, 15 (19 November 1981), p. 24.

1393   "Lullaby". Trans. M.H.K. Qureshi. *Toronto South Asian Review* (Toronto), 1, 3 (Fall 1982-Winter 1983), pp. 64-66.

1394   "Lullaby for a Palestinian child". Trans. Daud Kamal. *The Muslim* (Islamabad) (31 October 1986).

1395   "The massacre of Beirut". Trans. Daud Kamal. *The Muslim* (Islamabad) (14 July 1982).

1396   *Memory: poetry of Faiz Ahmad Faiz*. Trans. Sain Sucha. Sollentuna: Vudya Kitaban forlag, 1987. 66p.
Includes Urdu text.

1397   "The morning of freedom". Trans. Daud Kamal. *Pakistani Literature* (Islamabad) 1, 1 (1992), p. 21.

1398   "My companion". Trans. M.H.K. Qureshi. *Toronto South Asian Review* (Toronto), 1, 3 (Fall 1982-Winter 1983), pp. 64-66.

1399   "My heart". Trans. M.H.K. Qureshi. *Toronto South Asian Review* (Toronto), 1, 3 (Fall 1982-Winter 1983), pp. 64-66.

1400   "My visitors". Trans. M.H.K. Qureshi. *Toronto South Asian Review* (Toronto), 1, 3 (Fall 1982-Winter 1983), pp. 64-66.

1401   "Nimbus". Trans. Daud Kamal. *Frontier Post* (Lahore) (13 February 1987).

1402   "Nine poems". Trans. Alamgir Hashmi, Carolyn Kizer, Naomi Lazard. *Annual of Urdu Studies* 2 (1982), pp. 1-9.
— • "Bangladesh III".

—• "Chopins melody sounds".
—• "Elegy".
—• "If I were certain".
—• "Landscape".
—• "Let me think".
—• "My visitors".
—• "No sign of blood".
—• "Paris".

1403   "A nocturnal rhapsody". Trans. Daud Kamal. *The Muslim* (Islamabad) (10 June 1983).

1404   "Paris". Trans. Daud Kamal. *The Muslim* (Islamabad) (16 July 1982).

1405   "A prison evening". Trans. Daud Kamal. *The Muslim* (Islamabad) (25 February 1983).

1406   "Poem". Trans. Agha Shahid Ali. *Sonora Review* 8 (1985), p. 63.

1407   "Poems". Trans. Agha Shahid Ali. *Sonora Review* 8 (1985), pp. 28-41.

1408   "Poems". Trans. Daud Kamal. *Race and Class* 26, 3 (Winter 1985), pp. 1-8.
—• "August 1952 (Ghazal)".
—• "Battleground".
—• "Before you came".
—• "Blackout".
—• "City of lights".
—• "Don't ask me for that love again".
—• "India-Pakistan war: 1965".
—• "Lament for the death of time".
—• "Landscape".
—• "Last night".
—• "My visitors" (trans. Naomi Lazard).
—• "A prison daybreak".
—• "A prison evening".
—• "Spring comes".

1409   "Poems". Trans. Daud Kamal. *The Indian Literary Review* 3, 1 (January 1985), pp. 17-18.

1410   *Poems by Faiz.* Trans. Victor G. Kiernan. London: Allen and Unwin, 1971. 288p. Includes lengthy Introduction, notes and literal and poetic translations with Urdu text. Poems are taken from *Naqsh-i Faryadi, Dast-i Saba* and *Zindan Namah.*

1411   *Poems by Faiz.* Trans. Victor G. Kiernan. Lahore: Oxford University Press, 1973. 288p.

1412   *Poems by Faiz Ahmad Faiz.* Trans. Victor G. Kiernan. New Delhi: Peoples Publishing House, 1985. 85p.

1413   "A prison nightfall".   Trans. Mahmud Jamal.   In: *Stories from Asia*.   Ed. John Welch.   London: Oxford University Press, 1988, p. 112.

1414   "Remembrance".   Trans. Daud Kamal.   *The Muslim* (Islamabad) (31 December 1982).

1415   "Return from Dacca".   Trans. Daud Kamal.   *Frontier Post* (Lahore) (5 June 1987).

1416   "Scene".   Trans. Daud Kamal.   *Viewpoint* (Lahore) 8, 6 (16 September 1982), p. 24.

1417   "Selected poems".   Trans. C.M. Naim and Carlo Coppola.   *Mahfil* 1, 15, pp. 2-10.

1418   *"Selected poems of Faiz*.   Trans. Daud Kamal.   Karachi: Pakistan Publishing House, 1984. 80p.
Includes fifty poems; short autobiographical note by Faiz.

1419   "Six poems of Faiz".   Trans. Daud Kamal.   *Urdu Canada* 1, 1 (February 1986), pp. 22-31.

1420   "Speak".   Trans. Daud Kamal.   *The Muslim* (Islamabad) (25 March 1983).

1421   "Spiral".   Trans. Daud Kamal.   *The Muslim* (Islamabad) (16 March 1984).

1422   "Stay with me".   Trans. Daud Kamal.   *Viewpoint* (Lahore) 8, 6 (16 September 1982), p. 24.

1423   "Supplication".   Trans. Daud Kamal.   *Viewpoint* (Lahore) 10, 35 (4 April 1985), p. 5.

1424   "Three poems".   Trans. Ahmad Ali.   *Perspective* 1, 2-3 (August-September 1967), pp. 38-40.
— • "The blood of the rose".
— • "Peak".
— • "There is someone coming".

1425   "Three poems".   Trans. C.M. Naim, et al.   *Mahfil* 2, 2 (May 1965), pp. 39-42.
— • "The meeting".
— • "Wasukht".
— • "The window".

1426   *The true subject: selected poems of Faiz Ahmad Faiz*.   Trans. Naomi Lazard. Princeton, New Jersey: Princeton University Press, 1988. 136p. (Lockert Library of poetry in translation).

1427   "2 Ghazals from *Naqsh-i Farqadi*".   Trans. Shiv K. Kumar.   *Indian Literature* 31, 4 (July-August 1988), pp. 57-60.

1428   "Two poems".   Trans. Victor G. Kiernan.   *Contemporary Indian Literature* 2, 6 (June 1962), p. 8.
— • "Africa, come back".
— • "A few day's more"

1429   "Tyrant". Trans. Daud Kamal. *The Muslim* (Islamabad) (27 June 1986).

1430   "We, the poets". Trans. Daud Kamal. *The Muslim* (Islamabad) (20 April 1984).

1431   "We will see". Trans. Daud Kamal. *Frontier Post* (Lahore) (12 June 1987).

1432   "Why pray for eternal life?" Trans. Daud Kamal. *Viewpoint* (Lahore) 7, 8 (1 October 1981), p. 29.

1433   *Yaqub's selection and translation of poems by Faiz Ahmad Faiz.* Lenton Sands: Jacobs New Agents, 1987.

STUDIES

1434   **Ali, Agha Shahid**
"Homage to Faiz Ahmad Faiz". *New Quest* 51 (May-June 1985), pp. 167-168.

1435   **Ali, Mahir**
["A review of *Selected poems of Faiz in English*. Trans. Daud Kamal"]. *Annual of Urdu Studies* 5 (1985), pp. 140-142.
Reprinted from *The Herald* (Karachi), (January 1985), p. 110.

1436   **Ali, Masood Amjad**
"The poetry of Faiz". *Pakistan Review* 12 (January 1964), pp. 5-8.

1437   **Anand, Mulk Raj**
"Reminiscences of Faiz Ahmad Faiz". *Indian Literature* 28, 2 (March-April 1985), pp. 9-22.

1438   **Askari, Muhammad Hasan**
"Some personal reminiscences. Faiz: a life devoted to peace". *Viewpoint* (Lahore) 12, 27 (12 February 1987), pp. 13-14.

1439   **Azam, Ikram**
Poems from Faiz. Rawalpindi: Nairang-i Khayal Publications, 1982. 60p.
Includes "Faiz on literature" and translation of thirty-four poems from Faiz's *Mere dil mere musafir*.

1440   **Faiz, Alys**
Dear Heart: to Faiz in prison (1951-1955). Lahore: Ferozsons, 1985. 150p.
Alys Faiz's letters to her husband Faiz in prison.

1441   "Faiz Ahmad Faiz". *Pakistani Literature* (Islamabad) 1, 1 (1992), pp. 19-20.
Biographical sketch.

1442   **Faiz, Faiz Ahmad**
"Faiz on Faiz; a rare occasion on which Pakistan's foremost poet speaks about himself". Trans. Carlo Coppolla and Munibur Rahman. *Journal of South Asian literature* 10, 1 (Autumn 1974), pp. 131-139.

1443 — • "Future of "Ghazal"; "Poetry". *Sonora Review* 8 (1985), pp. 53-55.

1444 — • "On some poems". *Lotus Afro-Asian writings* 17 (1973), p. 134.

1445 — • *Faiz A. Faiz. The living word.* Tunisia: Lotus Books, 1987. 175p.
Collection of articles, interviews, translation of poems compiled in remembrance of Faiz, who was the editor-in-chief of *Lotus* magazine.

1446 Hasan, Khalid
"Faiz in London I: lonely but never alone". *Viewpoint* (Lahore) 6, 45 (11 June 1981), pp. 15-17.

1447 — • "Faiz in London II: the poet and the man". *Viewpoint* (Lahore) 6, 46 (18 June 1981), pp. 15-17.

1448 — • "Faiz Ahmad Faiz: in memoriam". *Race and Class* 26, 3 (Winter 1985), pp. 1-2.

1449 Hashmi, Alamgir
"Americanizing Faiz". *Viewpoint* (Lahore) 15, 21 (4 January 1990), p. 36.
Also in: *The Muslim Magazine* 4 (25 August 1989), p. 5.

1450 Husain, Imdad
An introduction to the poetry of Faiz Ahmad Faiz. Lahore: Vanguard Books, 1989. 153p.

1451 Husain, Karrar
"Faiz gave us the living word". *Viewpoint* (Lahore) 10, 28 (10 February 1985), pp. 11-12.

1452 "Interview". *Toronto South Asian Review* (Toronto), 1, 3 (Fall 1982-Winter 1983), pp. 58-63.
Interview conducted in English on September 26, 1982.

1453 Iqbal, Muzafar
"A conversation with Faiz Ahmed Faiz". *Pakistani Literature* (Islamabad) 1, 1 (1992), pp. 23-32.
Conversation held in Saskatoon, Canada, on 4 June 1981.

1454 — • "An interview". Trans. Khalid Hasan. *The Indian Literary Review* 3, 1 (January 1985), pp. 5-14.

1455 Iqbal, Muzafar and Hasan, Khalid
"Faiz on writers role". I. *Viewpoint* (Lahore) 11, 15 (21 November 1985), pp. 11-12, 30.

1456 — • "Faiz on writers role". II. *Viewpoint* (Lahore) 11, 16 (28 November 1985), pp. 27-28.

1457 Jones, Allen
"JSAL interviews Faiz Ahmed Faiz". *Journal of South Asian Literature* 10, 1 (Autumn 1974), pp. 141-144.

1458   **Joshi, Narendra K.**
"Faiz Ahmed Faiz: a study". *Contemporary Indian Literature* 2, 10, pp. 10-11; 2, 11, pp. 8-9, 17.

1459   **Kazakova, Rimma**
"A bouquet for Faiz. Poet and the modern age". *Viewpoint* (Lahore) 12, 28 (19 February 1987), pp. 10-12.

1460   **Kazmi, Izhar, H.**
"Faiz Ahmad Faiz: poetic expression and socio-political change". *Urdu Canada* 1, 2 (1986), pp. 26-27.

1461   **Kizer, Carolyn**
"Faiz Ahmed Faiz: excerpts from a Pakistan journal". *Sonora Review* 8 (1985), pp. 56-60.

1462   **Lall, Inder Jit**
"Faiz: poet of vitality". *Indian Literature* 18, 4 (1975), pp. 58-62.

1463   **Lazard, Naomi**
"Translating Faiz Ahmed Faiz: a memoir and a memoriam". *Sonora Review* 8 (1985), pp. 42-51.

1464   **Lodi, Yusuf**
Faiz/Bai Ell. Lahore: Vanguard Books, 1987. 176p.
Introductory matter in English; verses in Urdu. Cartoons, chiefly political, inspired by the verses of Faiz.

1465   **Malik, Muhammad Aslam**
"The Pakistani poet: Faiz Ahmed Faiz". *Lotus: Afro-Asian Writings* 22 (1974), p. 11.

1466   **Mohan, Indar**
"Faiz Ahmad Faiz". *Mainstream* 8, 44 (4 July 1970), p. 11.

1467   **Narang, Gopi Chand**
"The tradition and innovation in the poetry of Faiz". *Indian Literature* 28, 2 (March-April 1985), pp. 23-34.
Paper originally presented at the International Symposium on Faiz Ahmed Faiz, organized by the University of London, 9-10 July 1984.

1468   **Parker, Nevil**
"Faiz Ahmed Faiz". *Sonora Review* 8 (1985), pp. 24-27.

1469   **Rahman, Tariq**
"Faiz Ahmad Faiz: his poetry and politics". *The Muslim* (Islamabad) (8 June 1990).
Review of *Faiz: Shairi aur siyasat.*

1470   **Razdan, B.M.**
"Urdu ghazal and Faiz Ahmed Faiz". *New Quest* (Bombay) 74 (March-April 1989), pp. 123-126.

1471 Salganik, Maryam
"Faiz and his poetry today". *Viewpoint* (Lahore) 12, 28 (19 February 1987), p. 9.

1472 Shastry, S. Lakshman
"Faiz Ahmad Faiz". *Contemporary Indian Literature* (June 1962), p. 3.

1473 Zahir, Sajjad
"Faiz Ahmad Faiz and his poetry". *Contemporary Indian Literature* 3 (September 1963), pp. 6-7.

1474 Zia, A.Q.
"Faiz and his symbolism". *Urdu Canada* 1, 1 (February 1986), pp. 22-31.

FARAZ, AHMAD

TRANSLATIONS

1475 *The banished dreams.* Trans and Intro. M.H.K. Qureshi. Southall (UK): Shakti Communication, [1985?]. 133p.
Forty poems; with text in Urdu and in transliteration.

1476 "Brink" (a fragment)". *The Muslim* (Islamabad) (3 February 1984).

1477 "Departure". Trans. Daud Kamal. *Pakistan Times* (14 September 1984).

1478 "Doorknob". Trans. Daud Kamal. *Viewpoint* (Lahore) 9, 20 (22 December 1983), p. 32.

1479 "Ebony". Trans. Daud Kamal. *Viewpoint* (Lahore) 9, 27 (9 February 1984), p. 10.

1480 "The hurricane of remorse". Trans. Daud Kamal. *The Muslim* (Islamabad) (19 August 1983).

1481 "Incandescent beauty". Trans. Daud Kamal. *The Muslim* (Islamabad) (16 September 1983).

1482 "Mothers". Trans. Daud Kamal. *The Nation* (31 October 1986).

1483 "O life!" O life!" Trans. Daud Kamal. *Viewpoint* (Lahore) 9, 6 (15 September 1983), p. 29.

1484 "Shudder on the horizon". Trans. Daud Kamal. *Viewpoint* (Lahore) 9, 22 (5 January 1984), p. 26.

1485 "You and I". Trans. Daud Kamal. *The Muslim* (Islamabad) (2 September 1983).

STUDY

1486 **Nadeem, Shahid**
["An interview with Faraz"]. *Herald* (Karachi) (January 1986), pp. 111-114.

FARIDI, SHAMS

TRANSLATION

1487 "A nazm". Trans. K.K. Khullar. *Indian Literature* 23, 1-2 (1980), p. 540.

FAROOI, SAQI

TRANSLATIONS

1488 *A listening game*. Trans. Frances Pritchett. Ed. Shamsur Rahman Faruqi. London: Lokamaya Press, 1987.

1489 "The poster". Trans. Muhammad Umar Memon. *Denver Quarterly* 12, 2 (Summer 1977), p. 241.

1490 "Saqi Farooqi's The wounded cat in an empty sack: four versions". Trans. Rafey Habib, C.M. Naim, Faruq Hassan, and Alamgir Hashmi. *Annual of Urdu Studies* 3 (1983), pp. 41-46.
"Saqi Farooqi's poem "Khali bore men zakhmi billa", in its original Urdu with four different versions in English".

1491 "Six poems". Trans. Faruq Hassan, et al. *Annual of Urdu Studies* 3 (1983),
— • "A dog poem". Trans. Faruq Hassan. p. 22.
— • "Mistress". Trans. Faruq Hassan and C.M. Naim. p. 21.
— • "A rabbits tale". Trans. Rafey Habib and C.M. Naim. p. 25.
— • "Sher Imdad Ali's tadpole". Trans. Faruq Hassan, Rafey Habib and C.M. Naim. p. 22.
— • "That I may reach the Island". Trans. Faruq Hassan. p. 21.
— • "To a pig". Trans. Faruq Hassan and Rafey Habib. p. 24.

1492 "A wounded cat in a sack". Trans. M.H.K. Qureshi. *Urdu Canada* 1, 1 (February 1986), p. 68.

STUDIES

1493   Farrukhi, Asif Alam
"The living waters". *Newsline* 2, 1 (July 1990), p. 132.
Review of Saqi Farooqi's *Zinda pani sacha.*

1494   — • "If I write something which touches your heart, that is justification enough for my poetry". *Newsline* 2, 1 (July 1990), pp. 128-131.
Interview with Saqi Farooqi

1495   Hassan, Faruq
"Saqi Farooqi: a poet's progress". *Annual of Urdu Studies* 3 (1983), pp. 7-39.
Life and works of Saqi Farooqi.

1496   "Hasan kooza-gar". *Annual of Urdu Studies* 5 (1985), pp. 3-17.
A personal recollection of Saqi Farooqi's association with N.M Rashed.

FARUQI, EJAZ

TRANSLATIONS

1497   "A heavenly voice". Trans. Jamil Azar. *Urdu Canada* 1, 2 (1986), p. 74.

1498   "Time". Trans. Jamil Azar. *Urdu Canada* 1, 3 (1987), p. 88.

FARUQI, SHAMSUR RAHMAN

TRANSLATIONS

1499   "Ghazals". Trans. the author. *Indian Literature* 12, 5 (May-June 1988), pp. 136-139.
Three ghazals and one untitled poem.

1500   "Two poems". Trans. Gopi Chand Narang and David Paul Douglas. *Indian Writing Today* 4, 4 (October-December 1971), p. 241.
— • "A prayer".
— • "Underdone".

1501   "Poems". Trans. the author. *Indian Literature* 31, 3 (May-June 1988), pp. 136-139.
Three ghazals and one nazm.

FAZLI, NIDA

TRANSLATIONS

1502 "Five poems". Trans. Baidar Bakht and Leslie Lavigne. *Annual of Urdu Studies* 6 (1987), pp. 71-73.
—• "After a long time". p. 71.
—• "Just keep on living like this". p. 72.
—• "The last letter". p. 72.
—• "Masks". p. 73.
—• "The new disease". p. 71.

1503 "Four poems". Trans. Gopi Chand Narang, et al. *Mahfil* 6, 2-3 (1970), pp. 27-28.
—• "The God is silent".
—• "Love".
—• "Masks".
—• "A word".

1504 "Piecemeal". Trans. C.M. Naim. *Books Abroad* 43, 4 (Autumn 1969), pp. 546.

1505 "Seven poems". Trans. Baidar Bakht and Leslie Lavigne. *The Toronto South Asia Review* 4, 3 (Spring 1986), pp. 53-57.

FIRAQ GORAKHPURI, RAGHUPATHI SAHAI

TRANSLATIONS

1506 "Beggars all". Trans. Firaq Gorakhpuri. *Illustrated Weekly of India* (29 September 1963), pp. 61-65.

1507 "Broken links". Trans K.K. Khullar. *Indian Literature* 23, 1-2 (1980), p. 529.

1508 "The night is very sad and still". Trans. the author. *Illustrated Weekly of India* 19 (May 1963), p. 19.

1509 "A poem". Trans. S.H. Vatsyayan. In: *Modern Indian Poetry*. Ed. A.V. Rajeswara Rao. New Delhi: Kavita [1958], p. 53.

1510 "Song of the earth". Trans. P.C. Gupta. *Contemporary Indian Literature* 6, 8 (August 1966), p. 30.

STUDIES

1511 Firaq Gorakhpuri
"Some reflections". *Contemporary Indian Literature* 11, 1 (January 1971), pp. 8-9.
Speech delivered by Firaq when accepting Bharatiya Jnanpith award in Delhi, on 26 December 1970.

1512 "Firaq Gorakhpuri: an appreciation". *Mainstream* 8, 9 (8 August 1970), p. 35.

1513 "Grand old man of Urdu poetry honoured". *Times of India* (28 November 1970), p. 1: 5-7.

1514 Josan, C.J.S.
"Firaq Gorakhpuri: a poet of synthesis". *Books Abroad* 43, 4 (Autumn 1969), pp. 535-541.

1515 Kala, S.C.
"Firaq Gorakhpuri, poet of love and revolt". *Times of India* (16 August 1970), pp. 1-6.

1516 Khullar, K.K.
"Iqbal, Firaq and others". *Thought* 26, 48 (7 December 1974), pp. 15-17.

1517 Lall, Inder Jit
"Features and facets of Firaq's verse". *Indian Literature* 25, 3 (May-June 1982), pp. 40-49.

1518 — • "Firaq Gorakhpuri". *Thought* 25, 49 (8 December 1973), pp. 15-16.

1519 Narang, Gopi Chand
"Tradition and innovation in Urdu poetry". In: *Poetry and renaissance; Kumaran Asan birth centenary volume*. Ed. M. Govindan. Madras: Sameeksha, 1974, pp. 415-434.
Discusses the work of Firaq and Faiz.

1520 "Personalities: Firaq". *Link* 13, 17 (6 December 1970), p. 33.

1521 "Personalities: Raghupati Sahai Firaq". *Link* 11, 4 (8 September 1968), p. 37.

1522 Rattan H.R.
"Raghupati Sahai Firaq". *Contemporary Indian Literature* 3, 8 (August 1963), pp. 6-7.

1523 Sastri, D. Diptivilas
"Firaq Gorakhpuri". *Educational Review* (Madras) 78, 8 (August 1970), pp. 182-183.

1524 Shankar, V.
"Jnanpith Award-Winner Firaq Gorakhpuri". *Illustrated Weekly of India* 91, 47 (29 November 1970), p. 27.

GHALIB, MIRZA ASADULLAH KHAN

BIBLIOGRAPHY

1525 **Silver, B.Q.**
"A bibliography of English sources on Ghalib". *Mahfil* 5, 4 (1968-69), pp. 115-25.

TRANSLATIONS

1526 "Basilisk" (a ghazal). Trans. Daud Kamal. *Frontier Post* (Lahore) (5 June 1987).

1527 "Bequest". Trans. Daud Kamal. *The Muslim* (Islamabad) (13 July 1984).

1528 *Distracting words.* Trans. Mohammad Zakir. Delhi: Idara-e-Amini, 1976. 82p.
One hundred and thirty-two Persian and Urdu couplets. Includes Urdu text.

1529 "The eddying ash". Trans. Daud Kamal. *The Muslim* (Islamabad) (13 July 1984).

1530 "The fugitive shadow". Trans. Daud Kamal. *The Muslim* (Islamabad) (17 August 1984).

1531 "Geometry of the stars". Trans. Daud Kamal. *The Muslim* (Islamabad) (13 July 1984).

1532 *Ghalib; reverberations by Daul Kamal.* Trans. Daud Kamal. Karachi: Gold Block Works, 1970.
Includes free verse translations, Urdu text.

1533 *Ghalib's love poems.* Trans. P. Lal. Calcutta: Writers Workshop, 1971. 19p.
"A Writers Workshop Redbird Book".

1534 *Ghalib: selected poems.* Trans. Ahmad Ali and B.A. Dar, et al. Rome: Istituto Italiano per il Medio ed Estremo Oriente, 1969. 70, 25p.
Includes Urdu text.

1535 *Ghalib's lighter verse.* Trans. C.M. Naim. Calcutta: Writers Workshop, 1972. 24p.
Includes Urdu text.

1536 *Ghalib's passion flower.* Trans. Satya Deo Misra. Delhi: Movie Press, 1969. 177p.

1537 *Ghalib, Urdu and Persian ghazals.* Selected and Trans. Khurshidul Islam and Ralph Russell (in preparation), 1992.
Includes notes, lengthy introduction and an essay on translating Ghalib.

1538 "A ghazal". Trans. Daud Kamal. *Frontier Post* (Lahore) (30 January 1987).

1539 "Ghazal". Trans. M. Shahid Alam. *Journal of South Asian Literature* 13, 1-4 (1977-78), p. 307.

1540   *Ghazals of Ghalib: versions from the Urdu*. Ed. Aijaz Ahmad. New York: Columbia University Press, 1971. 174p.
Includes translations and poems by American poets inspired by Ghalib's work. Extensive notes, Urdu texts.

1541   *Hundred gems from Ghalib*. Trans. Shahabuddin Rahmatullah. Islamabad: National Book Foundation, 1980.

1542   *Hundred ghazals of Mirza Ghalib*. Ed. and trans. Pranab Bandyopadhyay. Calcutta: United Writers, 1975. 33p.

1543   "Life's maddening futility".   Trans. Daud Kamal.   *The Muslim* (Islamabad) (17 August 1984).

1544   "Lust for life". Trans. Daud Kamal. *The Muslim* (Islamabad) (17 August 1984).

1545   "Never have I seen". Trans. Daud Kamal. *Frontier Post* (Lahore) (13 March 1987).

1546   "Panacea". Trans. Daud Kamal. *The Muslim* (Islamabad) (10 August 1984).

1547   "The poem (Ghalib's) itself". Trans. C.M. Naim. *Mahfil* 5, 4 (1968-69), pp. 97-114.

1548   *Poems by Ghalib*. Trans. William Stafford and Adrienne Rich. Hudson Review Centennial Booklet, 1969.

1549   *Selected verses of Mirza Ghalib*. Ed. and trans. Sufia Sadullah. Beaconsfield: Darwin Finlayson, 1965. 134p.
Each verse is accompanied by an illustration by Colin David.

1550   *Selected verses of Mirza Ghalib*. Trans. Sufia Sadullah. Beaconsfield, England: Darwen Finlayson, 1965. 122p.

1551   *Selections from Ghalib*. Trans. H.S. Saraswat. New Delhi: R. Sarawati, 1965. 50p.

1552   *Selections from Ghalib and Iqbal*. Trans. K.N. Sud. New Delhi: Sterling Publishers, 1978. p. 110.

1553   "Selections from Ghalib". Trans. Qurratulain Hyder. *Illustrated Weekly of India* 90, 8 (1969), pp. 40-41.

1554   "The shifted cry". Trans. Daud Kamal. *The Muslim* (Islamabad) (13 July 1984).

1555   "Taut bow". Trans. Daud Kamal. *The Muslim* (Islamabad) (17 August 1984).

1556   "Three couplets". Trans. Daud Kamal. *Frontier Post* (Lahore) (29 May 1987).

1557   "Three renderings". Trans. Daud Kamal. *The Muslim* (Islamabad) (30 September 1983).

1558   "Transcience". Trans. Daud Kamal. *The Muslim* (Islamabad) (17 August 1984).

1559   "Translation of selected poems of Ghalib".   Trans. Naz.   *Pakistan Review* 17, 2 (February 1967), pp. 82-95.

1560   "Translations from Ghalib".   Trans. Ahmad Ali.   *Eastern Horizon* 4, 7 (July 1965), pp. 45-50.

1561   "Translations from Ghalib".   Trans. Muhammad Mujeeb.   *Link* 11, 27 (16 February 1969), p. 30.

1562   "Translations from Ghalib".   Trans. Qurratulain Hyder.   *Link* 11, 27 (16 February 1959), p. 30.

1563   "Translations from Ghalib".   *Shabkhun* 5, 52 (September 1970), pp. 5-12.

1564   *Twenty-five verses by Ghalib.*   Trans. C.M. Naim.   Calcutta: Writers Workshop, 1970.   46p.
Includes Urdu text.

1565   *Urdu ghazals of Ghalib.*   Trans. Yusuf Husain.   New Delhi: Ghalib Institute, 1977.   325, 114p.
Includes Urdu text.

1566   *Urdu letters of Mirza Asadullah Khan Ghalib.*   Trans. and annotated by Daud Rahbar.   New York: State University of New York Press, 1987. 628p.

1567   *Whispers of the angel.   Nawa-e Sarosh: selections from fourteen English translations of Ghalib.   With four paintings by eminent artists.*   New Delhi: Ghalib Academy, [1969].   52p.
Urdu text in Roman characters with verse translations.

1568   *Whispers from Ghalib.*   Trans. Sufi Abdul Qadeer.   Ed. Matiullah Dard.   Birmingham: Joseph Chamberlain College, 1985.   31p.

STUDIES

1569   **Abdul Aziz**
"Ghalib's mysticism".   *Pakistan Review*   17, 2 (February 1969), pp. 41-46.

1670   **Abdul Hakim, Khalifa**
"The genius of Ghalib".   *Iqbal Review*   10 (October 1969), pp. 17-23.

1571   **Abdul Haq**
"Mirza Ghalib: a leaf from his autobiography".   *Pakistan Review* 20, 1 (January 1972), pp. 31-32.

1572   **Abdullah, S.M.**
"Ghalib: precursor of Iqbal".   *Perspective* (Karachi) 2, 8-9 (February-March 1969), pp. 111-113.

1573   Abd al-Latif, Saiyid
Ghalib: a critical appreciation of his life and Urdu poetry. Hyderabad, Deccan, 1928. 104p.

1574   Ahmad, Aijaz
"Ghalib: the dew drop on the red poppy". *Mahfil* 5, 4 (1968-1969), pp. 59-69.

1575   Ahmad, Aquil
"Ghalib". *The Hindustan Times Weekly Magazine* (14 February 1956), p. 4.

1576   Ahmad, Jamiluddin
"Patriotic strain in Ghalib". *Perspective* 2, 8-9 (14 February 1956), p. 4.

1577   Ahmad, K.J.
"The originality in Ghalib". *Pakistan Review* 17, 2 (February 1969), pp. 72-73.

1578   Ali, Ahmad
"Ghalib's thought and poetry". *Perspective* 2, 8-9 (February-March 1969), pp. 107-110.

1579   Ali, Ahmad and Bausani, Alessandro
Ghalib: two essays. Rome: Istituto Italiano per il Medio ed Estremo Oriente, 1969.
167p. (Serie Orientale Roma, vol. 39, also numbered as vol. 3 of "Orientalia Romana").

1580   Ali, Ahmad and Dar, Bashir Ahmad, et al.
Aspect of Ghalib: five essays. Karachi: Pakistan American Cultural Centre, 1970. 94p.

1581   Amir, S. Javed
"Ghalib and Donne as love poets". *Pakistan Review* 17, 2 (February 1969), pp. 54-58.

1582   Anand, Mulk Raj, et al.
"Writer's tribute to Ghalib". *Contemporary Indian Literature* 9, 1 (January 1969), pp. 5-7.

1583   Ashraf, K.M.
"Ghalib and the revolt of 1857". In: *Rebellion 1857: a symposium.* Ed. P.C. Joshi. New Delhi: People's Publishing House, 1957, pp. 245-256.

1584   Babree, Laeeq
"Mood of Ghalib". *Pakistan Review* 17, 2 (February 1969), pp. 78-80.

1585   Baig, Safdar Ali
"The mystical poetry of Ghalib". *Islamic Culture* 43, 2 (April 1969), pp. 97-108.

1586   Baloch, S.K.
"The world of Ghalib". *Pakistan Review* 9, 6 (June 1961), pp. 9-12.

1587   — • "The greatness of Ghalib". *Pakistan Review* 17, 2 (February 1969), pp. 30-35.

1588   Bandyopadhyay, Pranab
Mirza Ghalib. Calcutta: United Writers, 1990. 64p.

1589 **Bausani, Allessandro**
"Mirza Asad Allah Khan Ghalib". In: *Encyclopaedia of Islam* 2 (1965), pp. 1000-1001.

1590 — • "The position of Ghalib (1796-1869) in the history of Urdu and Indo-Persian poetry: 1. Galib's Urdu Poetry". *Der Islam* 34 (September 1959), pp. 99-127.

1591 **Beg, Abdullah Anwar**
"The life and odes of Ghalib". *Pakistan Review* 17, 2 (February 1969), pp. 98-100
A review.

1592 — • "Mirza Ghalib of Delhi". *Pakistan Review* 16 (February 1968), pp. 12-16.

1593 **Bukhsh, Salahuddin Khan**
"Ghalib: an appreciation". *Hindustan Review* 21 (Janaury-June 1910), pp. 282-288.

1594 **Chand, Attar**
"Ghalib and national integration". *Socialist Congressman* 8, 19-20 (26 January 1969), pp. 19, 25.

1595 — • "Ghalib, poet of poets". *Young India* 14, 2 (February 1969), pp. 13-14, 54.

1596 **Chelyshev, Y.**
"Mirza Ghalib: a great poet and humanist". *Contemporary Indian Literature* 9, 3 (March 1969), pp. 14-15.

1597 **'Critic'**
"Ghalib's realistic ideals". *Pakistan Review* 7, 3 (March 1959), pp. 11-12.

1598 **Dar, Bashir Ahmad**
"Ghalib and Iqbal". *Iqbal Review* 10 (October 1969), pp. 25-43.

1599 "An early partisan of Ghalib". *Annual of Urdu Studies* 3 (1983), pp. 99-100.
Reproduced from *The Muslim* (Islamabad) of February 15, 1980, a letter that originally appeared in *The Mofussilite* (Delhi) in March 1868. Ghalib was then the Plaintiff in a libel case which had resulted from Ghalib's polemics against the author of the famous Persian dictionary *Burhān-e-Qāti'*.
Also includes an extract from Ghalib's letter, translated by Muhammad Sadiq.

1600 **Ebadat Brelvi**
"Literary importance of Ghalib's letters". *Pakistan Review* 19, 12 (Decemer 1971), pp. 40-43.

1601 "Excerpts from Ghalib's letters". Trans. Qurratulain Hyder. *Illustrated Weekly of India* 90, 8 (23 February 1969), pp. 36-39.

1602 **Faiz, Faiz Ahmad**
"Mirza Asadullah Khan Ghalib". *Perspective* 2, 8-9 (February-March 1969), pp. 93-105.

1603 **Faruqi, A.**
"Ghalib as a man and humanist". *Pakistan Review* 17, 2 (February 1969), pp. 47-49, 63.

1604   **Faruqi, Shamsur Rahman**
["A review of Annemarie Schimmel's *A dance of sparks*"]. *Annual of Urdu Studies* 3 (1983), pp. 107-111.

"1605 —• "Enjoyable and exasperating". *Indian Literature* 32, 3 (May-June 1989), pp. 153-161.
Review of P.K. Varma, *Ghalib: the man, the times* (1989).

1606   **Firaq Gorakhpuri**
"Ghalib - a memorial tribute". *Cultural Forum* 11, 3-4 (April-July 1969), pp. 81-89.

1607   —• "Some aspects of Ghalib's poetry". *Illustrated Weekly of India* 90, 8 (23 February 1969), pp. 29-31, 46.

1608   **Fyzee, A.A.A.**
"On translating Ghalib; review of J.L. Kaul's interpretion of Ghalib". *Indian Literature* 2, 1 (October 1958-March 1959), p. 82.

1609   —• "Ghalib centenary and our attitude towards Urdu". *Contemporary Indian Literature* 9 (1969), pp. 4-5.

1610   —• "Ghalib centenary number". *Pakistan Review* 17, 2 (February 1969), pp. 6-95.

1611   —• "Ghalib epic". *Link* 11, 29 (2 March 1969), pp. 37-38.

1612   —• "Ghalib: a self-portrait in words". *Mahfil* 5, 4 (1968-1969), pp. 1-5.

1613   —• "Ghalib: the man and his poetry". *Link* 11, 27 (16 February 1969), pp. 29-34.

1614   —• "Ghalib issue". *Mahfil* 5, 4 (1968-69).

1615   —• "Ghalib poems". *Link* 11, 27 (16 February 1969), pp. 30, 37.

1616   *Ghalib's life and work.* Delhi: Publications Division, Ministry of Information and Broadcasting, 1969. 39p.
"Issued on the occasion of the Ghalib centenary, 1969".

1617   **Gilani, A.C. Sayyid**
Ghalib: his life and Persian poetry. 2nd ed. Karachi: Azam Books Co., 1962. 296p.
Pt. 3 contains the Urdu text of verses from Ghalib's "Ghazals".

1618   **Habib, Kemal Muhammad**
"Ghalib: a great aesthete". *Vision* 18, 1-2 (February-March 1969), pp. 13-18.

1619   **Hali, Khwajah Altaf Husain**
Yadgar-i Ghalib: a biography of Ghalib. Trans. K.H. Qadiri. Delhi: Idarah-i Adabiyat-i Delhi, 1990. 321p.
Includes Persian and Urdu text.

1620   **Hamid, A.A.**
"The world of Mirza Ghalib". *Perspective* 2, 8-9 (February-March 1969), pp. 114-116.

1621   **Haq, Inamul**
"Ghalib's concept of God". *Journal Research Society of Pakistan* 22, 3 (July 1985), pp. 1-28.

1622   **Hasan, Ibnul**
"Ghalib: man and poet". *Perspective* 2, 1-2 (July-August 1968), pp. 53-56.

1623   **Hasan, Iqtida**
["Review of *Diwan-i-Ghalib*.   Ed. Imtiaz Ali Arshi"].   *Annali dell' Istituto Universitario Orientale di Napoli*, Nuova Serie, II, pp. 150-156.

1624   **Hasan, Masood**
"Mirza Ghalib: the great Urdu poet". *Indo-Iranica* 23, 1-2 (March-June 1970), pp. 102-105.

1625   **Hasan, Mohammad**
"Some important critics of Ghalib". Trans. Muhammad Umar Memon. *Mahfil* 5, 4 (1968-1969), pp. 31-43.

1626   — • "Urdu: Ghalib centenary year". *Indian Literature* 13, 4 (December 1970), pp. 106-113.

1627   **Hashmi, Alamgir**
"The letters of Mirza Ghalib". *The Pakistan Times: Midweek Edition* (23 May 1989), pp. A, D.

1628   — • "Mirza Ghalib and his Post Office". *The Muslim Magazine* 2, (2 December 1988), p. 5.
Also in: *Explorations* 13, 1 pp. 89-92.
On Ghalib's prose.

1629   **Hassan, N. Gardezi**
"Ghalib and the raj". *Viewpoint* (Lahore) 10, 30 (28 February 1985), pp. 27-29.

1630   **Hazeen Ludhianvi**
"Mirza Ghalib: a tribute". *Pakistan Review* 17, 2 (February 1969), p. 81.

1631   **Husain, Agha Iftikhar**
"Study of Ghalib in Europe". *Pakistan Review* 81, 2 (February 1970), pp. 37-42.

1632   **Husaini, M.A., et al.**
Ghalib: life and works. New Delhi: Publications Division, Ministry of Information and Broadcasting, 1969. 39p.

1633   *Interpretation of Ghalib.* Trans. J.L. Kaul. Delhi: Atma Ram, 1957. 92, 16p.

1634   **Ish, Kumar**
The melody of an angel: Mirza Ghalib, his mind and art. Chandigarh: Publication Bureau, Panjab University, 1982. 178p.

1635   **Iyenger, K.R. Srinivasa**
"Ghalib". *Swarajya* 14, 50 (13 June 1970), pp. 19-20.

1636   **Jafri, Ali Sardar**
"Ghalib and his poetry". Trans. Qurratulain Hyder. *Illustrated Weekly of India* 89, 10 (10 March 1968), pp. 39-41.

1637   **Jung, Annes**
"A man called Ghalib". *Times of India Magazine* (6 April 1969), pp. 4:1-5.

1638   **Kaleem, Siddiq**
"The contemporary relevance of Ghalib". *Pakistan Review* 14, 5 (May 1966), pp.7-8.
Also in his *Pakistan: a cultural spectrum.* Lahore: Arsalan Publications, 1973, pp. 170-175.

1639   — • "What Ghalib today means to me". *Pakistan Review* 17, 2 (February 1979), pp. 36-37.

1640   **Khan, Abdur Rahman**
"The universal genius of Ghalib". *Pakistan Review* 17, 2 (February 1969), pp. 38-40.

1641   **Khan, Hamid Ahmad**
"Ghalib - the early phase". *Pakistan Review* 5 (May 1966), pp. 4-6, 41.

1642   — • "Ghalib - the early phase". *Pakistan Review* 17, 2 (February 1969), pp. 19-22.

1643   — • "Ghalib's vision of man and nature". *Asia* (Spring 1970), pp. 38-51.

1644   **Khan, Nuzrat Yar**
"Ghalib: a profile. *Urdu Canada* 1, 1 (February 1986), pp. 48-52.

1645   **Khan, Shujaatullah**
"Ghalib: the monarch of Urdu poetry". *Eastern Horizon* 6, 1 (January 1967), pp. 49-52.

1646   **Khanna, R.**
"A couplet of Ghalib". *Advent* 23, 2 (April 1971), pp. 28-29.

1647   **Khorasanee, Ameen**
"Translation of selected poems of Ghalib". *Pakistan Review* 17, 2 (February 1969), pp. 91-95.

1648   **Khundmiri, S. Alam**
"Ghalib, our contemporary". Trans. Muhammad Umar Memon. *Annual of Urdu Studies* 3 (1983), pp. 85-98.

1649   **Kuldip, R.K.**
Mirza Ghalib: a critical appreciation of Ghalib's thought and verse. Calcutta: Intertrade Publications, 1967. 112p.

1650   **Lakhanpal P.L.**
Ghalib: the man and his verse. Delhi: International Books, 1960.

1651   **Lall, Inder Jit**
Candle's smoke: Ghalib's life and verse. Delhi: Saluja Prakashan, 1970. 64p.

1652   — • "Changezi—Ghalib's worst critic". *Times of India* (11 April 1971), pp. 9: 1-3.

1653   — • "Criticism on Ghalib". *Thought* 21, 30 (26 July 1969), pp. 14-15.

1654   — • "Evaluation of Ghalib". *Times of India* (28 February 1971), pp. 7:4-6.

1655   — • "An interpreter of Ghalib". *Thought* 26, 51 (28 December 1974), pp. 18-19.

1656   — • *A short biography of Mirza Ghalib.* Delhi: Saluja Prakashan, 1969. 41p.

1657   — • "Some recent works on Ghalib". *Indian Literature* 17, 3 (July 1974), pp. 86-88.

1658   **Latif, Sayyid Abdul**
Ghalib: critical appreciation of his life and Urdu poetry. Hyderabad: Chandrakanth Press, 1928. 104p.

1659   **Mahmud, Sayyid Fayyaz**
Ghalib: a critical introduction. Lahore: University of the Punjab, 1969. 518p.

1660   **Malik Ram**
"Ghalib: his life and times". *Illustrated Weekly of India* 90, 8 (23 February 1969), pp. 32-33.

1661   — • "Ghalib, the man and the poet". *Indian and Foreign Review* 6, 9 (15 February 1969), pp. 13-15.

1662   — • *Mirza Ghalib.* New Delhi: National Book Trust, 1968. 93p.
Includes biography and translations.

1663   — • "Mirza Ghalib". *Contemporary Indian Literature* 9, 1 (February 1969), pp. 8-10.

1664   **Marikar, M.A.S.**
"Mirza Ghalib". *Contemporary Indian Literature* 3, 5 (May 1963), pp. 8-9, 19-22.

1665   **Mehal, Muhammad Nazir**
"Ghalib during the war of independence". *Pakistan Review* 17, 2 (February 1969), pp. 26-27.

1666   — • "Mirza Ghalib: some reflections". *Weekend Review* 2, 26 (1 June 1968), pp. 30-32.

1667   **Misra, Satya Deo**
Ghalib's passion flower, consuming, flower-fresh, heady. Delhi, 1969. 177p.
Tributes and adaptations of selected poems of Ghalib.

1668   **Moghni, A**
"The significance of Ghalib's poetry: his thought and art". *Visvabharati Quarterly* 32, 3-4 (1966-67), pp. 259-266.

1669   **Mujeeb, Mohammed**
Ghalib. New Delhi: Sahitya Academy, 1969. 80p.
Includes biography and translations.

1670   — • "The personal and the universal in Ghalib". *Indian Literature* 12, 2 (June 1969), pp. 5-14.

1671   — • "Two kindred spirits: Mirza Ghalib and Emily Dickinson". *Asia* (Spring 1970), pp. 38-51.

1672   **Munawwar, Muhammad**
"Ghalib, as an egotist". *Pakistan Review* 17, 2 (February 1969), pp. 50-53.

1673   **Naim, C.M**
["Review of Kedar Nath Sud's *Selections from Ghalib and Iqbal*"]. *Annual of Urdu Studies* 3 (1983), p. 116.

1674   **Naqvi, Noorul Hasan**
Ghalib reveals himself. His life through his writings. Aligarh: Muslim University, 1972. 88p. (Ghalib Centenary Publications) .
Includes selected verses of Ghalib in Urdu and in translation.

1675   **Naqvi, S.A.H.**
"Ghalibs overall impact on Urdu poetry". *Pakistan Review* 17, 2 (February 1969), pp. 64-71.

1676   **Narang, Gopi Chand**
"Ghalib and the rebellion of 1857". *Indian Literature* 15, 1 (March 1972), pp. 5-20.

1677   **Nasir, Nasir-ud-Din**
"Ghalib's interplay on words". *Pakistan Review* 17, 5 (May 1969), pp. 25-28.

1678   — • "Ghalib: a poet par excellence". *Pakistan Review* 16 (February 1968), pp. 27-28.

1679   **Natesan, G.A.**
Ghalib: a sketch of his life and works. Madras: G.A. Natesan and Co., 48p.

1680   Nath, Kidar
"Ghalib and the mutiny". *The Century* 7, 37 (25 January 1969), pp. 12-24.

1681   — • "Ghalib's prose". *Illustrated Weekly of India* 84, 17 (28 April 1963), p. 43.

1682   — • "Ghalib as a prose writer". *Mainstream* 7, 24 (15 February 1969), pp. 21-.

1683   Naz
Ghalib: his life and thought. Karachi: Ferozsons, 1969. 125p.

1684   — • "Mirza Ghalib". *Pakistan Review* 17, 2 (February 1969), pp. 6-8.

1685   Pakistan American Culture Centre
Aspects of Ghalib: five essays. Karachi: Pakistan American Culture Centre, 1970. 94p.

1686   Paul, Harendra Chandra
"Mirza Ghalib: his life and philosophy". *Calcutta Review* 173 (November 1964), pp. 105-124.

1687   — • "Some odes of Mirza Ghalib". *Calcutta Review* 139, 3 (September 1956), pp. 252-254;
143, 3 (September 1957), pp. 129-132;
159, 2 (May 1961), pp. 207-209;
166, 1 (January 1963), pp. 4-8;
169, 2 (November 1963), pp. 219-223;
170, 1 (January 1974), pp. 85-89.

1688   Prigarina, N.I.
Mirza Ghalib. Moscow: Nauka, 1986. 282p.

1689   Qadir, C.A.
"Philosophy of Ghalib". *Journal of Research* (Humanities Punjab University, Lahore). 4 (January 1969), pp. 257-281.

1690   Qidwai, Sheik Wilayet Ally
"Ghalib the Urdu poet". *East and West* 8, 1 (January-June 1909), pp. 527-535.

1691   Rahbar, Daud
"Ghalib and the conversion of Hali". *Muslim World* 55, 4 (October 1965), pp. 304-310.

1692   — • "Ghalib and a debatable point of theology". (Installment II). *Muslim World* 51, 1 (January 1966), pp. 14-17.

1693   — • "Ghalib credo"... (Installment III). *Muslim World* 51, 2 (April 1966), pp. 104-107.

1694   Rahman, Tariq
"E.M. Forster and Ghalib". *American Notes and Queries* (January-February 1985), pp. 80-81.

1695 **Rahmatullah, Shahabuddin**
Hundred gems from Ghalib. Islamabad: National Book Foundation, 1980.

1696 **Raina, B.N.**
Raina's Ghalib: a transcreation of Mirza Ghalib's selected verse. Calcutta: Writers Workshop, 1984. 100p.

1697 **Rizvi, S.E.H.**
"The element of Ghalib's thought". Trans. C.M. Naim and Muhammad Umar Memon. *Mahfil* 5, 4 (1968-69), pp. 7-29.

1698 **Roome, John Clive**
"The prince among poets". *Pakistan Review* 17, 2 (February 1969), pp. 23-25.

1699 **Russell, Ralph and Islam, Khurshidul**
Ghalib, 1797-1869. Volume I: life and letters. Cambridge: HUP, 1969. 404p. (UNESCO)

1700 — • *Ghalib: life and letters.* London: George Allen and Unwin, 1969.
Includes translations of selected letters; interpretive commentary.

1701 **Russell, Ralph**
Ghalib: the poet and his age; papers read at the centenary celebrations at SOAS, University of London. London: George Allen and Unwin, 1972. 131p.

1702 — • "Ghalib's Urdu verse". *Mainstream* 7, 28 (15 March 1969), pp. 17-25.

1703 — • "Ghalib and the revolt of 1857". *Mainstream* 7, 26 (1 March 1969), pp. 31-33.

1704 — • "On translating Ghalib". *Mahfil* 5, 4 (1968-1969), pp. 71-87.

1705 — • ["Review of *Ghazals of Ghalib.* Ed. Aijaz Ahmad"]. *Journal of the Royal Asiatic Society* 1, pp. 78-82.

1706 **Saeed, Ahmad**
"Ghalib: after the war of independence till death". *Pakistan Review* 17, 2 (February 1969), pp. 28-29.

1707 **Saggar, R.L.**
"Was Ghalib a progressive?" *Times of India* (3 December 1972), pp. 13-14.

1708 **Saiyidain, Khwaja Ghulam**
Tagore lecture 1969 on Ghalib. Ahmedabad: Gujarat University, 1971. 78p.
Includes Urdu text.

1709 **Sami, A.**
Ghalib. Lyallpur, 1921. 52p.

1710 **Saran, Sarasvati**
Mirza Ghalib; the poet of poets. New Delhi: Munshiram Manoharlal, 1976. 231p.

1711 **Schimmel, Annemarie**
A dance of sparks: imagery of fire in Ghalib's poetry. New Delhi: Vikas Publishing House, 1979. 141p.

1712 **Shamsuddin**
"Mirza Ghalib: the poet of life and love". *Indo-Asian Culture* 18, 2 (April 1969), pp. 40-42
Also in: *United Asia* 21 (May-June 1969), pp. 124-126.

1713 **Shankhdher, B.M.**
"Ghalib and the press". *Modern Review* 124 (June 1969), pp. 416-417.

1714 **Siddiqui, M.A.**
"Ghalib: his mind and art". *Vision* 18, 4 (May 1969), pp. 4-5, 24.

1715 — • "Ghalib: a poet of life". *Perspective* 5, 8-9 (February-March 1972), pp. 45-48.

1716 — • "Special section on Ghalib". *Pakistan Quarterly* 17, 1 (Winter 1969), pp. 78-118.

1717 **Sud, Kedar Nath**
Eternal flame. Aspect of Ghalib's life and works. Delhi: Sterling Publishers, 1969. 136p.
Includes biography and translations.

1718 — • *Selections from Ghalib and Iqbal*. New Delhi: Sterling Publishers, 1978. 110p.

1719 **Sukhochev, A.S.**
"Altaf Husain Hali o Mirza Ghalib". In: *Mirza Ghalib - a great poet of east*. Moscow, 1983, pp. 119-121.

1720 **Tirmizi, S.A.I.**
Persian letters of Ghalib. New Delhi: Ghalib Academy and Asia Publishing House, 1969. 121p.
Includes lengthy introduction; bibliography; index, texts of letters in Persian.

1721 **Upadhyaya, B.S.**
"Ghalib and his times". *Mainstream* 7, 26 (1 March 1969), pp. 34-36.

1722 **Vahiduddin, Syed**
"Ghalib: the restless soul". *Aryan Path* 41, 1 (January 1970), pp. 29-34.

1723 **Varma, M.**
"Ghalib centenary; political exploitation of a minor poet". *Organiser* (26 July 1969), pp. 11-12.

1724 **Varma, Pavan K.**
Ghalib, the man, the times. New Delhi; New York; Viking, 1989. 224p.

1725 **Welch, A.T. and Cachia P.**
"Ghalib's qasida in honour of the prophet". In: *Islam: past influence and present challenge.*
Albany: State University of New York Press, 1979, pp. 188-209.

1726 **Wig, N.N.**
"A new evaluation of Ghalib and his poetry". *Indian Literature* 11, 1 (January-March 1968),
pp. 36-48.

1727 **Wijdani, J.D.**
"The tone and texture of Ghalib's poetry". *Pakistan Review* 17, 2 (February 1969), pp. 74-
77.

1728 "Writer's tribute to Ghalib". *Contemporary Indian Literature* 9 (February 1969),
pp. 5-7.

1729 **Zahir, Sajjad**
"Ghalib and progressive Urdu literature". *New Age* 17, 7 (16 February 1969), p. 5.

1730 **Zaidi, Ali Jawad**
"Research on Ghalib". *Lokrajya* 24, 20 (1 March 1969), pp. 2-5.

1731 **Zaidi, Nasir Hasan**
"Mirza Ghalib's letters". *Pakistan Review* 17, 2 (February 1969), pp. 59-63.

1732 **Zeno**
"Ghalib: archetype of the poet". *Pakistan Review* 17, 2 (February 1969), pp. 16-18.

HABIB, SHAISTA

STUDY

1733 **Janus**
"Shaista Habib's poetry". *Viewpoint* (Lahore) 5, 43 (1 June 1980), p. 27.

HAFIZ JALLANDAHRI, ABDUL ASAR

STUDY

1734 **Anela, Hafeez**
Poet son of India. Lahore: Majlis-e Urdu, 1943. 184p.
A biography.

HALI, KHVAJAH ALTAF HUSAIN

TRANSLATIONS

1735   *English translation of the Rubāiyāt and Qitaat of Hali* ...   Trans. Nibaran Chandra Chatterjee. Calcutta, 1918. 57p.

1736   "Homage to the silent". *Annual of Urdu Studies* 1 (1981), pp. 46-56. Translation of Hali's *Cup ki dad*.

1737   "Musaddas-e Hali: a fragment". Trans. Ross Masood. *Perspective* 2, 10 (April 1969), pp. 32-33.

1738   *Musaddas-i-Hali.* Trans. Anonymous. Karachi: Peermahomed Ebrahim Trust, 1975. 260p.
Prose translation.

1739   "Musaddas-i-Hali, selections. Khwaja Altaf Husain Hali". In: *Muslim self-statement in India and Pakistan 1857-1968.* Wiesbaden: Otto Harrassowitz, 1970, pp. 95-99.

1740   *Qitaāt - English translation of Rubaiyat and Qitaat of Hali.* Calcutta, 1918, pp. 23-57.
One of the Official Text books for the high proficiency examination in Urdu.

1741   *The quatrains of Hali - Maulvi Altaf Husain Ansari Panipati.* Ed. and Trans. G.E. Ward. London, Oxford [printed], New York, 1904. 84p.

1742   *The quatrains of Hali.* Trans. G.E. Ward and C.S. Tute. Oxford University Press, [1933?].
Includes Urdu text; literal translation by Ward; verse translation by Tute.

1743   *Rubaiyat and qitaat of Hali.* Trans. Nibacharan Chandra Chaterjee. Calcutta, 1914.

STUDIES

1744   **Bausani, Allessandro**
"Altaf Hussain Hali's ideas on ghazal". In: *Charisteria Orientalia.* Eds. F. Tauer, et al. Prague: Czekoslovenska Akademie Ved, (1956), pp. 38-55.

1745   **Dayaram, Bulchand**
"A modern Hindustani poet". *East and West* 4 (August 1905), pp. 884-891.
Includes translations of Hali's verse.

1746   **Husain, Mian Tasadduque**
Hali as poet, critic and biographer, and his influence on Urdu literature. Ph.D. thesis, University of London, 1935.

1747   **Jamil, M Tahir**
Hali's poetry: a study. Bombay: Taraporeval, 1938. 138p.

1748 Jhinghan, F.C.
"Poet Hali of Panipat". *Haryana Review* 9, 8 (August 1975), p. 30.

1749 Malik Ram
Hali. New Delhi: Sahitya Akademi, 1982. 75p.
Life and works of Hali.

1750 Minault, Gail
"Hali's *Majalis Un-Nissa:* purdah and woman power in nineteenth century India". In: *Islamic Society and Culture: essays in honour of Professor Aziz Ahmad*. Eds. Israel Milton and N.K. Wagle. New Delhi: Manohar Publications, 1983, pp. 39-49.

1751 Naim, C.M.
["Review of *Musaddas-i-Hali*"]. *Annual of Urdu Studies* 1 (1981), pp. 111-112.
Includes a letter from Sir Syed Ahmad Khan to Hali.

1752 Pulatova Sh.
"Altaf Husain Hali's *'Majlis un nisa'*". In: *Literatures of India*. Moscow: Nauka, 1979, pp. 103-113.

1753 Qureshi, Waheed
"Hali: poet and reformer". *Vision* 16, 8 (September 1967), pp. 6-8, 26.

1754 Rashid, Amina
"Maulana Altaf Husain Hali". *Pakistan Review* 14, 5 (May 1966), pp. 9-10.

1755 Steele, Laurel
"Hali and his muqaddamah: the creation of a literary attitude in nineteenth century India". *Annual of Urdu Studies* 1 (1981), pp. 1-45.

1756 Vasil'eva, L.
"Altaf Husain Hali: a biographical study". In: *Literatures of India*. Moscow, 1989, pp. 120-154.

1757 — • "Kompozitsionniye osobennosti musaddas Hali". In: *Literatures of India*. Moscow, 1979, pp. 113-121.

HAMDANI, IMDAD

STUDY

1758 Rahman, Tariq
"A poet with unpretentious diction". *Pakistan Times* (20 July 1990).
Review of Imdad Hamdani's *Sadaon ka samundar*.

HANFI, ABDULAZIZ AMIQ

TRANSLATIONS

1759   "Poems by Amiq Hanfi". Trans. Ain Rashed. *Illustrated Weekly of India* (1974), p. 21.

1760   "Selections from Sindbad". Trans. the author. *Poetry India* 1, 2 (April-June 1966), pp. 33-38.

HASAN, ABRARUL

TRANSLATION

1761   "I". Trans. Faruq Hassan. *Urdu Canada* 1, 2 (1986), p. 75.

STUDY

1762   **Hassan, Faruq**
["Review of Abrar-ul-Hasan's *Daire: nazmen*"]. *Annual of Urdu Studies* 4 (1984), pp. 107-110.

HASAN, MIR

TRANSLATION

1763   *The nasr-i Benazir, or the incomparable prose of Mir Hasan, literally translated into English by M.H.Court.* Calcutta, [1898?]. 121p.
From Bahadur Ali's prose version of the *Sihr al-bayan*.

STUDY

1764   **Russell, Ralph and Islam, Khurshidul**
"Mir Hasan's enchanting story". In their *Three Mughal Poets*. Cambridge: Harvard University Press, 1968, pp. 69-94.

HASRAT MOHANI, MAULANA FAZAL HASAN

TRANSLATIONS

1765 *Intikhab-i Divan-i Hasrat Mohani.* *(Selections from the poetical notes of Hasrat Mohani).* Pt 1. Cawnpur, 1922. 76p.
Revised by Hasrat Mohani in Sabarmati jail.
Includes Urdu text.

STUDIES

1766 "Hasrat Mohani the visionary". *Viewpoint* (Lahore) 3, 40 (May 1978), pp. 25, 32.

1767 **Qadiri, Khalid Hasan**
Hasrat Mohani. Delhi: Idarah-i Adabiyat-i Delhi, 1985. 450p.

1768 **Sayed, M. Hafiz**
"The late Maulana Hasrat Mohani". *Thought* 3, 22 (1 June 1951), p. 8.

1769 **Siddiq, Muhammad**
"Hasrat Mohani". *Journal of the Pakistan Historical Society* 32, 1 (1984), pp. 31-70.

HASSAN, FARUQ

TRANSLATIONS

1770 "Eight poems by Faruq Hassan". Trans. the author and Stanley Rajiva. *Urdu Canada* 1, 1 (February 1986), pp. 80-84.
— • "Her dreams and mine".
— • "If she were far ..."
— • "In a dream".
— • "In time".
— • "Messages".
— • "Persistence of memory".
— • "Search".
— • "Twenty years ago, a flower of hundred desires".

1771 "Six poems". Trans. Stanley Rajiva. *Annual of Urdu Studies* 4 (1984), pp. 43-48.
— • "Her dreams and mine". p. 47.
— • "If she were far ..." p. 46.
— • "In a dream". p. 43.
— • "In time". pp. 47-48.
— • "Messages". p. 45.
— • "Search". p. 44.

1772   "Two poems". Trans. the author and Stanley Rajiva. *The Toronto South Asian Review* 3, 3 (Spring 1985), pp. 70-71.
— • "Messages".
— • "Search".

STUDIES

1773 **Ahmad, Sohail**
"New and old Faruq Hassan". *Urdu Canada* 1, 1 (February 1986), pp. 77-79.
Review read at Pak Tea House, Lahore in January, 1984.

1774 **Iqbal, Muzaffar**
"Faruq Hassan's old and new poems". *Urdu Canada* 1, 1 (February 1986), pp. 71-76.

HUSSAIN, ASHFAQ

TRANSLATIONS

1775   "Poems by Ashfaq Hussain". Trans. Sheila Burney. *Urdu Canada* 1, 2 (1986), pp. 85-89.
— • "The curse of generations".
— • "In the neighbourhood of skyscrapers".
— • "Niagra falls".
— • "The portal of dreams".
— • "Raison d'etre".
— • "Remembance".
— • "A suggestion".
— • "Unkind Island".

1776   *That day will dawn.* Trans. Sheila Burney, et al. Toronto: Pakistan Canada Amity Forum, 1985. 144p.
Twenty-eight poems with Urdu text.

STUDIES

1777 **Sohail, M.K.**
["A review of *That day will dawn*"]. *Urdu Canada* 1, 2 (1986), pp. 81-84.

1778 **Voll, Linda**
["A review of *That day will dawn*"]. *Urdu Canada* 1, 2 (1986), pp. 78-80.

IMAN, AKHTARUL

TRANSLATIONS

1779   "Before sleeping" (written between 1936 and 1939). Trans. Leslie Lavigne and Baidar Bakht. *Urdu Canada* 1, 2 (1986), p. 66.

1780   "Compromise". Trans. Akhtarul Iman and Adil Jussawalla. In: *New writing in India.* Ed. Adil Jussawalla. Baltimore: Penguin Books, 1974, pp. 294-295.

1781   "Compromise". Trans. Leslie Lavigne and Baidar Bakht. *Urdu Canada* 1, 3 (1987), pp. 72-73.

1782   "Compromise". Trans. Gopi Chand Narang and David Paul Douglas. *Indian Literature* 23, 1-2 (1980), pp. 555.

1783   "Crystalline". Trans. Gopi Chand Narang and David Paul Douglas. *Indian Literature* 23, 1-2 (1980), p. 556.

1784   "Deprivation." (written between 1936 and 1939). Trans. Leslie Lavigne and Baidar Bakht. *Urdu Canada* 1, 2 (1986), p. 65.

1785   "Five poems". Trans. Baidar Bakht and Kathleen Grant Jaegar. *Annual of Urdu Studies* 3 (1983),
— • "The boy". p. 18-19.
— • "Confidence". p. 20.
— • "Man of glass". p. 20.
— • "Remedy". p. 17.
— • "Two mountains.". p. 17.

1786   "Four poems". Trans. M.H.K. Qureshi and Carlo Coppola. *Mahfil* 2, 3 (Summer 1965), pp. 36-38.

1787   "Inertness" (written between 1936 and 1939). Trans. Leslie Lavigne and Baidar Bakht. *Urdu Canada* 1, 2 (1986), p. 67.

1788   "Sequences". Trans. M.H.K. Qureshi and Carlo Coppola. *Phoenix* (University of Chicago) (Winter 1964), p. 9.

1789   "That house." (written between 1951 and 1961). Trans. Leslie Lavigne and Baidar Bakht. *Urdu Canada* 1, 2 (1986), p. 64.

1790   "Two poems". Trans. Inder Jit Lall. *Indian Literature* 8, 2 (1965), pp. 23-24.

STUDIES

1791   "Taking stock". Trans. Leslie Lavigne and Baidar Bakht. *Urdu Canada* 1, 2 (1986). pp. 7-12.
A translation of the foreword to Akhtarul Iman's collected works *Sar-O-saaman.*

1792   **Farrukhi, Asif Aslam**
["An interview with Akhtarul Iman"]. *Newsline* (Karachi), (December 1989), pp. 143-145.

INSHA

STUDY

1793   **Riaz, Ibne**
"Insha, a versatile genius". *Pakistan Review* 9, 12 (December 1961), pp. 39-40, 46.

IQBAL, MUHAMMAD

BIBLIOGRAPHY AND CATALOGUES

Entries from the following bibliographies are not included in the present bibliography.

1794   **Akhtar, Abdul Hafeez**
Analytical catalogue of books on Allama Mohammad Iqbal, 1877-1977. Karachi: Department of Libraries, 1978. 97, 182p.

1795   **Azhar, Malik Mueen Nawaz**
A bibliography of articles on Iqbal, 1900-1977. Lahore: Islamic Book Service, 1978. 63p.

1796   **Nur Illahi, Khwaja and Abdul Ghani**
Bibliography of Iqbal. Lahore: Bazm-i Iqbal, 1954. 267p.
All critical material included is in English.

1797   **Qarshi, Afzal Haq**
"Index of articles and reviews published in the Iqbal Review (1960-1983)". *Iqbal Review* 25, 3 (October 1984), pp. 129-152.

1798   **Siddiq, Muhammad**
Descriptive catalogue of Allama Iqbal's personal library. Lahore: Iqbal Academy, 1983. 110, 26, 82p.

1799   **Waheed, K.A.**
A bibliography of Iqbal. Karachi: Iqbal Academy, 1965. 224p.

TRANSLATIONS

1800   "Bal-i Jibril: thirteen ghazals". Trans. A.A. Shah. *Iqbal Review* 11, 3 (October 1970), pp. 1-16.

1801 "Bandagi-namah of Iqbal". Trans. K. Badar. *Iqbal* 12, 2 (January 1964), pp. 64-73.

1802 *Bang-i-dara.* Trans. Mohammad Sadiq Khan Satti. Islamabad: M.S.K. Satti, 1984.

1803 "The book of servitude". Trans. M. Hadi Husain. *Iqbal Review* 7, 1 (April 1966), pp. 83-94.

1804 *Botschaft des Ostens.* Trans. Annnemarie Schimmel. Wiesbaden, 1963.
German verse translation.

1805 *Buch der Ewigkeit.* Trans. Annemarie Schimmel. München, 1957.
German verse translation.

1806 *'Complaint' and 'Answer'; Shikwa and Jawab-i-Shikwa.* Trans. A.J. Arberry. Lahore: Shaikh Muhammad Ashraf, 1955. 79p.

1807 "The conquest of nature; Translation of Iqbal's *'Tashkhir-i-fitrat'* from *Payam-i-Mashriq*". Trans. M. Hadi Husain. *Iqbal Review* 6, 3 (October 1965), pp. 37-40.

1808 *The development of metaphysics in Persia; a contribution to the history of Muslim philosophy.* Lahore: Bazm-i Iqbal, 1964. 149p.

1809 *Gabriel's wing.* Trans. Syed Akbar Ali Shah. Islamabad: Modern Book Depot, 1979. 162p.
Translation in English verse of sixty-one ghazals from Iqbal's *Bal-e-jibril.* Includes notes, explanations and glossaries.

1810 "Gulshan-i raz-i jadid: the new garden of mystery". Trans. B.A. Dar. *Iqbal* 5, 3 (January 1957), pp. 1-47.

1811 *Gulshan-i raz-i jadid. New garden of mystery and Bandagi namah, Book of servitude.* Trans. B.A. Dar. Lahore: Institute of Islamic Culture, 1964. 58p.

1812 "Iqbal's Shikwa in English". Trans. Khushwant Singh. *Viewpoint* (Lahore) 5, 8 (September 1979), pp. 23-24, 30.
An extract from the complete translation of Mohammed Iqbal's Shikwa ... by Khushwant Singh.

1813 *Javid Nama.* Trans. A.J. Arberry. London: George Allen and Unwin, 1967.

1814 *Khizri-raah; presentation in English.* Trans. A.Q. Niaz. Friends in Council Publishers, 1951.

1815 *Longer poems of Iqbal.* Trans. A.R. Tariq. Lahore: Shaikh Ghulam Ali, 1978. 206p.

1816 *Message de l'Orient.* Trans. E. Meyerovitch and Mohammad Achena. Paris, 1956.
French prose-translation.

1817   *A message from the east: a translation of Iqbal's Payam-i mashriq.* 2nd. ed. Trans. M. Hadi Hussain. Lahore: Iqbal Academy, 1977. 189p.

1818   *The mystery of selflessness. Rumuz-i bekhudi.* Trans. A.J. Arberry. London: J. Murray, 1953
English verse-translation.

1819   "The new rose garden of mystery". Trans. M. Hadi Husain. *Pakistan Review* 16, 5 (May 1968), pp. 28-29.

1820   *'The new rose garden of mystery' and 'The book of slaves'; verse translations of 'Gulshan-i-raz-Jadid' and 'Bandagi-namah'.* Trans. M. Hadi Husain. Lahore: Shaikh Muhammad Ashraf, 1969. 66p.

1821   *Pilgrimage of eternity, being an English translation of Muhammad Iqbal's Javid nama.* Trans. Shaikh Mahmud Ahmad. Lahore: Institute of Islamic Culture, 1961. 187p.

1822   "A poem from Javed Namah". Trans. the author. *Pakistani Literature* (Islamabad) 1, 1 (1992), p. 11.

1823   *Poems from Iqbal. Translated from the Urdu.* Selected and trans. Victor G. Kiernan. Bombay: Kutub Publisher, 1974.

[Another ed.] London: John Murray, 1955.

1824   *Poesie di Muhammad Iqbal.* Trans. Alessandro Bausani. Parma, 1956.

1825   *Poselství z východu.* Trans. J. Marek. Prague, 1960.
Czech translation of selected poems, with illustrations.

1826   *The reconstruction of religious thought in Islam.* London: Oxford University Press, 1934. 192p.
On Islamic religious philosophy in context of the 20th century; seven lectures by Iqbal.

1827   *The reconstruction of religious thought in Islam.* Ed. and annotated by Saeed Sheikh. Lahore: Institute of Islamic Culture, 1986. 249p.

1828   *The rod of moses: versified English translation of Iqbal's 'Zarb-i-Kalim'.* Lahore: Iqbal Academy Pakistan, 1983. 170p.

1829   *Rubayiat of Iqbal.* Trans. A.R. Tariq. Lahore: Shaikh Ghulam Ali, 1973. 220p.

1830   *The secrets of the self.* Trans. R.A. Nicholson. London, 1920.
English prose-translation.
Review of this translation: E.G. Browne, *Translations of the Royal Asiatic Society* (1921), p. 128; E.M. Forster, *Athenaeum*, London, 1921.

[Another ed.] Lahore, 1955.

1831 *'Shikwah' and 'Jawab-i-Shikwah'*. Trans. Altaf Husain. Lahore: Shaikh Muhammad Ashraf, 1943. 14, 72p.

1832 *Shikwa aur jawab-i Shikwa: complaint and answer: Iqbal's dialogue with Allah.* Trans. Khushwant Singh. Delhi: Oxford University Press, 1981. 96p.

1833 "Translation of two poems from Iqbal's *Bal-i-jibrail*". Trans. Qazi Abdul Kabir. *Pakistan Review* 14, 4 (April 1966), pp. 24-25.

1834 *The tulip of Sinai.* Trans. A.J. Arberry. London, 1947.
English verse translation of the first part of *Lae-i Tur*.

1835 *A voice from the east: the poetry of Iqbal.* Trans. Sardar Umrao Singh. Lahore: Mercantiel Electric Press, 1922. 47p.

1836 *Zarb-i-kalim. The rod of Moses: versified English translation of Iqbal's Zarb-i-kalim.* Trans. Syed Akbar Ali Shah. Lahore: Iqbal Academy Pakistan, 1983. 170p.

STUDIES

1837 **Abdul Hai, Saiyed**
Iqbal: his contribution. Dacca: Bureau of National Reconstruction, 1968. 24p.

1838 **Abdul Hakim, Khalifa**
"Concept of love in Rumi and Iqbal". *Islamic Culture* 14, 3 (July 1940), pp. 266-273.

1839 — • "Reconstruction of religious thought in Islam: Iqbal's concept of God." *Pakistan Calling* 4, 2 (1 January 1951), pp. 18, 19.

1840 — • "Time and space in Iqbal's philosophy". *Pakistan Calling* 4, 8 (April 1951), pp. 8, 9.
Also in: *Pakistan Times* (21 April 1951), p. 8.

1841 — • "Allama Muhammad Iqbal". *Pakistan Quarterly* 8, 2 (1959).

1842 **Abdullah, Dr S.M.**
"Nachruf auf Iqbal". *Moslemische Revue* 14 (Berlin 1938).

1843 — • "The nature of Dante's influence on Iqbal". *Iqbal Review* 24, 1 (April 1983), pp. 25-31.

1844 **Abdur Rahim, Khawaja**
Iqbal, the poet of tomorrow. Lahore: Markaziyya Majlis-i Iqbal, 1968. 273p.

1845 **Abid Ali, Syed**
"Baba Tahir Uryan and Iqbal". *Iqbal* 5, 1 (July 1956), pp. 54-81.

1846 Abid, Mahfooz Jan
"Iqbal and Matthew Arnold: a comparative study". *Iqbal Review* *23*, 3 (October 1982), pp. 85-93.

1847 Ahmad, Absar
Concept of self and self-identify in contemporary philosophy: an affirmation of Iqbal's doctrine. Lahore: Iqbal Academy Pakistan, 1986. 335p.

1848 — • "The Hegelian key to understanding Iqbal". *Iqbal Review* 21, 3 (October 1980), pp. 31-41.

1849 Ahmad, Aziz
"Iqbal's political theory". *Islamic Culture* (October 1944), pp. 377-393.

1850 — • *Iqbal and the recent exposition of Islamic political thought.* Lahore: Shaikh Muhammad Ashraf, 1965. 64p.

1851 — • "Sources of Iqbal's idea of the perfect man". *Iqbal* 7, 1 (July 1958), pp. 1-17.

1852 Ahmad, Doris
Iqbal, as I knew him. Lahore: Iqbal Academy Pakistan, 1986. 54p.
Reminiscences of Iqbal's German housekeeper.

1853 Ahmad, Jamiluddin
Iqbal's concept of Islamic polity. Karachi: Pakistan Publications, 1968. 23p.

1854 Ahmad, Khurshid
"Iqbal and the Islamic aims of education". *Iqbal Review* 2, 3 (October 1961), pp. 51-70.

1855 Ahmad, M.A.
"Iqbal's political theory." *Islamic Culture* 18, 4 [1944?], pp. 337-393.

1856 — • "Rumi (1207-1273) and Iqbal". *Islamic Review and Arab Affairs* 40 (April 1952), pp. 31-37.

1857 Ahmad, Dr M.M.
"Iqbal's appreciative self". *Iqbal Review* 2, 3 (October 1961), pp. 14-17.

1858 Ahmad, Muhammad Saleem
"Iqbal and politics - I". *Pakistan Studies* 11, 3 (Winter 1983-84), pp. 63-84.

1859 — • "Iqbal and politics - II". *Pakistan Studies* 11, 4 (Summer 1984), pp. 64-83.

1860 Ahmad, S. Hasan
Iqbal, his political ideas at crosswords: a commentary on unpublished letters to Prof. Thompson, with photographic reproductions of the original letters. Aligarh: Printwell Publications, 1979. 98p.

1861   **Ahmad, Z.**
"Relationship between east and west in Iqbal's thoughts". *Islamic Review and Arab Affairs*
54 (October 1966), pp. 13-16.

1862   **Ahmad, Ziauddin**
"Iqbal's concept of deracialisation". *Islamic Literature* 8, 8 (August 1956).

1863   **Ahsan, Abdushakur**
An appreciation of Iqbal's thought and art. Lahore: Research Society of Pakistan, University
of the Punjab, 1985. 260p.

1864   **Ahsan, Mumtaz Hasan**
"Side-lights on Iqbal: Iqbal as a man." *Pakistan Calling* 6, 8 (1952), pp. 8, 9.

1865   **Ahsan, Syed Ali**
"Poetry and philosophy in Iqbal". *Bengal Literary Review* 5 (November 1960), pp. 1-7.
Also in: *Iqbal Review* 1, 3 (October 1960), pp. 21-25.

1866   **Ajmal, Muhammad**
"Iqbal and mysticism". *Iqbal Review* 29, 3 (October-December 1988), pp. 11-30.

1867   **Akbar, Mojahid**
"Iqbal: a view". *Pakistan Review* 7, 10 (October 1959), pp. 33, 35.

1868   **Akhtar, Saleem**
"Herbert Read on Dr Iqbal". *Iqbal Review* 24, 1 (April 1983), pp. 33-37.

1869   **Aks, Ameena**
"Iqbal: a personal appreciation". *Weekend Review* 2, 20 (20 April 1968), pp. 15-16.

1870   **Alam, M. Jehangir**
"Two unpublished letters of Iqbal". *Iqbal Review* 24, 1 (April 1983), pp. 43-44.

1871   **Ali, Abdullah Yusuf**
"The doctrine of human personality in Iqbal's poetry".   In: *Essays by diverse hands.*   Ed.
St. John Ervine. London: Oxford University Press, 1940, pp. 89-105.

1872   **Ali, Ahmad**
"Iqbal: a Pakistan view". *Illustrated Weekly of India* 95, 34 (20 October 1974), pp. 15-19.

1873   **Ali, Bishop Michael J. Nazir**
"Iqbal and Rumi". *Iqbal Review* 29, 3 (October-December 1988), pp. 31-46.

1874   **Ali, Shaikh Akbar**
Iqbal: his poetry and message. Lahore: Qaumi Kutub Khana, 1932. 304p.

1875   **Ali, S. Amjad**
"Iqbal in foreign lands". *Pakistan Quarterly* 3, 1 (1953), pp. 30-35.

1876   **Allana, G.**
"Iqbal: as political philosopher". *Iqbal Review* 14, 3 (October 1973), pp. 61-68.

1877   **Anand, Mulk Raj**
"Poetry of Sir Muhammad Iqbal". *Indian Art and Letters* 5, 1 (1937), pp. 19-39.

1878   **Anikeev, N.P.**
"Obshchestvenno-politicheskie vzgliady M. Iqbala". *Sovetskoe Vostokovedeniia* (March 1958).

1879   **Ansari, A.A.**
"Iqbal as poet and thinker". *Iqbal Review* 27, 1 (April-September 1986), pp. 121-134.

1880   **Ansari, Aslub Ahmad**
Iqbal: essays and studies. New Delhi: Ghalib Academy, 1978. 332p.
Includes quotations in Urdu.

1881   — • "Iqbal's relevance to our times". *Islamic Culture* 50, 2 (April 1976), pp. 81-85.

1882   **Ansari, Zafar Ishaq**
"Iqbal and nationalism". *Iqbal Review* 2, 1 (April 1961), pp. 51-89.

1883   **Anwar Beg, A.**
"Iqbal: poet of humanity". *Pakistan Review* 8 (June 1960), pp. 19-21, 28.

1884   **Arberry, A.J.**
"Pakistan - Iqbal's concept". *Pakistan Review* 16, 4 (April 1968), p. 32.

1885   — • *Notes on Iqbal's Asrar-i khudi.* Lahore: Bazm-i Iqbal, 1955.

1886   — • "Iqbal and Milton, interesting comparison of art and thought." *Civil and Military Gazette* (16 November 1959).

1887   — • "Review on S.A Vahid's book, *Iqbal his art and thought*". *Islamic Review* 18, 3 (March-April 1960), pp 45-46.

1888   **Aslam, Qazi Mohammad**
"Iqbal at a College reception in Lahore". *Iqbal Review* 11, 3 (October 1970), pp. 17-27.

1889   **Ashraf, S.E.**
A critical exposition of Iqbal's philosophy. Patna: Associated Book Agency, 1978.

1890   **Atiya Faizi**
Iqbal. Bombay: Academy of Islam, 1947.

1891   — • "Iqbal as I knew him". *Pakistan Times Supplement* (21 April 1950), pp. 10, 11.

1892   **Azad, Jagan Nath**
Iqbal, his poetry and philosophy. Mysore: Prasaranga, University of Mysore, 1981. 76p.

1893 — • *Iqbal: mind and art*. Ed. and Intro. Mohammad Maruf. Lahore: National Book House, 1983. 232p.
Compilation of the author's previously published articles on Iqbal.

1894 — • "Iqbal's philosophy of life". *Illustrated Weekly of India* 94, 34 (26 August 1973), pp. 28-31.

1895 — • "Iqbal: poet - son of India". *Indian and Foreign Review* 10, 13 (15 April 1973), pp. 19-21.

1896 — • "Iqbal and Schopenhauer". *Cultural Forum* 15, 3-4 (April-July 1973), pp. 70-73.

1897 — • "Pandit Anand Narain Mulla as a translator of Iqbal". *Iqbal Review* 23, 1 (April 1982), pp. 37-45.

1898 Azam, Muhammad
"A few moments with Allama Iqbal". *Pakistan Review* 14, 8 (August 1966), pp. 21-22.

1899 Azeez, A.M.A
"Iqbal: a poet of Islam". *Pakistan Review* 2, 4 (1954), pp. 22, 23.

1900 Azeez, S.A.
"Sorrow of Iqbal". *Civil and Military Gazette* (21 April 1954), p. 4.

1901 Azhar, A.D.
"Iqbal as a Seer". *Iqbal Review* 2, 3 (October 1961), pp. 1-9.

1902 Azhar, M.A.
"Iqbal". *Pakistan Review* 1 (May 1953), pp. 23, 24.

1903 Bahar, A.C.
"Milton and Iqbal". *Modern Review* 123, 12 (December 1968), pp. 918-923.

1904 Baig, Safdar Ali
"Doctor Iqbal's optimism". *Islamic Culture* 44, 2 (April 1970), pp. 91-100.

1905 — • "Poet Iqbal's dynamism". *Triveni* 36, 3 (October 1967), pp. 35-41.

1906 Baloch, S.K.
"Idealism in Iqbal's poetry". *Pakistan Review* 16, 4 (April 1968), pp. 22-25.

1907 Bannerth, E.
"Islam in modern Urdu poetry. A translation of Dr. M. Iqbal's *Shikwah and Jawab-i Shikwah*". *Anthropos* 37-60, (1942-1945).

1908 Barni, Sayyid Muzaffar Husain
Muhibb-i vatan Iqbal. Iqbal, poet-patriot of India. Trans. Syeda Saiyidain Hameed. New Delhi: Vikas Publishing House, 1987. 136p.
Nationalism and secularism in the poetry of Iqbal. Includes Urdu text in Roman characters.

1909   Basham, A.L.
"Three poems of Iqbal". In: *Islamic society and culture: essays in honour of Professor Aziz Ahmad*. Eds. M. Israel and N.K. Wagle. New Delhi: Manohar, 1983, pp. 117-12.

1910   Bausani, Alessandro
"Classical Muslim philosophy in the work of a Muslim modernist: Mohammad Iqbal (1877-1938)". *Archiv für Geschichte der Philosophie* (Berlin) 42, 3 (1960), pp. 272-288.

1911   — • "The concept of time in the religious philosophy of Iqbal". *Die Welt des Islams* 3 (1954), pp. 158-186.

1912   — • "Dante and Iqbal". *Pakistan Quarterly* 1, 6 (Summer 1951), pp. 51-54, 72. Also in: *East and West* 2 (1951), pp. 77-81.

1913   — • "Iqbal". *Pakistan Quarterly* 2, 3 (Summer 1952), pp. 16-19, 54.

1914   — • *Il Poema Celeste*. Roma, 1952 (Istituto per il Medio ed Estremo Oriente).

1915   — • "Iqbal's philosophy of religion and the west". *Pakistan Quarterly* 2, 3 (1952), pp. 16-19, 54.

1916   — • "Mohammad Iqbal's message in east and west". *Oriental Modern* 1 (1950), pp. 137-140.

1917   — • "The life and work of Iqbal". Trans. A.K.M. *Iqbal Review* 14, 3 (October 1973), pp. 45-60.

1918   — • "Satan in Iqbal's philosophical and poetical works". Trans. R.A. Butter. *Iqbal Review* 9, 3 (October 1968), pp. 68-118.

1919   — • "Satana nell'opera filosofico-poetica di Muhammad Iqbal". *Rivista degli Studi Orientali* 30 (1957).

1920   Beg, Abdullah Anwar
The poet of the east: the life and works of Dr Shaikh Sir Muhammad Iqbal the poet philospher. Lahore: Khawar Publishing Cooperative Society, 1961.   323p.
First published 1939.

1921   — • "The poet of the east". *Islamic Literature* 13, 4 (April 1967), pp. 5-10. Also in: *Pakistan Review* 16, 4 (April 1968), pp. 4-8.

1922   — • "The poet of Islam". *Islamic Literature* 15, 3 (March 1969), pp. 53-62.

1923   Bhajjan, S.V.
"Iqbal the poet". *Henry Martyn Institute of Islamic Studies Bulletin* 54, 4 (January 1966), pp. 15-34.

1924   Bhatti, A.M.A.
"A line from Iqbal". *Pakistan Review* 2 (April 1954), pp. 34-36.

1925 Bilgrami, H.H.
Glimpses of Iqbal's mind and thought; brief lectures on Iqbal, delivered at London, Cambridge and Oxford. Lahore: Shaikh Muhammad Ashraf, 1966. 110p.

[Another ed.] Lahore: Orientalia, 1954. 124p.

1926 — • "British centenary of Muhammad Iqbal". *Indo-Iranica* 26, 4 (December 1973), pp. 60-64.

1927 — • "Iqbal's concept of democracy based on Islamic principles". *Islamic Literature* 6, 4 (1954), pp. 197-202.

1928 — • "Iqbal's theory of knowledge and its significance in his poetry." *Islamic Literature* 3, 5 (1951), pp. 244-254.

1929 Brohi, A.K.
"Iqbal as a philospher poet". *Iqbal Review* 2, 1 (April 1961), pp. 1-21.

1930 Bürgel, J.C.
"The pious rogue: a study in the meaning of qalandar and rend in the poetry Muhammad Iqbal". *Edebiyat* (Philadelphia) 4, 1 (1979), pp. 43-64.

1931 — • *Steppe im Staubkorn.* (Texte aus der Urdu-Dichtung Muhammad Iqbals). Freiburg: Universitätsverlag Freiburg, 1982. 194p.

1932 Chagla, Ahmed C.
"Some aspects of Iqbal's thought." *Triveni* 18, 2 (June 1946), pp. 93-102.

1933 Chawdhury, Kabir
"Iqbal: an appreciation". *Iqbal Review* 2, 3 (October 1961), pp. 79-85.

1934 Chopra, Hira Lall
"Iqbal and India". *Indo-Iranica* 15 (June 1962), pp. 27-33.

1935 — • "Iqbal and his message". *Indo-Iranica* 8, 3 (September 1955), pp. 20-28.

1936 Christopher, C.B.
"Individual and society: a study of the social philosophy of Iqbal". *Pakistan Review* 3 (April 1955), pp. 26-28.

1937 Clavel, L.S.
"Islamic allusions in the poetry of Iqbal". *Asian Studies* 8 (1970), pp. 378-85.

1938 Dar, Bashir Ahmad
"Ghalib and Iqbal". *Iqbal Review* 10, 3 (October 1969), pp. 25-44.

1939 — • "The idea of satan in Iqbal and Milton". *Iqbal* 1, 1 (July 1952), pp. 83-108.

1940 — • "Iqbal and Bergson". *Iqbal* 3, 1 (July 1954), pp. 34-86.

1941 — • *Letters and writings of Iqbal*. Karachi: Iqbal Academy, 1967. 129p.

1942 — • *Iqbal and Post-Kantian voluntarism*. Lahore: Bazm-i Iqbal, 1956. 498p.

1943 — • "New Iqbal material". *Iqbal Review* 10, 3 (October 1969), pp. 83-96.

1944 — • *A study in Iqbal's philosophy*. Lahore: Shaikh Muhammad Ashraf, 1944. 422p. Appendices include two short notes by Iqbal: "Self in the light of relativity" and "McTaggart's philosophy".

1945 **Dickie, James**
"Muhammad Iqbal: a reappraisal". *Islamic Review and Arab Affairs* 53, 4 (April 1965), pp. 31-34.
Also in: *Iqbal Review* 9, 1 (April 1968), pp. 67-74.

1946 **Enver, Ishrat Hasan**
The metaphysics of Iqbal. Lahore: Shaikh Muhammad Ashraf, 1963. 105p.
First published 1944, 1955.

1947 — • "Ethics of Iqbal". *Islamic Literature* (September 1956), pp. 43-45.

1948 — • "The essential Iqbal I". *Viewpoint* (Lahore) 9, 38 (April 1984), pp. 18-19.

1949 — • "The essential Iqbal II". *Viewpoint* (Lahore) 9, 39 (May 1984), pp. 26-28.

1950 **Faiz, Faiz Ahmad**
"Iqbal day at Karachi: Iqbal as a poet". *Iqbal Review* 8 (April 1967), pp. 119-133.

1951 **Farooqi, A.**
"A comparative study of Iqbal's thought". *Pakistan Review* 14, 4 (April 1966), pp. 11-19.

1952 — • "The impact of Khawaja Hafiz on Iqbal's thought". *Iqbal Review* 14, 1 (April 1973), pp. 33-60.

1953 — • "Iqbal's conception of God". *Islamic Literature* 11, 2 (September 1965), pp. 27-32.

1954 — • "Iqbal and the doctrine of reincarnation". *Studies in Islam* 5 (July 1968), pp. 120-128.

1955 — • "Iqbal's perfect man". *Pakistan Review* 12 (March 1964), pp. 18-21

1956 — • "Iqbal's pilgrimage of eternity". *Pakistan Review* 19, 8 (August 1971), pp. 20-26.

1957 — • "The problem of good and evil as viewed by Iqbal". *Iqbal Review* 13, 3 (October 1972), pp. 33-43.

1958 — • "Zorastrianism and Iqbal". *Iqbal Review* 5, 3 (October 1964), pp. 1-20.

1959   Farooqi, Dr M.A.
"The poetic art of Iqbal". *Iqbal Review* 2, 3 (October 1961), pp. 24-50.

1960   Faruqi, K.A.
"Iqbal: the humanist". *Indian Literature* 22, 3 (1979), pp. 97-114.

1961   Faruqi, Shamsur Rahman
"Iqbal's dilemma". *Humanities Review* (New Delhi) 3, 2 (July-December 1981), pp. 15-20.

1962   — • "Iqbal from the inside". *Indian Literature* 28, 5 (September-October 1985), pp. 207-211.

1963   — • "Iqbal in proper light". *Indian Literature* 31, 1 (January-February 1988), pp. 145-147.
Review of S.M.H. Burney's *Iqbal: Poet-patriot of India* (New Delhi, 1987).

1964   Fayyaz, Muhammad
"Self and synthesis: an interpretation of Iqbal's dialectical thought". *Urdu Canada* 1, 3 (1987), pp. 12-22.

1965   Fernandez, A.
"Man's divine quest, appreciation of the philosophy of the ego according to Sir Muhammad Iqbal". *Annali Lateranensis* 20 (Rome, 1956).

1966   Figar, Abdur Rahman
"Iqbal's philosophy of revolution". *Pakistan Quarterly* 9, 4 (Winter 1959), pp. 26-29.

1967   Forster, E.M.
"Iqbal". *Pakistan Review* 1 (January 1953), pp. 12-13.

1968   Fück, J.W.
"Muhammad Iqbal und der indomuslimische Modernismus". In: *Westöstliche Abhandlungen, Rudolf Tschundi zum 70. Geburtstag.* Wiesbaden, 1954.

1969   Ghareeb, Mamoun
"Iqbal: the philosopher and the poet". *Iqbal Review* 9, 1 (April 1968), pp. 18-21.

1970   "Gleanings from Iqbal. Allama Muhammad Iqbal (1874-1938)". *Pakistani Literature* (Islamabad) 1, 1 (1992), pp. 9-10.
Biographical sketch of Iqbal.

1971   *All-Guiana Council on Muslim Rights, Historical and Cultural Committee.*
In commemoration of the 25th anniversary of Iqbal day, 21st April, 1963. Ed. M.H. Ganie. Georgetown, British Guiana, 1963. 20p.

1972   Habib, Kamal Muhammad
"A Bang-i Dara poem studied: 'Muhabbat', (Love)". *Iqbal Review* 17, 1 (April 1976), pp. 47-56.

1973 — • "Iqbal and Tagore: an essay on two contrasting sensibilities". *Vision* (Karachi) (October 1967), pp. 13-20, (November 1967), pp. 13-20.

1974 — • "Iqbal as the poet of time". *Iqbal Review* 18, 4 (January 1978), pp. 149-170.

1975 — • "Iqbal's poetic achievement". *Pakistan Quarterly* 14, 4 (Spring 1967), pp. 30-36.

1976 — • "Some aspects of Iqbal's poetry: a discussion of his imagery and symbols". *Vision* 17, 7 (August 1968), pp. 7-17.

1977 — • "Studies in Iqbal's longer poems". *Iqbal Review* 6, 1 (April 1965), pp. 1-32.

1978 Haider, Sajjad
"Iqbal and his philosophy". *Iqbal Review* 9, 1 (April 1968), pp. 1-17.

1979 Halepota, A.J.
"Affinity of Iqbal with Shah Waliyullah". *Iqbal Review* 15, 1 (April 1974), pp. 65-72.

1980 Hamid, Khwaja Abdul
"Iqbal's philosophy of human ego". *Vishvabharati Quarterly* N.S. 9 (September 1943).

1981 Harre, R.
"Iqbal: a reformer of Islamic philosophy". *The Hibbert Journal* (London) 56 (July 1958), pp. 333-339.

1982 Hasan, Mohammad
A new approach to Iqbal. New Delhi: Publications Division, Ministry of Information and Broadcasting, 1987. 102p.
Includes Urdu text.

1983 Hasan, Mumtaz
Tribute to Iqbal. Lahore: Iqbal Academy Pakistan, 1982. 120p.

1984 — • "A day in Iqbal's life". In: *Mohammad Iqbal: poet and philosopher*. Pakistan-German Forum. Karachi: Din Muhammad Press, 1960.

1985 — • "Iqbal as a Seer". *Iqbal Review* 7, 1 (April 1966), pp. 43-62.

1986 Hasan, N.
"Iqbal's conception of art". *Eastern World* (London) 7 (February 1955), pp. 27-29.

1987 Hasan, Reyazul
"Il poeta musulmano indiano Mohammad Iqbal". *Oriente Moderno* 20 (Rome 1940), pp. 605-623.
Biography and translations in Italian of Iqbal's poetry.

1988 Hasan, Riffat
"Iqbal's ideal person and Rumi's influence". *Iqbal Review* 24, 3 (October 1983), pp. 119-126.

1989 — • "Iqbal's philosophy of art". *Iqbal Review* 26, 3 (October-December 1985), pp. 19-44.

1990 — • "Some thoughts on Iqbal's aesthetics". *Pakistan Review* 16, 4 (April 1968), pp. 18-20.

1991 — • *The sword and the sceptre: a collection of writings on Iqbal, dealing mainly with his life and poetical works.* Lahore: Iqbal Academy Pakistan, 1977. 394p.

1992 **Hassan, Masudul**
Life of Iqbal: general account of his life. Lahore: Ferozsons, 1978. 2 vols.

1993 **Hassan, Parveen Feroze**
The political philosophy of Iqbal. Lahore: Publishers United, 1970. 426p.

1994 **Hayit, Dr B.**
Mohammad Iqbal und die Welt des Islam. Köln, 1956.

1995 **Haywood, John A.**
"The wisdom of Muhammad Iqbal: some considerations of form and content". *Iqbal Review* 9, 1 (April 1968), pp. 22-33.

1996 **Horani, Jamilur Rahman**
"Iqbal: the problem of poetic belief". *Iqbal Review* 4 (April 1964), pp. 23-47.

1997 **Houben, J.J.**
"The individual in democracy and Iqbal's conception of khudi". *Pakistan Quarterly* 4, 1 (Spring 1954), pp. 18-21, 63-67.

1998 **Husain, A.**
Aspect of Iqbal, articles and addresses of Iqbal day for Inter-Collegiate Muslim Brotherhood. Lahore, 1938.

1999 — • "15th anniversary of the poet Iqbal". *Indian Art and Letters* NS 27 (1953).

2000 **Husain, Rofe**
"Spiritual message of Iqbal". *Islamic Literature* (April 1953), pp. 23-25.

2001 **Husain, S. Sajjad**
"Iqbal and Wordsworth". *Iqbal Review* 24, 1 (April 1983), pp. 21-23.

2002 **Hussain, Riaz**
"American, West European and Soviet attitudes to Iqbal". *Iqbal Review* 26, 3 (October-December 1985), pp. 97-112.

2003 — • "The evolution of Iqbal's poetic thought - a myth exploded". *Iqbal Review* 18, 1 (April 1977), pp. 19-22.

2004 **Ibrahim, A.M.M.**
"Iqbal's philosophy of love." *Islamic Literature* 7, 6 (July 1955), pp. 27-36.

2005 — • "Iqbal's conception of the Islamic State". *Islamic Literature* (January-February 1965), pp. 143-152.

2006 — • "Iqbal's conception of time". *Islamic Literature* 8, 10 (October 1956), pp. 27-36.

2007 Iftikhar, M.
"Aml-e Chughatai - illustrations of Allama Iqbal's verse". *Pakistan Review* 17, 4 (April 1969), pp. 50-53.

2008 Iqbal, A.
"Rumi and Iqbal". *Pakistan Philosophical Journal* 1, 4 (1958), pp. 63-72.

2009 Iqbal Academy, Karachi
In memorium III, Iqbal day speeches and articles. Karachi: Iqbal Academy, 1969. 63p.

2010 Iqbal Centenary Symposium, Delhi, 1977.
Multi disciplinary approach to Iqbal: Iqbal Centenary Symposium. New Delhi: Ratnedeep Press, 1977. 69p.
Organised by the Centre of Indian languages, Jawaharlal Nehru University, in collaboration with the Department of Urdu, University of Delhi.

2011 Iqbal, Javed
Stray reflections: a notebook of Allama Iqbal. Lahore: Shaikh Ghulam Ali and Sons, 1961. 161p.

2012 — • "Iqbal as a father". *Pakistan Quarterly Supplement* (1960).

2013 — • "Iqbal and Nietzsche": In: *Mohammad Iqbal: poet and philosopher.* Karachi: Din Muhammad Press, 1960.

2014 — • *Iqbal as a thinker: collected essays by eminent scholars on Iqbal's thought and teachings.* Lahore: Shaikh Muhammad Ashraf, 1960. 304p.
First published 1944, 1952.

2015 — • *Mohammad Iqbal: poet and philosopher.* Pakistan-German Forum. Karachi, 1960.

2016 Iqbal, Muhammad
Botschaft des Ostens: Ausgewählte Werke. (Aus den Pers. und Urdu ausgew. und übers. von Annemarie Schimmel). Tübingen und Basel: Horst Erdmann Verlag, 1977. 368p.

2017 "Observations on the main characteristics of mystic experience". *Pakistani Literature* (Islamabad) 1, 1 (1992), pp. 12-14.

2018 — • "On the nature of human experience". *Pakistani Literature* (Islamabad) 1, 1 (1992), pp. 15-16.
Extract from the philosophical text of the revelations of religious experience.

2019 — • "The human ego - his freedom and immortality". *Pakistani Literature*

2020 — • "In defence of Asrar-i Khudi". (Iqbal's letter to Dr Nicholson). *Dawn* (21 April 1949), p. 4.

2021 **Iqbal, S.M.**
"Iqbal on the doctrine of absolute unity". *Islamic Review and Arab and Affairs* 47 (May 1959), pp. 7-12.

2022 **Iqbal Singh**
The ardent pilgrim. An introduction to the life and work of Mohammad Iqbal. Bombay: Orient Longmans, 1951. 246p.

2023 **Ishaq, Khalid**
"Three great thinkers: Ghazali, William James, Iqbal". *Pakistan Quarterly* 3, 1 (1953), pp. 24-28.

2024 **Islam, Muhammad Ziaul**
"Iqbal's internationalism and humanism". *Pakistan Review* 17, 5 (May 1969), pp.1 2-16.

2025 **Jafri, Ali Sardar**
"Iqbal: poet of the east". Trans. Qurratulain Hyder. *Illustrated Weekly of India* 90, 17 (27 April 1969), pp. 30-33.

2026 **Jafri, Ali Sardar and Duggal, K.S.**
Iqbal: commemorative volume. New Delhi: All India Iqbal Centenary Celebrations Committee, [1980?]. 318p.

2027 **Jafri, Farid S.**
"Inspiration from Iqbal". *Morning News* (23 April 1967), p. 17.

2028 **Jilani, Dr Ghulam**
"Iqbal as a reformer". *Iqbal Review* 1, 3 (October 1960), pp. 5-16

2029 **Jordan, W.M.**
"Iqbal's mystic insight". *Pakistan Review* 9, 8 (August 1961), pp. 7-8.

2030 **Kaaf, G.**
"Iqbal's 'Masjid-i Qurtuba' ". *Pakistan Review* 2 (April 1954), pp. 37-39.

2031 **Kaleem, Siddiq**
"The tone and temper of Iqbal's poetry". In his *Pakistan: a cultural spectrum.* Lahore: Arsalan Publications, 1973, pp. 176-179.

2032 **Kalia, H.S.**
"Iqbal: scholar-poet of eminence". *Times of India* (19 March 1961).

2033 **Kamal, R.**
"Iqbal's concept of man". *Islamic Culture* 37 (January 1963), pp. 30-48.

2034   **Karim, A.H.**
"The nature of experience in the philosophy of self". *Iqbal Review* 1, 3 (October 1960), pp. 41-57.

2035   **Kamran, Gilani**
"Iqbal's *Javid namah"*. *Iqbal Review* 25, 1 (April 1984), pp. 59-62.

2036   **Khan, Jaliluddin Ahmad**
"Iqbal as poet with a message to the modern world". *Iqbal Review* 4 (July 1963), pp. 85-94.

2037   **Khan, Masud Husain**
"Iqbal's concept of art. After the formation of his philosophy of ego or the self". Trans. Mirza Khalil A. Beg. *Indian Literature* 10, 9 (September-October 1985), pp. 212-220. An essay from *Iqbal ki nazari-o-amali sheriyar.*

2038   **Khan, N.A.**
"Tagore and Iqbal". *Indo-Iranica* 14, 3 (September 1961), pp. 44-56.

2039   **Khan, Sadaat Ali**
"A note on Iqbal". *Indian Art and Letters* (17 November 1943), pp. 71-73.

2040   **Khan, Zulfiqar Ali**
A voice from the east: or, the poetry of Iqbal. Karachi: Iqbal Academy, 1966. 42p. First published. Lahore, 1922.

2041   — • "A voice from the east or the poetry of Iqbal". *Iqbal Review* 7, 1 (April 1966), pp. 1-42.

2042   **Khanum, Sajida Adeeb**
Iqbal as a philosopher. Hyderabad: Abul Kalam Azad Oriental Research Institute, 1982. 113p.

2043   **Khatoon, Jamilah**
"Iqbal's perfect man". *Iqbal* 1, 1 (July 1952), pp. 57-64.

2044   — • "Iqbal's theory of knowledge". *Iqbal Review* 1, 1 (April 1960), pp. 91-104.

2045   — • *The place of God, man and universe in the philosophical system of Iqbal.* Karachi: Iqbal Academy, 1969.

2046   **Khawar, Rafiq**
"Iqbal: a re-examination, his thoughts". *Illustrated Weekly of Pakistan* 5, 28 (26 April 1952), pp. 12-33.

2047   **Khayal, Taj Muhammad**
Iqbal as a thinker. Lahore: Shaikh Muhammad Ashraf, 1944. 304p.

2048   — • "Iqbal's conception of satan". *Iqbal* 2, 1 (July 1953), pp. 1-17.

2049 Khorasnee, Ameen
"A ghazal". *Iqbal Review* 9, 1 (April 1968), pp. 76-79.

2050 Khrishniah, S.
"The spirit of Iqbal". *Thought* 6, 33 (14 August 1954), pp. 10-11.

2051 —• "Iqbal: poet of socialism". *Link* 15, 29 (25 February 1973), p. 33.

2052 Khullar, K.K.
"Iqbal, Firaq and others". *Thought* 26, 48 (7 December 1974), pp. 15-17.

2053 Khundmiri, Alam
"Iqbal and the revaluation of man". In: *Poetry and renaissance: Kumaran Asan birth centenary volume*. Ed. M. Govindan. Madras: Sameeksha, 1974, pp. 107-114.

2054 —• *Some aspects of Iqbal's poetic philosophy*. Srinagar: Iqbal Institute on behalf of the University of Kashmir, 1980. 74p.
Includes Persian and Urdu text.

2055 Khwaja Masud
"Iqbal on creativity". *Viewpoint* (Lahore) 6, 40 (May 1981), pp. 28-30.

2056 —• "Iqbal's mission: destruction of false gods". *Viewpoint* (Lahore) 9, 14 (November 1983), pp. 11-32.

2057 Kidwai, Saleem
"Iqbal - philosophic poet". *Indian Literature* 18, 3 (July-September 1975), pp. 71-82.

2058 Koehler, Wolfgang
Muhammad Iqbal und die drei Reiches des Geistes. Muhammad Iqbal and the three realms of the spirits. Hamburg: Deutsch-Pakistanisches Forum, 1977. 278p.
Research paper.

2059 Lall, Inder Jit
"Muhammad Iqbal: a poet of stress and struggle". *The Statesman* (22 April 1967), pp. 6: 4.

2060 —• "Muhammad Iqbal - star of the east". *Thought* 25, 16 (21 April 1973), pp. 19-20.

2061 Lamb, Christopher
"Iqbal and interfaith dialogue". *Iqbal Review* 29, 3 (October-December 1988), pp. 115-120.

2062 Latif, Saiyyid Abdul
"Iqbal and world order". *Osmania Magazine* 11, 5 (Hyderabad, Deccan, 1938).

2063 Mahmood, Fayyaz
"Iqbal's attitude towards God". In: *Thinker*. (Lahore, 1944).

2064 **Mahmud, Sayyid Fayyaz**
"The man of action in Iqbal's poetry". *Iqbal* 15, 1 (July 1966), pp. 47-55.

2065 **Maitre, Luce-Claude**
Introduction to the thought of Iqbal. Trans. M.A.M. Dar. Karachi: Iqbal Academy, 1961. 53p.

2066 — • "Un grand humaniste oriental: Mohammad Iqbal". *Orient* 4, 13 (1960), pp. 81-94.
Also in: "Iqbal, a great humanist". *Iqbal Review* 11, 1 (April 1961), pp. 22-34.

2067 — • *Introduction à la Pensée d'Iqbal.* Paris, 1955.
Translated into English by M.A.M. Dar, *Introduction to the thought of Iqbal,* Karachi: Iqbal Academy, 1961.

2068 **Majeed, A.**
"An analysis of a couplet in Iqbal's *Bang-e-Dara".* *Pakistan Review* 19, 6 (June 1971), pp. 10-11.

2069 **Majid, M.A.**
"Anecdotes pertaining to Allama Iqbal". *Pakistan Review* 14, 4 (April 1966), pp. 13-15.

2070 — • "An appreciation of Guru Nanak in Iqbal's poetry". *Studies in Islam* 5 (July 1968), pp. 46-160.

2071 — • "Iqbal and Girami - anecdotes". *Pakistan Review* 15, 4 (April 1967), pp. 30-31.

2072 — • "Random recitals from Iqbal". *Pakistan Review* 14, 4 (April 1966), pp. 20-21.

2073 **Malik, Ghulam Rasool**
Iqbal and the English romantics. New Delhi: Atlantic Publishers and Distributors, 1988.

2074 **Malik, Hafeez**
"Iqbal's conception of ego". *Muslim World* 60, 2 (April 1970), pp. 160-169.
Presented at the American Oriental Society Annual Meeting, New Haven, Conn., on March 23, 1967.

2075 — • *Iqbal: poet-philosopher of Pakistan.* New York: Columbia University Press, 1969. 441p.

2076 **Malik, Mohammad Jafar**
"Iqbal's concept: conflict between good and evil". *Viewpoint* (Lahore) 5, 14 (11 November 1979), pp. 7-8; 5, 16 (25 November 1979), pp. 7-8, 30.

2077 **Marek, Jan**
"The date of Muhammad Iqbal's birth". *Archiv Orientalni* 26 (Prague, 1958), pp. 617-620.

2078 — • "Socialist ideas in the poetry of Muhammad Iqbal". *Studies in Islam* 5 (July 1968), pp. 167-179.

2079   Maricar, N.M. Sultan
"Iqbal: the Muslim International poet". *Islamic Review and Arab Affairs* 50 (April 1962), pp. 28-31.

2080   Maruf, Mohammed
Iqbal and his contemporary western religious thought. Lahore: Iqbal Academy Pakistan, 1987. 312p.

2081   — • *Contributions to Iqbal's thought.* Lahore: Islamic Book Service, 1977.

2082   — • *Iqbal's philosophy of religion: a study in the cognitive value of religious experience.* Lahore: Islamic Book Service, 1977. 267p.

2083   Masud-ul-Hasan
Life of Iqbal: general account of his life. Lahore: Ferozsons, 1976.

2084   May, Lini S.
Iqbal: his life and times, 1877-1938. Lahore: Shaikh Muhammad Ashraf, 1974. 347p.

2085   — • "Iqbal". *Iqbal* (Lahore) 1, 6 (January 1958), pp. 28-60.
Brief biography and summary of Iqbal's philosophy.

2086   McCarthy, Edward
"Iqbal as a poet and philosopher". *Iqbal Review* 2, 3 (October 1961), pp. 18-23.

2087   Memon, Muhammad Umar
Iqbal: poet and philsopher between east and west. Madison: South Asian Studies, University of Wisconson, Publication No. 4, 1979. 119p.

2088   Menon, K.P.S.
"Message of Iqbal". *Indian Review* (1925), pp. 506-509.

2089   Minai, I.A.
"Iqbal: The realist". *Illutrated Weekly of Pakistan* (18 June 1950), pp. 9-27.

2090   Mohan Singh
"Tagore, Puran Singh and Iqbal". *Sikh Review* 18, 190 (May 1969), pp. 36-37.

2091   Muhar, P.S.
"Political philosophy of Sir Muhammad Iqbal". *Indian Journal of Political Science* (Aligarh) 18, 3-4 (April 1966), pp. 22-25.

2092   Muizuddin, Mohammad
"Iqbal and Cambridge". *Pakistan Studies* 11, 1-2 (Spring 1983), pp. 70-74.

2093   Mujahid, Sharif
Allama Iqbal: poet philosopher of the east. 2nd ed. Karachi: Quaid-i-Azam Academy, 1986. 57p.

2094   **Munawwar, Muhammad**
"Allama Iqbal and the young generation". *Iqbal Review* 27, 1 (April-September 1986), pp. 63-80.

2095   — • "Allama Iqbal refusing to be called a poet". *Iqbal Review* 29, 1 (April-June 1988), pp. 209-235.

2096   — • *Dimensions of Iqbal.* Lahore: Iqbal Academy Pakistan, 1986. 165p.

2097   — • *Iqbal centenary papers.* Lahore: Dept. of Iqbal Studies, University of the Punjab, 1982. 2 vols.
English and Urdu.
Vol. 2 has title: *Maqalat: Jashn-i Iqbal Sadi.*
Papers of the International Congress on Allama Muhammed Iqbal sponsored by the University of the Punjab, Lahore, December 2-8 1977.

2098   — • "Iqbal - epoch making poet-philosopher". *Iqbal Review* 25, 3 (October 1984), pp. 107-128.

2099   — • "Iqbal - man of faith and vision". *Iqbal Review* 23, 3 (October 1982), pp. 1-33.

2100   — • "Iqbal on man's metaphorical death". *Iqbal Review* 24, 3 (October 1983), pp. 99-118.

2101   — • *Iqbal: poet-philosopher of Islam.* Lahore: Islamic Book Foundation, 1982. 207p.

2102   **Murshed, S.M.**
"Allama Iqbal". *Pakistan Review* 14, 8 (August 1966), pp. 6-7, 27; 14, 9 (September 1966), pp. 28-29.

2103   — • "Iqbal day at Lahore". *Iqbal Review* 8 (April 1967), pp. 1-12.

2104   — • "Iqbal's political thought". *Pakistan Review* 14, 10 (October 1966), pp. 6-7, 13.

2105   **Mustafa, Ghulam**
"The idea of God and Universe in Tagore and Iqbal". *Iqbal Review* 1, 3 (October 1960), pp. 26-34.

2106   — • "Iqbal: the philosopher-poet". *Iqbal Review* 1, 1 (April 1960), pp. 43-53.

2107   **Nadwi, Abul Hassan Ali**
Glory of Iqbal; Nuqush-i Iqbal. Trans. Muhammad Asif Kidwai. Lucknow: Academy of Islamic Research and Publications, 1973. 220p.

2108   **Nafiçy, Said**
"Mysticism in Iqbal's poetry". *Iqbal Review* 1, 1 (April 1960), pp. 5-9.

2109   **Naib, Raja Mohammad**
"Political philosophy of Iqbal". *Pakistan Review* 13, 10 (October 1965), pp. 16-21.

2110   **Naim, C.M.**
"The 'pseudo-dramatic' poems of Iqbal". In: *Iqbal: poet and philosopher between east and west*. Ed. Muhammad Umar Memon. Madison: University of Wisconsin Press, 1979, pp. 82-104.

2111   — • "The pseudo-dramatic of Iqbal". *Iqbal Review* 20, 1 (April 1979), pp. 1-12.

2112   **Naimuddin, Sayyid**
"The concept of love in Rumi and Iqbal". *Islamic Culture* 42, 4 (October 1968), pp. 185-210.

2113   — • "Evil and freewill in Rumi and Iqbal". *Islamic Culture* 46, 3 (July 1972), pp. 227-234.

2114   — • "The ideal man in Rumi and Iqbal". *Islamic Culture* 40, 2 (April 1971), pp. 81-94.

2115   **Nallino, M.**
"Recente Eco indo-Persiana della Divina Commedia: Mohammad Iqbal": *Oriente Moderno* 12, (Rome, 1932), pp. 210-223.

2116   **Namus, M. Shuja**
A discussion on Iqbal's philosophy of life. Lahore: Lion Press, 1974. 164p.
First published 1948.

2117   **Naqvi, S.A.H.**
"The concept of Iqbal's art". *Perspective* 4, 10 (April 1971), pp. 23-26.

2118   **Niaz A.Q.**
Iqbal's superman. Lahore, 1960. 122p.

2119   **Niazi, Shaheer**
"Diotima, Tahira and Iqbal". *Iqbal Review* 15, 3 (October 1974), pp. 22-29.

2120   **Niazi, S. Nasir**
"Conversation with Iqbal". In: *Mohammad Iqbal: poet and philosopher*. Karachi: Din Muhammad Press, 1960.

2121   **Nicholson, R.A.**
"Iqbal's 'Message of the east'". *Iqbal Review* 13, 3 (October 1972), pp. 6-16.

2122   — • "The secrets of the self: a Muslim poet's interpretation of vitalism". *The Quest* (July 1920).

2123   — • "Summary of the paper on the 'Asrar-i khudi'". *Journal of the Royal Asiatic Society* (January 1920), pt. 1, pp. 142, 143.

2124   **Pakistan-German Forum**
Mohammad Iqbal, poet and philosphers. Karachi, 1960.

2125 **Pirzada, S.A.A.**
"Iqbal's concept of self". *Pakistan Review* 14, 4 (April 1966), pp. 10-12.

2126 *Poèzia Muhammad Iqbala.* Moscow: Nauka, 1972. 193p.

2127 *Poètika tvorchestva Muhammada Iqbal.* Moscow: Nauka, 1978.

2128 **Prigarina, N.I.**
"A new Soviet book on Iqbal". *Viewpoint* (Lahore) 5, 25 (January 1980), p. 25.

2129 **Qadir, Qazi A.**
"Physical world and the principle of cosmic dynamics (about the concept of 'ishq')", *Iqbal Review* 2, 1 (April 1961), pp. 45-50.

2130 **Qarshi, Afzal Haq**
"A rare writing of Iqbal". *Iqbal Review* 24, 1 (April 1983), pp. 39-42.

2131 **Qasimi, Ahmad Nadim**
Allama Muhammad Iqbal, 1877-1938. Trans. M. Salim-ur-Rahman. Lahore: Board for Advancement of Literature, 1977.

2132 **Qureshi, M.A.**
"Some aspects of Iqbal's biography". *Iqbal* 7, 1 (July 1958), pp. 63-71.

2133 — • "Iqbal and Firaq". *Iqbal* (April 1960).

2134 — • "Iqbal in the witness box". *Iqbal Review* 2, 1 (April 1961), pp. 35-44.

2135 **Rafique, M.**
"The problem of suffering in Iqbal's philosophy". *Studies in Islam* 5, 2-3 (April 1968), pp. 114-119.

2136 — • *Sri Aurobindo and Iqbal: a comparative study of their philosophy.* Aligarh: Aligarh Muslim University, 1974.

2137 **Rafiuddin, Dr Mohammad**
"Iqbal's idea of the self". *Iqbal Review* 4, 3 (October 1963), pp. 1-31.

2138 — • "Iqbal's concept of evolution". *Iqbal Review* 1, 1 (April 1960), pp. 20-42.

2139 — • "The philosophy of Iqbal, its nature and importance". *Iqbal Review* 2, 3 (October 1961), pp. 86-129.

2140 **Rahman, Khwaja Abdul**
"Iqbal's philosophy of the self". *Iqbal* 2, 1 (July 1953), pp. 35-45.

2141 — • *Iqbal, the poet of tomorrow.* Lahore: Markaziyya Majlis-i-Iqbal, 1968. 273p.

2142 **Rahman, Fazlur**
"Some aspects of Iqbal's political thought". *Studies in Islam* 5, 2-3 (April 1968), pp. 161-166.

2143 **Rahmatullah, Shahabuddin**
"Art in Iqbal's poetry". *Illustrated Weekly of Pakistan* (21 April 1957), p. 32.

2144 — • "Imagery in Iqbal". *Iqbal Review* 16, 1 (April 1975), pp. 6-13.

2145 **Raju, Dr P.T.**
"The idealism of Sir Muhammad Iqbal". *Vishvabharati Quarterly* NS 6, 2 (August-October 1940).

2146 **Ras, Venkata**
"The secrets of the self: a study of Iqbal's poem 'Asrar-i khudi'". *Trivani* 14, (1942).

2147 **Raschid, M.**
"Iqbal - poet and thinker". *Pakistan Review* 13 (April 1965), pp. 3-71.

2148 **Rastogi, Tara Charan**
Western influence in Iqbal. New Delhi: Ashish Publishing House, 1987. 282p.

2149 **Rasul, Abdar**
"Iqbal and the reconstruction of mankind". *Islamic Literature* 10, 5 (May 1958), pp. 43-48.

2150 **Rasul, M.G.**
"Rumi and Iqbal". *Islamic Literature* 6, 4 (April 1954), pp. 31-36.

2151 **Riaz, Muhammad**
"Arberry and his translation of Iqbal's works". *Journal of Pakistan Historical Society* 29, pt. 4 (October 1981), pp. 223-237.

2152 — • "Influence of Baba Faghani's style on Iqbal". *Journal of the Pakistan Historical Society* 16 (October 1968), pp. 220-230.

2153 **Rizvi, J.H.**
"Iqbal as a poet". *Perspective* 2, 10 (April 1969), pp. 14-18.

2154 **Rofe, Husein**
"The spiritual message of Iqbal". *Islamic Literature* 5, 4 (April 1953), pp. 23-26.

2155 **Roy, N.B.**
"The background of Iqbal's poetry". *Visvabharati Quarterly* 20, 4 (Spring (1955), pp. 321-331.

2156 **Saeed, Ahmad**
"Iqbal on Tipu Sultan". *Pakistan Review* 17, 4 (April 1969), pp. 41-44.

2157 **Safiullah, Syed**
"Nationalism and Dr Mohammed Iqbal". *Annals of Oriental Research* 31, 2 (1983), pp. 1-6.

2158 Sahsrami, Kalim
"Eqbal's philosophy of Muslim renaissance". *Islamic Literature* 6, 4 (April 1954), pp. 43-46.

2159 Saiyidain, Khwaja Ghulam
Iqbal's educational philosophy. Lahore: Shaikh Muhammad Ashraf, 1954. 248p.
Partly published first in *Islamic Culture* (Hyderabad, Deccan, 1938).

2160 Schimmel, Annemarie
"The ascension of the poet", In: *Mohammad Iqbal: poet and philosopher*. Pakistan-German Forum. Karachi: Din Muhammad Press, 1960.

2161 — • *Classical Urdu literature from the beginning to Iqbal*. Wiesbaden: Otto Harrassowitz, 1975. (*A history of Indian literature*. Ed. Jan Gonda, vol. 8, fasc. 3).

2162 — • *Gabriel's wing: a study into the religious ideas of Sir Muhammad Iqbal*. Leiden: E.J. Brill, 1963. 428p.
Includes extensive bibliography.

2163 — • "The idea of prayer in the thought of Iqbal". *The Muslim World* 68 (July 1958). Reprinted in *Mohammad Iqbal: poet and philosopher*. Pakistan-German Forum. Karachi: Din Muhammad Press, 1960.

2164 — • "Ikbal, Muhammad". In: *Encyclopaedia of Islam*. New ed. 3 (1968-1971), pp. 1057-1059.

2165 — • "Iqbal and Hallaj". In: *Mohammad Iqbal: poet and philosopher*. Pakistan-German Forum. Karachi: Din Muhammad Press, 1960.

2166 — • "Iqbal in foreign countries". *Morning News* (22 April 1962), p. 7.

2167 — • "The *Javidname* in the light of the comparative history of religions". *Pakistan Quarterly* 6, 4 (1956), pp. 29-32.

2168 — • "Muhammad Iqbal as seen by a European historian of religion". *Studies in Islam* 5, 2-3 (April 1968), pp. 53-82.

2169 — • "Muhammad Iqbal: the ascension of the poet". *Die Welt des Islam* 3 (Leiden, 1954).

2170 — • "Mohammad Iqbal and German thought". In: *Mohammad Iqbal: poet and philosopher*. Pakistan-German Forum. Karachi: Din Muhammad Press, 1960.

2171 — • "Time and eternity in Muhammad Iqbal's work". *Proceedings X. Congress for the History of Religions*, Marburg, 1962.

2172 — • "The western influence on Sir Muhammad Iqbal's thought". *Proceedings of the International Congress for the History of Religions,* Tokyo 1960.
Reprinted in *Civil and Military Gazette* (Lahore, 21 April 1962).
Also in : *Pakistan Times* (21 April 1961), p. 10.

2173　—• "Where east meets west". *Pakistan Quarterly* (1 August 1966), pp. 18-20.

2174　—• *Iqbal and education* (papers read at the seminar sponsored by Jamia College, Karachi, on April 22-24, 1966). Karachi: Jamia Institute of Education, 1966. 132p.

2175　**Shafi, Ahmad**
"A poet of Islam - Sir Muhammad Iqbal". *Modern Review* (Allahabad) 54 (December 1933), pp. 619-624.

2176　**Shahid, Muhammad Haneef**
"Iqbal and the Saudi scholars". *Iqbal Review* 29, 1 (April-June 1988), pp. 157-167.

2177　**Shaikh, H.**
"Iqbal's flaming passion". *Dawn* (21 April 1957).

2178　**Shakir, Moin**
"Mohammad Iqbal". *Quest* 101 (May-June 1976), pp. 27-32.

2179　—• "Secularism and Iqbal". *Mainstream* 10, 8 (23 October 1971), pp. 24-26.

2180　**Shamsi, Muhammad Ahmad**
"Iqbal and the western thought". *Iqbal Review* 21, 1 (April 1980), pp. 47-60.

2181　**Sharif, M.M.**
About Iqbal and his thought. Lahore: Institute of Islamic Culture, 1964. 116p.

2182　—• "The genesis of Iqbal's aesthetics". *Iqbal* 1, 1 (1952), pp. 19-40.

2183　—• "Iqbal's conception of God". *Islamic Culture* (Hyderabad, Deccan 1942). Reprinted in: *Thinker* (Lahore 1944).

2184　—• "Iqbal on the nature of time". *Iqbal Review* 1, 3 (October 1960), pp. 35-40.

2185　—• "Iqbal's theory of art". *Iqbal* 2, 3 (January 1954), pp. 1-8.

2186　**Sharif, Saad**
"Iqbal - an appreciation". *Pakistan Review* 16, 5 (May 1968), pp. 26-27.

2187　**Sheikh, Hasiena**
"Iqbal on national character". *Evening Star* (21 April 1962), p. 2.

2188　**Sheikh, M. Saeed**
Studies in Iqbal's thought and art. Select articles from the *Quarterly Iqbal*. Lahore: Bazm-i-Iqbal, 1972. 518p.

2189　**Siddiqi, M. Raziuddin**
"Iqbal and free will". *Pakistan Quarterly* 4, 3 (August 1954), pp. 19-23, 50-52.

2190　**Siddiqui, Marghub**
"Iqbal represents cultural dead lock". *Civil and Military Gazette* (21 April 1954).

2191   **Siddiqui, Misbah-ul-Haq**
Iqbal: a critical study. Lahore: Farhan Pub., 1977. 257p.

2192   **Siddiqui, Muhammad Mazharuddin**
Concept of Muslim culture in Iqbal. Islamabad: Islamic Research Institute, 1970.
Reprinted 1983. 144p.

2193   — • *The image of the west in Iqbal*. Lahore: Bazm-i-Iqbal, 1964. 148p.

2194   — • "An historical study of Iqbal's views of sufism". *Islamic Studies* 5, 4 (December
1966), pp. 411-427.

2195   — • "Iqbal's principle of movement and its application to the present Muslim
society". *Islamic Studies* 5, 1 (March 1966), pp. 9-42.

2196   **Siddiqui, Nazir**
Iqbal and Radhakrishnan: a comparative study. New Delhi: Sterling Publishers, 1989. 122p.
Includes Urdu text.

2197   **Sinha, Sachchidananda**
Iqbal: the poet and his message. Allahabad: Ram Narain Lal, 1947. 512p.

2198   **Slomp, Jan**
"The triangle: Hafiz, Goethe and Iqbal". In: *Main currents of contemporary thought in
Pakistan*. Ed. Hakim Muhammad Said. Karachi: Hamdard Academy, 1973, pp. 388-414.

2199   **Smith, Wilfred Cantwell**
"Iqbal". In his: *Modern Islam in India*. Lahore: Minverva Book Shop, 1943, 475p.

2200   **Sorley, Herbert Tower**
"Iqbal". In: *Musa Pervagans*. Aberdeen: Aberdeen University Press, 1953, pp. 169-203.

2201   **Sprengling, M.**
"A tonal tribute to Iqbal". *Pakistan Quarterly* 6, 2 (1957).

2202   **Stepanyants, M.T.**
"Problem of ethics in Mohammad Iqbal's philosophy". *Iqbal Review* 14, 1 (April 1973),
pp. 1-8.

2203   **Subhan, A.**
"Relevance of Iqbal's message to India". *Indian and Foreign Review* 13, 14 (May 1976),
pp. 22-23.

2204   **Sud, Kedar Nath**
"Iqbal and Pakistan". *Mainstream* 7, 33 (19 April 1969), pp. 32-33.

2205   — • *Iqbal and his poems; a reappraisal*. Delhi: Sterling Publishers, 1969. 137p.

2206   **Sultana, Farrukh**
"Iqbal's concept of power". *Pakistan Review* 14, 11 (November 1966), pp. 6-8.

2207   — • "Iqbal - the poet philosopher". *Pakistan Review* 17, 4 (April 1969), pp. 45-47.

2208   — • "Iqbal on social reconstruction". *Islamic Literature* 12, 4 (April 1966), pp. 27-32.

2209   — • "Status of women in Iqbal's thought". *Pakistan Review* 16, 5 (May 1968), pp. 35-36.
Also in: *Islamic Literature* 17, 1 (January 1971), pp. 49-54.

2210   **Syed, J.W.**
"Poetry: an expression of the self". *Iqbal Review* 2, 3 (October 1961), pp. 71-78.

2211   **Tafferel, G.**
"Notice biografiche su Mohammad Iqbal". *Oriente Moderno* 18 (Rome, 1938), pp. 322-323.

2212   **Talib, Gurbachan Singh**
"Iqbal's poetic achievement: an estimate". *Indian P.E.N.* 41, 2. pp. 6-9.

2213   **Tariq, A.S.**
"The Javedname". *Pakistan Quarterly* 6, 4, pp. 29-32.

2214   **Tariq, A.R.**
"Iqbal and nationalism". *Pakistan Review* 15, 4 (April 1967), pp. 13-17.

2215   — • "Iqbal's dream of Pakistan". *Pakistan Review* 14, 4 (April 1966), pp. 4-6.

2216   — • "Iqbal in the Persian speaking world". *Pakistan Review* 15, 4 (April 1967), pp. 12-15.

2217   — • *Speeches and statements of Iqbal.* Lahore: Shaikh Ghulam Ali, 1973. 246p.

2218   **Taseer, M.D.**
"Iqbal and the ghazal". *Pakistan Quarterly* 1, 1 (April 1949), pp. 28-40.

2219   — • "Iqbal's theory of art and literature". *Pakistan Quarterly* 1, 3 (1949), pp. 15, 71.

2220   — • *Iqbal: the universal poet.* Lahore: Munib Pub., 1977. 75p.

2221   — • "Iqbal: the universal poet". *Pakistan Quarterly* 5, 3 (1955), pp. 40, 41.

2222   **Thapar, R.**
"Muhamed Iqbal". *Eastern World* 9 (August 1955), pp. 35-36.

2223   "Three unpublished letters of Iqbal's". Trans. K.A. Nizami. *Studies in Islam* 5 (July 1968), pp. 188-192.

2224   *Tributes to the late Professor Muhammad Iqbal (1894-1948) by his friends and family.*
Trans. Daud Rahbar. Hartford, 1964. 116p.

2225 **Tufail, Mian Muhammad**
Iqbal's philosophy and education. Lahore: Bazm-i-Iqbal, 1966. 144p.

2226 *Tvorchestvo Muhammada Iqbala: sbornik statei*. Moscow: Nauka, 1982. 251p.
Articles by soviet scholars.

2227 **Usmani, Muhammad Ahmad**
Khudi through sex, and other philosophical essays. Lahore: Philosophical Publciations, 1967.
159p.

2228 **Vahid, Syed Abdul**
"A.J. Arberry, a great student of Iqbal". *Iqbal Review* 13, 1 (April 1972), pp. 37-50.

2229 — • "Date of Iqbal's birth". *Iqbal Review* 5 (October 1964), pp. 21-32.

2230 — • *Glimpses of Iqbal*. Karachi: Iqbal Academy, 1974. 240p.

2231 — • "The greatness of Iqbal". *Iqbal Review* 15, 1 (April 1974), pp. 8-12.

2232 — • *Introduction to Iqbal*. Karachi: Pakistan Publications, 1952. 67p.

2233 — • "Iqbal and Afghanistan". *Pakistan Review* 15, 3 (March 1967), p. 17.

2234 — • "Iqbal and Browning". *Iqbal Review* 6, 1 (April 1965), pp. 73-95.

2235 — • "Iqbal and Dante". *Pakistan Quarterly* 1, 6, pp. 51-54, 72.

2236 — • "Iqbal and his greatness". *Pakistan Times* (21 April 1961), p. 3.

2237 — • "Iqbal and Italy". *Pakistan Review* 15, 4 (April 1967), pp. 9-11.

2238 — • *Iqbal, his art and thought*. Hyderabad (Deccan), 1944.

[Another ed.] London: John Murray, 1959.

2239 — • "Iqbal and his critics". *Iqbal Review* 5, 1 (April 1964), pp. 1-13.

2240 — • "Iqbal and his poetry". *Islamic Review* 13, 4 (1954), pp. 30-34.

2241 — • "Iqbal as a poet". *Pakistan* 1, 1 (September 1948), pp. 12-23.

2242 — • "Iqbal and Milton". *Pakistan Quarterly* 7, 2 (1957).
Reprinted in *Iqbal: his art and thought*. London, 1959.

2243 — • "The message of Iqbal for our time". *Perspective* 2, 10 April 1969), pp. 7-11.

2244 — • "On translating Iqbal". *Pakistan Review* 15, 10 (October 1967), pp. 28-34.

2245 — • "Iqbal - a survey of his work". *Iqbal Review* 14, 1 (April 1973), pp. 61-68.
Also in: *Studies in Islam* 5 (July 1968), pp. 129-145.

2246 — • *Studies in Iqbal*. Lahore: Shaikh Muhammad Ashraf, 1967. 364p.

2247 — • *Thoughts and reflections of Iqbal*. Lahore: Shaikh Muhammad Ashraf, 1964. 381p.

2248 **Vahiduddin, Syed**
"Iqbal and mysticism". *Studies in Islam* 5 (July 1968), pp. 180-187.

2249 — • "Tradition and modernity in Iqbal's philosophical thought". *Islamic Culture* 61, 3 (July 1987), pp. 1-29.

2250 **Valiuddin, Mir**
"Iqbal's concepts of love and reasons". *Studies in Islam* 5, 2-3 (April 1968), pp. 83-113.

2251 — • *A voice from the east: the poetry of Iqbal*. Trans. Sardar Umrao Singh. Lahore: Mercantile Electric Press, 1922. 47p.
Includes translations and texts from Urdu and Persian.

2252 **Victor Courtois, S.J.**
"Sir Muhammad Iqbal, poete, philosophe et apologiste indien". *Terre d'Islam* 13, 4 (Trim. 1938), 3. Sér., No. 4.

2253 **Waheeduddin, Fakir Syed**
Iqbal in pictures. Karachi: Lion Art Press, 1965.
A pictorial biography of Iqbal.

2254 **Waliur Rahman**
"Iqbal's doctrine of destiny". *Islamic Culture* 13, 2 (April 1930), pp. 150-175.

2255 **Waqarur Rahman**
"Iqbal's role in the Pakistan Movement". *Pakistan Review* 16, 6 (June 1968), pp. 14-18.

2256 **Wheeler, R.S.**
"The individual and action in the thought of Iqbal". *Muslim World* 52, 3 (July 1962), pp. 197-206.

2257 **Yahya al-Khash-Shab**
"Iqbal". *Iqbal Review* 16, 1 (April 1975), pp. 66-70.

2258 **Zaidi, Nasir Hasan**
"Imagery in Iqbal's poetry". *Pakistan Review* 17, 4 (April 1969), pp. 38-40.

2259 — • "Iqbal's view of art". *Pakistan Review* 6, 10 (October 1958), pp. 43-44.

2260 **Ziauddin, M.**
"Iqbal the poet-philosopher of Islam". *Vishvabharati Quarterly* NS 4, 1 (May-July 1938).

2261   **Zu al Fakar Ali Khan**
A voice from the east: or the poetry of Iqbal. Lahore, 1922. 47p.
Translation from Hindustani by Umrao Singh.
Translation from Persian by R.A. Nicholson.
Includes extracts from Iqbal's Persian and Hindustani poetry in the original and in English translations.

ISLAM, KHURSHIDUL

2262   "Thirst". Trans. Inder Jit Lall. *Indian Literature* 13, 3 (July 1974), pp. 134-135.

JAFRI, ADA

TRANSLATIONS

2263   "Three poems". Trans. Rafiq Khawar. *Perspective* 3, 12 (June 1970), pp. 91-96.
— • "Aqsa Mosque".
— • "al-Fatah".
— • "Mother".

STUDY

2264   **Noorani, Asif**
["An interview with Ada Jafarey"]. *The Herald* (Karachi), (September 1989), pp. 111-114.

JAFRI, ALI SARDAR

TRANSLATIONS

2265   "Robe of sparks". Trans. Gopi Chand Narang and Richard H. Robinson. *Indian Literature* 10, 2 (1967), p. 21.

2266   "Who is the enemy? Evening of Tashkent". Trans. C.M. Naim. *Journal of Asian Studies* 28 (February 1969), pp. 278-80.

STUDY

2267   "Ali Sardar Jafri in town". *Viewpoint* (Lahore) 8, 44 (9 June 1983), p. 26.

JALIB, HABIB

2268   ["An interview with Habib Jalib"]. *The Herald* (Karachi), (March 1985), pp. 112-117.

JIGAR MURADABADI, ALI SIKANDER

TRANSLATIONS

2269   "Ghazal". Trans. Rahm Ali al Hasmi and Tembimuttur. *Poetry* 93, 4 (January 1959), pp. 235-237.

2270   "A poem". Trans. P. Machwe. In: *Modern Indian poetry*. Ed. A.V. Rajeswara Rao. New Delhi: Kavita, 1958.

STUDIES

2271   **Hasan, Mohammad**
"Jigar Muradabadi's *Atish-i gul*". *Indian Literature* 2, 2 (April-September 1959), pp. 121-126.

2272   **Lall, Inder Jit**
"Jigar Moradabadi - an introductory note". *Poetry India* 1, 3 (July-September 1966), pp. 47-50.

2273   **Mittal, Gopal**
"Jigar Moradabadi - an appreciation". *Thought* 12, 42 (15 October 1960), pp. 12-13.

JOSH MALIHABADI, SHABBIR HASAN KHAN

TRANSLATIONS

2274   "Poets of India". Trans. Ajit Kumar. *Indian Literature* 30, 3 (May-June 1987), pp. 14-16.
Indexes a version in Roman characters - entitled 'Shair-e-Hindustani'.

2275   "Girl looking for light". Trans. Alamgir Hashmi. In: *Nimrods sin: treason and translation in a multilingual world*. Ed. Norman Simms. Hamilton, New Zealand: Outrigger Publishers, 1983, p. 23.

STUDIES

2276   Ali, Mirza Nasir
"Josh Malihabadi". *Quest* 34 (November 1962), pp. 51-58.

2277   "Josh Malihabadi". *Quest* 35 (October 1962), pp. 57-70.

2278   Haidar, Iqbal
Josh: the poet of the century. Calgary: Josh Literary Society, 1986. 80p.
Proceedings of a Conference held in 1985.

2279   Kohli, Suresh
"Of Josh and Firaq". *Viewpoint* (Lahore) 8, 45 (June 1982), pp. 30-31.

2280   Shamsi, Mohammad Ahmad
"Josh: an agnostic or a believer". *Journal of the Pakistan Study Centre* (University of Peshawar) 1, 3 (Spring 1981), pp. 9-23.

JURAT, QALANDAR BAKHSH

STUDIES

2281   Ansari, A.S. Bazmee
"Djurat". In: *Encyclopaedia of Islam* 2, (1965), p. 602.

2282   Faruqi, Shamsur Rahman
"Jurat's *sahr-asob*: an afterword". *Annual of Urdu Studies* 3 (1983), pp. 11-16.

2283   "In the presence of the nightingale: a sahr-ashob". Trans. Shamsur Rahman Faruqi and Frances W. Pritchett. *Annual of Urdu Studies* 3 (1983), pp. 1-10.

KAMRAN, GILANI

TRANSLATIONS

2284   "Bird, o bird". Trans. Alamgir Hashmi. *Orbis* (England) 46-47 (1982), pp. 32-33.

2285   "The old bookseller". Trans. C.M. Naim. *Mahfil* 2, 2 (May 1965), p. 51.

2286   "Urdu poems". Trans. Alamgir Hashmi. *Translation* 7 (Fall 1980), pp. 147-149.

KAZMI, BASIR SULTAN

TRANSLATION

2287   "Eyes". Trans. Alamgir Hashmi. *Orbis* (England) 46-47 (1982), pp. 32-33.

KHAN, INAYAT

TRANSLATION

2288   *Diwan of Inayat Khan.* Trans. Jessie Duncan Westbrook. London: Sufi Publishing Society, 1915. 48p.

KHUSRAU, AMIR

STUDIES

2289   **Abdurrahman, Sabahuddin**
Amir Khusrao or a genius. Delhi: Idarah-i Adabiyat-i Delhi, 1982. 125p.
Quotations in Persian and Urdu.

2290   *Amir Khusrau: memorial volume.* New Delhi: Publications Division, Ministry of Information and Broadcasting, 1975. 208p.

2291   **Ansari, Noorul Hasan**
"Amir Khusrao, the poet and patriot". *Indo-Iranica* 3, 9 (1986), pp. 1-4, pp. 88-99.

2292   **Enayatullah, Anwar**
"Amir Khusrau". *Pakistan Review* 7, 1 (January 1959), pp. 31-32.

2293   **Habib, Muhammad**
Hazrat Amir Khusrao of Delhi. Bombay: D.B. Taraporevala Sons and Co., 1927. 110p.

2294   **Haider, Azimusshan**
"The romance of Deval Rani and Khizr Khan; 'Ashiqa' - a historical mathnavi of Amir Khusrao". *Perspective* 1, 12 (June 1968), pp. 43-48.

2295   **Lall, Inder Jit**
"Amir Khusrau". *Century* 1, 43 (14 March 1964), p. 10

2296   **Mirza, Muhammad Wahid**
The life and works of Amir Khusrao. Lahore: University of the Punjab, 1962. 262p.

2297   — • "Amir Khusrau: review of life and works of Amir Khusrao". *Islamic Culture*
8 (1935), pp. 165-1968.

2298   **Naidu, S.S.R.**
"Amir Khusro and his contribution to Hindi language and literature". *Annals of Oriental Research* 21, 2 (1967), pp. 1-9.

2299   **Samnani, Saiyid Ghulam**
Amir Khusrao. New Delhi: National Book Trust, 1968. 78p.

KOMAL, BALRAJ

TRANSLATIONS

2300   "Empty vessel". Trans. the author. In: *New generation three*. Eds. Ramlal and
Syeda Naseem Chishti. Lucknow: New Generation, 1968, pp. 84-93.

2301   "Infirm sandy shore". *Thought* 6, 24 (12 June 1954), p. 11.

2302   "Leisure". *Thought* 6, 22 (29 May 1954), p. 10.

2303   *Selected poems of Balraj Komal*. Ed. and trans. Leslie Lavigne and Baidar Bakht.
Delhi: Educational Publishing House, 1989. 113p.
Includes Urdu text.

2304   "Three Poems. Trans. the author. *Poetry India* 2, 1 (January-March 1967), pp. 20-21.
— • "The circus horse".
— • "The Martyr".
— • "The tin parrots".

2305   "Two poems". Trans. Baidar Bakht and Leslie Lavigne. *Annual of Urdu Studies* 6
(1987), p. 42.
— • "Communication".
— • "Poem".

2306   "Two poems of Balraj Komal".   Trans. the author.   *Indian Literature* 29, 5
(September-October 1986), pp. 232-236.
— • "A river of falling stars".
— • "A sky full of birds".
Selection from *Parindon bhara asman*.

STUDY

2307   **Hanfee, Ameeq**
"An Urdu modern: Balraj Komal". *Poetry India* 2, 1 (January-March 1967), pp. 41-46.

MADANI, AZIZ HAMID

TRANSLATIONS

2308   "The final night". Trans. M. Salim-ur Rahman. *Pakistani Literature* (Islamabad) 1, 1 (1992), p. 65.

MAHDI, BAQIR

TRANSLATIONS

2309   "The black verse". Trans. K.K. Khullar. *Indian Literature* 23, 1-2 (1980), pp. 533-534.

2310   "The final cry". Trans. Baqir Mahdi and Adil Jussawalla. In: *New writing in India*. Ed. Adil Jussawalla. Baltimore: Penguin Books, 1974, pp. 207-208.

2311   "Haridwar". Trans. K.K Khullar. *Indian Literature* 23, 1-2 (1980), p. 537.

2312   "Nadan". Trans. K.K. Khullar. *Indian Literature* 23, 1-2 (1980), pp. 534-536.

MAHROTRA, SHANTI

TRANSLATION

2313   "On the canvas". Trans. Helen Ullrich and C.J.S. Jossan. *Books Abroad* 43, 4 (Autumn 1969), p. 549.

MAJAZ LAKHNAVI, ASRARUL HAQ

TRANSLATION

2314   "The vagabond". Trans. K. Shahid Husain. *Pakistan Quarterly* 10, 1 (Spring 1960), pp. 46-47.

STUDIES

2315   **Coppola, Carlo**
"Asrarul Haq Majaz: the progressive poet as revolutionary romantic". *Indian Literature* 24, 4 (July-August 1981), pp. 46-62.

2316   **Mittal, Gopal**
"Majaz, the double addict".   *Thought* 8, 7 (18 February 1956), p. 14.

2317   **Naqvi, S.A.H.**
"Asrarul Haq Majaz".   *Pakistan Review* 18, 7 (July 1970), pp. 34-36, 39.

2318   **Saleem, Ahmad**
"Asrarul Haq Majaz: his relevance".   *Viewpoint* (Lahore) 9, 27 (9 February 1984), pp. 27, 29.

2319   **Vasil'eva, L.**
"Lirika Majaza".   In: *Literatura i Vremia.* Moscow: Nauka, 1973, pp. 35-42.

MAKHDUM MOHIUDDIN

TRANSLATIONS

2320   "The hush".   Trans. Wahab Hyder.   *Century* 2, 2-3 (6 June 1964), p. 21.

2321   "Poems".   Trans. Shiv K. Kumar.   *Indian Literature* 28, 1 (January-February 1985), pp. 9-14.
— • "Baptism of fire".
— • "Dancing together".
— • "Darkness".
— • "The heart of silence".
— • "Prison".

STUDIES

2322   **Chandar, Krishan**
"Makhdoom: the warrior poet".   *Illustrated Weekly of India* 90, 39 (28 September 1969), pp. 51-52.

2323   **Coppola, Carlo**
"Two modes in the poetry of Makhdum Mohiyuddin".   *Indian Literature* 26, 1 (January-February 1983), pp. 43-68.

2324   **Gour, Raj Bahadur**
Makhdoom: a memoir. New Delhi: Communist Party Publication, 1970. 30p.

2325   "Makhdum Mohiuddin".   *Link* 12, 3 (31 August 1969), p. 33.

2326   **Sukhochev, A.S.**
Makhdum Mahiuddin. Moscow: Nauka, 1989.

MEERA JI

TRANSLATIONS

2327   "The story of the night in the guise of day".   Trans. Muzaffar Iqbal.   *Pakistani Literature* (Islamabad) 1, 1 (1992), pp. 47-49.

STUDY

2328   **Pashi, Kumar**
"Meeraji - a baffling poet".   *Pakistan Review* 13, 9 (September 1965), pp. 23-24.

MIR, SAFDAR

TRANSLATIONS

2329   "Poems".   Trans. Victor G. Kiernan.   *Annual of Urdu Studies* 6 (1987), pp. 68-70.
— • "City of the dead". p. 68.
— • "Dawn". p. 68.
— • "Snowfall". p. 69.
— • "War". pp. 69-70.

MIR TAQI MIR

TRANSLATIONS

2330   **Verma, Rajinder Singh**
Pick of Mir.   New Delhi: Enkay Publishers, 1989.   216p.

STUDIES

2331   **Ali, Ahmad**
"The anguished heart: Mir and the romantic imagination".   *Eastern Horizon* 6 (October 1967), pp. 52-57; (November 1967), pp. 44-48.

2332   "And now the pen brings forth some jokes".   Trans. C.M. Naim.   *Annual of Urdu Studies* 2 (1982), pp. 49-51.
Fifteen jokes taken from Mir Taqi Mir's autobiography in Persian called *Zikr-i Mir*.

2333   **Garcin de Tassy, Joseph Héliodore Sagesse Vertu**
Conseils aux mauvais poètes, poème de Mir Taki, traduit de l'hindostani.   Paris, 1826.   18p.

2334 **Hassan, Faruq**
"Mir and his poetry". *Pakistan Review* 10 (October 1962), pp. 28-31.

2335 **Ish, Kumar**
Mir Taqi Mir. New Delhi: Sahitya Akademi, 1972. 100p.
Life and works of Mir Taqi Mir.

2336 **Naz**
"Mir Taqi Mir". *Pakistan Review* 15 (July 1967), pp. 15-23.

2337 **Russell, Ralph**
"Themes of eighteenth century lyric poetry in the verse of Mir". In: *Sasibhusan Dasgupta commemoration volume.* Eds. R.K. Dasgupta and Sisir Kumar Das. Calcutta: New Age Publishers, [1968?], pp. 125-152.

2338 **Russell, Ralph and Islam, Khurshidul**
"The love poetry of Mir". In their *Three Mughal poets.* Cambridge: Harvard University Press, 1968, pp. 95-277.
Includes two other essays on Mir.

2339 **Siddiqi, Zaheer Ahmad**
["Review of *Mir Taqi Mir - Hayat aur shairi* by Khavaja Ahmad Faruqi"]. *Indian Literature* 26, 1 (1983), pp. 151-152.

2340 **Zain, Syed Abu Zafar**
"Mir Taqi Mir". *Pakistan Review* 13 (April 1965), pp. 16-17.

MISHRA, K.

TRANSLATION

2341 "Middle class family". Trans. R.O. Susan and C.J.S. Jossan. *Books Abroad* 43 (Autumn 1969), p. 549.

MITTAL, GOPAL

TRANSLATIONS

2342 "False dawn". *Thought* 6, 20 (15 May 1954), p. 10.

2343 "A poem". *Thought* 12, 2 (1960), p. 12.

2344 "The quest's end". Trans. Satindra Singh. *Thought* 14, 22 (2 June 1962), p. 11.

2345   "With the pen". *Thought* 15, 8 (23 February 1963), p. 13.

MOMIN, MOMIN KHAN

STUDY

2346   "Translation of Ghalib and Momin". Trans. Sufia Sadulla. *Pakistan Quarterly* 12, 2 (Winter 1964), p. 29.

NAHEED, KISHWAR

TRANSLATIONS

2347   "I am not that woman". Trans. Mahmud Jamal. In: *Stories from Asia*. Ed. John Welch. London: Oxford University Press, 1988, p. 109.

2348   "Poems by Kishwar Naheed". Trans. Baidar Bakht and Derek M. Cohen. *Urdu Canada* 1, 3 (1987), pp. 74-76.

2349   *The price of looking back: poems of Kishvar Naheed. Fitnah samani-yi dil.* Ed. Baidar Bakht. Trans. Baidar Bakht and Derek M. Cohen. Lahore: Book Traders, 1987. 112p.
With parallel Urdu text.

2350   *The scream of an illegitimate voice. Selection of poems of Kishwar Naheed.* Trans. Baidar Bakht, Leslie Lavigne and Derek M. Cohen. Lahore: Sang-e-Meel Publications, 1991. 166p.
A selection of one hundred poems. Includes notes on the author and the translators.

2351   "Three poems". Trans. C.M. Naim. *Annual of Urdu Studies* 4 (1984), pp. 75-77.
— • "Confession".
— • "The end of exploitation".
— • "I feel in my bones".

NASIKH, SHAIKH IMAM BAKHSH

TRANSLATION

2352   "Ghazal". Trans. Carl R. Petievich and Kenneth Bryant. *Urdu Canada* 1, 2 (November 1986), p. 76.

NAUSHAHI, GAUHAR

TRANSLATION

2353   "Come snake, bite my heel". Trans. C.M. Naim. *Mahfil* 2, 2 (May 1965), p. 52.

NAZ

TRANSLATION

2354   "Brain to the heart". *Pakistan Review* 16, 4 (April 1968), p. 33.

STUDY

2355   **Bashir, Saquib**
"Naz - writer of great potential". *Pakistan Review* 18, 8 (August 1970), pp. 19-20.

NAZIR AKBARABADI

TRANSLATIONS

2356   "The gipsy". Trans. Ahmad Ali. *Perspective* 4, 6 (December 1970), pp. 35-38.

2357   "The vile world carnival: a sahr-asob". Trans. Shamsur Rahman Faruqi and Frances
W. Pritchett. *Annual of Urdu Studies* 4 (1984), pp. 25-35.
With parallel Urdu text.

STUDIES

2358   **Glebov, N.V.**
"Narodnyi poet Indii Nazir Akbarabadi". In: *The poetry of peoples of India*. Moscow:
Nauka, 1962, pp. 76-103.

2359   **Hasan, Mohammad**
Nazir Akbarabadi. New Delhi: Sahitya Akademi, 1973. 72p.
On the life and poetry of Nazir Akbarabadi.

2360   "People's poet of India: Nazir Akbarabadi". In: *Problems of Modern Indian
Literature*. Calcutta: Statistical Publishing Society, pp. 28-147.

NAZMI, AKHTAR JAMIL

STUDY

2361   Shamsuddin. "Akhtar Jameel Nazmi - a young Urdu poet". *Indian Literature* 13, 4 (October 1973), pp. 19-20.
Includes Urdu text in roman characters.

NIAZI, MUNIR

TRANSLATIONS

2362   "Always late". Trans. Daud Kamal. *The Muslim* (Islamabad) (12 October 1984).

2363   "Another day wasted". Trans. Daud Kamal. *Frontier Post* (Lahore) (12 June 1987).

2364   "Bird that flew away". Trans. Daud Kamal. *Frontier Post* (Lahore) (13 February 1987).

2365   "Compass of stars". Trans. Daud Kamal. *Frontier Post* (Lahore) (13 February 1987).

2366   "The curve of an audible dream". Trans. Daud Kamal. *The Muslim* (Islamabad) (6 January 1984).

2367   "Death's premature rose". Trans. Daul Kamal. *Viewpoint* (Lahore) 8, 33 (Lahore) (24 March 1983), p. 13.

2368   "Dreams are not to live". Trans. Daud Kamal. *The Muslim* (Islamabad) (21 September 1984).

2369   "A dream of paradise in the shadow of war". Trans. Daud Kamal. *The Muslim* (Islamabad) (4 February 1983).

2370   "Eagle of the morning sun". Trans. Daud Kamal. *The Muslim* (Islamabad) (17 February 1984).

2371   "Ghazal". Trans. Daud Kamal. *Viewpoint* (Lahore) 9, 30 (1 March 1984), p. 29.

2372   "Gravestones". Trans. Daud Kamal. *Viewpoint* (Lahore) 8, 33 (24 March 1983), p. 13.

2373   "A half open window at midnight". Trans. Daud Kamal. *Viewpoint* (Lahore) 8, 19 (16 December 1982), p. 27.

2374   "Horizons". Trans. Daud Kamal. *The Muslim* (Islamabad) (16 November 1984).

2375   "New year". Trans. Daud Kamal. *Frontier Post* (Lahore) (6 February 1987).

2376   "Now is not the time". Trans. Daud Kamal. *Frontier Post* (Lahore) (6 February 1987).

2377   "A page from forgotten album". Trans. Daud Kamal. *Pakistan Times* (22 October 1982).

2378   "The point of intersection". Trans. Daud Kamal. *Pakistan Times* (1 May 1986).

2379   "Relics of a lost reality". Trans. Daud Kamal. *The Muslim* (Islamabad) (3 June 1983).
Also in: *Frontier Post* (Lahore) (13 March 1987).

2380   "Signalling to a friendly star to keep shining". Trans. Daud Kamal. *The Nation* (10 October 1986).

2381   "Sisyphean Essay". Trans. M. Salim-ur-Rahman. *Pakistani Literature* (Islamabad) 1, 1 (1992), p. 66.

2382   "The stained lights of my city". Trans. Daud Kamal. *The Muslim* (Islamabad) (8 October 1982).

2383   "Still-life". Trans. M. Salim-ur-Rahman. *Pakistani Literature* (Islamabad) 1, 1 (1992), p. 66.

2384   "Thinking of other universe". Trans. Daud Kamal. *Pakistan Times* (15 January 1982).

2385   "Thought nymph". Trans. Daud Kamal. *Pakistan Times* (11 February 1983).

2386   "Trees". Trans. Daud Kamal. *Frontier Post* (Lahore) (23 January 1987).

STUDIES

2387   **Ahmed, Zafaryab**
"Interview: Munir Niazi - in full form". *Viewpoint* (Lahore) 14, 50 (27 July 1989), pp. 24-25.

NIGAH, ZEHRA

STUDY

2388   "Interview". *The Herald* (Karachi) (November 1984), pp. 91-94.

PARTAU, ROHILA

STUDY

2389 **Rahman, Tariq**
"The poetry of Partau Rohila". *Dawn* (23 March 1990).

PASHI, KUMAR

TRANSLATIONS

2390 "Self portrait". Trans. K.K. Khullar. *Indian Literature* 23, 1-2 (1980), p. 539.

2391 "Symphony of silence". Trans. K.K. Khullar. *Indian Literature* 23, 1-2 (1980), p. 538.

PUECH, GEORGE

STUDY

2392 **Lall, Inder Jit**
"George Puech - a European Urdu poet". *Thought* 13, 38 (23 September 1961), pp. 16-17.

QAIM CHANDPURI, MUHAMMAD QIYAMUDDIN

STUDIES

2393 **Hasan, Iqtida**
"Qaim Chandpuri. His life and poetry". *Oriental College Magazine* 41 (Lahore, 1965), pp. 1-30.

2394 **Mohi, S.A.**
"Qaim Chandpuri: his life and art". *Indica* 4, 1 (March 1967), pp. 61-64.

QAISER, NAZIR

STUDY

2395 Rogers, Kristine M.
"A triumph of imagination: the poetry of Nazir Qaiser". *Annual of Urdu Studies* 7 (1990), pp. 88-92.

QALIL DALTONGANJVI

STUDY

2396 "Life and literature: a conversation with Qalil Daltonganjvi". *Annual of Urdu Studies* 7 (1990), pp. 126-129.

QASIMI, AHMAD NADIM

TRANSLATIONS

2397 "Artefact". Trans. Daud Kamal. *The Muslim* (Islamabad) (28 October 1983).

2398 "Blindfolded bull". Trans. Daud Kamal. *The Muslim* (Islamabad) (10 June 1983).

2399 "The bridled passion". Trans. Daud Kamal. *Frontier Post* (Lahore) (5 June 1987).

2400 "Four poems from the Urdu". Trans. Raja Changez Sultan. *Translation* 3 (Winter 1976), pp. 95-97.

2401 "Ghazal" (A fragment). *Pakistan Times* (9 September 1983).

2402 "Ghost town". Trans. Daud Kamal. *Viewpoint* (Lahore) 8, 6 (16 September 1982).

2403 "Green cliffs". Trans. Daud Kamal. *The Muslim* (Islamabad) (1 May 1986).

2404 "Guide". Trans. Daud Kamal. *The Muslim* (Islamabad) (16 August 1982).
Also in: *Viewpoint* (Lahore) 8, 6 (16 September 1982), p. 24.

2405 "The inner arctic". Trans. Daud Kamal. *Pakistan Times* (5 November 1982).
Also in: *Viewpoint* (Lahore) 8, 33 (24 March 1983), p. 13.

2406 "Introduction". Trans. Daud Kamal. *The Muslim* (Islamabad) (8 October 1982).
Also in: *Viewpoint* (Lahore) 8, 19 (16 December 1982), p. 27.

2407   "A lament". Trans. Shelah S. Bhatti. *Pakistani Literature* (Islamabad) 1, 1 (1992), pp. 81-88.

2408   "Mist". Trans. Daud Kamal. *Pakistan Times* (26 November 1982).

2409   "Outlandish poetry". Trans. Daud Kamal. *The Muslim* (Islamabad) (11 November 1983).

2410   "Page from an explorer's diary". Trans. M. Salim-ur-Rahman. *Pakistani Literature* (Islamabad) 1, 1 (1992), p. 50.

2411   "Remoteness". Trans. Daud Kamal. *Pakistan Times* (12 October 1984).

2412   "Resurgence". Trans. Daud Kamal. *The Muslim* (Islamabad) (22 July 1983).

2413   "September 6, 1965". Trans. C.M. Naim. *Journal of Asian Studies* 28 (February 1969), p. 282.

2414   "The stillborn revolution". Trans. Daud Kamal. *The Muslim* (Islamabad) (9 September 1983).

2415   "Stone". Trans. Daud Kamal. *The Muslim* (Islamabad) (24 June 1983).

2416   "Whole perspective?". Trans. Daud Kamal. *Viewpoint* (Lahore) 8, 33 (24 March 1983), p. 13.

QULI QUTUB SHAH, MOHAMMAD

STUDIES

2417   Iqbal, Najmuddin
"Quli Qutub Shah: author of Urdu's first divan". *Perspective* 3, 2 (May 1970), pp. 16-17.

2418   Matthews, David J.
"The kulliyat of Muhammad Quli Qutb Shah: problems and prospects". In: *Urdu and Muslim South Asia*. Ed. C. Shackle. London: School of Oriental and African Studies, University of London, 1989, pp. 39-48.

2419   Sherwani, H.K.
Muhammad-Quli Qutb Shah, founder of Hyderabad. London, 1967.

QURESHI, ABU SAID

TRANSLATION

2420 "After the atomic war. Trans. S. Amjad Ali. *Pakistan Quarterly* 13, 2-3 (Summer-Winter 1965), p. 51.

RAHBAR, MUHAMMAD DAUD

TRANSLATION

2421 *The cup of Jamshid: a collection of original ghazal poetry*. Trans. the author. Cape Cod, Mass.: Claude Stark, 1974. 199p.

RAHMAN, HUMAIRA

TRANSLATION

2422 "Poem by Humaira Rahman". Trans. Mamun Aiman. *Urdu Canada* 1, 3 (1987), pp. 80-81.

RANGIN, SAADAT YAR KHAN

TRANSLATION

2423 *The faras-nama-i-Rangin, or The book of the horse by Rangin*. Trans. D.C. Phillott. London, 1911. 83p.

RASHED, N.M.

TRANSLATIONS

2424 "Afraid of life, are you?" Trans. Mohammed Zakir. *Indian Literature* 23, 1-2 (1980), pp. 558-559.

2425 "Four poems". Trans. M.H.K. Qureshi, et al. *Mahfil* 2, 2 (May 1965), pp. 1-5.

2426   "Four poems". Trans. M.H.K. Qureshi and Carlo Coppola. *The Beloit Poetry Journal* (Winter 1962-63), pp. 47-50.

2427   "Hasan, the potter". Trans. Rafey Habib, Faruq Hassan and Stanley Rajiva. *Pakistani Literature* (Islamabad) 1, 1 (1992), pp. 35-46.

2428   "Nine poems". Trans. Carlo Coppola, et al. *Mahfil* 7, 1-2 (Spring-Summer 1971), pp. 21-30

2429   "Sheba". Trans. M.H.K. Qureshi. *Urdu Canada* 1, 1 (February 1986), pp. 6.

2430   "Three poems". Trans. M.H.K. Qureshi. *Toronto South Asian Review* 1, 2 (Summer 1982), pp. 62-64.

2431   "What mystery do we solve?" Trans. Mohammad Zakir. *Indian Literature* 23, 1-2 (1980), pp. 559-560.

STUDIES

2432   Ahmad, Nazir
"N.M. Rashed's poet achievement: a critical appraisal". *Explorations* (Lahore) 2, 1, pp. 49-68.

2433   Chaudhary, Mukhtar
"N.M. Rashed's 'New dance'." *Annual of Urdu Studies* 7 (1990), pp.109-110. Includes Urdu text.

2434   "The fruits of labour are sweeter than the gifts of fortune by Nazr-i-Muhammad (grew up to become N.M. Rashed)". *Annual of Urdu Studies* 3 (1983), pp. 101-102.

2435   "Interview with N.M. Rashed". *Mahfil* 7, 1-2 (Spring-Summer 1971), pp. 1-20.

2436   "N.M. Rashid". *Pakistani Literature* (Islamabad) 1, 1 (1992), p. 33-34. Biographical sketch.

2437   Zakir, Mohammed
"The poetry of Nun Mim Rashid". *Indian Literature* 23, 5 (1980), pp. 41-55.

RIAZ, FAHMIDA

TRANSLATIONS

2438   "Four poems". *Annual of Urdu Studies* 4   (1984),
— • "The beauty contest". p. 79-80.
— • "The doll". p. 79.

— • "Iqleema". p. 80.
— • "The soft fragrance of my jasmine". p. 80.

2439   "The lone hill". Trans. Nazir Ahmad. *Pakistan Quarterly* 15, 1-2 (Spring-Summer 1971), p. 97.

2440   **Documents**
[Reproduced from *Mainstream*]. *Annual of Urdu Studies* 6 (1987), pp. 131-132.
Letter to the Prime Minister of Pakistan sent on 27 June 1987 by Fahmida Riaz, who with her family has been living in exile for over six years in India.   (New Delhi, 11 July 1987, p. 30).

SAGHAR NIZAMI

TRANSLATION

2441   "The new storm-wave".   Trans. Abrar Ahmad Farooki.   *Contemporary Indian Literature* 2, 10 (October 1962), p. 5.

STUDY

2442   **Bhattacharya, Vivek**
"The poetry of Saghar Nizami". *Thought* 20, 17 (27 April 1968), pp. 14-15.

SAHIR LUDHIANVI, ABDUL HAYE

TRANSLATIONS

2443   *The bitter harvest: selections from Sahir Ludhianvi's verse*.   Trans. Riffat Hasan. Lahore: Aziz Pub., 1977. 196p.

2444   "Brothers". Trans. Carlo Coppola and M.H.K Qureshi. *Literature East and West* 10, 1-2 (1966), p. 89.

2445   *Shadows speak*. Trans. Khwaja Ahmad Abbas. Bombay: PPH Bookstall, 1958.

2446   *Sorcery (Sahri) - Urdu poetry of Sahir Ludhianvi*. Trans. Sain Sucha. Sweden: Vudya Kitabun Forlag, 1989. 114p.
Includes parallel Urdu text.

2447   "Three poems". Trans. M.H.K. Qureshi and Carlo Coppola. *Mahfil* 2, 4, pp. 10-11.

STUDIES

2448   Akhtar, Hamid
"Sahir Ludhianvi: his words will live". *Viewpoint* (Lahore) 6, 13 (November 1980), pp. 9, 25.

2449   Coppola, Carlo and M.H.K. Qureshi
"A note on Sahir Ludhianvi, poems by Sahir Ludhianvi". *Literature East and West* 10 (June 1966), pp. 86-97.

2450   — • "Political, social criticism and Indian film songs: the case of Sahir Ludhianvi". *Journal of Popular Culture* 10, 4 (Spring 1977), pp. 897-902.

2451   Gul, Ijaz
"Art: Sahir's gift to cinema". *Viewpoint* (Lahore) 6, 14 (November 1980), p. 31.

2452   Jalib, Habib
"Homage to Sahir". *Viewpoint* (Lahore) 6, 14 (November 1980), p. 32.

SAIDI, MAKHMUR

TRANSLATION

2453   "Possibility". Trans. Inder Jit Lall. *Indian Literature* 17, 3 (July 1974), p. 135.

SALAM MACHLIDSHAHRI

TRANSLATION

2454   "Allusion". Trans. S.O. Samanahi. *Thought* 14, 19 (12 May 1962), p. 14.

SARA SHAGUFTA

STUDY

2455   Pritam, Amrita
"A woman called Sara". Trans. Krishan Ashant. *Indian Literature* 29, 2 (March-April 1986), pp. 166-173.
Extract from a biography of Sara Shagufta.

SARHADI, MIRZA MAHMUD

STUDY

2456   "Poets and politicians: the pests of Pakistan". *Pakistan Journal of the Pakistan Study Centre* (University of Peshawar) (Autumn 1981), p. 4.
On the satirical verses of Mirza Mahmood Sarhadi.

SARUR JAHANABADI

STUDIES

2457   **Goher, Inder Jeet**
"Sarur Jahanabadi: nation poet of Urdu". *Thought* (30 July 1960), pp. 13-14.

2458   **Lall, Inder Jit**
"Saroor Jahanabadi: an Urdu poet of renaissance". *Indian Literature* 10, 1 (1967), pp. 102-109.

SAUDA, MUHAMMAD RAFI

TRANSLATIONS

2459   "An ode from Souda". Trans. John Gilchrist. *Asiatick Miscellany* 1, (1885), pp. 376-379.
First example of Urdu translation into English and probably the first example of Urdu printing in India.

2460   "The ruined city". Trans. Qurratulain Hyder. *Pakistan Quarterly* 7, 2 (1957), pp. 12-13.

2461   **Court, Henry**
Selections from kulliyat or complete works of Mirza Rafi-Oos-Sauda. Simla, 1872. 50p.
Literal translations, with notes, of ten selections from the non-ghazal poetry of Sauda "being the parts appointed for the high proficiency examination in Oordoo".

STUDIES

2462   **Haque, Ishrat**
"Society and polity as reflected in Sawda's poetry". *Islamic Culture* 59, 3 (July 1985), pp. 229-242.

2463 **Harley, Alexander Hamilton**
"Sauda, the satirist of Hindustan". *Calcutta Review* (August 1922), pp. 214-224.

2464 **Jarret, H.S.**
Muntakhab-i masnawiyat-i Sauda. Selections from the masnavis of Sauda. Calcutta, 1875. 45p.

2465 **Narang, Gopi Chand**
"The Princeton manuscript of Kulliyat-e Sauda". *Journal of the American Oriental Society* 93 (1973), pp. 539-541.

2466 **Russell, Ralph**
"An eighteenth century Urdu satirist". *Indian Literature* 2, 1 (October 1958-March 1959), pp. 36-43.

2467 **Russell, Ralph and Islam, Khurshidul**
"The satires of Sauda". In their *Three Mughal poets*. Cambridge: Harvard University Press, 1968, pp. 37-68.

SHAD AZIMABADI

2468 "Rubaiyat of Shad Azimabadi". *Annual of Urdu Studies* 2 1982, pp. 101-110.
Excerpt from a book, *Rubaiyat of Shad Azimabadi*, compiled by Hameed Azimabadi (Patna: Hameed Azimabadi, 1946). Urdu text and facing English translation. The English verse translation is by Nizamat Jung Bahadur of Hyderabad (Deccan), based on Hameed Azimabadi's translation.

SHAHEEN

TRANSLATIONS

2469 "Four poems. Trans. Faruq Hassan and Stanley Rajiva. *Annual of Urdu Studies* 6 (1987),
— • "The ball". p. 76.
— • "Black muddy slush". pp. 74-75.
— • "My dreams are wild". p. 76.
— • "Tell him". p. 75.

2470 "The last word". Trans. Leslie Lavigne and Baidar Bakht. *Urdu Canada* 1, 1 (February 1986), p. 70.

2471 "Rendez-vous". Trans. Leslie Lavigne and Baidar Bakht. *Urdu Canada* 1, 1 (February 1986), p. 69.

STUDIES

2472 Hassan, Faruq
["Review of *Be-nishán*"]. *Annual of Urdu Studies* 5 (1985), pp. 127-130. (Publication funded by the Directorate of Multiculturalism, Department of the Secretary of State, Ottawa, Canada.)

2473 Khan, Nuzrat Yar
Dreams and destinations: Shaheen and his poetry. Ottawa-Hull: Canada Pakistan Association, [1987?].

SHAHIDI, PARVEZ

TRANSLATIONS

2474 *Dialogue five: selected poems of Parvez Shahedi.* Trans. A.A.M. Ghani. Calcutta: Satyabrata Pal, 1969. 16p.

2475 *Selected poems.* Trans. A.A.M. Ghani. Calcutta: Satyabrata Pal, 1968. 16p.

STUDY

2476 Rauf, A.
"Pervez Shahidi: a poem analysed". *Calcutta Review* 180, 2 (August 1966), pp. 113-116.

SHAHIR, SAYYID MUHAMMAD HASAN

TRANSLATION

2477 "Four poems". Trans. Najmul Hasan. *Thought* 14, 17 (28 April 1962), p. 12.

SHAHRYAR

TRANSLATIONS

2478 "Day feeling the attack of night". Trans. Gopi Chand Narang and David Paul Douglas. *Indian Literature* 23, 1-2 (1980), p. 557.

2479 "From one moment to another". Trans. Gopi Chand Narang and David Paul Douglas. *Indian Literature* 23, 1-2 (1980), p. 557.

2480   "The gates of dreams are barred". Trans. Gopi Chand Narang. *Indian Literature* 31, 2 (March-April 1988), p. 58.
Includes a note on poetry, "Poems of today" by Shahryar, translated by Gopi Chand Narang.

2481   "Still life". Trans. Gopi Chand Narang. *Indian Literature* 31, 2 (March-April 1988), p. 59.

STUDY

2482   Komal, Balraj
"Dreams are forever". *Indian Literature* 31, 5 (September-October 1988), pp. 185,188.
A review of Shahryar's collection *Khwab ka dar band hai.*

SHAHRYAR, MASUD

TRANSLATIONS

2483   "Poem". Trans. Muhammad Umar Memon. *Denver Quarterly* 12, 2 (Summer 1977), p. 242.

2484   "New day, new torment". Trans. C.M. Naim. *Books Abroad* 43, 4 (Autumn 1969), p. 546.

SHAIR, HIMAYAT ALI

TRANSLATION

2485   *Flowers in flames: an Urdu poem on world peace.* Trans. Rajinder Singh Verma. Karachi: al Musannefeen, 1985. 120p.
Verse translation of Shair's long poem, 'Bangal se Koriya tak'. Includes Urdu text.

SHAKIR, PARWEEN

TRANSLATIONS

2486   "Six poems". Trans. C.M. Naim. *Annual of Urdu Studies* 4 (1984),
— • "Obstinate". p. 81.
— • "A poem for the Iranian poetess, Farugh Farrukhzad 1934-1967". p. 82.
— • "A simple request". p. 82.
— • "Something to remember". p. 81.

—• "To a friend". p. 81.
—• "What will happen to flowers?" p. 82.

SHAUQ, MIRZA

TRANSLATIONS

2487   *Zahr-i-ishq, or the poison of love; (a love narrative from Awadh)*. Trans. Shah Abdus Salam and Jeffrey Donaghue. Delhi: D.K. Publications, 1982. 141p.
Includes Urdu text with glossary and notes.

STUDIES

2488   **Abbas, S.M.M.**
"Masnavi Zehr-i ishq". *Pakistan Review* 2 (May 1954), pp. 37-40.

2489   **Minault, Gail**
["A review of *Zahr-i ishq, or the poison of love. (A love narrative from Awadh)*. Trans. Shah Abdus Salam, et al."] *Annual of Urdu Studies* 4 (1984), pp. 110-111.
A review

SIDDIQI, MUKHTAR

TRANSLATIONS

2490   "Khayal darbari".   Trans. Farmanullah Khan.   *Pakistan Quarterly* 13, 1 (Spring 1965), pp. 58-59.

2491   "Thatha". Trans. C.M. Naim. *Mahfil* 2, 2 (May 1965), pp. 63-66.

SIDDIQI, M. NAIM

TRANSLATIONS

2492   "From burning maples to bleeding olives".   *Pakistan Review* 15, 11 (November 1967), pp. 9-10.
Includes Urdu text.

2493   "A way farer". *Pakistan Review* 16, 6 (June 1968), pp. 30-38.
Includes Urdu text.

SIDDIQI, SAHIR

STUDY

2494   **Ahmad, K. Jamil**
"Sahir Siddiqi - a talented Urdu poet". *Pakistan Review* 14, 11 (November 1966), pp. 44-45.

SOHAIL, K.

TRANSLATION

2495   "The wind"; "My persuasive companion". Trans. Linda Voll. *Urdu Canada* 1, 3 (1987), pp. 78-79.

TABAN, GHULAM RABBANI

TRANSLATION

2496   "A ghazal". Trans. S. Zimnan. *Thought* 15, 24 (15 June 1963), p. 15.

TALKH, MANMOHAN

TRANSLATION

2497   "Untenable plaint". Trans. Vijay Mathur and Rajendra Mathur. *Thought* 12, 19 (7 May 1960), p. 10.

TAMKEEN, QAISER

TRANSLATION

2498   "Sorry, no lift". *Urdu Canada* 1, 3 (1987), pp. 67-71.

TANWEER ANJUM

TRANSLATIONS

2499 "Three poems". Trans. C.M. Naim. *Annual of Urdu Studies* 4, (1984),
— • "I could've become just a dream". p. 83.
— • "Poem". p. 84.
— • "Termites". p. 83.

TUFTA, HAR GOPAL

TRANSLATION

2500 "Tibet". Trans. Inder Jit Lall. *Thought* 15, 5 (2 February 1963), p. 13.

VALI DAKHANI, SHAMSUDDIN

STUDIES

2501 **Hashimi, Nurulhasan**
Wali. New Delhi: Sahitya Akedemia, 1986. 71p.
Urdu text in Roman characters.

2502 **Haywood, John A.**
"Wali Dakhani and the development of Dakhani - Urdu Sufi Poetry". *Acta Orientalia* 28
(1964), pp. 153-174.

2503 **Sadiq, Muhammad**
"Vali: his age, life and poetry". *Iqbal* 8, 3 (January 1960), pp. 29-43.

2504 *Les oeuvres de Wali. Traduction et notes par M. Garcin de Tassy.* Paris, 1836. 67p.

VASHISHT, JAVED

STUDY

2505 **Lall, Inder Jit**
"Javed Vashisht - Urdu poet". *Indian P.E.N.* 40, 1 (January 1974), pp. 10-11.

ZAFAR, MUHAMMAD BAHADUR SHAH

TRANSLATION

2506   "Three ghazals of Bahadur Shah Zafar". Trans. Ahmad Ali. *Pakistan Quarterly* 7, 2 (1957), pp. 4-5.

STUDIES

2507   **Haider, Azimusshan**
"Bahadur Shah Zafar's poetry". *Perspective* 3, 7 (January 1970), pp. 52-56.

2508   "The first truly popular poet of Urdu". *Pakistan Perspective* 3, 3-4 (August-September 1977), pp, 16-17.

2509   **Lall, Inder Jit**
"Bahadur Shah - the Emperor and poet". *Thought* 15, 33 (17 August 1963), pp. 13-14.

2510   **Rabiunnisa**
"Bahadur Shah Zafar". *Perspective* 4, 4 (November 1970), pp. 14-16.

ZAHIR, SAJJAD

TRANSLATIONS

2511   "Three Urdu poems". Trans. the author. *Indian Literature* 14, 1 (March 1971), pp. 76-77.
— • "I sometimes fear".
— • "Less with lips".
— • "The river".

STUDIES

2512   **Ansari, Zoe**
"Sajad Zahir as I knew him". *Indian P.E.N.* 39, 12 (December 1973), pp. 8-11.

2513   **Baquer, Ali**
A tribute to Sajjad Zaheer. The pen and the vision. New Delhi: Seema Publications, 1987. 123p. photographs.
Includes tributes from Faiz Ahmad Faiz, Mulk Raj Anand, Ali Sardar Jafri, Ismat Chughtai and Kartar Singh Duggal. Also includes Sajjid Zahir's articles on the Indian Progressive Writers Association, Afro-Asian Writers Movement, his letters to friends and family and reminiscences of friends.

2514   **Shastry, S. Lakshman**
"Sajjad Zaheer". *Contemporary Indian Literature* 6, 1 (January 1966), p. 30.

ZAIDI, MUSTAFA

TRANSLATION

2515   "Rendering of late Mustafa Zaidi's last poem". Trans. Naz. *Pakistan Review* 18, 11 (November 1970), pp. 20-21.
Dedicated to Shahnaz Lala Rukh.

ZAIDI, SAJIDA

TRANSLATION

2516   "I am everywhere ... everywhere". Trans. K.K. Khullar. *Indian Literature* 23, 1-2 (1980), pp. 552-553.

ZAIDI, ZAHIDA

TRANSLATIONS

2517   "Dark mirrors". Trans. K.K. Khullar. *Indian Literature* 23, 1-2 (1980), p. 533?

2518   "Four poems". In: *The voice of the Indian poets, and Anthology of Indian poetry*. Ed. Pranab Bandyopadhyay. Calcutta: United Writers, 1975, pp. 128-132.

2519   "Slumbering sparks". Trans. K.K. Khullar. *Indian Literature* 23, 1-2 (1980), pp. 531-532.

2520   "Three poems". Trans. the author. In: *VAK: an anthology of poems and translations*. Ed. Sibnarayan Ray. Calcutta: Writers Workshop, 1975, pp. 38-40.

2521   "Two poems". Trans. C.M. Naim. *Annual of Urdu Studies* 4 (1984), p. 78.
— • "In the unfinished city".
— • "Life's poison".

ZAUQ, SHAIKH MUHAMMAD IBRAHIM

STUDY

2522 **Chagla, Ahmed G.**
"The master Zauq". *Scintilla* 2 (October 1961), pp. 45-48.

POETRY

Anthologies

2523   Ahmad, Rukhsana
Beyond belief: contemporary feminist Urdu poetry. Trans. Rukhsana Ahmad. Lahore: ASR Publications, 1990. 78p.
Includes works of: Ishrat Aafreen, Saeeda Gazdar, Kishwar Naheed, Fehmida Riaz, Neelma Sarwar, Sara Shagufta, Zehra Nigah.
Includes introduction and brief biographical notes on each poetess.

2524   — • *We sinful women.* London: The Women's Press, 1990. 193p.
Reprint of the above.

2425   Ali, Ahmad
The bulbul and the rose. Karachi: Maktaba Jamia, Talim-e-Milli, 1960. 115p.

2526   — • *The falcon and the hunted bird.* Karachi: Kitab Publishers, 1950. 98p.
Includes works of: Muhammad Vali, Sauda, Dard, Mir Taqi Mir, Insha Allah Khan Insha, Bahadur Shah Zafar, Atish, Zauq, Ghalib, Momin, Dagh.
Includes biographical sketches of each poet.

2527   — • *The golden tradition: an anthology of Urdu poetry.* New York: Columbia University Press, 1973. 286p.
Includes works of: Muhammad Vali, Siraj, Sauda, Dard, Mir Taqi Mir, Nazir Akbarabadi, Mir Hasan, Insha Allah Khan Insha, Bahadur Shah Zafar, Atish, Zauq, Ghalib, Momin, Mir Anis, Dagh.

2528   — • "Selections from Urdu poetry". *Eastern Horizons* 4, pp. 15-20; 5, p. 39; 6, pp. 32-37; 7, pp. 45-50; 8, pp, 38-42.

2529   Allana, Ghulam Ali
Presenting Pakistani poetry. Karachi: Pakistan Writers Guild, 1961. 206p.
Includes works of: Iqbal, Zafar Ali Khan, Akhtar Shirani, Josh Malihabadi, Hafiz Jallandhiri, Faiz Ahmad Faiz, N.M. Rashid, Ahsan Danish, Mukhtar Siddiqi, Ahmad Nadim Qasimi, Jamiluddin Aali, Shanul Haq Haqqi, Ibne Insha, Abdul Aziz Khalid, Khalilur Rahman, Qayyum Nazar, Yusaf Zafar, Shaikh Ayaz, Aziz Ahmad Aziz.
Urdu selections: pp. 6-43.

2530   *An anthology of short stories and poems.* Moka, Mauritius: Mahatma Gandhi Institute, 1979. 67p.
English, French, Hindi and Urdu.

2531   Bakht, Baidar and Jaeger, Kathleen Grant
An anthology of modern Urdu poetry. Vol. 1. Delhi: Educational Publishing House, 1984. 251p.
Includes works of: Makhdoom Mohiuddin, N.M. Rashed, Faiz Ahmad Faiz, Meera Ji, Ali Sardar Jafri, Akhtarul Iman, Munibur Rahman.
Includes Urdu text.

2532   **Barker, M.A.R. and Salam, Shah Abdus**
Classical Urdu poetry. Vol. II. Ithaca, New York: Spoken Language Services, 1977.
Includes works of: Quli Qutb Shah, Mulla Vajahi, Mulla Ghawwas, Ibne Nishati, Shahi,
Nusrati, Hashimi Bijapuri, Muhammad Vali, Afzal, Sauda, Dard, Mir Taqi Mir, Mir Hasan,
Nazir Akbarabadi, Insha Allah Khan Insha, Mushafi, Jurat, Rangin, Nasikh, Atish, Nasim,
Shauq, Mir Anis, Dabir, Jan Sahib, Zauq, Momin, Ghalib, Zafar, Amir Minai, Dagh, Hali,
Akbar Allahabadi, Iqbal.

2533   **Batra, Satish**
New generation two: an anthology of Urdu writers. Lucknow: New Generation, 1967.
Includes works of: Wazir Agha, Balraj Komal, Kumar Pashi, Krishna Mohan, Sayyid H.
Hashmi.

2534   **Hashmi, Alamgir**
The worlds of Muslim imagination. Islamabad: Gulmohar, 1986. 270p.
Contemporary literature of the last fifty years. Includes works of: N.M. Rashed, Zahid Dar,
Wazir Agha, Fehmida Riaz, Sarmad Sehbai, Faiz Ahmad Faiz, Ahmad Nadim Qasimi, Munir
Niazi, Majeed Amjad.

2535   **Hollings, W.C.**
*A translation of popular rekhta songs, with the English and Hindustani facing each other in
each page.* Calcutta, 1852. 78p.

2536   *Indian poetry today.* New Delhi: Indian Council for Cultural Relations 1974-1981.
Selection of Indian language poetry, including Urdu.

2537   **Jain, Champat Rai**
Gems of Islam. New Delhi: Today and Tomorrow's Printers and Publishers, 1975. 2 vols.
Reprint of London, 1940 edition.
Includes translations from Urdu mystic poets.

2538   **Jamal, Mahmud**
The Penguin book of modern Urdu poetry. Harmondsworth: Penguin, 1986. 165p.
Includes works of: Iftikhar Arif, Kishwar Naheed, Fehmida Riaz, N.M. Rashed, Ali Sardar
Jafri, Akhtarul Iman, Munir Niazi, Saqi Farooqi, Faiz Ahmad Faiz, Ahmad Faraz.

2539   **Jussawall, Adil**
New writing in India. Harmondsworth: Penguin, 1977. 320p.
Includes works of: Baqar Mehdi, Akhtarul Iman.

2540   **Kanda, K.C.**
Masterpieces of Urdu ghazal from the 17th to the 20th century. New Delhi: Sterling
Publishers, 1990. 334p.
Urdu text in Roman and Persian characters.

2541   **Khan, Inayat and Westbrook, Jessie Duncan**
Hindustani lyrics rendered from Urdu. Southampton: Book Depot for Sufi Literature, 1919.
59p.

2542   **Khwaja, Waqas Ahmad**
Cactus: an anthology of Pakistan literature. Lahore: Writers Group Publications, 1985.
112p.

2543   — • *Masterpieces of Urdu ghazal from the 17th to the 20th century.* Trans.
K.C. Kanda. New York: Sterling Publishers, 1990. 334p.
Includes Urdu in roman and Arabic characters.

2544   — • *Mornings in the wilderness. Readings in Pakistani literature.* Trans. Waqas
Ahmad Khwaja. Lahore: Sang-e-Meel Publications, 1988. 320p.
Includes works of: Nasir Kazmi, Majeed Amjad, Kishwar Naheed, N.M. Rashed, Faiz
Ahmad Faiz, Zahid Dar, Munir Niazi, Javed Shaheen.
Includes biographical notes on each poet.

2545   **Krivitskiĭ, A. Iu. and Palladin, A.I.**
Poeziĭ Aziĭ: sbornik. Moscow: Nauka, 1957. 911p.
Russian translations of short poems of Indian authors.

2546   **Mahmud, Shabana**
Anthology of women's poetry in Urdu: From 1800 to the present. Trans. Khwaja Mahmudul
Hasan. (In preparation 1992).

2547   **Matthews, David J. and Shackle, Christopher**
An anthology of classical Urdu love lyrics. London: Oxford University Press, 1972. 283p.
Includes works of: Quli Qutb Shah, Vali, Siraj, Hatim, Mazhar, Sauda, Dard, Mir Taqi Mir,
Jurat, Mushafi, Insha Allah Khan Insha, Nasikh, Atish, Zauq, Ghalib, Bahadur Shah Zafar,
Momin, Shefta, Dagh, Hali, Iqbal, Hasrat Mohani.
Includes Urdu text.

2548   **Mirza, Baldev**
Skylark (Aligarh) *Urdu Number* 17, 3 (March 1976), pp. 395-424.
Includes works of: Abbas Akhtar, Shahab Jafri, Salam Machlidshahri, Khalilur Rahman
Azmi, Munibur Rahman, Sulaiman Arib, Wahid Akhtar, Amiq Hanfi, Balraj Komal, Kumar
Pashi, Shahryar, Sajida Zaidi, Adil Mansuri, Qazi Salim, Muhammad Alvi, Zahida Zaidi,
Nida Fazli, Zubair Rizvi, Shamim Hanfi, Munir Niazi...

2549   **Nagi, Anis**
Modern Urdu poems from Pakistan. Lahore: Swad Noon Publications, 1974. 220p.
Includes works of: Faiz Ahmad Faiz, N.M. Rashed, Meera Ji, Ahmad Nadim Qasimi,
Majeed Amjad, Zahir Kashmiri, Zia Jallandhri, Mohammad Safdar, Munir Niazi, Gilani
Kamran, Iftikhar Jalib, Abbas Athar, Zahid Dar, Salahuddin Mahmud, Anis Nagi, Salim-ur-
Rahman, Kishwar Naheed, Muhammad Salim-ur-Rahman, Aijaz Faruqi, Fahmida Riaz, Yusuf
Kamran, Sarmad Sahbai, Sadat Saidi, Aftab Iqbal Shamim, Fahim Jozi, Riaz Majid.
Includes biographical notes on each poet.

2550   **Nandy, Pritish**
Modern Indian poetry. New Delhi: Arnold-Heinemann, 1974. 231p.
Includes works of: Adil Mansuri, Akhtarul Iman, Ali Sardar Jafri, Amir Hanfi, Asrarul Haq
Majaz, Balraj Komal, Kaifi Azmi, Makhdum Mohiuddin, Nida Fazli, Sahir Ludhianvi.

2551   **Niaz, A.Q.**
Cries in the night: an anthology of modern Pakistani Urdu poetry, presented in English. 2nd. ed. Lahore: Majmael-Bahrain, 1957. 287p.

2552   **Oesterheld, Christina**
Auswahl zeitgenössischer Urdu-Lyrik und -Prosa (Haus der Kulturen der Welt). Berlin: Das Arabische Buch, 1991. 124p. (Gesteht's! die Dichter des Orients sind grösser; 4).
Includes works of: Iftikhar Arif, Balraj Komal, Jamiluddin Aali.

2553   **Pakistan Writer's Guild**
The Nation (January 1963): Pakistani Writers' Guild Number. Karachi 1963. 88p.
Includes works of: Josh Malihabad, Hafiz Jallandhri, Faiz Ahmad Faiz, N.M. Rashed, Jamiluddin Aali, Ahmad Nadim Qasimi, Abdul Aziz Khalid, Ibne Insha, Shanul Haq Haqqi, Ahsan Danish, Mukhtar Siddiqi, Yusuf Zafar, Qayyum Nazar.

2554   **Qureshi, M.H.K.**
"Urdu poetry in Canada". *Toronto South Asian Review* (Toronto) 1, 1 (Winter 1982), pp. 83-97.
Includes works of: Javed Shaheen, Nuzhat Siddiqui, Munibur Rahman and M.H.K. Qureshi. Various translators.

2555   **Ramlal, Chishti, Syeda Naseem**
New generation three. Lucknow: New Generation, 1968. 148p.
Includes works of: Makhdum Mohiuddin, Ghulam Rabbani Taban, Wazir Agha, Balraj Komal, Khalilur Rahman Azmi, Wahid Akhtar, Shaz Tamkanat, Zubair Rizvi, Bashar Nawaz, Muhammad Alvi, Shahryar, Raj Narain Raz, Kumar Pashi, Hali, Nasim Muzaffarpuri.

2556   **Shah, Sirdar Iqbal Ali**
The golden treasury of Indian literature. London, 1938. 293p.
Includes works of: Hali, Iqbal, Ghalib, Bahadur Shah Zafar, Zauq, Mir Hasan, Dard, Sauda.

2557   **Verma, Rajinder Singh**
Contemporary Urdu verse: hundred masterpieces of eight major Urdu poets. Trans. Rajinder Singh Verma. Delhi: Atma Ram, 1989. 112p.

POETRY

History and Criticism

2558   Afzal, Qaiser
"New trends in Urdu poetry". *Pakistan Review* 8 (September 1960), pp. 7-8.

2559   Ahmad, Shaikh Mahmud
"Urdu poetry today". *Vision* 16, 12 (January 1968), p. 8, 26.

2560   Ahmer, Yunus
"Prose poem: a new trend in Urdu". *Pakistan Perspective* 3, 8-9 (February-March 1978), pp. 30-31.

2561   Ali, Ahmad
"Introduction to Urdu poetry". *Eastern Horizon* 4, 3, pp. 23-45.
Also in: *Pakistan* 2, 2 (Autumn 1948), pp. 26-42.
Includes translated selections.

2562   Allahabadi, T.
"Modern Urdu poetry". *Pakistan Review* 3 (October 1955), pp. 44-45.

2563   Anjum, A.R.
"English literary tradition and Urdu poetry". *Explorations* (Lahore) 2, 1, pp. 31-42.

2564   Babree, Laeeq
"Facet of modern Urdu poetry". *Pakistan Review* 18, 2 (February 1970), pp. 30-32.

2565   Barker, M.A.R. and Salam, Shah Abdus
Classical Urdu poetry. Ithaca, New York: Spoken Language Services, 1977. 3 vols.
Cassette tapes of poetry are also available.

2566   Barker, M.A.R., et al.
A reader of modern Urdu poetry. Montreal: McGill University Institute of Islamic Studies, 1968. 274p.

2567   Bukhari, Syed Abdul Wahab
"A brief history of the origin of Urdu and Hindi poets of the Urdu language". *Journal of the Annamalai University Part A, Humanities* 25 (1964), pp. 80-112.

2568   Chakbast, Braj Narain
"Hindustani poetry". *Hindustan Review* 11 (July-December 1911), pp. 74-80, 215-221.

2569   Dasgupta, Alokeranjan
Gelobt sei der Pfau. Indische Lyrik der Gegenwart. München: Schneekluth, 1986. 208p.
Includes translations from Shahryar, Zubair Rizvi, Adil Mansuri, Nida Fazli.

2570   Dearing, Lewis
"Past and present in modern Indian and Pakistani poetry. Part 1". *Literature East and West* 10 (1966), pp. 69-85.

2571   **Dulai, Surjit Singh**
"Urdu poetry and its advent in English". *Journal of South Asian Literature* 10, 1 (Fall, 1974). pp. 167-176.
A review article on Ahmed Ali's *The golden tradition* (New York), 1973.

2572   **Faiz, Ahmed Faiz**
"The concept of beauty". *Viewpoint* (Lahore) 6, 16 (November 1980), p. 18.

2573   — • "Faiz on writers' role - II". *Viewpoint* (Lahore) 11, 16 (28 November 1985), pp. 27-28, 33.

2574   — • "Realism and romanticism". *Viewpoint* (Lahore) 6, 13 (November 1980), pp. 18-19

2575   **Farrukhi, Aslam**
"Urdu poetry since independence". *Pakistan Quarterly* 15, 1-2 (Summer-Autumn 1967), pp. 273-277.
Includes select bibliography of Urdu poetry since independence.

2576   **Garcin de Tassy, Joseph Héliodore Sagesse Vertu**
Allégories récits poétiques et chants populaires. 2nd ed. Paris, 1876. 639p.

2577   **Glebov, N.V.**
"Natsional'nye i demokraticheskiye motivi v klassicheskoĭ poëzii Urdu". In: *Poetry of Indian peoples*. Moscow, 1962, pp. 54-75.

2578   **Gorekar, N.S.**
"Modern Urdu poetry". *Indica* 5, 2 (September 1968), pp. 133-138.

2579   **Gulati, Azad**
"The Urdu scene: poetry and criticism dominate". *Indian Literature* 30, 6 (November-December 1987), pp. 221-228.

2580   **Hasan, Ibnul**
"Urdu literature in the seventies". *Pakistan Pictorial* 16 (July-August 1975), pp. 38-39.

2581   **Hasan, Iqtida**
"Later Mughals as represented in Urdu poetry". *Annali Dell'* Nuova Serie 12, pp. 129-152.

2582   **Hasan, Mohammad**
"Urdu: awaiting its moment of truth; Poetry 1960-1970". *Indian Literature* 14, 1 (March 1971), pp. 9-19.

2583   **Hashmi, Alamgir**
"Some directions of contemporary Urdu poetry in Pakistan: from 1965 to the present". *South Asia* New Series, 1, 2 (September 1979), pp. 67-79.

2584   **Husain, Mumtaz**
"Form and spirit in Muslim poetry". *Pakistan Quarterly* 6, 3 (1956), pp. 20-24, 69.

2585   **Ikram Barelvi**
"Pain and grief in Urdu poetry". *Pakistan Perspective* 2, 10-11 (March-April 1977), pp. 15-22, 30.

2586   **Jha, Amarnath**
Urdu poets and poetry. Allahabad: Leader Press, 1956. 220, 130p.

2587   **Kamran, Gilani**
South Asian Muslim creative mind. Lahore: National Book House, 1980. 146p.

2588   **Khatoon, Uzera**
"Poetry of life". *Pakistan Quarterly* 2, 4 [1952], pp. 20-24, 65.

2589   **Khundmiri, S. Alam**
"The changing idiom in modern Urdu poetry". *Illustrated Weekly of India* 2 (October-December 1967), pp. 53-56.

2590   **Lall, Inder Jit**
"Aspects of Urdu verse". *Thought* 25, 25 (23 June 1973), pp. 17-19.

2591   **Madhi, S.A.**
Parallelism in English and Urdu poets. Lucknow, 1965. 285p.

2592   *Masterpieces of Urdu ghazal from the 17th to the 20th century.* Trans. K.C. Kanda. New Delhi: Sterling Publishers, 1990. 334p.
Includes Urdu text in Roman and Arabic characters.

2593   **Mohan Singh**
Some characteristics and tendencies of modern Urdu poetry as explained through select representative poems published from 1867-1925. Lahore: Lahore Art Electric Press, 1931. 143p.

2594   **Naim, C.M.**
Readings in Urdu: prose and poetry. Honolulu: EWCP, 1965. 396p.

2595   — • "Yes, the poem itself". *Literature East and West* 15, 1, pp. 7-16.

2596   **Narang, Gopi Chand**
"The tradition and conventions of classical Urdu poetry". *New Orient* 5 (April 1966), pp. 50-53.

2597   — • "Tradition and innovation in Urdu poetry". In: *Poetry and Renaissance; Kumaran Asan Birth Centenary volume.* Ed. M. Govindan. Madras: Sameeksha, 1974, pp. 415, 434.
Discusses the work of Firaq and Faiz.

2598   — • "Urdu poetry". In: *Indian Poetry Today* 4. New Delhi: Indian Council for Cultural Relations, 1981, pp. 391-470.

2599   Pashi, Kumar.
"The new poem in Urdu". *Pakistan Review* 12 (October 1964), pp. 13-14.

2600   Qureshi, M.H.K.
"A preliminary analysis of an Urdu poetic tradition". *Alberta Anthropologist* 1, 2 (1967), pp. 24-29.

2601   Qureshi, Regula
"Tarannum: the chanting of Urdu poetry". *Journal of the Society for Ethnomusicology* 13, 3 (September 1969), pp. 425-468.

2602   Rahman, Anisur
"Some recent English translations of modern Urdu poetry". *Journal of South Asian Literature* 24, 2 (Summer, Fall 1898), pp. 203-214.

2603   Rahmatullah, Shahabuddin
Art in Urdu poetry. Dacca: The Pakistan Cooperative Book Society, [1955?], 120p.; 22 plates. English-Urdu.

2604   Rashed, N.M.
"Urdu poetry in Pakistan today". *Pakistan Quarterly* 1, 5 (Winter 1950), pp. 17-22, 49.

2605   Raza, Rahim
"Poeti orientali contro la guerra". *Plural, semestrale di letteratura internazionale* 5, 9 (1991), pp. 97-106.

2606   Russell, Ralph
"Some problems of the treatment of Urdu metre". *Journal of the Royal Asiatic Society* (April 1960), pp. 48-58.

2607   Sadiq, Muhammad
"Modern Urdu poetry". *Iqbal* 18, 3 (January-March 1971), pp. 1-14.

2608   Saksena, Ram Babu
European and Indo-European poets of Urdu and Persian. Lucknow: Naval Kishore Press, 1941. 407p.

2609   Saraswati, Saran
Development of Urdu poetry. New Delhi: Discovery Publishing House, 1990. 277p. Urdu text in Roman characters.

2610   Sayeed, Banu Tahira
"Urdu poetry of today". In: *Symposium on poetry India*. Madras: Krishna Srinivas, 1973, pp. 81-87.

2611   Schimmel, Annemarie
"Poetry, religion, and calligraphy: thoughts about Sadequain's work". In: *Calligraphy in modern art*. Ed. Hillman von Halem. Karachi: Pakistan-German Forum, 1975, pp. 61-65.

2612   Scott, T.
"Hindustani poets and poetry". *Calcutta Review* 72 (1881), p. 185.

2613   Saeed, Ahmad
"Three Lahori Urdu humorous poets". *Pakistan Review* 12 (June 1964), pp. 10-12.

2614   Shadani, Andaleeb
"Urdu poets of Bengal". *Pakistan Review* 14, 10 (October 1966), pp. 10-11.

2615   Shaikh, Zahurul H.
"Modern trends in Urdu poetry". *Explorations* 1, 1, pp. 93-99.

2616   Shakoor, A.
"Modern Urdu poetry". *The Hindustan Times Weekly Magazine* (13 September 1953), p. 4.

2617   Shaukat, Sameena
"Emperor Shah Alam II and his literary gatherings of the Diwan-i-Khas". *Indo-Iranica* 2, 14 (December 1961), pp. 45-74.

2618   Siddiqui, M.A.
"New voices in Urdu poetry". *Vision* 17, 12 (January 1969), pp. 5-6, 24.

2619   Siddiqui, Shujaatullah
Glimpses into the past. Karachi: All-Pakistan Multilingual Mushaira Committee, 1983. 117p.

2620   Thiesen Finn
A manual of classical prosody with chapters on Urdu, Karakhanidic and Ottoman prosody. Wiesbaden: Otto Harrassowitz, 1982.

2621   — • "Urdu poetry needs qualitative change in aesthetic image". *New Age* 16, 52 (December 1968).

2622   Yazdani, Malik Ghulam
"Modern Urdu poets of Hyderabad". *Islamic Culture* 20, 4 (1947), pp. 16-36.

2623   Zahir, Sajjad
"New voices in Urdu poetry". *Century* 1, 2 (1 June 1963), p. 15.

2624   Zaidi, Ali Jawad
"Urdu: poetry, the centre of attraction". *Indian Literature* 29, 6 (November-December 1986), pp. 171-177.
A survey of the 1985 writings.

2625   Zia, A.Q.
Urdu poetry in contemporary setting: a study in historical perspective. Hong Kong: Asian Research Service, 1985. 62p.
A cursory survey of the poetry of the last twenty-five years.

GHAZAL

2626   Ansari, Aslub Ahmad
"A critical approach to ghazal". *Annual of Urdu Studies* 5 (1985), pp. 139-140.
A review of Khwajah Manzur Husain's *Tahrik-e jidd-o jihad ba-taur-e mauzu-e sukhan.*
Reprinted from *Studies in Islam* (New Delhi), 16, 1 (January 1979), pp. 71-72.

2627   Bausani, Alessandro and Blachere, R.
"Ghazal - in Urdu literature". In: *Encyclopaedia of Islam* 2 (1965), pp. 1028-1036.

2628   Faiz, Faiz Ahmad
"Thoughts on the future of 'ghazal'". *Viewpoint* (Lahore) 6, 5 (September 1980), pp. 18-19.

2629   Faruqi, Shamsur Rahman
"Ghazal, old and new". *The Hindustani Times Weekly Magazine* (17 April 1960), p. 5

2630   — • *The secret mirror: essays on Urdu poetry.* Delhi: Academic Literature, 1981.
160p.
Includes articles on the poetry of Mir Anis, Ghalib and Iqbal.

2631   Faruqi, Shamsur Rahman and Pritchet, Frances W.
"Lyric poetry in Urdu: ghazal and nazm". *Journal of South Asian literature* 19, 2 (Summer-Fall 1984), pp. 111-127.

2632   "The future of the ghazal: a symposium: Muhammad Ahsan Farooqi; N.M. Rashed; Wazir Agha; Saleem Ahmad". Trans. Muhammad Umar Memon. *Annual of Urdu Studies* 4 (1984), pp. 1-23.
"*Naya Daur* invited some distinguished intellectuals to comment on the subject".
Also in: *Naya Daur* (Karachi), 61-62 (n.d.), pp. 45-74.

2633   Kinany, A.K.
The development of ghazal in Arabic literature: Pre-Islamic and early Islamic periods.
Damascus, 1951. 282p.

2634   Lall, Inder Jit
"Ghazal: a sustainer of spasms". *Thought* 19, 20 (20 May 1967), pp. 14-15.

2635   — • "Poetry: the ghazal through the centuries". *Design* 11, 7 (July 1967), pp. 150-153.

2636   — • "Three doyens of Urdu ghazal". *Thought* 14, 17 (28 April 1962), pp. 12-13.

2637   Naim, C.M.
"Ghazal and taghazzul: the lyric, personal and social". In: *The literatures of India: an introduction.* Ed. Edward C. Dimock, et al. Chicago: University of Chicago Press, 1974, pp. 181-197.

2638   — • "Traditional symbolism in the modern Urdu ghazal". In: *Language and Areas: Studies presented to George V. Bobrinskoy.* Chicago: Division of the Humanities, University of Chicago, 1967, pp. 105-111.

2639   Nath, Kidar
"Masters of Urdu ghazal". *Illustrated Weekly of India* (15 July 1962), pp. 30-31.

2640   Pritchett, Frances W.
"Convention in the classical Urdu ghazal". *Journal of South Asian and Middle Eastern Studies* 3, 1 (Fall 1979), pp. 60-77.

2641   Rahman, Tariq
"Boy-love in the Urdu ghazal". *Paidika* (Amsterdam) 2, 1 (Summer 1989), pp. 10-27.
An abridged version in *Annual of Urdu Studies* 7 (1990), pp. 1-20.

2642   Randhir, L.C.
Ghazal, the beauty eternal. New Delhi: Milind Publications, 1982. 216p.
A survey of Urdu ghazal from Mir to Firaq; includes a chapter on the singing of ghazals. Urdu quotations in Devanagari characters.

2643   Rattan, H.R.
"Ghazal today". *The Hindustan Times Weekly Magazine* (14 February 1960), p. 4.

2644   Russell, Ralph
"The pursuit of the Urdu ghazal". *Journal of Asian Studies* 29, 1 (November 1969), pp. 107-124.

2645   — • "The Urdu ghazal in Muslim society". *South Asian Review* 3, 2 (January 1970), pp. 141-149.

2646   Schimmel, Annemarie
["Review of Shamsur Rahman Faruqi's *The secret mirror: essays on Urdu poetry*"]. *Annual of Urdu Studies* 3 (1983), pp. 103-106.

2647   Suzuki, Takeshi
"The evolution of Urdu ghazal and some of its important features". *Area and Culture Studies* (Tokyo) 26, pp. 123-144.

MARSIYA

2648   Krenkow, F.
"Marthiya". In: *Encyclopaedia of Islam* 3 (1936), pp. 306-307.

2649   Naim, C.M.
"The art of the Urdu marsiya". In: *Islamic society and culture: essays in honour of Professor Aziz Ahmad.* Eds. Milton Israel and N.K. Wagle. New Delhi: Manohar Publications, (1983), pp. 101-116.

2650   Qureshi, Regula B.
"Islamic music in an Indian environment: the Shia majlis". *Ethnomusicology* 24, 1 (January 1981), pp. 41-71.

2651   Shackle, Christopher
"The Multani marsiya". In: *Der Islam* 55 (1978), pp. 281-311.

2652   Shinozani, S. Fazal Abbas
"Marsiya tradition in Urdu poetry". *Perspective* 4, 8 (February 1971), pp. 81-82.

2653   Sud, Kedar Nath
"The elegy in Urdu". *Thought* 17, 48 (26 November 1966), pp. 16-17.

MASNAVI

2654   Ithape, Usha G.
"My readings of some verses of the Qutab Mushtari, a mathnawi in Dakhani Hindi".
Oriental Institute Journal, Maharaja Sayajirao (University of Baroda), n.d.

2655   Levy, R.
"Mathnawi". In: *Encylopaedia of Islam* 3 (1936), pp. 410-412.

2656   Narang, Gopi Chand
"Some social and cultural aspects of Urdu masnavis". *Mahfil* 3, 2-3 (1966), pp. 55-64.

MUSHAIRA

2657   Ahmad, Zamiruddin
"Mushaira as an institution". *Pakistan Quarterly* 12, 2 (Winter 1969), pp. 19-22.

2658   Anderson, David D.
"The Mushaira". *Literature East and West* 12, 2-4 (December 1968), pp. 217-222.

2659   Beg, Farhatullah
Dihli ki akhiri sham. The last mushairah of Delhi: a translation into English of Farhatullah Baig's modern Urdu classic, Dihli ki akhri shama. New Delhi: Orient Longman, 1979. 126p.
Introduction, notes, glossary, and bibliography by Akhtar Qamber.

2660   — • *The last mushairah of Delhi.* Trans. Akhtar Qamber. New Delhi: Orient Longman, 1979. 126p.
Annotated translation of the essay by Mirza Farhatullah Beg.

2661   Maswani, A.M.K.
"The Mushaira: Urdu poetical symposium". *Perspective* 3, 11 (May 1970), pp. 9-13.

2662   Naim, C.M.
["Review of *The last mushaira of Delhi*"]. *Annual of Urdu Studies* 1 (1981), pp. 113-115.

2663   — • "Poet-audience interaction at Urdu musha'iras". In: *Urdu and Muslim South Asia*. Ed. Christopher Shackle. London: School of Oriental and African Studies, University of London, 1989, pp. 167-173.

2664   **Pyami, Zafar**
"Shankar-Shad mushaira". *Link* 8, 34 (3 April 1966), p. 38.

2665   **Rahman, Munibur**
"The Musha'irah". *Annual of Urdu Studies* 3 (1983), pp. 75-84.
On the institution of mushaira, 'a poetical contest', and its significant role in the evolution of Urdu Poetry. Revised version of an article originally presented at the Fourth National Convention of the Popular Cultural Association held at Milwaukee, Wisconsin, May 2-4 1974.

PATRIOTIC AND WAR POETRY

2666   **Ahmad, K. Jamil**
"Patriotism in Urdu poetry". *Pakistan Review* 17, 3 (March 1969), pp. 30-39.

2667   **Ahmad, Saeed**
"Glimpses of Urdu and Panjabi war poetry". *Pakistan Review* 9 (September 1966), pp. 16-18, 29.

2668   **Alvi, Sajida S.**
"Urdu literature from prison: some reflections on the writings of Pakistani prisoners of war in India". *Journal of the Research Society of Pakistan* (Lahore), 19, 3 (July 1982), pp. 43-54.

2669   **Ashraf, Syed Ali**
"The poetry of freedom". *Pakistan Quarterly* 4, 1, pp. 28-33.

2670   **Ashraf, Syed Waheed**
"Nationalism in Urdu poetry". *Annals of Oriental Research* (Madras), 31, pt. 2 (1983), pp. 1-10.

2671   **Ebadat Barelvi**
"The poetry of freedom". Trans. S. Amjad Ali. *Pakistan Quarterly* 10, 4 (1962), pp. 54-61.

2672   **Faruqi, Muhammad Hamza**
"The war of 1857 and Urdu poetry". *Journal of the Research Society Pakistan* 22, 2 (April 1985), pp. 45-61.

2673   **Majeed, M.A.**
"Role of our poets in the war". *Pakistan Review* 14, 2 (February 1966), pp. 3-6, 20.

2674   — • "Role of our poets in the September 1965 war". *Pakistan Review* 20, 1 (January 1972), pp. 33-38.

2675   **Minault, Gail**
"Urdu political poetry during the Khilafat Movement". *Modern Asian Studies* 8, 4 (October 1974), pp. 459-471.

2676   **Narang, Gopi Chand**
"The Indian freedom struggle and Urdu poetry". *Indian Literature* 29, 4 (July-August 1986), pp. 127-139.

2677   **Siddiqui, Abul Lais**
"Sami-ullah Khan, Mohsin-ul-Mulk and Hali". In: *History of the Freedom Movement* II (1831-1905), Pt. 2. Karachi: Pakistan Historical Society, pp. 543-555.

PROGRESSIVE WRITERS MOVEMENT

2678   **Alam, Qaiser Zoha**
"Progressive poetry and propaganda". *Indian Literature* 26, 1 (January-February 1983), pp. 69-78.
A critique of Kalimuddin Ahmad's criticism on Progressive Urdu poetry.

2679   **Coppola, Carlo**
Urdu poetry 1935-1970: the Progressive episode. Ph.D. thesis, University of Chicago, 1975.

2680   **Jafri, Ali Sardar**
"Progressive Movement and Urdu poetry - I." *Viewpoint* (Lahore) 8, 45 (16 June 1983), pp. 27-29.

2681   — • "Progressive Movement and Urdu poetry - II." *Viewpoint* (Lahore) 8, 46 (23 June 1983), pp. 27-29.

2682   — • "Progressive Movement and Urdu poetry". *Urdu Canada* 1, 1 (February 1986), pp. 1-21.
Originally presented at the Urdu Conference held in September, 1982 under the auspices of the Urdu Society of Canada, Toronto.

QASIDA

2683   **Siddiqi, Atiq Ahmad**
"Qasida in Urdu". *Indian Literature* 30, 1 (January-February 1987), pp. 72-80.

RELIGIOUS POETRY

2684   **Bausani, Alessandro**
"The religious spirit in muslim poetry". *Pakistan Quarterly* 5, 2 (Summer 1955), pp. 44-48, 62-63.

2685   — • "Can we speak of Muslim poetry?" *Pakistan Quarterly* 7, 4 (Winter 1957).

2686   **Hussain, Syed Safdar**
"Islamic influence on modern Urdu poetry". *Islamic Literature* 14, 5 (May 1968), pp. 55-60.

2687   **Jain, Champat Rai**
Gems of Islam. New Delhi: Today and Tomorrow's Printers and Publishers, 1975. 2 vols.
Reprint of London, 1940 edition.
Includes translations from Urdu mystic poets.

2688   **Narang, Gopi Chand**
"A critical perspective. The impact of Islamic mysticism on Urdu poetry". *Indian Literature* 32, 2 (March-April 1989), pp. 155-170.

2689   **Schimmel, Annemarie**
"Reflections on popular Islamic poetry". *Contributions to Asian Studies* 17 (1982), pp. 91-94.

RUBAIYAT

2690   **Masse, Henri**
"Rubai". In: *Encyclopaedia of Islam* 3 (1936), pp. 1167-1168.

2691   **Taseer, M.D.**
"Rubaiyat in Urdu and English". *Pakistan Quarterly* 1, 2 (1949), pp. 27-28, 46.

SHAHR ASHOB

2692   **Hasan, Iqtida**
"Later Mughals as represented in the light of the Shahr ashob from Hatim, Sauda and Nazir". *Annali dell' Istituto Universitario Orientale di Napoli*, Nuova Serie, 9 (1959), pp. 131-153.

2693   **Naim, C.M.**
"A note on sahr-asob". *Annual of Urdu Studies* 4 (1984), p. 42.

2694   **Pritchett, Frances W.**
"The world turned upside down: sahr-asob as a genre". *Annual of Urdu Studies* 4 (1984), pp. 37-41.

2695   **Sukhochev, A.S.**
"Shahrashob v literature Urdu". In: *Theory of genre of Oriental literatures.* Moscow: Nauka, 1985, pp. 59-74.

SUFI POETRY

2696   Ali, Ahmad
"Mysticism and poetry". *Pakistan Quarterly* 3, 2 [1953], pp. 49-52.

2697   Haywood, John A.
"Wali Dakhani and the development of Dakhani - Urdu Sufi poetry". *Acta Orientalia* 28, 1-2 (Copenhagen, 1964), pp. 153-174.

2698   Pritchett, Frances W. and Khaliq, Ahmad Khaliq
Urdu meter: a practical handbook. Madison: South Asian Studies, University of Wisconsin, 1987. 147p.

WOMEN'S POETRY

2699   Garcin de Tassy, Joseph Héliodore Sagesse Vertu
Les femmes poètes dans l'Inde (Revue de l'Orient). Paris, 1854.

2700   Schimmel, Annemarie
Liebe zu dem Einen: Texte aus der mystischen Tradition des indischen Islam. Ausgew. aus dem Pers., Arab., Urdu und Sindhi. Trans and Intro. Annemarie Schimmel. Zürich u. a.: Benziger Verlag, 1986. 173p.

2701   — • "A nineteenth century anthology of poetesses". In: *Islamic society and culture: essays in honour of Professor Aziz Ahmad.* Eds. Milton Israel and N.K. Wagle. New Delhi: Manohar, 1983.

PROSE

Individual Authors

BIBLIOGRAPHY

2702   **Narang, Gopi Chand**
"A bibliography of Urdu short stories in English translation".   *Mahfil* 3, 2-3 (1966), pp. 55-64.

2703   **Narang, Gopi Chand and Seidlinger, Mary**
"A bibliography of Urdu short stories in English translation".   *Mahfil* 4, 2 (1967), pp. 23-29.

ABBAS, GHULAM

TRANSLATIONS

2704   "Anandi".   In: *Contemporary Pakistani short stories*.   Ed. and trans. Nisar Ahmad Farooki.   Lahore: Ferozsons Ltd., 1955, pp. 99-109.
Also in: *Stories from Pakistan*.   Ed. Krishan Gopal Abid.   New Delhi: India Paperbacks, 1977, pp. 55-63.

2705   "Anandi".   Trans. Jai Ratan.   *Illustrated Weekly of India* (8 January 1984), pp. 55-58.

2706   "Bombay-wallah".   Trans. Qaisar Afzal.   *The Nation* (January 1963), [*Pakistan Writer's Guild Number,* Karachi 1963],   pp. 49-51.

2707   "Fancy haircutting saloon".   Trans. C.M. Naim.   *Annual of Urdu Studies* 3 (1983), pp. 65-73.

2708   "Fancy haircutting saloon".   In: *Mornings in the wilderness*.   Ed. and trans. Waqas Ahmad Khwaja.   Lahore: Sang-e-Meel Publications, 1988, pp. 169-181.

2709   "The gamblers".   Trans. the author.   In: *Ten years of vision*.   Ed. Yunus Said. Karachi: Pakistan Publishing House, 1963, pp. 22-30.

2710   "Ghaazi mard".   Trans. Karen Leonard and Gopi Chand Narang.   *Mahfil* 7, 1-2 (Spring-Summer 1971), pp. 131-135.

2711   "His wife".   Trans. Sadiq Hussain.   In: *Modern Urdu short stories from Paksitan*. Ed. S. Viqar Azim.   Islamabad: R.C.D. Cultural Institute of Pakistan, 1977, pp. 40-53.

2712   "Overcoat".   Trans. Zainab Ghulam Abbas.   *Pakistani Literature* (Islamabad) 1, 1 (1992), pp. 73-79.

2713   "The overcoat". Trans. Abdul Khair Kashfi and Janet M. Powers. *Arizona Quarterly* 22, 3 (Autumn 1966), pp. 206-216.

2714   "The overcoat". Trans. Zainab Ghulam Abbas. *Perspective* 1, 1 (July 1967), pp. 57-62.

2715   "The overcoat". Trans. S. Amjad Ali. *Pakistan Quarterly* 5, 2 (Summer 1955), pp. 59-61.
Also in: *Pakistan Perspective* 2, 10-11 (March-April 1977), pp. 9-13.

2716   "The shadow". Trans. Yasmin Hosain. In: *Modern Urdu short stories from Pakistan.* Ed. S. Viqar Azim. Islamabad: R.C.D. Cultural Institute of Pakistan, 1977, pp. 27-39.

2717   "The tombstone". Trans. Sabiha Hasan. *Pakistan Quarterly* 3, 1 pp. 55-60.

2718   "White man's burden". Trans. Khalid Hasan. In: *A touch of reality: contemporary Pakistani stories.* Ed. Faruq Hassan. Montreal: Dawson College, [197-?], pp. 7-13.

ABBAS, KHWAJA AHMAD

TRANSLATIONS

2719   "A debt to pay". Trans. Khushwant Singh. In: *Writings of India's partition.* Eds. Ramesh Mathur and Mahendra Kulasrestha. Delhi: Simant Publications, 1987.

2720   "The death of Shaikh Burhanuddin". In: *Land of five rivers.* Ed. and trans. Khushwant Singh. Bombay: Jaico Publishing House, 1965.

2721   "The dumb cow". Trans. the author. *Mahfil* 4, 2 (1968), pp. 5-14.

2722   *I am not an island: an experiment in autobiography.* New Delhi: Vikas Publishing House, 1977. 551p.

2723   "Maharaja's elephant". Trans. the author. In: *Modern Indian short stories.* Vol. 1. Ed. K.S. Duggal. New Delhi: Indian Council for Cultural Relations, 1975, pp. 123-127.

2724   "The miracle of Haji Ali". Trans. the author. *Illustrated Weekly of India* (12 May 1985), pp. 56-59.

2725   "Naya inteqam". Trans. Anwar Enayetullah. *The Herald* 12, 11 (November 1981), pp. 72-77.

2726   "Rafiq". Trans. Helmut Nespital. In: *Der Tigerkönig.* Berlin: Verlag Volk und Welt, 1966, pp. 423-443.

AHMAD, ASHFAQ

TRANSLATIONS

2727 "Baba". Trans. [S. Amjad Ali?]. *Pakistan Quarterly* 3, 3 [1953], pp. 53-56, 60. Abridged.

2728 "Gato". In: *Stories from Pakistan*. Ed. Krishan Gopal Abid. New Delhi: India Paperbacks, 1977. pp. 122-149.

2729 "The lost night". Trans. Khalid Hasan. In: *Under the green canopy*. Ed. Khalid Hasan. Lahore: Afro-Asian Book Club, 1966.
Also in: *Perspective* 1, 10-11 (April-May 1968), pp. 23-31.
Also in: *A touch of reality: contemporary Pakistani stories*. Ed. Faruq Hassan. Montreal: Dawson College, [197-?], pp. 68-74.

2730 "Mohsin Mohalla". Trans. Faruq Hassan. *Urdu Canada* 1, 3 (1987), pp. 54-56.

2731 "The search". Trans. Salma Mahmud. In: *Modern Urdu short stories from Pakistan*. Ed. S. Viqar Azim. Islamabad: R.C.D. Cultural Institute of Pakistan, 1977, pp. 163-178.

2732 "Stony-hearted". In: *Mornings in the wilderness*. Ed. and Trans. Waqas Ahmad Khwaja. Lahore: Sang-e-Meel Publications, 1988, pp. 221-235.

AHMAD, AZIZ

TRANSLATIONS

2733 *The shore and the wave. Aisi bulandi aisi pasti*. Trans. Ralph Russell. London: G. Allen and Unwin, 1971. 167p.
Novel.

STUDY

2734 **Banerjee, Sumanta**
["Review of *The shore and the wave*"]. *Indian Literature* 25, 1 (1972), pp. 76-81.

AHMAD, NAZIR

TRANSLATIONS

2735   *The bride's mirror: a miratularus.* Vocabulary and notes by G.E. Ward. London, 1899. 371p.
Urdu in Roman characters.

2736   *The bride's mirror: a tale of domestic life in Delhi forty years ago.* Trans. G.E. Ward. London: Henry Frowde, 1903. 187p.

2737   *Mirror of the bride: Mirat-ul-Urus.* Trans. M. Kempson. Madras: The Hogarth Press, [1934].

2738   *Mirror: or, Miratul-Arus of Maulavi Nazir Ahmad.* Ed. E. Ward. London, 1899. 371p.
Urdu in Roman characters.

2739   *Mirror. A tale of domestic life in Delhi forty years ago ...* Trans. G.E. Ward. London, 1903. 157p.

2740   *Mubtala; or a tale of two wives.* Trans. Khwaja Khan. Madras: The Hogarth Press, 1934. 87p.
Abridged.

2741   *The repentance of Nussoh; Taubatun Nusuh.* Trans. G.E. Ward. Madras: The Hogarth Press, 1934.

2742   *The repentance of Nussoh.* Trans. M. Kempson. London: Wm. H. Allen and Co., 1884. 118p.

STUDIES

2743   **Kalsi, A.S.**
"The influence of Nazir Ahmad's *Mirat al-Arus* (1869) on the development of Hindi fiction". *Annual of Urdu Studies* 7 (1990), pp. 31-44.

2744   **Rabiunnisa**
"Maulvi Nazir Ahmad: a pioneer of Urdu novel"./*Perspective* 5, 1 (July 1971), pp. 77-80.

2745   **Rashid, S**
"Nazir Ahmad Khan: a pioneer of Urdu novel". *Pakistan Review* 7 (December 1959), p. 45.

2746   **Sukhochev, A.S.**
"Lectures of Nazir Ahmad as a source for study of Indian enlightenment". In: *Problems of modern Indian literature*. Calcutta: Statistical Publishing Society, pp. 191-202.

AHMAD, RAZI FASIH

TRANSLATION

2747   "Blossoms in the dust".   Trans. M.N. Khan.   *Perspective* 5, 10 (April 1972), pp. 75-81.

AHMAD, ZAMIRUDDIN

TRANSLATION

2748   "A slap in the face".   Trans. the author.   *Vision* 12, 10 (December 1963), pp. 40-43, 51-59.
Abridged.

2749   "Purvai, the easterly wind".   Trans. Muhammad Umar Memon.   *The Toronto South Asian Review* 8, 1 (Summer 1989), pp. 25-33.

AHMAR JAIPURI, RASHID AHMAD

STUDY

2750   **Bora, Ramchandra**
"Writ large: Rashid Ahmad Ahmar Jaipuri".   *Thought* 27, 23 (7 June 1975), pp. 9-10.

AHMED, AFTAB

STUDY

2751   "A legacy of sweetness and light".   *Viewpoint* (Lahore) 10, 28 (February 1985), pp. 10, 32.

AKHTAR HUSAIN RAIPURI

TRANSLATIONS

2752   "The burning ghat".   Trans. the author.   In: *Ten years of vision*.   Ed. Yunus Said. Karachi: Pakistan Publishing House, 1963,   pp. 17-21.

2753   "Flock of sheep". In: *Contemporary Pakistani short stories*. Ed. and trans. Nisar Ahmad Farooki. Lahore: Ferozsons Ltd., 1955, pp. 21-36.

2754   "Flock of sheep". In: *Stories from Pakistan*. Ed. Krishan Gopal Abid. New Delhi: India Paperbacks, 1977, pp. 108-121.

2755   "The heart is dark". Trans. Yunus Said. *Vision* 12, 10 (December 1962), pp. 27-30.

2756   "An image of stone". Trans. Qaiser Afzal. *The Nation.* (January 1963), [*Pakistan Writer's Guild Number,* Karachi 1963], pp. 45-48, 69.

STUDY

2757   **Janus**
"Akhtar Husain Raipuri". *Viewpoint* (Lahore) 8, 13 (4 November 1982), p. 27.

AKHTAR, SALIM

TRANSLATION

2758   "Miss Ahmed, B.A., B.T." In: *Modern Urdu stories*. Ed. and Trans. Agha Iqbal Mirza. Calcutta: Writers Workshop, 1975.

ALI, AHMAD

TRANSLATIONS

2759   "Before death".   Trans. the author.   *New Directions* 15 (International Issue), pp. 132-147.

2760   "Our lane". In: *Indian short stories*. Eds. and trans. Mulk Raj Anand and Iqbal Singh. London: New India Publishing Co., 1946.

2761   "Our lane". In: *Ten years of vision*. Ed. Yunus Said. Karachi: Pakistan Publishing House, 1963, pp. 3-16.

2762   "The sentimental lover". Trans. [S. Amjad Ali?]. *Pakistan Quarterly* 3, 4, pp. 46-48.

STUDY

2763   **Brander, L.**
"Two novels by Ahmed Ali". *Journal of Commonwealth Literature* (3 July 1967), pp. 76-86.

AMIN, RAFIA MANZURUL

TRANSLATIONS

2764 "Bakhtavar". Trans. Manzurul Amin. In: *New generation 2: an anthology of Urdu writers*. Ed. Satish Batra. Lucknow: New Generation, 1967, pp. 47-56.

2765 "Crossroad". In: *Modern Urdu stories*. Ed. and trans. Agha Iqbal Mirza. Calcutta: Writers Workshop, 1975.

AMJAD, RASHID

TRANSLATIONS

2766 "Fading identity". Trans. Rajinder Singh Verma. *Urdu Canada* 1, 2 (1986), pp. 49-52.

2767 "The muffled voices". In: *Modern Urdu stories*. Ed. and trans. Agha Iqbal Mirza. Calcutta: Writers Workshop, 1975.

ANSARI, HAYATULLAH

TRANSLATION

2768 "Banke bahadur". Trans. Muhammad Hamid Siddiqi. *Illustrated Weekly of India* 93, 1 (2 January 1972), pp. 25-27, 53.
An excerpt from the novel.

ANWAR

TRANSLATION

2769 "Blood". In: *Stories from Pakistan*. Ed. Krishan Gopal Abid. New Delhi: India Paperbacks, 1977, pp. 64-78.

ASGHAR, KHALIDA

TRANSLATION

2770   "The wagon". Trans. Muhammad Umar Memon. In: *Twenty years of the Urdu short story. Indian Literature* 19, 6 (November-December 1976), pp. 119-131.

ASGHAR, MASUD

TRANSLATION

2771   "Trees and doors". Trans. Linda Wentink. *Journal of South Asian Literature* 16, 2 (Summer-Fall 1981), pp. 133-137.

ASHK, UPENDRA NATH

STUDY

2772   **Farrukhi, Asif Aslam**
"I consider myself a Pakistani writer: Interview with Upendra Nath Ashk". *Newsline* 1, 8 (February 1990), pp. 109-112.

ASHRAF, SYED MOIN

TRANSLATION

2773   "Reborn". Trans. the author. *Urdu Canada* 1, 2 (1986), pp. 53-58.

ASKARI, MIRZAH

TRANSLATION

2774   "Lady of Hiroshima". In: *Contemporary Pakistani short stories*. Ed. and trans. Nisar Ahmad Farooki. Lahore: Ferozsons Ltd., 1955, pp. 53-78.

ASKARI, MUHAMMAD HASAN

TRANSLATIONS

2775   "Bitch". In: *Contemporary Pakistani short stories*. Ed. and trans. Nisar Ahmad Farooki. Lahore: Ferozsons Ltd., 1955, pp. 79-97.

2776   "The bitch". In: *Stories from Pakistan*. Ed. Krishan Gopal Abid. New Delhi: Indian Paperbacks, 1977, pp. 91-107.

AZAD, ABUL KALAM

STUDIES

2777   **Engineer, Asghar Ali**
"Theological creativity of Abul Kalam Azad". *Indian Literature* 31, 4 (July-August 1988), pp. 17-29.

2778   **Faruqi, Khwaja Ahmad**
"Maulana Azad as a man of letters". *Indian Literature* 1, 2   (April-September 1958), pp. 6-13.

2779   **Saroor, Aley Ahmad**
"The literary contribution of Maulana Azad". *Indian Literature* 31, 4 (July-August 1988), pp. 7-16.

AZIM, ANWAR

TRANSLATIONS

2780   "The blackmailer". Trans. Iqbal Akhtar. *Indian Literature* 22, 2 (1979), pp. 24-46.

2781   "Cinderella". Trans. Iqbal Akhtar. *Indian Literature* 19, 6 (1976), pp. 62-86.

AZIMI, FAHIN

TRANSLATION

2782   "The second statue of liberty". Trans. the author. *Urdu Canada* 1, 2 (1986), pp. 29-33.

BADIUZZAMAN

TRANSLATIONS

2783   "The agony that was ecstasy". Trans. N.N. Abbasi. *Thought* 21, 5 (1 February 1969), *Short Story Supplement,* pp. 9-12.

2784   "The panorama of life". Trans. N.N. Abbasi. *Thought* 20, 49 (7 December 1968), *Short Story Supplement*, pp. 3-4.

BALWANT SINGH

TRANSLATIONS

2785   "How far - yet how near". Trans. Jai Ratan. *Illustrated Weekly of India* (2 August 1964), pp. 19-21.

2786   "Webley - 38". Trans. Jai Ratan. *Thought* (29 June 1963), pp. 11-13.

2787   "Soorma Singh". In: *Land of five rivers*. Ed. and trans. Khushwant Singh. Bombay: Jaico Publishing House, 1965.

BANO, JEELANI

TRANSLATIONS

2788   "Revenge". Trans. B.A. Farooqui. *Urdu Canada* 1, 3 (1987), pp. 46-49.

2789   "The surety". Trans. Jai Ratan. *Indian Literature* 26, 1 (January-February 1983), pp. 110-117.

BATRA, SATISH

TRANSLATIONS

2790   "Ones own country". Trans. the author. *Urdu Canada* 1, 3 (1987), pp. 63-66.

2791   "The wedding gown". Trans. the author. In: *New generation 2; an anthology of Urdu writers*. Ed. Satish Batra. Lucknow: New Generation, 1967, pp. 29-35.

BEDI, RAJINDER SINGH

TRANSLATIONS

2792 "Beyond the terminus". Trans. Jai Ratan. In: *Modern Indian short stories*. Vol. 1. Ed. K.S. Duggal. New Delhi: Indian Council for Cultural Relations, 1975, pp. 128-143.

2793 "Bhola". Trans. Jai Ratan. *Indian Literature* 30, 2 (March-April 1987), pp. 102-112.

2794 "Eclipse". Trans. Jai Ratan. *Thought* (8 February 1964), pp. 11-13. Also in: *Indian Literature* 28, 3 (May-June 1985), pp. 34-44.

2795 "Give me your sorrows". Trans. Karen Leonard and Gopi Chand Narang. *Indian Literature* 11, 2 (1968), pp. 20-48.

2796 "Intermittent fever". Trans. Jai Ratan. *Illustrated Weekly of India* 97 (21-23 May 1976), pp. 43-47.

2797 *I take this woman*. Trans. Khushwant Singh. Delhi: Hind Pocket Books, 1967. 103p. Translation of Bedi's Sahitya Akademi Award novel *Ek chadar maili si*.

2798 "Lajwanti". Trans. the author. In: *Contemporary Indian short stories*. Vol. 2. Ed. Bhabani Bhattacharya. Delhi: Sahitya Akademi, (1967), pp. 201-214.

2799 "Lajwanti". Trans. Anwar Enayetullah. *The Herald* (Karachi) 12, 4 (April 1981), pp. 56-64.

2800 "Lajwanti". In: *Land of five rivers*. Ed. and trans. Khushwant Singh. Bombay: Jaico Publishing House, 1965.

2801 "Lajwanti". In: *Writings of India's partition*. Eds. Ramesh Mathur and Mahendra Kulasrestha. Delhi: Simant Publications, 1976.

2802 "Lajwanti". Trans. Mark Pegors. *Annual of Urdu Studies* 5 (1985), pp. 67-76.

2803 "The pawnshop". Trans. Manmohan Singh. *Thought* 12, 48 (26 November 1960), pp. 11-12.

2804 "Prabodh and Maitriya". Trans. C.M. Naim. *Annual of Urdu Studies* 5 (1985), pp. 98-100. Translation of an introduction written by Rajinder Singh Bedi for his novel *Ek cadar maili si*, published by Star Publications (Delhi) in 1964. The translation is based on the text that appeared in *Ajkal* (Delhi), (October 1984), pp. 4-5 and 22.

2805 *Selected short stories*. Ed. Gopi Chand Narang. Trans. Jai Ratan. New Delhi, 1989. 259p.

2806   "Sculptress and the antique dealer". Trans. Kuldip Singh. *Illustrated Weekly of India* 90, 47 (23 November 1969), pp. 48-49.

2807   "The warm coat". In: *Modern Urdu stories*. Ed. and trans. Agha Iqbal Mirza. Calcutta: Writers Workshop, 1975.

2808   "When I was little". Trans. Ralph Russell. *Adam International Review. Passages from India* 355-360 (1971), pp. 355-360.

2809   "A woman". Trans. C.M. Naim. *Annual of Urdu Studies* 5 (1985), pp. 77-80.

2810   "Zenu". Trans. Jai Ratan. *Indian Literature* 22, 2 (1979), pp. 12-23.

STUDIES

2811   **Abbas, Khawja Ahmad**
"Bedi, the last of the triumvirate". *Indian Literature* 28, 3 (May-June 1985), pp. 25-28.

2812   **Dulai, Surjit Singh**
["Review of Rajinder Singh Bedi's *I take this woman*"]. *Mahfil* 5, 1-2 [1968], pp. 110-115.

2813   **Emzedd**
"Bedi is no more". *Viewpoint* (Lahore) 10, 15 (November 1984), pp. 28-29.

2814   **Feldman, Jamila**
"To be or not to be a Goddess: Rajinder Singh Bedi's women characters". *Annual of Urdu Studies* 7 (1990), pp. 67-73.

2815   **Flemming, Leslie A.**
"Chekhovian elements in the short stories of Rajinder Singh Bedi". *Literature East and West* 21, 1-4 (1977), pp. 65-76.

2816   — • "Progressive writers, progressive filmaker: the films of Rajinder Singh Bedi". *Annual of Urdu Studies* 5 (1985), pp. 81-97.

2817   **Gulati, Azad**
"The art of Rajindar Singh Bedi". *Indian Literature* 28, 3 (May-June 1985), pp. 29-33.

2818   **Kakar, Sudhir**
Intimate relations: exploring Indian sexuality. New Delhi: Viking (Penguin), 1989. 161p. Contains analysis of films and literary texts, including Bedi's *Ek chadr maili si*.

2819   **Lall, Inder Jit**
"Rajinder Singh Bedi". *Indian P.E.N.* 33, 3 (March 1967), pp. 73-74.

2820   "Mahfil interviews Rajinder Singh Bedi". *Mahfil* 8, 2-3 (Summer-Autumn 1972), pp. 139-158.

2821   **Narang, Gopi Chand**
"Bedi's art and style, it's metaphorical and mythical roots".   Trans. Jai Ratan.   *Urdu Canada*
1, 3 (1987), pp. 33-48.

BEG, MIRZA HAMID

TRANSLATIONS

2822   "The Mughal Inn".   Trans. C.M. Naim.   *The Toronto South Asian Review* 3, 1
(Summer 1984), pp. 35-39.
Also in: *Urdu Canada* 1, 3 (1987), pp. 59-62.

BIN RAZAQ, SALAAM

TRANSLATION

2823   "Full circle".   Trans. Jai Ratan.   *Indian Literature* 29, 3 (May-June 1986),
pp. 85-100.

BUKHARI, A.S.

TRANSLATIONS

2824   "Constancy rewarded".   Trans. M.N. Khan.   *Perspective* 5, 2-3 (August-September
1971), pp. 83-87.

2825   "The dear departed".   Trans. S. Amjad Ali.   *Pakistan Quarterly* 9, 2 (Summer 1959),
pp. 55-61."

2826   "Memorium".   In: *Mornings in the wilderness*.   Ed. and trans. Waqas Ahmad
Khwaja.   Lahore: Sang-e-Meel, Publications, 1985,   pp. 187-202.

2827   "The seven-year itch".   Trans. M.N. Khan.   *Perspective* 6, 2-3 (August-September
1971), pp. 85-90.

STUDIES

2828   **Vahid, Syed Abdul**
"A.S. Bokhari".   *Pakistan Quarterly* 9, 2 (Summer 1959), p. 54.

2829   **Yusafzai, Mazhar**
"A.S. Bokhari 'Patras'". *Pakistan Pictorial* 2, 1-2 (January-February 1978), p. 23.

CHANDAR, KRISHAN

TRANSLATIONS

2830   "All-India Heroine's Conference". *Thought* 20, 40 (5 October 1968), *Short Story Supplement*, pp. 3-7.

2831   "At the Hotel Firdaus". Trans. Jai Ratan. *Imprint* 13, 11 (February 1974), pp. 73-89.

2832   "Bachan Singh". Trans. Jai Ratan. *Thought* 22, 16 (18 April 1970), pp. 13-14.

2833   "The carpet". Trans. Jai Ratan. *The Literary Review* (Teaneck, New Jersey) 4, 4 (Summer (1961), pp. 539-550.

2834   "The cat and the minister". Trans. Jai Ratan. *Imprint* 14, 2 (May 1974), pp. 47-50.

2835   "The dreamer". Trans. Jai Ratan. *Thought* 19, 25 (24 June 1967), pp. 13-15.

2836   *The dreamer.* Trans. Jai Ratan. Delhi: Hind Pocket Books, 1970. 160p.
Includes eleven stories.

2837   *Flame and the flower.* Trans. the author. Bombay: Current Book House, 1951. 99p.
Includes fifteen stories.

2838   "The Four-anna aunt". Trans. Jai Ratan. *Thought* 16, 26 (27 June 1964), pp. 11-14.
Also in: *Writings on India's partition.* Eds. Ramesh Mathur and Mahendra Kulasrestha. Delhi: Simant Publications, 1976.

2839   "Heaven is a garbage bin". Trans. Jai Ratan. *Illustrated Weekly of India* 94, 49 (9 December 1973), pp. 49-57.
Also in: *Stories from India.* Eds. Khushwant Singh and Qurratulain Hyder. New Delhi: Sterling Publishers, 1974.

2840   "Higher mathematics". Trans. Jai Ratan. *Illustrated Weekly of India* 97, 17 (25 April 1976), pp. 49-53.

2841   "Ich werde Schuhe tragen". Trans. Helmut Nespital. *Der Tigerkönig*. Berlin: Verlag Volk und Welt, 1966, pp. 459-470.

2842   *I cannot die; Ann-data.* Trans. Khwaja Ahmad Abbas. Poona: Kitab Publishers, [1945?]. 52p.

2843 "Kalu Bhangi". Trans. Ralph Russell. In: *Tales from modern India*. Ed. K. Natwar-Singh. New York: MacMillian, 1966, pp. 179-196.

2844 *Krishan Chander: selected short stories*. Ed. Gopi Chand Narang. Trans. Jai Ratan. New Delhi: Sahitya Akademi, 1990. 263p.

2845 "Lakhpati bannayka nuskha". *The Herald* (Karachi) 12, (6 June 1981), pp. 72-82.

2846 "Mirrors are lonely". Trans. D.P. Pandey. New Delhi. 1977.

2847 *Mr Ass comes to town; Ek gadhe ki sarguzasht*. Trans. L. Babman. Delhi: Hind Pocket, 1968. 167p.

2848 "On the pavement". Trans. L. Hayat Bouman. *Illustrated Weekly of India*
91, 5 (1 February 1970), pp. 19-23.
91, 6 (8 February 1970), pp. 25-29;
91, 7 (15 February 1970), pp. 25-29;
91, 8 (22 February 1970), pp. 25-28;
91, 9 (1 March 1970), pp. 25-29.

2849 "The Peshawar express". In: *Writings on India's partition*. Eds. Ramesh Mathur and Mahendra Kulasreshta. Delhi: Simant Publications, 1976.

2850 "The pit". Trans. C.J.S. Jossan. *Journal of South Asian Literature* 13, 1-4 (1977-78), pp. 225-232.

2851 "Sartaj". Trans. Anwar Enayetullah. *The Herald* (Karachi) (October 1983), pp. 88-97.

2852 *Seven faces of London*. Trans. L. Hayat Bouman. New Delhi: Paradise Publications, 1968. 175p.

2853 "The shoe". In: *Modern Urdu stories*. Ed. and trans. Agha Iqbal Mirza. Calcutta: Writer's Workshop, 1975.

2854 "The soldier". Trans. the author. In: *Modern Indian short stories*. Vol. 1. Ed. K.S. Duggal. New Delhi: Indian Council for Cultural Relations, pp. 113-121.
Also in: *Tales from Modern India*. Ed. K. Natwar-Singh. New York: MacMillan, 1966, pp. 168-178.
Also in: *Modern Indian short stories*. Comp. and ed. Suresh Kohli. New Delhi: Arnold Heineman, 1974, pp. 71-79.

2855 "Son". Trans. Jai Ratan. *Thought* 21, 31 (2 August 1969) [*Short Story Supplement*], pp. 13-14.

2856 "Tai eesree". Trans. Khushwant Singh. In: *Land of five rivers*. Ed. and trans. Khushwant Singh. Bombay: Jaico Publishing House, 1965.

2857 "Those thirty minutes". Trans. Jai Ratan. *Illustrated Weekly of India* 90, 21 (25 May 1969), pp. 25-27.

2858 *Virgin and the well.* Trans. the author. Dehra Dun: EBD Publishing and Distributing Company, 1968. 146p.
Includes eight stories.

STUDIES

2859 Azeem, Anwer
"Krishan Chander". (Letter) *Indian Express* (18 December 1968), p. 6: 3.

2860 Bachan Singh
"Krishan Chander". *Thought* 22, 16 (18 April 1970), pp. 13-14.

2861 Chandar, Krishan
"I believe". *Illustrated Weekly of India* 90, 48 (30 November 1969), pp. 34-35.

2862 Gupta, N.K.
"Krishan Chander". (Letter) *Indian Express* (7 December 1968), p. 6: 5.

2863 Gupta, Prakash C.
"Krishan Chander". *Contemporary Indian Literature* 3, 2, pp. 5, 13.

2864 "Krishan Chander honoured". *Link* 11, 14 (17 November 1968), p. 40

2865 "R.S."
"Not malice alone: Ghalib and Krishan Chander". *Thought* 20, 46 (23 November 1968), p. 21.

2866 Sharma, Reoti S.
"Krishan Chander". *Indian Express* (26 November 1968), p. 6: 3.
Also in: *Times of India* (29 November 1968), p. 10: 6.

2867 Suchochev, A.S.
Krishan Chandar. Moscow: Nauka, 1983.

2868 Sud, Kedar Nath
"Urdu fiction and Krishan Chander". *Indian Literature* 20, 4 (1977), pp. 122-127.

CHAWLA, HARCHARAN

TRANSLATIONS

2869 "Anguish of a horse". Trans. Satish Batra. *Urdu Canada* 1, 2 (1968), pp. 59-63.

2870 *The broken horizon.* Trans. Satish Batra. Lucknow: A.I.N.M.U.W.C. (All-India Non-Muslim Urdu Writer's Conference), 1974. 68p.

CHUGHTAI, ISMAT

TRANSLATIONS

2871   "Dosa". Trans. Satish Batra. In: *New generation 2; an anthology of Urdu writers.* Ed. Satish Batra. Lucknow: New Generation, 1967, pp. 36-46.

2872   "Giving her away". Trans. Jai Ratan. *Indian Literature* 29, 2 (March-April 1986), pp. 208-214.

2873   "Housewife". Trans. Fatima Ahmad. In: *Modern Indian short stories.* Ed. K.S. Duggal. New Delhi: Indian Council for Cultural Relations, 1975, pp. 144-153.

2874   "Housewife". *Indian Horizons* 22, 1 (January 1973), pp. 84-95.

2875   "Kallu". Trans. Jan Brzezinski. *Annual of Urdu Studies* 7 (1990), pp. 93-107. Two versions of the story, one written in 1957, and the other at a later date.

2876   "Kalu bhangi". Trans. Ralph Russell. *Indian Literature* 2, 2 (April-September 1959), pp. 54-70.

2877   "The liar". Trans. Fatima Ahmad. *The Toronto South Asian Review* 3, 3 (Spring 1985), pp. 42-46.

2878   "Little mother". Trans. Ahmad Ali. In: *Indian short stories.* Eds. and Trans. Mulk Raj Anand and Iqbal Singh. London: New India Publishing Co., 1946.

2879   "Mirror unto me". Trans. Satish Batra. In: *New generation three.* Eds. Ramlal and Syeda Naseem Chishti. Lucknow: New Generation, 1968, pp. 123-128.

2880   "The quilt". Trans. Surjit Singh Dulai and Carlo Coppola. *Mahfil* 8, 2-3 (Summer-Fall 1972), pp. 2-3.

2881   *The quilt and other stories.* Trans. Tahira Naqvi and Syed S. Hameed. New Delhi: Kali For Women, 1990. 224p.

[Another ed.] London: The Women's Press, 1987.

2882   "Sleep". Trans. Hardev Singh. *Thought* 21, 14 (5 April 1969) [*Short Story Supplement*], pp. 7-10.

2883   "Tiny's granny". Trans. Ralph Russell. In: *Contemporary Indian short stories* Vol. 1. New Delhi: Sahitya Akademi, 1959, pp. 117-129.
Also in: *The Literary Review* (Teaneck, New Jersey) 4, 4 (Summer 1961), pp. 506-518.
Also in: *Truth tales: contemporary writing by Indian women.* New Delhi: Kali for women, 1986; London: The Women's Press, 1987, pp. 167-184.

2884   "Two hands". Trans. Steven M. Poulos. *Journal of South Asian Literature* 16, 2 (Summer-Fall 1981), pp. 123-130.

2885   "Wedding clothes".   Trans. Suzanne Schwartz.   *Mahfil* 8, 2-3 (Summer-Autumn 1972), pp. 203-214.

STUDIES

2886   Chughtai, Ismat
"Interview".   The *Herald* (Karachi), (April 1985), pp. 114-117.

2887   Latif, Khalid
"Ismat Chughtai - personality sketch".   Trans. Carlo Coppola and M.A. Beg.   *Mahfil* 8, 2-3 (Summer-Autumn 1972), pp. 189-194.

2888   "Mahfil interviews Ismat Chughtai".   *Mahfil* 8, 2-3 (Summer-Autumn 1972), pp. 169-188.

FAKHR ZAMAN

TRANSLATION

2889   *The lost seven; and dead man's tale.*   Trans. Khalid Hasan.   Delhi: Ajanta Publications, 1989.   116p.
"Two most controversial novels banned in Pakistan".

FARIDI, SHAH NASIR

TRANSLATION

2890   "The price is my heart".   Trans. the author and Srivirinchi.   *Indian Literature* 24, 5 (1981), pp. 63-68.

FAROOKI, NISAR AHMAD

TRANSLATION

2891   "Moonshine".   In: *Contemporary Pakistani short stories*.   Ed. and trans. Nisar Ahmad Farooki.   Lahore: Ferozsons Ltd., 1955,   pp. 247-263.

FATIMA, ALTAF

TRANSLATION

2892   *"Dastak na dō"*. Trans. Anwar Enayetullah. *The Herald* (Karachi). Novel serialized in the journal during 1980-1981.

FAZLI, KARIM

TRANSLATION

2893   *The Jamadar*. Trans. Rafiq Khawar. London: Cassell, [1961?]. Novel.

FIKR TAUNSVI

TRANSLATION

2894   "The city". Trans. Inder Jit Lall. *Thought* 25, 20 (19 May 1973), pp. 13-14.

GAZDAR, SAEEDA

TRANSLATION

2895   "Hindustani Pakistani". Trans. Anwar Enayetullah. *The Herald* (Karachi), (June 1983), pp. 52-58.

HAIDER, FIRDAUS

TRANSLATION

2896   "Majazi Khuda". Trans. Anwar Enayetullah. *The Herald* (Karachi), 12, 5 (May 1981), pp. 66-75.

HAMESH, AHMAD

TRANSLATION

2897   "The fly". Trans. Javaid Qazi. In: *Twenty years of the Urdu short story*. *Indian Literature* 19, 6 (November-December 1976), pp. 165-187.

HAMID, ABDUL

TRANSLATIONS

2898   "The chasm". Trans. Khalid Hasan. In: *Under the green canopy*. Lahore: Afro-Asian Book Club, 1966.
Also in: *A touch of reality: contemporary Pakistani stories*. Ed. Faruq Hassan. Montreal: Dawson College, [197-?], pp. 75-80.

HARDEV SINGH

TRANSLATION

2899   "The prayer". Trans. the author. *Thought* 20, 31 (3 August 1963), *Short Story Supplement*, p. 12.

HASHMI, JAMILA

TRANSLATION

2900   "The orange mist". Trans. Zahida Khanum. In: *Under the green canopy*. Lahore: Afro-Asian Book Club, 1966.

HINA, ZAHIDA

TRANSLATIONS

2901   "Achilles heel". Trans. Muhammad Umar Memon. *Annual of Urdu Studies* 6 (1987), pp. 86-93.

2902   "To be or not to be".   Trans. C.M. Naim.   *Annual of Urdu Studies* 4 (1984), pp. 69-73.

HUSAIN, ALI ABBAS

TRANSLATIONS

2903   "The snow slab".   In: *Contemporary Pakistani short stories*.   Ed. and trans. Nisar Ahmad Farooki.   Lahore: Ferozsons Ltd., 1955,   pp. 189-199.

2904   "Wirsa".   Trans. Anwar Enayetullah.   *The Herald* (Karachi) (July 1983), pp. 94-98.

HUSAIN, INTIZAR

TRANSLATIONS

2905   "The back room".   Trans. Caroline J. Beeson and Muhammad Umar Memon. *Journal of South Asian Literature* 18, 2 (Summer, Fall 1983), pp. 41-48.

2906   "The city of sorrows".   Trans. Muhammad Salim-ur-Rahman.   In: *Modern Urdu short stories from Pakistan*.   Ed. S. Viqar Azim.   Islamabad: R.C.D.   A Cultural Institute of Pakistan, 1977,   pp. 128-145.

2907   "Dust and ashes".   Trans. Qaiser Afzal.   *The Nation.* (January 1963) [*Pakistan Writer's Guild Number.*]   Karachi 1963, pp. 62-63.

2908   "A frame of bones".   In: *Mornings in the wilderness*.   Ed. Waqas Ahmad Khawja. Lahore: Sang-e-Meel Publications, 1988,   pp. 209-221.

2909   "The last man".   Trans. Leslie A. Flemming.   *Journal of South Asian Literature* 18, 2 (Summer, Fall 1983), pp. 56-60.

2910   "The last man".   Trans. Riaz Hassan, et al.   In: *Under the green canopy*.   Lahore: Afro-Asian Book Club, 1966.
Also in: *Journal of South Asian Literature* 18, 2 (Summer, Fall 1983), pp. 90-102.
Also in: *A touch of reality: contemporary Pakistan stories*.   Ed. Faruq Hassan.   Montreal: Dawson College, [197-?],   pp. 103-106.

2911   "The legs".   Trans. Nancy D. Gross. *Journal of South Asian Studies* 18, 2 (Summer, Fall 1983), pp. 90-102.

2912   "The legs".   Trans. Qurratulain Hyder.   *Illustrated Weekly of India* 91, 36 (6 September 1970), pp. 34-37.

2913   "Metamorphosis". Trans. C.M. Naim. *Mahfil* 1, 1, pp. 22-29.

2914   "The lost ones". Trans. Muhammad Umar Memon. *Pakistani Literature* (Islamabad) 1, 1 (1992), pp. 89-102.

2915   "The lost ones". Trans. Muhammad Umar Memon. *Journal of South Asian Literature* 18, 2 (Summer, Fall 1983), pp. 121-132.

2916   "The monkeys". Trans. Wayne R. Husted and Muhammad Umar Memon. *Annual of Urdu Studies* 6 (1987), pp. 83-85.

2917   "The prisoner". Trans. C.M. Naim. *Journal of South Asian Literature* 18, 2 (Summer, Fall 1983), pp. 115-120.

2918   "The shadow". Trans. Muhammad Umar Memon. *Journal of South Asian Literature* 18, 2 (Summer, Fall 1983), pp. 72-81.

2919   "The stairway". Trans. Muhammad Umar Memon. *Journal of South Asian Literature* 18, 2 (Summer, Fall 1983), pp. 20-30.
Also in: *Twenty years of the Urdu short story. Indian Literature* 19, 6 (November-December 1976), pp. 87-102.

2920   "A stranded railroad car". Trans. Muhammad Umar Memon. *Journal of South Asian Literature* 18, 2 (Summer, Fall 1983), pp. 49-55.

2921   "Towards his fire". Trans. Muhammad Umar Memon. *Journal of South Asian Literature* 18, 2 (Summer, Fall 1983), pp. 31-40.

2922   "Turtles". Trans. Nancy D. Gross. *Journal of South Asian Literature* 18, 2 (Summer, Fall 1983), pp. 103-114.

2923   *An unwritten epic and other stories*. Lahore: Sang-e-Meel Publications, 1987. 278p. Fourteen stories and a short but succinct introduction.

2924   "An unwritten epic". Trans. Leslie A. Flemming and Muhammad Umar Memon. *Journal of South Asian Literature* 18, 2 (Summer, Fall 1983), pp. 6-19.

2925   "Weggefahrten". Trans. Sandra Joost. In: *Auswahl zeitgenossischer Urdu-Lyrik und -Prosa (Haus der Kulturen der welt)*. Ed. Christina Oesterheld. Berlin: Das Arabische Buch, 1991, pp. 56-71. (Gesteht's die Dichter der Orients sind grösser; 4)

2926   "The yellow dog". Trans. Faruq Hassan. In: *A touch of reality: Contemporary Pakistani stories*. Ed. Faruq Hassan. Montreal: Dawson College, [197-?], pp. 94-102.

2927   "The yellow cur". Trans. Daud Rahbar. *Journal of South Asian Literature* 18, 2 (Summer, Fall 1983), pp. 61-71.

STUDIES

2928 Farrukhi, Asif Aslam
"Today a writers domicile has become more important than his poetry". *Newsline* 9, (March 1990), pp. 88-90.
Interview with Intizar Husain.

2929 Husain, Intizar
"Diary of a Pakistani: milestone to milestone". *Pakistan Quarterly* 15 (Summer-Autumn 1967), pp. 85-90.

2930 — • "Conversation between Intizar Husain and Muhammad Umar Memon". Trans. Bruce R. Pray. *Journal of South Asian Literature* 18, 2 (Summer, Fall 1983), pp. 153-186.

2931 Janus
"Intizar in Roop Nagar". *Viewpoint* (Lahore) 5, 23 (January 1980), p. 9.

2932 Memon, Muhammad Umar
"An enriched white-bread novel". *Journal of South Asian Literature* 18, 2 (Summer, Fall 1983), pp. 206-208.

2933 "The lost ones (A requim for the self by Intizar Hussain)". *Edebiyat, a Journal of Middle Eastern Literature* 3, 2 (1978), pp. 139-156.

2934 — • "Pakistani Urdu creative writing on national disintegration: the case of Bangladesh". *Journal of South Asian Studies* 43, 1 (1983), pp. 105-127.

2935 — • "Partition literature: a study of Intizar Husain". *Modern Asian Studies* 14, 3 (1980), pp. 377-410.

2936 — • "Reclamation of memory, fall, and the death of the creative self: three moments in the fiction of Intizar Hussain". *International Journal of Middle East Studies* 13, 1 (1981), pp. 73-91.

2937 — • "Shi'ite consciousness in a recent Urdu novel: Intizar Husain's *Basti*". In: *Urdu and Muslim South Asia*. Ed. Christopher Shackle. London: School of Oriental and African Studies, University of London, 1989, pp. 139-150.

2938 — • "The writings of Intizar Hussain". *Journal of South Asian Literature* 18, 2 (Summer, Fall 1983), 222p.
Thirteen stories and three articles by Intizar Hussain in translation and an interview with him, plus criticism, reviews and bibliography.

2939 Pritchett, Frances W.
"Narrative modes in Intizar Husain's short stories". *Journal of South Asian Literature* 18, 2 (Summer, Fall 1983), pp. 192-199.

2940 Qazi, Javaid
"The significance of being human in Intizar Husain's fictional world". *Journal of South Asian Literature* 18, 2 (Summer, Fall 1983), pp. 187-191.

2941   Salim-ur-Rahman, Muhammad
"Four Reviews". *Journal of South Asian Literature* 18, 2 (Summer, Fall 1983), pp. 200-205.

2942   Wentink, Linda
"Curfew in Kufa". *Annual of Urdu Studies* 2 (1982), pp. 123-130.
A review of Intizar Husain's novel *Basti.*

2943   Zeno
"The world of Intizar Hussain". *Dawn* (Karachi), 17 (February 1984), p. 4.

HUSAIN, KHALIDA

TRANSLATIONS

2944   "The wagon". Trans. Muhammad Umar Memon. *Pakistani Literature* (Islamabad)
1, 1 (1992), pp. 103-114.

STUDY

2945   Salim-ur-Rahman, Muhammad
["Review of *Pahchan*"]. *Annual of Urdu Studies* 4 [1984], pp 111-114.
Reprinted with few changes from the *Pakistan Times* (Lahore), 12 (July 1982), p. 4.

HUSAIN, SADIQ

TRANSLATION

2946   "A pair of gold bangles". Trans. the author. In: *Modern Urdu short stories from
Pakistan*. Ed. S. Viqar Azim. Islamabad: R.C.D. Cultural Institute of Pakistan, 1977,
pp. 107-113.

HUSSEIN, ABDULLAH

TRANSLATIONS

2947   "The brook". Trans. Muhammad Umar Memon. *Mahfil* 7, 1-2 (Spring-Summer
1971), pp. 93-124.

2948   *Downfall by degrees and other stories*. Ed. and trans. Muhammad Umar Memon.
Toronto: TSAR Publications, 1987. 197p.

2949   "The exile". Trans. Ahmed Nadeem Anwer. In: *Twenty years of the Urdu short story*. *Indian Literature* 19, 6 (November-December 1976), pp. 132-144.

2950   "Exile". In: *Mornings in the wilderness*. Ed. and Trans. Waqas Ahmad Khwaja. Lahore: Sang-e Meel Publications, 1988, pp. 237-248.

2951   "The little stream". Trans. Faruq Hassan. In: *A touch of reality: contemporary Pakistani stories*. Ed. and trans. Faruq Hassan. Montreal: Dawson College, [197-?], pp. 126-146.

2952   "The tale of the old fisherman". Trans. C.M. Naim and Gordon Roadarmel. *Mahfil* 2, 2 (May 1965), pp. 7-16.

2953   *Night and other stories*. Trans. Muhammad Umar Memon. New Delhi: Orient Longman, 1984. 171p.
Includes:
— • "The little brook".
— • "Night".
— • "The sea".

STUDIES

2954   **Blecher, George**
["Review of *Night and other stories*"]. *Annual of Urdu Studies* 5 (1985), pp. 136-137.

2955   **Farrukhi, Asif Aslam**
"Faces of the soul". *Newsline* 2, 3 (September 1990), pp. 121-22.
Review of *Downfall by degrees and other stories*.

2956   **Iqbal, Muzaffar**
Abdullah Husain (from sad generations to a lonely tiger). Madison: The South Asian Studies Centre, University of Wisconsin, 1985. 113p.
A study of Abdullah Hussein's fiction.

2957   — • "The writer's context". *Pakistani Literature* (Islamabad) 1, 1 (1992), pp. 115-120.

2958   — • "A tale of sad generations". *Pakistani Literature* (Islamabad) 1, 1 (1992), pp. 121-148.

2959   **Janus**
Culture: "Abdullah Husain in town I". *Viewpoint* (Lahore) 6, 12 (October 1980), p. 30.

2960   — • Culture: "Abdullah Husain in town II". *Viewpoint* (Lahore) 6, 13 (October 1980), p. 27.

2961   — • Culture: "Abdullah Husain in town III". *Viewpoint* (Lahore) 6, 14 (December 1980), p. 19.

2962 **Khan, Alam**
"Need literature of protest". Trans. Ikramrul Haq. *Viewpoint* (Lahore) 7, 5 (September 1982), pp. 30-31.
An interview with Abdullah Hussein.

2963 **Memon, Muhammad Umar**
"Abdullah Hussein: a profile". *The Toronto South Asian Review* 4, 1 (Summer 1985), pp. 26-43.

HYDER, QURRATULAIN

TRANSLATIONS

2964 "A chapter from *Aag ka darya*". Trans. the author and Gauri Deshpande. In: *Indian writing today* 5, 3 (July-September 1971), pp. 179-183.

2965 "Confessions of St. Flora of Georgia". Trans. the author. *Indian Literature* 29, 2 (March-April 1986), pp. 215-241.

2966 "Der Berg der Fkire". "Faqiro ki pahari". Trans. Christina Oesterheld. *Erkundungen-23 Erzählungen aus Indien.* Berlin: Verlag Volk und Welt, 1990, pp. 65-177.

2967 "Dervish". Trans. the author. In: *Modern Indian short stories.* Ed. Suresh Kohli. New Delhi: Arnold Heinemann, 1974, pp. 123-131.

2968 "Die wechselvollen Schicksale der Andalib Bano". Trans. Christina Oesterheld. In: *Auswahl zeitgenössischer Urdu-Lyrik und -Prosa (Haus der Kulturen der welt).* Ed. Christina Oesterheld. Berlin: Das Arabische Buch, 1991, pp. 38-53. (Gesteht's! die Dichter des Orients sind grösser; 4).

2969 "The exiles". Trans. Faruq Hassan. In: *A touch of reality: Contemporary Pakistani Stories.* Ed. Faruq Hassan. Montreal: Dawson College, [197-?], pp. 35-58.
Also in: *Urdu Canada* 1, 3 (1987), pp. 23-45.

2970 "From river of fire". Trans. the author. In: *New writing in India.* Ed. Adil Jussawalla. Baltimore: Penguin Books, 1974, pp. 39-49.

2971 "Honour". Trans. the author. *Illustrated Weekly of India* 94 (18 March 1973), pp. 29-31.

2972 "I Tiresias". Trans. the author. *Illustrated Weekly of India* 90, 28 (13 July 1969), pp. 25-29.
Also in: *Stories from India.* Eds. Khushwant Singh and Qurratulain Hyder. New Delhi: Sterling Publishers, 1974.

2973   "Memories of an Indian childhood".   Trans. the author. *Illustrated Weekly of India*
91, 12 (22 March 1970).
Also in: *Modern Indian short stories*. Vol. 1. Ed. K.S. Duggal. New Delhi: Indian Council
for Cultural Relations, 1975, pp. 160-173.

2974   "Mooted on other banks". In: *Contemporary Pakistani short stories*. Ed. and Trans.
Nisar Ahmad Farooki. Lahore: Ferozsons Ltd., 1955, pp. 235-246.

2975   "My aunt Gracie". *Illustrated Weekly of India* 93, 36 (3 September 1972), pp. 28-33.

2976   "The photographer". Trans. B.A. Farooqi. *The Toronto South Asian Review* 5, 3
(Spring 1987), pp. 66-77.

2977   "The sermons of Haji Gul Baba Bektashi". Trans. the author. In: *Twenty years of
the Urdu short stories*. *Indian Literature* 19, 6 (November-December 1976), pp. 51-61.

2978   "Stateless". Trans. Qurratulain Hyder. In: *New writing in India*.   Ed. Adil
Jussawalla. Baltimore: Penguin Books, 1974, pp. 39-49.
Novel excerpt from *Aga ka darya*.

2979   *A woman's life*. Trans. the author. New Delhi: Chetna Publications, 1979. 96p.
Two novellas:
— • "A woman's life".
— • "Tea gardens of Sylhet".

STUDIES

2980   **Asaduddin, M.**
"The novels of Qurratulain Hyder". *Indian Literature* 34, 2 (March-April 1991), pp. 82-108.
Includes select bibliography of Qurratulain Hyder's works.

2981   **Farrukhi, Asif Aslam**
"The other side of Qurratulain Hyder". *Newsline* 2, 4 (October 1990), pp. 163-164.
Review of Qurratulain Hyder's novel, *Chandni Begum*.

2982   **Flemming, Leslie A.**
"Muslim self-identity in Qurratulain Hyder's *Ag ka darya*". In: *Studies in the Urdu ghazal
and prose fiction*. Ed. Muhammad Umar Memon. Madison, 1979, pp. 243-256.

2983   **Naim, C.M.**
["Review of *Kar-i jahan daraz hai. Fann our fankar*"]. *Annual of Urdu Studies* 1 (1981),
pp. 105-107.

2984   **Janus**
"Qurat-ul-Ain's plaint". *Viewpoint* (Lahore) 5, 26 (February 1980), p. 10.

2985 Oesterheld, Christina
Zum Romanschaffen der Urdu-Schriftsteller in Qurratul-ain Haider. Untersuchung der Entwicklung der literarischen Methode anhand der Romane "Mere bhi sanamkhane", "Ag ka darya", und "Akhir-i-sab ke hamsafar". Ph.D. thesis, Berlin, 1986.

2986 "Personalities: Qurratulain Haidar". *Link* 10, 31 (10 March 1968), p. 33.

2987 Pritchett, Frances W.
"A woman's life". Annual of Urdu Studies 2 (1982), pp. 136-142.
A review of Qurratulain Hyder's novel, *Agle janam mohe bitiya na kijo,* translated by Qurratulain Hyder.

2988 Rashid, S.
"Qurrat-ul-ain Hyder: critical appreciation". *Pakistan Review* 8 (June 1960), pp. 27-28.

INAYATULLAH, ANWAR

TRANSLATIONS

2989 "Life is for living". Trans. M.N. Khan. *Perspective* 4, 1 (July 1970), pp. 35-39.

2990 "The longest hour". Trans. M.N. Khan. *Perspective* 4, 9 (March 1971), pp. 81-86.

IQBAL, MUZAFFAR

TRANSLATION

2991 "A journey through time". Trans. the author. *Annual of Urdu Studies* 7 (1990), pp. 53-61.
Translation of chapters three and four of *Inxila*, Book 1 of a trilogy (*Hijraten*) published by al-Daira, Lahore, 1987.

ISSAR, DAVINDAR

TRANSLATIONS

2992 "The man unknown". Trans. Raj Abhey. *The Statesman* (23 March 1958).

2993 "Margaret". Trans. Anwar Enayetullah. *The Herald* (Karachi) (December 1983), pp. 52-57.

JAHAN, BILQIS

TRANSLATION

2994   "Life and lamentation". Trans. Ahmad Ali. In: *Under the green canopy*. Lahore: Afro-Asian Book Club, 1966.

JAHAN, RASHID

TRANSLATIONS

2995   "Iftari". *Mainstream* 14, 1-5 (1973), pp. 153-156.

2996   "Woman". A play in one act. Trans. Steven M. Poulos. *Annual of Urdu Studies* 1 (1986), pp. 70-88.

STUDIES

2997   "In memoriam. Rashid Jahan". *Indian Literature* 1 (1952).

2998   **Poulos, Steven M.**
"Rashid Jahan of *Angare*, her life and work". *Indian Literature* 30, 4 (July-August 1987), pp. 108-118.

JAHAN, S.M.

TRANSLATION

2999   "The red clock". Trans. Inder Jit Lall. *Thought* (16 February 1963), p. 11.

JALAL, HAMID

TRANSLATION

3000   "Agony of an ecstasy". In: *A touch of reality: contemporary Pakistani stories*. Ed. Faruq Hassan. Montreal: Dawson College, [197-?].

JAMAL, AKHTAR

STUDY

3001 **Rahman, Tariq**
"The short stories of Akhtar Jamal". *Dawn* (8 June 1990).

KHALID, FAROOQ

TRANSLATIONS

3002 *Black mirrors*. Trans. Eric Cyprian. London: Jonathan Cape, 1987. 284p.
Novel. First published in Pakistan in 1977 under the title *Siah ainey*, it was awarded the
Adamji Award in 1978.

3003 "Black mirrors". Trans. Eric Cyprian. *Urdu Canada* 1, 3 (1987), pp. 68-81.

STUDY

3004 **Hashmi, Alamgir**
"The novel as mirror or lens". *The Muslim Magazine* (19 May 1989), p. 5

KHAN, SAYYID AHMAD

STUDIES

3005 **Abdul Khaliq**
"Ethics of Sir Sayyid Ahmad Khan". *Iqbal* 18, 1 (July 1969), pp. 62-78.

3006 **Ahmad, Naseer**
"Sir Syed Ahmad Khan - writer and reformer". *Pakistan Review* 16, 3 (March 1966),
pp. 26-27.

3007 **Ahmad, Ziauddin**
"Sir Syed Ahmad Khan". *Perspective* 5, 2-3 (August-September 1971), pp. 59-64.

3008 — • "Syed Ahmad Khan and Aligarh Movement". *Pakistan Pictorial* 2, 1-2
(January-February 1978), pp. 12-15.

3009 **Aminuddin, M.**
"The genius of Sir Sayyid Ahmad Khan". *Perspective* 3, 8-9 (February-March 1970),
pp. 89-92.

3010 **Baljon, J.M.S.**
The reforms and religious ideas of Sir Sayyid Ahmad Khan. 3rd ed. Lahore: Shaikh Muhammad Ashraf, 1964. 160p.

3011 **Daabla, Basheer A.**
"Muslim political thought in colonial India: a comparative study of Sir Sayyid Ahmad Khan and Mawlana Abu al Kalam Azad". *Islamic Culture* 61, 2 (April 1987), pp. 24-50.

3012 **Dar, Bashir Ahmad**
Religious thought of Sayyid Ahmad Khan. Lahore: Institute of Islamic Culture, 1957. 304p.

3013 **Graham, George Farquhar Irving**
The life and notes of Sir Syed Ahmad Khan. Karachi: Oxford University Press, 1974. 298p. First published Edinburgh, 1885.

3014 — • *The life and work of Syed Ahmad Khan, KCSI.* 3rd ed. London, 1909.

3015 **Hali, Khawaja Altaf Husain**
Hayat-i Javed. Trans. Khalid Hasan Qadiri and David J. Matthews. Delhi, 1979.

3016 **Husain, M. Hadi**
Syed Ahmad Khan: pioneer of Muslim resurgence. Lahore: Institute of Islamic Culture, 1970. 259p.

3017 **Jain, M.S.**
The Aligarh Movement: its origin and development 1858-1906. Agra: Sri Ram Mehra and Co., 1965. 201p.

3018 **Khan, Kazim Ali**
Sir Syed and Muslim University, Aligarh. Lucknow: Prakashan Kendra, [1967?]. 38p.

3019 **Khan, Syed Ahmad**
"*Sirat-i faryidiya*". Trans. Christopher Shackle. *Islamic Culture* 46, 4 (December 1972), pp. 307-336.
A memoir.

3020 — • *Writings and speeches of Sir Syed Ahmad Khan.* Ed. and comp. Shan Muhammad. Bombay: Nachiketa Publications, 1972. 272p.

3021 **Malik, Hafeez**
Sir Sayyid Ahmad Khan and Muslim modernization in India and Pakistan. New York: Columbia University Press, 1980. 340p.

3022 — • "Sir Sayyid Ahmad Khan's role in the development of Muslim nationalism in the Indo-Pakistan subcontinent". *Islamic Studies* 5, 4 (December 1966), pp. 385-410.

3023 **Moin, Mumtaz**
The Aligarh Movement: origin and early history. Karachi: Salman Academy, 1976. 273p.

3024 **Muhammad, Shan**
Sir Syed Ahmad Khan: a political biography. Meerut: Meenakshi, 1969. 272p.

3025 **Nizami, K.A.**
Sayyid Ahmad Khan. Delhi: Publications Division, Ministry of Information and Broadcasting, 1966. 184p.

3026 **Rawlinson, H.G.**
"Sir Sayyid Ahmad Khan". *Islamic Culture* 4, 3 (1930), pp. 389-396.

3027 **Shakir, Moin**
"The political ideas of Sir Syed Ahmad". *Quest* 57 (April 1968), pp. 57-62.

3028 **Troll, Christian W.**
"A note on an early topographical work of Sayyid Ahmad Khan: *Asar al-Sanadid".* *Journal of the Royal Asiatic Society* (1972), pp. 134-146.

3029 — • *Sayyid Ahmad Khan, a reinterpretation of Muslim theology.* New Delhi, 1978.

KHATUN, AMTUL RAHMAN

STUDY

3030 **Rashid, S.**
"Our women novelists: A.R. Khatoon". *Pakistan Review* 6, 10 (October 1958), pp. 33, 35.

KOMAL, BALRAJ

TRANSLATION

3031 "The well". Trans. the author. *Indian Literature* 29, 1 (January-February 1986), pp. 58-64.

LAL, INDAR JIT

TRANSLATIONS

3032 "The faded visage". Trans. the author. *Thought* (6 July 1963), p. 11.

3033 "The finale". Trans. the author. *Thought* (18 January 1964), pp. 11-12.

LAM AHMAD AKBARABADI

STUDY

3034   Hasan, Masood
"Lam Ahmad Akbarabadi". *Indian Literature* 14, 2 (March-April 1976), pp. 64-72.
A veteran Urdu writer and a pioneer in the field of modern Urdu short story.

MAJID, IQBAL

TRANSLATIONS

3035   "Two men, slightly wet". Trans. C.M. Naim. In: *Twenty years of the Urdu short story. Indian Literature* 19, 6 (November 1976), pp. 209-218.

3036   "The parasite". Trans. Muhammad Umar Memon. *Indian Literature* 19, 2 (March-April 1976), pp. 52-63.

MANRA, BALRAJ

TRANSLATIONS

3037   *The altar and other stories*. Trans. Muhammad Umar Memon. Delhi: Writers Forum, 1967.

3038   "The box of matches". Trans. K. Mukadam and Adil Jussawalla. In: *New writing in India*. Ed. Adil Jussawalla. Baltimore: Penguin Books, 1974, pp. 243-248.

3039   "The colour of ashes". Trans. K. Kumar. *Thought* (15 August 1964), pp. 13-14.

3040   "Composition one". Trans. Muhammad Umar Memon. In: *Twenty years of the Urdu short story. Indian Literature* 19, 6 (November-December 1976), pp. 115-118.

3041   "The matchbox". Trans. Muhammad Umar Memon. *Short Story International* (September 1965), pp. 45-51.
Also in: *Pakistan Review* 13, 10 (October 1964), pp. 25-27.

3042   "Portrait in black and blood". Trans. Muhammad Umar Memon. *Aawesh* 68 (Delhi) 1, 3 (1969).

3043   "The sleeping city". Trans. K. Kumar. *Thought* (16 May 1964), pp. 11-12.

3044   "The tremendous treasure". Trans. Sagar Sethi. *Thought* (19 October 1963), pp. 11-12.

MANTO, SAADAT HASAN

TRANSLATIONS

3045   "The angel". Trans. Linda Wentink. *Journal of South Asian Literature* 20, 2 (Summer, Fall 1985), pp. 101-106.

3046   "Ashok Kumar". Trans. Leslie A. Flemming. *Journal of South Asian Literature* 20, 2 (Summer, Fall 1985), pp. 113-120.

3047   *Kingdom's end and other stories*. Trans. Khalid Hasan. London: Verso, 1987. 257p.

3048   "Black borders". Trans. Nathan Rabe, Alan Zinser and John Zylla. *Journal of South Asian Literature* 20, 2 (Summer, Fall 1985), pp. 36-55.

3049   "Black margins". Trans. Saroj Vashishtha. In: *Writing's on India's partition*. Eds. Ramesh Mathur and Mehendra Kulasreshta. Delhi: Simant Publications, 1976.

3050   *Black milk*. Trans. Hamid Jalal. Lahore: al-Kitab, 1956. 254p.
Includes eleven stories and a biographical essay by the translator.

3051   *The best of Manto: a collection of his short stories*. Ed. and Trans. Jai Ratan. New Delhi: Sterling Publishers, 1989. 158p.

3052   "Black marginalia. Saadat Hasan Manto's *siyah hashiye*". Trans. Jai Ratan. *Indian Literature* 28, 1 (January-February 1985), pp. 21-36.

3053   "Black shalwar". Trans. Hamid Jalal. In: *Span*. Ed. Lionel Wigmore. London, 1959.

3054   "Black shalwar". Trans. Tahira Naqvi. *Journal of South Asian Literature* 20, 2 (Summer, Fall 1985), pp. 26-35.

3055   "Black veil". In: *Contemporary Pakistani short stories*. Ed. and Trans. Nisar Ahmad Farooki. Lahore: Ferozsons Ltd., 1955, pp. 145-165.

3056   "Black veil". In: *Stories from Pakistan*. Ed. Krishan Gopal Abid. New Delhi: India Paperbacks, 1977, pp. 9-27.

3057   "By God". Trans. Leslie A Flemming and Gopi Chand Narang. *Journal of South Asian Literature* 13, 1-4 (1977-78), pp. 161-164.

3058   "By God". "Khuda ki qasm". *Pakistan Review* 13 (April 1965).

3059   "Coachman and the new constitution". "Naya Qanun". In: *Indian short stories*. Eds. Mulk Raj Anand and Iqbal Singh. London: New India Publishing Co., 1946.

3060   "Cold, like ice". "Thanda gosht". Trans. C.M. Naim and Ruth L. Schmidt. *Journal of South Asian Literature* 1, 1 [1964?], pp. 14-19.

3061   "Cold like ice". Trans. C.M. Naim and Ruth L. Schmidt. *Mahfil* 1, 1 [1965], pp. 12-19.

3062   "Cough mixture". Trans. Madan Gupta. *Thought* (11 May 1963), pp. 11-12.

3063   "Coward". Trans. Faruq Hassan. *Urdu Canada* 1, 1 (February 1986), pp. 61-65. Also in: *Pakistani Literature* (Islamabad) 1, 1 (1992), pp. 67-72.

3064   "The dancing sisters". "Swaraj ke liye". Trans. Hamid Jalal. In: *Ten years of vision*. Ed. Yunus Said. Karachi: Pakistan Publishing House, 1963.

3065   "The dog of Tithwal". In: *Writings on India's partition*. Eds. Ramesh Mathur and Mehendra Kulasreshta. Delhi: Simant Publications, 1976.

3066   "The dove". Trans. S. Amjad Ali. *Pakistan Quarterly* 17, 3-4 (Autumn-Winter 1970), pp. 127-133.

3067   "Empty bottles, empty boxes". Trans. Leslie A. Flemming. *Journal of South Asian Literature* 20, 2 (Summer, Fall 1985), pp. 56-60.

3068   "An episode from 1919". Trans. Madan Gupta. *Indian Literature* 30, 1 (1987), pp. 29-37.

3069   "Exchange of lunatics". "Tobah Tek Singh". In: *Land of five rivers*. Ed. and trans. Khushwant Singh. Bombay: Jaico Publishing House, 1965.

3070   "The eyes". Trans. Nusrat Ali. *Pakistan Review* 14 (November 1966).

3071   "Five days of grace". Trans. Avtar Singh Judge. *Thought* 9, 51 (21 December 1957), pp. 9-11.

3072   "For the sake of independence". Trans. Riaz Ahmad. *Journal of South Asian Literature* 20, 2 (Summer, Fall 1985), pp. 71-86.

3073   "The insult". Trans. Nisar Ahmad Farooqi. In: *Contemporary Pakistani short stories*. Ed. and trans. Nisar Ahmad Farooki. Lahore: Ferozsons Ltd., 1955, pp. 111-143.

3074   "The insult". Trans. Hamid Jalal. In: *Pakistani short stories*. Ed. Nisar Ahmad Farooki. Lahore: Ferozsons, 1955.

3075   "The insult". Trans. Leslie A. Flemming. *Journal of South Asian Literature* 20, 2 (Summer, Fall 1985), pp. 4-14.

3076   "In this maelstrom". "Is manjdhar men". Trans. Muhammad Umar Memon. *Annual of Urdu Studies* 2 (1982), pp. 11-38.

3077   "Khushia". Trans. Hamid Jalal. In: *A touch of reality: contemporary Pakistani short stories*. Ed. Faruq Hassan. Montreal: Dawson College, [197-?].
Also includes 6 other stories of Manto.

2nd ed. entitled *Nothing but the truth: Pakistani short stories*. 1978.

3078   "The last salute". Trans. Avtar Singh Judge. *Thought* 10, 11 (15 March 1958), pp. 9-11.

3079   "Manzoor". Trans. Desh Raj Gopal. *Thought* (3 February 1962), pp. 11-13.

3080   "A mother's craving". Trans. Nusrat Ali. *Pakistan Review* 14, 5 (May 1966), pp. 34-35.

3081   "Mozel". Trans. Moazzam Siddiqi. *Journal of South Asian Literature* 20, 2 (Summer, Fall 1985), pp. 87-100.

3082   "Mozelle". Trans. C.M. Naim. *Illustrated Weekly of India* 91, 51 (20 December 1970), pp. 40-49.

3083   "My son Yazid." "Yazid". Trans. Hamid Jalal. *Perspective* 1, 7 (January 1968), pp. 11-18.

3084   "New constitution". Trans. Hamid Jalal. In: *Modern Urdu short stories from Pakistan*. Ed. S. Viqar Azim. Islamabad: R.C.D. Cultural Institute of Pakistan, 1977, pp. 1-2.
Also in: *A touch of reality: contemporary Pakistan stories*. Ed. Faruq Hassan. Montreal: Dawson College, [197-?], pp. 14-20.

3085   "The new law". Trans. Carlo Coppola. *Phoenix* (University of Chicago) (Winter 1964), pp. 28-36.

3086   "Nikki". Trans. M. Salim-ur-Rahman. In: *Modern Urdu short stories from Pakistan*. Ed. S. Viqar Azim. Islamabad: R.C.D. Cultural Institute of Pakistan, 1977, pp. 13-24.

3087   "Nothing but the truth". Trans. Hamid Jalal. In: *Under the green canopy*. Trans. Khalid Hasan et al. Lahore: Afro-Asian Book Club, 1956.
Also in: *A touch of reality: contemporary Pakistani stories*. Ed. Faruq Hassan. Montreal: Dawson College, [197-?].

3088   "Odour". Trans. Hamid Jalal. In: *A treasury of modern Asian stories*. Eds. Daniel L. Milton and William Clifford. New York, 1961.
Also in: *A touch of reality: Contemporary Pakistani stories*. Ed. Faruq Hassan. Montreal: Dawson College, [197-?], pp. 26-29.

3089   "Open it". In: *Mornings on the wilderness*. Ed. and trans. Waqas Ahmad Khwaja. Lahore: Sang-e-Meel Publications, 1988, pp. 183-186.

3090   "Open up". Trans. Leslie A Flemming and Gopi Chand Narang. *Journal of South Asian Literature* 13, 1-4 (1977-78), pp. 157-159.

3091   "The photo". Trans. M. Iqbal. *Thought* 9, 7 (16 February 1957), p. 6.

3092   "Progressive". Trans. Munibur Rahman and Carlo Coppola. *Journal of South Asian Literature* 20, 2 (Summer, Fall 1985), pp. 20-25.

3093   "Progressive grave-yards". Trans. Madan Gupta. *Indian Literature* 26, 3 (May-June 1983), pp.15-22.

3094   "Sakina". Trans. Hamid Jalal. In: *A touch of reality: contemporary Pakistan stories.* Ed. Faruq Hassan. Montreal: Dawson College, [197-?], pp. 65-67.

3095   "Sharda". Trans. Hamid Jalal. *Vision* 8, pp. 9-10 (1958), pp. 22-28, 53.

3096   "Sharifan". In: *Writings on India's partition.* Eds. Ramesh Mathur and Mehendra Kulasreshta. Delhi: Simant Publications, 1976.

3097   "The side of the road". Trans. Faruq Hassan. *Journal of South Asian Literature* 20, 2 (Summer, Fall 1985), pp. 67-70.

3098   "Siraj". Trans. Fatima Ahmad. *Illustrated Weekly of India* 94, 32 (12 August 1973), pp. 61-65.

3099   "A story". Trans. Douglas Brown. *Journal of South Asian Literature* 13, 1-4 (1977-78), pp. 165-170.

3100   "Suicide". Trans. M. Iqbal. *Thought* 8, 47 (24 November 1956), pp. 9-10.

3101   "Tassels". Trans. Linda Wentink. *Journal of South Asian Literature* 20, 2 (Summer, Fall 1985), pp. 107-112.

3102   "The Tetwal dog". Trans. Tahira Naqvi. *Journal of South Asian Literature* 20, 2 (Summer, Fall 1985), pp. 61-66.

3103   "These women". Trans. Hardev Singh. *Thought* 20, 40 (5 October 1968); [*Short Story Supplement*], pp. 10-12.

3104   "Three annas and two piece". Trans. Avtar Singh Judge. *Thought* 8, 51 (22 December 1956).

3105   "Timid". Trans. Faruq Hassan. *Journal of South Asian Literature* 20, 2 (Summer, Fall 1985), pp. 15-19.

3106   "Toba Tek Singh". Trans. Hamid Jalal. *Vision* 12, 10 (December 1963), pp. 18-21, 49.

3107   "Toba Tek Singh". Trans. Robert B. Haldane. *Journal of South Asian Literature* 6, 2-3 (1970), pp.19-23.

3108   "Toba Tek Singh". Trans. M. Iqbal. *Thought* 8, 32 (August 1956), pp. 9-10.

3109   "Urinal". Trans. C.M. Naim. *Journal of South Asian Literature* 4, 2 (Winter 1968), pp. 21-22.

3110   "The will of Gurmukh Singh". In: *Writings on India's partition*. Eds. Ramesh Mathur and Mehendra Kulasreshta. Delhi: Simant Publications, 1976.

3111   "Zubeda" ("Aulaad"). Trans. Madan Gupta. *Thought* (6 June 1964), pp. 11-12. Also in: *Call it a day*. Eds. M.C. and Gwen Gabriel. Delhi: Siddhartha Publications, 1968, pp. 141-144.

STUDIES

3112   **Akhtar, Salim**
"Is Manto necessary today?" Trans. Leslie A. Flemming. *Journal of South Asian Literature* 20, 2 (Summer, Fall 1985), pp. 1-3.

3113   **Flemming, Leslie A.**
Another lonely voice: the life and works of Saadat Hasan Manto. Lahore: Vanguard Books, 1985. 306p.
In two parts, the first is a reprint of Lesley Flemming's earlier book by the same name; the second contains seventeen short stories translated by Tahira Naqvi.

3114   — • *Another lonely voice: the Urdu short stories of Saadat Hasan Manto*. Berkeley: Center for South and South east Asia studies, University of California, 1979. 133p.

3115   — • "Another lonely voice: the Urdu short stories of Saadat Hasan Manto". *Annual of Urdu Studies* 2 (1982), pp. 131-135.

3116   — • "Leslie A. Flemming interviews Ahmad Nadim Qasimi". *Journal of South Asian Literature* 20, 2 (Summer, Fall 1985), pp. 147-151.
A friend and colleague of Manto reminisces.

3117   — • *The life and works of Saadat Hasan Manto: a critical survey*. Madison: University Microfilms, 1973.

3118   — • "Other reflections: the minor writings of Saadat Hasan Manto". *Journal of South Asian Literature* 20, 2 (Summer, Fall 1985), pp. 131-146.

3119   — • "The post-partition stories of Saadat Hasan Manto". *Journal of South Asian Literature* 13, 1-4 (1977-78), pp. 99-109.

3120   — • "Riots and refugees: the post-partitions stories of Saadat Hasan Manto". *Journal of South Asian Literature* 13 (1977-8), pp. 99-109.

3121   — • "A study in contrasts: the topical essays of Saadat Hasan Manto". *Literature East and West* 17, (2-4), (1973), pp. 212-227.

3122 — • "The writings of Saadat Hasan Manto". Guest editor Leslie A. Flemming. *Journal of South Asian Literature* 20, 2 (Summer, Fall 1985), 162p.

3123 **Hasan, Khalid**
"Saadat Hasan Manto: not of blessed memory". *Annual of Urdu Studies* 4 (1984), p. 85. An account of author's meeting with Saadat Hasan Manto.

3124 **Hashmi, Alamgir**
"Manto's maimed kingdom". *Dawn Magazine* (31 March 1989), p. 4

3125 **Hassan, Faruq**
"The agony of an ecstasy". (Manto mamon). Trans. Hamid Jalal. In: *A touch of reality: Contemporary Pakistani short stories*. Ed. Faruq Hassan. Montreal: Dawson College, [197-?], pp. 147-61.

3126 **Janus.**
"Manto's royalties". *Viewpoint* (Lahore) 6, 10 (October 1980), p. 29.

3127 **Kaplan, Frederick I. and Dulai, S.S.**
"Humanity at bay: the conflict between man and the world in the stories of Gorki and Manto". *Journal of South Asian Literature* 13, 1-4 (1977-78), pp. 1-8.

3128 **Nardella, U**
"Il novellista urdu Sa'adat Aasan Manto". *Annali del Istituto Orientale di Napoli* N.S. 21, (1971), pp. 41-73; 23 (1973), pp. 47-60; 24 (1974), pp. 217-246.

3129 **Rahman, Tariq**
"Modernist anti-humanitarianism in Manto". *Dawn* (16 November 1990).

3130 **Wentink, Linda**
"Manto as a modernist". *Journal of South Asian Literature* 20, 2 (Summer, Fall 1985), pp. 121-130.

MANZAR, HASAN

TRANSLATIONS

3131 "The beggar boy". Trans. Muhammad Umar Memon. *Annual of Urdu Studies* 4 (1984), pp. 53-68.

3132 "The drizzle". Trans. Muhammad Umar Memon. *The Toronto South Asian Review* 3, 1 (Summer 1984), pp. 48-57.

3133 "The poor dears". Trans. Muhammad Umar Memon. *Urdu Canada* 1, 3 (1987), pp. 50-58.

3134   "White man's world". Trans. Faruq Hassan. *The Toronto South Asian Review* 5, 2 (Fall-Winter 1986), pp. 66-77.

MASRUR, HAJRA

TRANSLATIONS

3135   "The private stuff". Trans. Qaiser Afzal. In: *The Nation* (January 1963), [*Pakistan Writer's Guild Number.*] pp. 58-61.

3136   "Some one like you". Trans. M. Salim-ur-Rahman. In: *Modern Urdu short stories from Pakistan.* Ed. S. Viqar Azim. Islamabad: R.C.D. Cultural Institute of Pakistan, 1977, pp. 199-210.

3137   "The wounded monkey". Trans. Evelyn D. Vardy. *Journal of South Asian Literature* 13, 1-4, pp. 91-97.

MASTUR, KHADIJA

TRANSLATIONS

3138   "The hand pump". Trans. Salma Mahmud. In: *Modern Urdu short stories from Pakistan.* Ed. S. Viqar Azim. Islamabad: R.C.D. Cultural Institute of Pakistan, 1977, pp. 180-197.

3139   "Mainun lay chalay babla way". Trans. Anwar Enayetullah. *The Herald* (Karachi) (September 1983), pp. 82-86.

MATEEN, IQBAL

TRANSLATION

3140   "A flower and a butterfly". Trans. B.A. Farooqi. *The Toronto South Asian Review* 7, 3 (Spring 1989), pp. 77-81.

MAZHARUL, ISLAM

TRANSLATION

3141   "Prefaces". In: *Mornings in the wilderness*. Ed. and Trans. Waqas Ahmad Khwaja. Lahore: Sang-e-Meel Publications, 1988, pp. 253-257.

MEMON, MUHAMMAD UMAR

TRANSLATIONS

3142   "The apocalypse". Trans. the author. In: *Twenty years of the Urdu short story*. *Indian Literature* 19, 6 (November-December), pp. 145-157.

3143   "The dark alley". Trans. and abridged. Faruq Hassan. *Urdu Canada* 1, 2 (1986), pp. 37-48.

3144   "Lost moments". Trans. the author. *Thought* 16, 22 (30 May 1964), pp. 11-12. Also in: *Pakistan Review* 13, 10 (October 1965), pp. 31-33.

3145   "The worm and the sunflower". Trans. the author. *Toronto South Asian Review* (Toronto), 1, 3 (Fall 1982-Winter 1983), pp. 17-30.

MUFTI, MASUD

TRANSLATIONS

3146   "Agreement". In: *Modern Urdu stories*. Ed. and trans. Agha Iqbal Mirza. Calcutta: Writers Workshop, 1975.

3147   "Woman". Trans. Faruq Hassan. In: *A touch of reality: Contemporary Pakistan stories*. Ed. Faruq Hassan. Montreal: Dawson College, [197-?], pp. 88-93.

3148   "Nayey paimaney". Trans. Anwar Enayetullah. *The Herald* (Karachi), 12, 12 (December 1981), pp. 71-78.

MUFTI, MUMTAZ

TRANSLATIONS

3149   "Apa". Trans. J. Ershed. *Pakistan Quarterly* 1, 6 (August 1951), pp. 29-34, 60.

3150 "The frozen spark". Trans. Khalid Hasan, et al. In: *Under the green canopy.* Lahore: Afro-Asian Book Club, 1966.

3151 "Sister". In: *Contemporary Pakistani short stories*. Ed. and trans. Nisar Ahmad Farooki. Lahore: Ferozons Ltd., 1955, pp. 37-51.

3152 "Sister". In: *Stories from Pakistan*. Ed. Krishan Gopal Abid. New Delhi: India Paperbacks, 1977, pp.79-90.

STUDY

3153 **Farrukhi, Asif Aslam**
"Mufti, Mumtaz". *Herald* (Karachi) (June 1986), pp. 134-138.
Interview with Mumtaz Mufti.

MUHAMMAD, GHOLAM

STUDY

3154 **Farrukhi, Asif Aslam**
"Those who began writing just after 1971 did not try to see things objectively". *Newsline* 1, 11 (May 1990), pp. 76-78.
Interview with Gholam Mohammad.

MUHAMMADI BEGUM

STUDY

3155 **Naqvi, S.A.H.**
"An early woman novelist of Urdu". *Perspective* (Karachi) 3, 12 (June 1970), pp. 59-60.

NIAZ FATEHPURI

STUDY

3156 **Naqvi, S.A.H.**
"Niaz Fatehpuri". *Pakistan Review* 19, 1 (January 1971), pp. 28-29, 40.

PAUL, JOGINDER

TRANSLATIONS

3157   "Access". Trans. Krishna Paul and Shahab Afsar. *Indian Literature* 22, 2 (1979), pp. 47-63.

3158   "And graves for the dead". Trans. Krishna Paul. *Indian Literature* 23, 3-4 (1980), pp. 275-281.

3159   "The milk soured". Trans. Rajinder Singh Verma. *Indian Literature* 31, 2 (March-April 1988), pp. 107-120.

3160   "The second look". Trans. Krishna Paul. *Indian Literature* 25, 2 (1982), pp.144-153.

3161   "Those who stayed behind". Trans. Jai Ratan. *Indian Literature* 26, 6 (1983), pp. 26-37.

STUDIES

3162   **Agha, Wazir**
"Joginder Paul's *Nadeed*". Trans. Jai Ratan. *Urdu Canada* 1, 1 (February 1987), pp. 85-88.

3163   **Farrukhi, Asif Aslam**
"The writer has to catch hold of the particular truth of his age". *Newsline* 2, 3 (September 1990), pp. 123-125.
Interview with Joginder Paul.

3164   **Paul, Joginder**
"Yatra to Pakistan". *Urdu Canada* 1, 1 (February 1986), pp. 32-47.

PRADIP, VISHVESHWAR

TRANSLATION

3165   "The old coat". Trans. Satish Batra. In: *New generation three*. Eds. Ramlal and Syeda Naseem Chishti. London: New Generation, 1968, pp. 77-83.

PRAKASH, SURENDAR

TRANSLATIONS

3166   "Another man's drawing room".   Trans. Gopi Chand Narang and Leslie A. Flemming. *Indian Literature* 13, 3 (September 1970), pp. 29-35.

3167   "Autobiography". Trans. C.M. Naim. *Annual of Urdu Studies* 7 (1990), pp. 62-66.

3168   *Bazgoi*. Trans. Shamsur Rahman Faruqi. Delhi: Educational Publishing House, 1988. 203p.

3169   "The Curio". Trans. Jai Ratan. *Indian Literature* 31, 1 (January-February 1988), pp. 81-84.

3170   "Das Weinen". Trans. Sandra Joost. In: *Auswahl zeitgenössischer Urdu-Lyrik und -Prosa (Haus der Kulturen der Welt)*, Ed. Christina Oesterheld. Berlin: Das Arabische Buch, 1991, pp. 78-85. (Gesteht's! die Dichter des Orients sind grösser; 4).

3171   "Die vogelschenche". Trans. Christina Oesterheld. In: *Auswahl zeitgenössischer Urdu-Lyrik und-Prosa (Hans der Kulturen der welt)*, Ed. Christina Oesterheld. Berlin: Das Arabische Buch, 1991, pp. 78-85. (Gesteht's! die Dichter des Orients sind grosser; 4).

3172   "Jipizan". Trans. Muhammad Umar Memon. In: *Twenty years of the Urdu short story*. *Indian Literature* 19, 6 (November-December 1976), pp. 158-164.

3173   "Journey into the night". Trans. Jai Ratan. *Indian Literature* 30, 2 (March-April 1987), pp. 113-129.

3174   "Talqarmas". Trans. Linda Wentink. *Indian Literature* 23, 3-4 (1980), pp. 151-155.

STUDIES

3175   **Farrukhi, Asif Aslam**
"Writing is the business of the dervesh". *Newsline* 2, 10 (April 1991), pp. 132-134.
Interview with Surendra Prakash

3176   **Faruqi, Shamsur Rahman**
"A major statement". *Indian Literature* 33, 4 (July-August 1990), pp. 116-122.
Review of Surendra Prakash's novel *Bazgoi,* with an excerpt from the novel.

PREM CHAND, DHANPAT RAI SHRIVASTAN

TRANSLATIONS

3177   "The chess players". Trans. Gurdial Mallick. *Triveni* 17 (October 1945), pp. 178-187.

3178   "The chess players". Trans. Bhisham Sahni. *Illustrated Weekly of India* 85, 7 (16 February 1964), p. 22.

3179   "The child". Trans. Madan Gupta. *Thought* 9, 19 (12 May 1956), pp. 9-10.
Also in: *Contemporary Indian short stories*. Ed. Krishna Kripalani. New Delhi: Sahitya Akademi, 1959, pp. 36-42.
Also in: *Indian Horizons* 21, 2-3 (April-July 1972), pp. 127-136.

3180   "Daughter of a noble family". Trans. B.B. Bhandarkar. *Thought* 8, 5 (4 February 1956), pp. 9-11.

3181   *Deliverance and other stories*. Trans. David Rubin. Harmondsworth: Penguin Books, 1988.

3182   "A feast for the holy man". Trans. David Rubin. *Mahfil* 4, 2 (Winter 1968), pp. 18-20.

3183   "Food for the holy man". *Thought* 21, 27 (5 July 1969) [*Short Story Supplement*], p. 8.

3184   "Fragment of an autobiography". Trans. Madan Gopal. *Illustrated Weekly of India* 84, 21 (26 May 1963), pp. 32-33.

3185   "Girdhari". Trans. Madan Gupta. *Thought* 14, 1 (6 January 1962), pp. 11-13.

3186   "God lives in the Panch". In: *Indian short stories*. Ed. Manmohan Saksena. Oxford, 1950.
Also in: *Thought* 3, 29 (20 July 1951), pp. 9-12.

3187   *A handful of wheat and other stories*. Trans. P.C. Gupta. New Delhi: People's Publishing House, 1955. 230p.
Includes fifteen stories.

3188   "Jamid the devout". Trans. Madan Gupta. *Illustrated Weekly of India* 81, 4 (24 January 1960), pp. 29-30.

3189   "Miss Malti". Trans. Jai Ratan and P. Lal. In: *A treasury of modern Asian stories*. Eds. D.L. Milton and W. Clifford. New York: New American Library, 1961, pp. 48-60.
Novel excerpt from *Godan*.

3190   "The necklace". Trans. Madan Gupta. *Thought* 10, 2 (11 January 1958), pp. 9-10.

3191   *Nirmala: a novel*. Trans. David Rubin. Delhi: Vision Books, 1988. 168p.

3192   "Panchayat: the voice of God". Trans. Madan Gopal. *Illustrated Weekly of India* 81, 9 (28 February 1960), pp.18-21.

3193   "Pandit Chander Dhar". Trans. Madan Gupta. *Thought* 23, 48 (27 November 1971), pp. 13-15.

3194   "The path of salvation". Trans. Ram Singh. *Thought* 21, 23 (7 June 1969) [*Short Story Supplement*], pp. 6-8.

3195   *Prem Chand: an anthology*. Ed. Dr. Nagendra. New Delhi: Knnark, 1987. 232p.

3196   "The Procession". *Century* 5, 13 (15 August 1967), pp. 37-39.

3197   "Repentance". Trans. Madan Gupta. *Thought* 11, 11 (14 March 1959), pp. 9-11.

3198   "Resignation". Trans. D. Anand. In: *Tales from modern India*. Ed. K. Natwar Singh. New York: MacMillan, 1966, pp. 81-91.

3199   "Resignation". In: *Indian short stories*. Eds. and Trans. Mulk Raj Anand and Iqbal Singh. London: New India Publishing Co., 1946.

3200   "Sacrificed". Trans. Madan Gupta. *Illustrated Weekly of India* 84, 20 (19 May 1964), pp. 34-37.

3201   "Salvation". Trans. Madan Gupta. *Thought* 7, 30 (23 July 1955), pp. 8-10.

3202   "The secret". Trans. P. Lal. *Thought* 5, 23 (6 June 1953), p. 8.

3203   *The secret culture and other stories*. Trans. Madan Gupta. Delhi: Jaico Publishing House, 1960. 192p.
Includes twenty stories and a critical essay by Madan Gopal.

3204   *The shroud and twenty other stories by Prem Chand*. Trans. Madan Gopal. New Delhi: Sagar Publications, 1972. 278p.

3205   *Short stories of Prem Chand*.   Trans. Gurdial Mallick.   Bombay: Nalanda Publications, 1946. 166p.
Includes eleven stories.

3206   *Twenty-four stories by Premchand*. Trans. Nandir Nopani and P. Lal. New Delhi, 1980.

3207   "The lottery". Trans. Madan Gupta. *Thought* 8, 48 (December 1956), pp. 9-10, 8; 49 (8 December 1956), pp. 9-10.
Also in: *Illustrated Weekly of India* 81, 12 (20 March 1960), pp. 19-21.

3208   *The world of Prem Chand: selected stories of Prem Chand*. Trans. David Rubin. London: George Allen and Unwin, 1969. 215p.
Includes two autobiographical sketches and twenty-three stories.

3209   "The shroud". Trans. Madan Gopal. *Indian Literature* 5, 2 (1962), pp. 31-38.
Also in: *Tales from modern India*. Ed. K. Natwar Singh. New York: MacMillan, 1966, pp. 71-80.

3210   "The shroud". Trans. A.B.M. Habibullah. *Triveni* 12, 5 (November 1939), pp. 17-22.

3211   "The shroud". In: *A treasury of modern Asian stories*. Eds. D.L. Milton and W. Clifford. New York: New American Library, 1961, pp. 60-67.

3212   "The sinner and the sin". Trans. Madan Gupta. *Thought* 24, 17 (22 April 1972), pp. 13-14.

3213   "Someone to lean on". Trans. Madan Gupta. *Thought* 7, 39 (21 July 1963), pp. 25-27.

3214   "The son-in-law". Trans. Madan Gupta. *Thought* 7, 39 (24 September 1955), pp. 9-11.

3215   "The stepmother". Trans. Madan Gupta. *Thought* 15, 11 (16 March 1963), pp. 11-12.

3216   *Stories from Prem Chand*. Ed. and Trans. Rajinder Singh Verma. Delhi: Surya Prakashan. 1989. 112p.

3217   "Subhagi". Trans. Madan Gupta. *Illustrated Weekly of India* 84, 7 (17 February 1963), pp. 19-21.

3218   "The test". Trans. Roberts. *Mahfil* 1, 2 (1963), pp. 18-21.

3219   "A toy for Hamid". Trans. Krishna Kant. *Illustrated Weekly of India* 82, 45 (5 November 1961), pp. 21-27.

STUDIES

3220   **Agrawal, Kedar Nath**
"The heritage of Premchand and progressive writing". *Indian Culture* 36, 1 (1981), pp. 14-22.

3221   **Agyeya**
"Prem Chand". *Thought* 6, 32 (7 August 1954), pp. 11-12.

3222   **Asnani, Shyam M.**
"An Indian Gorki". *Indian Literature* 18, 2 (April-June 1975), pp. 62-72.

3223   **Azam, Muhammad**
"Premchand's mood and his Urdu short stories". *Indian Literature* 21, 1 (January-February 1978), pp. 85-92.

3224 — • "Premchand's Urdu-Hindi short stories". *Indian Literature* 18, 2 (April-June 1975), pp. 56-61.

3225 **Bald, Suresht Renjen**
"Power and powerlessness of rural and urban women in Premchand's *Godan*". *Journal of South Asian Literature* 21, 2 (Summer-Fall 1986), pp. 1-15.

3226 **Bandopadhaya, Manohar**
Life and works of Premchand. New Delhi: Publication Division, 1981. 200p.

3227 **Butalia, Subhadra**
"The world of Dickens and Prem Chand". *Times of India* (17 January 1971), pp. 3, 1-5.

3228 **Chandola, Anoop**
"Objective signalling: subjectivity in Premchand". *Journal of South Asian Literature* 21, 2 (Summer-Fall 1986), pp. 16-20.

3229 **Chandra, Sudhir**
"Premchand and Indian nationalism". *Modern Asian Studies* 16, 4 (October 1982), pp. 601-621.

3230 **Chelyshev, Y.**
"Premchand". *Contemporary Indian Literature* 2, 11, pp. 12-13, 17.

3231 **Coppola, Carlo**
"Premchand's address to the first meeting of the All-India Progressive Writers Association: some speculations". *Journal of South Asian Literature* 21, 2 (Summer-Fall 1986), pp. 21-39.

3232 — • "A review of Munshi Premchand; a literary biography by Madan Gopal". *Literature East and West* (June 1966), pp. 186-187.

3233 **Dwivedi, Ramagyan**
"Premchand - my teacher". *Hindi Review* 1, 7 (August 1956), pp. 37-39.

3234 **Gopal, Madan**
Munshi Prem Chand: a literary biography. New York: Asia Publishing House, 1964. 462p.

3235 — • "Premchand: a study". *Thought* 4, 44 (1 November 1952), pp. 10-12.

3236 **Goswamy, Kewal**
"Prem Chand through his letters". *Indian Literature* 27, 3 (May-June 1984), pp. 98-110.

3237 **Gupta, Prakash Chandra**
"The art of Premchand". *Hindustan Review* 4 (1959), pp. 356-361.

3238 — • *Prem Chand*. New Delhi: Sahitya Akademi, 1968. 56p.

3239 — • *Prem Chand: eminent Hindi novelist and story writer*. New Delhi: Sahitya Akademi, 1970. 56p.

3240 **Jain, Nirmala**
"Women in Premchand's writing". *Journal of South Asian Literature* 21, 2 (Summer-Fall 1986), pp. 40-44.

3241 **Jain, Pratibha**
"Premchand's Ranghbhumi: a historical evaluation". *Indian Literature* 16, 1-2 (January-June 1973), pp. 28-35.

3242 **Joshi, P.C.**
"Premchand and rural India". *Viewpoint* (Lahore) 6, 40 (May 1981), pp. 17-22.

3243 **Khanum, Zahida**
"Premchand, a pioneer of modern Urdu novel". *Scintilla* 1, 4 (January 1961), pp. 56-58.

3244 **Kumar Prem**
"Archetypal patterns in Premchand's early novels". *Journal of South Asian Literature* 21, 2 (Summer-Fall 1986), pp. 45-56.

3245 **Lal, P.**
"Premchand: an appreciation". *Indian International Centre Quarterly* 7, 1 (March 1980), pp. 15-24.

3246 **Machwe, Prabhakar**
"Premchand". *Thought* 5, 33 (15 August 1953), pp. 11-12.

3247 **Madan, Indar Nath**
Premchand, an interpretation. Lahore: Minverva Book Shop, 1946. 178p.

3248   — • "Premchand". *Hindi Review* 1, 8 (September 1956), pp. 7-11.

3249   — • "Premchand: a social analysis". *Research Bulletin (Arts) of the University of Punjab* [Hoshiarpur], 1951.

3250 **Misra, Shiv Kumar**
Premchand: our contemporary. New Delhi: National Publishing House, 1986. 240p.
Twenty-one essays by diverse writers.

3251 **Naravane, Vishwanath S.**
Premchand: his life and work. New Delhi: Vikas, 1980. 291p.

3252 **Obeyesekere, Ranjini**
"Women's rights and roles in Premchand's *Godan*". *Journal of South Asian Literature* 21, 2 (Summer-Fall 1986), pp. 57-64.

3253 **Pandey, Geetanjah**
"North Indian intelligentsia and Hindu-Muslim question: a study of Prem Chand's writing". *Economic and Political Weekly* (20 September 1984), pp. 1664-1670.

3254   — • "How equal? Women in Premchand's writings". *Economic and Political Weekly* 21, 50 (13 December 1986), pp. 2183-2187.

3255 — • "Premchand and the west". *New Quest* 48 (November-December 1984), pp. 347-354.

3256 **Prem Chand**
"How I write a story". Trans. P. Lal. *Thought* 5, 1 (3 January 1953), p. 14.

3257 — • "The place of literature in life". Trans. Bhisham Sahni. *Hindi Review* 5, 3 (April 1960), pp. 113-118; 5, 4 (May 1960), pp. 152-155.

3258 **Pritchett, Frances W.**
"*The chess-players*: from Premchand to Satyajit Ray (from short story to film)". *Journal of South Asian Literature* 21, 2 (Summer-Fall, 1986), pp. 65-78.

3259 **Rahbar, Hans Raj**
Prem Chand: his life and works. Trans. P. Lal. Delhi: Atma Ram and Sons, 1957. 184p.

3260 **Rai, Amrit**
Premchand: a life. Trans. Harish Trivedi. New Delhi: People's Publishing House, 1982. 413p.

3261 **Ram, Syam M.**
"Prem Chand: the Indian Gorky". *Modern Review* 133, 6 (December 1973), pp. 415-420.

3262 **Rizvi, A.A.**
"Munshi Premchand: a study". *Scintilla* 5 (October 1964), pp. 54-57.

3263 **Roadarmel, Gordon**
[A review of *Munshi Premchand:* a *literary biography* by Madan Gopal]. *Mahfil* 2, 4 (1966), pp. 44-48.

3264 **Rottger-Hogan, Elizabeth**
"*Rasa*, Idealism, and Realism: Premchand's literary essays". *Journal of South Asian Literature* 21, 2 (Summer-Fall 1986), pp. 79-85.

3265 **Rubin, David**
The world of Premchand. Selected stories ... translated by David Rubin. London: George Allen and Unwin, 1969. 215p.

3266 **Sahni, Bhisham and Paliwal, D.P.**
Prem Chand: a tribute. Delhi: Prem Chand Centenary Celebrations Committee, 1980. 114p. Includes translations of three stories.

3267 **Saksena, Usha**
"Western influence on Premchand". *Yearbook of Comparative and General Literature* [Bloomington, Indiana] 11 (1962), *Supplement*, pp. 129-132.

3268 **Schomer, Karine**
"Premchand's Premasram, Gandhism, and the imagination: a review article". *Journal of South Asian Literature* 21, 2 (Summer-Fall, 1986), pp. 86-98.

3269 Schulz, Siegfried
Premchand: a western appraisal. New Delhi: Indian Council for Cultural Relations, 1981.
42, 34p. (Azad Memorial Lectures, 1981).

3270 Shapiro, Michael C.
"The language of humour in Premchand's short stories". *Journal of South Asian Literature*
21, 2 (Summer-Fall, 1986), pp. 99-111.

3271 Sharma, Arvind
"Gold, dust, or gold dust?: religion in the life and writings of Premchand". *Journal of South
Asian Literature* 21, 2 (Summer-Fall, 1986), pp. 112-122.

3272 Sharma, Govind Narain
"Prem Chand's myth of the east and west: a reading of Premashram". *The International
Fiction Review* 5, 1 (1978), pp. 40-45.
On the novel *Gos-a-e-afiyat*.

3273 Singh, K.P.
"Premchand and Gandhism". *Indian Journal of Politics* 17, 2 (June 1983), pp. 103-108.

3274 —• "Peasant movement in Premchand". *Indian History Congress: Proceedings
(Delhi), 47th* (1986), pp. 664-670.

3275 Sprinker, Michael
"Marxism and nationalism: ideology and class struggle in Premchand's *Godan*". *Social Text*
23 (Fall-Winter 1989), pp. 59-82.

3276 Swan, Robert Oscar
Munshi Premchand of Lamhi Village. Durham, N.C.: Duke University Press, 1969. 149p.

3277 —• "Pattern in Premchand's short stories". *Journal of South Asian Literature* 21,
2 (Summer-Fall 1986), pp. 123-132.

3278 Tarsikar, M.S.
"Premchand: the novelist". Trans. M.S. Tarsikar. *Conservative* (1 August 1963), pp. 23-24.

3279 Upadhyaya, Devraj
"Psychology in Premchand's fiction". *Hindi Review* 1, 5 (June 1956), pp. 29-35.

QASIMI, AHMAD NADIM

TRANSLATIONS

3280 "Aasaib". Trans. Anwar Enayetullah. *The Herald* (Karachi) (August 1983),
pp. 76-82.

3281 "The chopper". Trans. Farida Ahmad. In: *Modern Urdu short stories from Pakistan*. Ed. S. Viqar Azim. Islamabad: R.C.D. Cultural Institute of Pakistan, 1977, pp. 55-73.

3282 "Compulsions". Trans. Ralph Russell. In: *Short stories from India, Pakistan and Bangladesh*. London: Harrap, 1980, pp. 96-107.

3283 "Deaths innumerable". Trans. Qaiser Afzal. In: *The Nation* (January 1963) [*Pakistan Writer's Guild Number*], pp. 55-57.

3284 "Fashion". *Modern Urdu stories*. Ed. and Trans. Agha Iqbal Mirza. Calcutta: Writers Workshop, 1975.

3285 "The ghost". Trans. M.N. Khan. *Perspective* 5, 8-9 (February-March 1972), pp. 38-42.

3286 "A lament". Trans. Shelah S. Bhatti. *Annual of Urdu Studies* 6 (1987), pp. 77-82.

3287 "Praise be to Allah". Trans. M. Salim-ur-Rahman. In: *Modern Urdu short stories from Pakistan*. Ed. S. Viqar Azim. Islamabad: R.C.D. Cultural Institute of Pakistan, 1972, pp. 74-105.

3288 "The reckoning". Trans. Jai Ratan. *Illustrated weekly of India* 20 (January 1985), pp. 54-57.

3289 *Selected short stories of Ahmad Nadeem Qasimi*. Trans. Sajjad Shaikh. Karachi: National Book Foundation, 1981. 128p.

3290 "Sultan". Trans. Bruce R. Pray. *Pakistan Quarterly* 17, 3-4 (Autumn-Winter 1970), pp. 116-119.
Also in: *Mahfil* 8, 2-3 (Summer-Autumn 1972), pp. 159-165.

3291 "To the head of the state". In: *Mornings in the wilderness*. Ed. and trans. Waqas Ahmad Khwaja. Lahore: Sang-e-Meel Publications, 1988, pp. 203-208.

3292 "The unwanted". Trans. Khalid Hasan. In: *Under the green canopy*. Lahore: Afro-Asian Book Club, 1966.
Also in: *A touch of reality: Contemporary Pakistan stories*. Ed. Faruq Hassan. Montreal: Dawson College, [197-?], pp. 81-87.

3293 "The wild woman". Trans. Abul Khair Kashfi and Janet M. Powers. *Mahfil* 2, 2 (May 1965), pp. 43-48.

3294 "The witch". In: *Stories from Pakistan*. Ed. Krishan Gopal Abid. New Delhi: India Paperbacks, 1977, pp. 28-54.

STUDIES

3295   Malik, Safdar Jamal
"Urdu-Kurzgeschichten: Ahmad Nadim Qasimi".   In: *Pakistan: Destabilisierung durch Kontinuität.* Wuppertal: Südasienbüro, pp. 86-91.

3296   Siddiqui, M.A.
"An evaluation of Ahmad Nadeem Qasimi". *Pakistan Perspective* 3, 1-2 (June-July 1977), pp. 36-37.

QUDSIA, BANO

TRANSLATION

3297   "The heed-seeker". Trans. Hina Babar Ali. *Journal of South Asian Literature* 19, 1 (Winter, Spring 1984), pp. 89-100.

STUDY

3298   Salim-ur-Rahman, Muhammad
["A review of *Raja Gidh*"]. *Annual of Urdu Studies* 4 (1984), pp. 114-116.
Reprinted with few changes from *The Pakistan Times* (Lahore) (10 August 1981), p. 4.

RAFIQ, SHAKILA

TRANSLATION

3299   "A roof overhead". Trans. Muhammad Umar Memon. *Annual of Urdu Studies* 6 (1987), pp. 94-98.

RAMLAL

TRANSLATIONS

3300   "The amusement". Trans. B.A. Farooqi. *Indian Literature* 20, 3 (May-June 1987), pp. 83-87.

3301   "The court-yard". In: *New generation 2; an anthology of Urdu writers.* Ed. and trans. Satish Batra. Lucknow: New Generation, 1967, pp. 11-18.

3302 "Back from hell". Trans. Jai Ratan. *Indian Literature* 31, 1 (January-February 1988), pp. 79-80.

3303 "From darkness to darkness". Trans. Jai Ratan. *Urdu Canada* 1, 2 (1986), pp. 34-36.

3304 "Entertainment". Trans. C.M. Naim. *Denver Quarterly* 12, 2 (Summer 1977), pp. 238-241.

3305 "The headless Budha". In: *New generation 2; an anthology of Urdu writers.* Ed. and trans. Satish Batra. Lucknow: New Generation, 1967, pp. 19-28.

3306 "The rest room". Trans. Satish Batra. In: *New generation three.* Eds. Ramlal and Syeda Naseem Chishti. Lucknow: New Generation, 1968, pp. 59-65.

3307 *Ramlall and his four stories.* Trans. Satish Batra and Jai Ratan. Eds. K.P. Saxena. Lucknow: New Generation, 42p.
A biographical note by K.P. Saxena.

STUDY

3308 **Vardy, Evelyn**
"Evelyn Vardy interviews Ram Lall". *Journal of South Asia Literature* 16, 2 (Summer, Fall 1981), pp. 195-202.

RASHID, SAJID

TRANSLATIONS

3309 "Die Sanduhr". Trans. Christina Oesterheld. *Erkundungen - 23 Erzählungen aus Indien.* Berlin: Verlag Volk und Welt, 1990, pp. 201- 205.

RATTAN SINGH

3310 "Thousand-year-long night". Trans. B.A. Farooqui. *The Toronto South Asian Review* 6, 1 (Summer 1987), pp. 81-82.

RAZAQ, SALAAM BIN

TRANSLATIONS

3311 "Es ist Blut geflossen". "Khunbaha". *Erkundungen - 23 Erzählungen aus Indien.* Berlin: Verlag Volk und Welt, 1990, pp. 185-200.

3312 "Full circle". Trans. Jai Ratan. *Indian Literature* 29, 3 (May-June 1986), pp. 85-100.

RIZVI, NASIR

3313 "Yadgar". Trans. Anwar Enayetullah. *The Herald* (Karachi) (November 1983), pp. 76-79.

RUSWA, MIRZA MUHAMMAD HADI

TRANSLATIONS

3314 *The courtesan of Lucknow (Umrao Jan Ada).* Trans. Khushwant Singh and M.A. Husaini. Delhi: Hind Pocket Books, 1961, 240p.

[Another ed.] Calcutta: Orient Longmans, 1961. 187p.

3315 *The courtesan of Lucknow (Umrao Jan Ada).* Trans. Khushwant Singh and M.A. Husaini. Delhi: Hind Pocket Books, 1970. 240p. First published 1899.

3316 *Die Kurtisane von Lakhnau Umrao Jan Ada.* Aus dem Urdu übers., und erl. von Ursula Rothen-Dubs. Zürich: Manesse, 1971. 437p.

STUDIES

3317 **Ghosh, S.L.** ["Review of *The courtesan of Lucknow*"]. *Indo-Asian Culture* 19, 3 (July 1970), pp. 55-57.

3318 **Mujeeb, Muhammad** ["Review of *Umrao Jan Ada*"]. In his *Islamic influence on Indian society.* Meerut: Meenakshi Prakashan, (1972), pp. 161-164.

SAEED DIHLAVI

TRANSLATION

3319   *Isabella*. Trans. Rahm Ali al-Hasmi. Delhi: Dini Book Depot, 1974. 188p.
A novel based on a comparative study of Islam and Christianity.

SAID, IBNE

TRANSLATION

3320   "The lady of Hiroshima". Trans. Nisar Ahmad Farooki. In: *Ten years of vision*.
Ed. Yunus Said. Karachi: Pakistan Publishing House, 1963, pp. 30-45.

SAJJAD, ENWAR

TRANSLATIONS

3321   "Anarkali". In: *Mornings in the wilderness*. Ed. and trans. Waqas Ahmad Khwaja.
Lahore: Sang-e-Meel Publications, 1988, pp. 249-252.

3322   "Conspirators". Trans. C.M. Naim. *Mahfil* 7, 1-2, pp. 149-151.

3323   "The cow". Trans. Yasmin Hosain. In: *Modern Urdu short stories from Pakistan*.
Ed. S. Viqar Azim. Islamabad: R.C.D. Cultural Institute of Pakistan, 1977, pp. 212-216.

3324   "The garden of delights". Trans. Linda Wentink. *Journal of South Asian Literature*
16, 2 (Summer-Fall 1981), pp. 143-145.

3325   "The grass, the wind and the cripple". Trans. Khalid Hasan. In: *Under the green
canopy*. Lahore: Afro-Asian Book Club, 1966.

3326   "The seedling". Trans. Iqbal Akhtar. In: *Twenty years of the Urdu short story*.
Indian Literature 19, 6 (November-December 1976), pp. 103-114.

STUDY

3327   **Wentink, Linda**
"Envar Sajjad's *The garden of delight*: a study of technique - from painting to prose".
Journal of South Asian Literature 16, 2 (Summer, Fall 1981), pp. 147-151.

SALEEM-UR RAHMAN, MUHAMMAD

TRANSLATIONS

3328 "A childhood of sleep". Trans. Faruq Hassan. *Toronto South Asian Review* 1, 3 (Fall 1982-Winter 1983), pp. 76-80.

3329 "Kerb". Trans. Sandra Joost. In: *Auswahl Zeitgenössischer Urdu-Lyrik und -Prosa (Haus der Kulturen der Welt)*. Ed. Christina Oesterheld. Berlin: Das Arabische Buch, 1991, pp. 94-100. (Gesteht's! die Dichter des Orients sind grösser; 4).

3330 "Ruckkehr und Aufbruch". Trans. Christina Oesterheld. In: *Auswahl Zeitgenössischer Urdu-Lyrik und -Prosa (Haus der Kulturen der Welt)*, Ed. Christina Oesterheld. Berlin: Das Arabische Buch, 1991, pp. 94-100. (Gesteht's! die Dichter des Orients sind grösser; 4).

SARATHI, O.P. SHARMA

TRANSLATION

3331 "Die Fesseln der Entfremdung". Trans. Christina Oesterheld. *Erkundungen - 23 Erzählungen aus Indien*. Berlin: Verlag Volk und Welt, (1990), pp. 178-184.

SARSHAR, RATAN NATH DAR

STUDIES

3332 **Dar, Bishan Narayan**
"Ratan Nath Dar (Sarshar): a study". *The Kayastha Samachar* (April 1902), pp. 381-397. Also in *Annual of Urdu Studies* 2 (1982), pp. 85-100.

3333 **Husain, Firoz**
The life and work of Ratan Nath Sarshar. Ph.D. thesis, University of London, 1984.

3334 **Sadiq, Muhammad**
"Ratan Nath Sarshar: a study". *Iqbal* 9 (1961), pp. 11-25.

SATINDRA SINGH

TRANSLATIONS

3335   "Comrade Bhupee". Trans. Jaipal Nangia. *Thought* 7, 29 (16 July 1955), pp. 9-11.

3336   "Match-making". Trans. Jaipal Nangia. *Thought* 7, 1 (1 January 1955), pp. 9-11.

3337   "The Mlechcha". Trans. G.P. Grewal. *Thought* 7, 2 (12 January 1955), pp. 9-10.

SAULAT RUKHSANA

STUDY

3338   **Wentink, Linda**
["Review of *Gile harf*"]. *Annual of Urdu Studies* 1 (1981), pp. 107-111.

SEEMA NIGHAT

TRANSLATION

3339   "Majboor".   Trans. Anwar Enayetullah.   *The Herald* (Karachi) (May 1983), pp. 52-58.

SHAHAB, QUDRATULLAH

TRANSLATIONS

3340   "Maaji". Trans. Salma Mahmud. In: *Modern Urdu short stories from Pakistan.* Ed. S. Viqar Azim. Islamabad: R.C.D. Cultural Insitute of Pakistan, 1977, pp. 115-126.

3341   "Mainly autobiographical". Trans. Qaiser Afzal. In: *The Nation* (January 1963) [*Pakistan Writer's Guild Number*], pp. 41-44.

3342   "The pauper". Trans. Qaiser Afzal. *Inspirations* 2, 1 (1963), pp. 17-19.

STUDY

3343   **Enayetullah, Anwar**
"Qudratullah Shahab". *Scintilla* 4 (October 1963-January 1964), pp. 76-77.

SHARAR, ABDUL HALIM

TRANSLATIONS

3344 *Lucknow: the last phase of the Oriental culture.* Trans. E.S. Harcourt and Fakhir Husain. London, 1975.

3345 *Paradise on earth. Firdaus-i Birin.* Trans. Masudul Hassan. Lahore: Ferozsons, 1978. 135p.

SHAUKAT THANVI

TRANSLATIONS

3346 "The good neighbour". Trans. M.N. Khan. *Perspective* 3, 7 (January 1970), pp. 67-71.

3347 "Health is a great curse". Trans. Abdul Qayyum. *Pakistan Review* 18, 1 (January 1970), pp. 20-25.

3348 "Rehana". Trans. M.N. Khan. *Perspective* 3, 3 (September 1969), pp. 57-62.

SHAUKAT USMANI, ALSO KNOWN AS SIKANDAR SUR

TRANSLATION

3349 *Night of the eclipse.* Karachi, 1951. 74p.
Includes eight short stories.

SHIBLI NUMANI, MUHAMMAD

TRANSLATION

3350 *Allamah Shibli's 'Sirat al-Nabi'.* Trans. Fazlur Rahman. Karachi: Pakistan Historical Society, 1970-71. 2 vols.

STUDIES

3351 **Bhajiwalla, Rustom P.**
Maulana Shibli and Umar Khayyam. Surat: Irish Presbyterian Mission Press, 1932. 118p.

3352 **Murad, Mehr Afroz**
Intellectual modernism of Shibli Numani: an exposition of his religious and political ideas.
Lahore: Institute of Islamic Culture, 1976. 135p.

3353 **Rashid, Aisha**
"Shibli Numani: a life sketch". *Pakistan Review* 10 (September 1962), pp. 25-26.

SHIRIN, MUMTAZ

3354 "Awakening". In: *Stories from Pakistan*. Ed. Krishan Gopal Abid. New Delhi: India Paperbacks, 1977, pp. 150-167.

3355 "Awakening". Trans. the author. *Pakistan Quarterly* 1, 5, pp. 29-31, 58, 62.

3356 "Awakening". In: *Contemporary Pakistani short stories*. Ed. and trans. Nisar Ahmad Farooki. Lahore: Ferozsons Ltd., 1955, pp. 167-187.

3357 "Defeat". Trans. S. Amjad Ali. *Pakistan Quarterly* 6, 4 (Winter 1956), pp. 59-65. Also in: *Span*. Ed. Lionel Wigmore. London, 1959.

3358 "Descent". Trans. the author. In: *Under the green canopy*. Trans. Khalid Hasan, et al. Afro-Asian Book Club, 1966.

3359 "Passing clouds". Trans. Shahnaz Hashmi. *Pakistan Quarterly* 11, 2 (Winter 1962), pp. 54-59.

STUDY

3360 "A writer's faith". *Perspective* 1, 7 (January 1968), pp. 9-10.

SIDDIQI, ABDUL RAHMAN

TRANSLATION

3361 "A day in the life of Abdul Basit". Trans. Khalid Hasan. In: *A touch of reality: contemporary Pakistani stories*. Ed. Faruq Hassan. Montreal: Dawson College, [197-?], pp. 116-125.

SIDDIQI, RASHID AHMAD

STUDY

3362 **Lall, Indar Jit**
"R.A. Siddiqui: Urdu essayist". *Thought* 24, 45 (4 November 1972), pp. 15-16.

SIDDIQI, SHAUKAT

TRANSLATIONS

3363 "Behind the wall". In: *Modern Urdu stories*. Ed. and Trans. Agha Iqbal Mirza.
Calcutta: Writers Workshop, 1975.

3364 "The Colonel's ghost". Trans. Qaiser Afzal. In: *The Nation* (January 1963)
[*Pakistan Writer's Guild Number*], pp. 52-54.

3365 "A dog's life". Trans. M. Salim-ur-Rahman. In: *Modern Urdu short stories from
Pakistan*. Ed. S. Viqar Azim. Islamabad: R.C.D. Cultural Institute of Pakistan, 1977,
pp. 147-161.

3366 "God's own country, a chapter from *Khuda ki basti*". *Pakistan Quarterly* 15, 4
(Spring 1868), pp. 89-93.

3367 "Tantiyah". Trans. Abul Khair Kashfi and Janet M. Powers. *Arizona Quarterly*
(Spring 1966).

STUDY

3368 ["Interview with Shaukat Siddiq"]. *The Herald* (Karachi) (January 1985),
pp. 118-121.

TABASSUM, BEGUM

STUDY

3369 **Chandra, P. Agrawal**
"Dreams, schemes and rebellion in the fiction of Begum Tabassum". *Journal of South Asian
Literature* 12 (Spring-Summer 1977), 3-8, pp. 45-54.
An expanded version of a paper read at the annual meeting of the Michigan Academy of
Science, Arts and Letters, Ann Arbor, April 1975.

TUFAN, BRAJ MOHAN

TRANSLATION

3370   "The soap king. Trans. C.L. Revri. *Thought* 10, 33 (16 August 1958), pp. 9-10.

VARMA, SHRAVAN KUMAR

TRANSLATIONS

3371   "Deep as the ocean". Trans. Muhammad Umar Memon. In: *Twenty years of the Urdu short story*. *Indian Literature* 19, 6 (November-December 1976), pp. 188-208.

3372   "The retreat". Trans. Muhammad Umar Memon. *The Nation* (Karachi) (July 1962), pp. 19-20.
Also in: *The Eve* 1, 4 (November 1963), pp. 17-19, 35, entitled "The prodigal returns".

WAJEDA TABASSUM

TRANSLATION

3373   "Used clothes". Trans. B.A. Farooqui. *Urdu Canada* 1, 3 (1987), pp. 57-62.

YAD, MOHAMMAD MANSHA

TRANSLATION

3374   "Kashi". Trans. Jamil Azar. *Under Canada* 1, 3 (1987), pp. 63-67.

YAZDANI, MALIK GHULAM

TRANSLATION

3375   "The exodus". Trans. M.A. Qadri. In: *Ten years of vision*. Ed. Yunus Said. Karachi: Pakistan Publishing House, 1963, pp. 113-123.

YUSUFI, MUSHTAQ AHMED

STUDY

3376 **Farrukhi, Asif Aslam**
"The best place to meet a writer is between the covers of a book: an interview with Mushtaq Ahmed Yusufi". *Newsline* (Karachi) (October 1989), pp. 109-112.

ZAHIR, RAZIA SAJJAD

TRANSLATIONS

3377 "Know her?" Trans. Firaq Gorakhpuri. *Illustrated Weekly of India* (31 May 1964), pp. 19-20.

3378 "Resignation". *The Sunday Standard* (20 December 1964).

3379 "The story of a story". Trans. the author. In: *Modern Indian short stories*. Vol. 1. Ed. K.S. Duggal. New Delhi: Indian Council for Cultural Relations, 1975, pp. 154-159.

PROSE: Anthologies

SHORT STORIES

3380 Abid, Krishan Gopal
Stories from Pakistan. New Delhi: India Paperbacks, 1977. 167p.
Includes works of: Saadat Hasan Manto, Ahmad Nadim Qasimi, Ghulam Abbas, Anwar Azim, Mumtaz Mufti, Hasan Askari, Akhtar Husain Raipuri, Ashfaq Ahmad, Mumtaz Shirin.

3381 Ali, Ahmad
Selected stories from Pakistan: Urdu. Islamabad: Pakistan Academy of Letters, 1983.
Fourteen stories; diverse translators. Many of the translations have been published elsewhere.

3382 Anand, Mulk Raj and Iqbal Singh
Indian short stories. London: New India Publishing Co., 1946. 194p.
Includes works of: Prem Chand, Saadat Hasan Manto, Ahmad Ali, Ismat Chughtai, Ahmad Abbass.

3383 Anis Nagi
Modern Urdu stories from Pakistan. Lahore: Swad Noon Publications, 1982. 129p.
Fifteen stories by fourteen authors, from Manto to Nagi.

3384 Azim, Viqar
Modern Urdu short stories from Pakistan. Islamabad: R.C.D. Cultural Institute, Pakistan, [1977]. 216p.
Includes works of: Saadat Hasan Manto, Ghulam Abbas, Ahmad Nadim Qasimi, Sadiq Hussain, Qudratullah Shahab, Intizar Husain, Shaukat Siddiqi, Ashfaq Ahmad, Khadija Mastur, Hajra Masrur, Anwar Sajjad.

3385 Batra, Satish
New generation 2; an anthology of Urdu writers. Lucknow: New Generation, 1967.
Includes works of: Ramlal, Satish Batra, Harcharan Chawla, Rafia Manzurul Amin.

3386 Duggal, Kartar Singh
Contemporary Indian short stories. New Delhi: Sahitya Akademi, 1959. 132p.
Consists of one story selected from each of the fifteen Indian languages depicting a cross-section of contemporary Indian literature.

3387 *Modern Indian short stories.* New Delhi: Indian Council for Cultural Relations, 1975. 210p. Vol. 1.
Includes works of: Krishan Chandar, K.A. Abbas, Rajindar Singh Bedi, Fatima Ahmad, Razia Sajjad Zahir, Qurratulain Hyder.

3388 Enayetullah, Anwar
This also happened: an anthology of Pakistani short stories. Karachi: Saad Publications, 1986. 197p.
Two Sindhi and sixteen Urdu short stories, with brief notes on individual authors. Most of the translations have been previously published in *Herald* (Karachi).

3389   Farooki, Nisar Ahmad
Contemporary Pakistan short stories. Lahore: Ferozsons Ltd., 1955. 264p.
Includes works of: Akhtar Husain Raipuri, Ghulam Abbas, Hasan Askari, Ali Abbas Husaini, Quratulain Hyder, Saadat Hasan Manto, Mumtaz Mufti, Mirza H. Askari, Nisar Ahmad Farooki.

3390   Faruqi, Ziyaul Hasan
Urdu: an anthology of Indian literature. Ed. K. Santhanam. New Delhi: Gandhi Peace Foundation, 1969.

3391   Gupta, Madan
A bunch of stories. Aurangabad: Parimal, 1982. 230p.
Translated from Hindi and Urdu.

3392   Hasan, Khalid
Under the green canopy. Lahore: Afro-Asian Book Club, 1966. 308p.
Includes works of: Ashfaq Ahmad, Abdul Hamid, Jamila Hashmi, Intizar Husain, Bilqis Jahan, Saadat Hasan Manto, Mumtaz Mufti, Mumtaz Shirin, Ahmad Nadim Qasimi, Anwar Sajjad.

3393   Hassan, Faruq
A touch of reality: contemporary Pakistani stories. Montreal: Dawson College, [197-?].
Includes works of: Saadat Hasan Manto, Ghulam Abbas, Qurratulain Hyder, Ashfaq Ahmad, Abdul Hamid, Ahmad Nadim Qasimi, Masud Mufti, Intizar Husain, Abdul Rahman Siddiqi, Abdullah Hussein.

3394   Hassan, Faruq and Hasan, Khalid
Nothing but the truth: Pakistani short stories. Montreal: Private, 1978. 397p.
Two English stories and twenty-four Urdu stories in translation from Pakistan. An expanded version of Faruq Hassan's earlier anthology *A touch of reality* (Montreal, n.d.).

3395   — • *Versions of truth: Urdu short stories from Pakistan.* New Delhi: Vikas, 1983. 273p.

3396   Hyder, Qurratulain and Khushwant Singh
Stories from India. New Delhi: Sterling Publishers, 1974. 206p.
Some translated from Indian languages, previously published in *The Illustrated Weekly of India.*

3397   Jussawalla, Adil
New writing in India. Harmondsworth: Penguin Books Ltd., 1977. 320p.
Includes works of: Qurratulain Hyder, Balraj Manra.

3398   Khushwant Singh
Land of five rivers. Bombay: Jaico Publishing House, 1965.
Includes works of: K.A. Abbas, Balwant Singh, Rajindar Singh Bedi, Krishan Chandar, Saadat Hasan Manto.

3399   **Khwaja, Waqas Ahmad**
Cactus: an anthology of Pakistani literature. Lahore: Writer's Group Publications, 1985. 112p.

3400   **Mathur, Ramesh and Kulasrestha, Mahendra**
Writings on India's partition. Delhi: Simant Publications, 1976. 247p.
Includes works of: Saadat Hasan Manto, Krishan Chandar, K.A. Abbas, Rajindar Singh Bedi.

3401   **Milton, Daniel L. and Clifford, William**
A treasury of modern Asian stories. New York: New American Library, 1961.

3402   **Mirza, Aghal Iqbal**
Modern Urdu stories. Calcutta: Writers Workshop, 1975. 94p.
Includes works of: Salim Akhtar, Rafia Manzurul Amin, Rasheed Amjad, Rajindar Singh Bedi, Krishan Chandar, Masud Mufti, Ahmad Nadim Qasimi, Shaukat Siddiqi.

3403   *The Nation* (January 1963) [*Pakistan Writer's Guild Number*], Trans. Qaisar Afzal. 88p.
Includes works of: Qudratullah Shahab, Akhtar Husain Raipuri, Ghulam Abbas, Shaukat Siddiqui, Ahmad Nadim Qasimi, Hajra Masrur, Intizar Husain.

3404   **Ratan, Jai**
Contemporary Urdu Short Stories: an anthology. New Delhi: Sterling Publishers, 1991. 219p.
Includes works of: Prem Chand, Saadat Hasan Manto, Rajindar Singh Bedi, Krishan Chandar, Mumtaz Mufti, Ismat Chughtai, Ahmad Nadim Qasimi, Ghulam Abbas, Balwant Singh, Qurratulain Hyder, Ashfaq Ahmad, Intizar Husain, Khalida Hussain, Ramlal, Joginder Paul, Anvar Sajjad, Jeelani Bano, Harcharan Chawla, Surendra Prakash, Iqbal Majid, Mansha Yad, Salaam Bin Razaq, Rasheed Amjad, Zahida Hina, Salim Agha, Qazalbash Sultan, Jamil Nasim.

3405   — • *Modern Urdu short stories*. New Delhi: Allied Publishers, 1987. 200p.

3406   **Said, Yunus**
Ten years of vision. Karachi: Pakistan Publishing House, 1963. 338p.
Includes works of: Ahmad Ali, Akhtar Husain Raipuri, Ghulam Abbas, Ibne Said, Saadat Hasan Manto, Malik Ghulam Yazdani.

3407   **Shah, Sirdar Iqbal**
The golden treasury of Indian literature. London, 1983. 293p.

3408   *Selected short stories from Pakistan*. Intro. and notes by Ahmad Ali. Islamabad: Pakistan Academy of Letters, 1983. 234p.
Includes biographical notes on authors, pp. 231-234.

3409   *Twenty years of the Urdu short story*. *Indian Literature* 19, 6 (November-December 1976).
Includes works of: Qurratulain Hyder, Anwar Azim, Intizar Husain, Anwar Sajjad, Balraj Manra, Khalida Asghar, Abdullah Hussein, Muhammad Umar Memon, Surendar Prakash, Ahmad Hamesh, Shravan Kumar Verma, Iqbal Majid.

3410   **Welch, John**
Stories from South Asia. Oxford: Oxford University Press, 1988. 170p.
Includes prose and poetry of different Indian languages.
Includes works of: Surendra Prakash.

PROSE

History and Criticism

3411 **Abdullah, S.M.**
Urdu prose. Lahore: Muhammad Ashraf, 1940. 186p.

3412 — • *The spirit and substance of Urdu prose under the influence of Sir Sayyid Ahmad Khan*. Lahore, 1940.

3413 **Anjum, A.R.**
Conspectus: articles on Pakistani themes and some literary essays. Lahore: Arsalan Publications, 1979. 126p.

3414 **Ansari, M.A., and Ansari, D.**
Chrestomathie der Urdu-Prosa des 19. und 20. Jahrhunderts. Leipzig: Verlag Enzyklopädie, 1965. 139p.

3415 **Chughtai, Ismat**
"The heroine in Urdu fiction". *Asian Horizon* (London) 1, (Summer 1948), pp. 36-43.

3416 **Das, Veena**
"The structure of marriage preferences: an account from Pakistani fiction". *Man* 8, 1 (March 1973), pp. 30-58.

3417 **Enayetullah, Anwar**
"Urdu's answer to Mills and Boon?". *The Herald* (Karachi) (July 1983), pp 89-90. Popular romances in Urdu.

3418 **Faruqi, Khwaja Ahmad**
"Contemporary prose style in Urdu". *Indian P.E.N.* 26 (August 1960), pp. 231-235.

3419 **Faruqi, Muhammad Hamza**
"Reflections of the war of 1857 in contemporary prose". *Journal of the Research Society of Pakistan* 22, 4 (October 1985), pp. 15-29.

3420 **Khan, A.G.**
"Reality in contemporary Urdu, Marathi and American fiction". In: *Essays on comparative literature and linguistics*. Ed. G.S. Amur. New Delhi: Sterling, 1984, pp. 151-158.

3421 **Khundmiri, S. Alam**
"Recent Urdu writing". *Indian Writing Today* 1, 1 (July-September 1967), pp. 78-85.

3422 **Kumar, Sukrita Paul**
"'Modernism' in Urdu fiction: a discussion with Mohammad Ali Siddiqui". *Urdu Canada* 1, 2 (1986), pp. 19-25.

3423 "Modernity in Urdu fiction: an interview with Wazir Agha". *Urdu Canada* 1, 2 (1986), pp. 13-18.

3424   Naim, C.M.
Readings in Urdu: prose and poetry. Honolulu: EWCP, 1965. 396p.

3425   Narang, Gopi Chand
Urdu: reading in literary Urdu prose. Madison: Published for the Department of Indian Studies by the University of Wisconsin Press, 1968 (ie. 1969), 382p.

3426   Rahman, Salimur
"The big mix-up: *Fasana-i Azad* after a hundred years". *The Pakistan Times, Magazine Section* (19 December 1980).

3427   Rais, Qamar
"Modern Urdu fiction and the new morality". *Indian Literature* 21, 5 (September-October 1978), pp. 69-75.

3428   Rauf, Abdur
"Sab-ras, the first specimen of literary Urdu prose". *Calcutta Review* 165 (November 1962), pp. 112-122.

3429   Sud, Kedar Nath
"The origins of Urdu fiction". *Thought* 20, 11 (16 March 1968), pp. 14-15.

3430   Sukhochev, A.S.
Ot dastanak romanu is istoric khudozhestvennă rozy. Moscow: Nauka, 1971.

3431   Tahsin, Mir M.H.A.K.
"Sayyad Sajjad. An early prose-writer of modern Urdu". *Islamic Culture* 13, 1 (1939), pp. 60-75.

NOVEL

3432   Ahmad, Jalaluddin
"The modern Urdu novel". *Pakistan Quarterly* 4 (August 1950), pp. 47-50.

3433   Anderson, David D.
"Ahmad Ali and *Twilight in Delhi*: the genesis of a Pakistani novel". *Mahfil* 7, 1-2 (1971), pp. 81-86.

3434   Butt, Nisar Aziz
"Urdu novel in perspective". *Pakistan Quarterly* 13, 1 (Spring 1965), pp. 44-49.

3435   Issar, Davendra
"The Urdu novel". *Century* 3, 4 (12 June 1965), pp. 1-12.

3436   Naqvi, S.A.H.
"An early woman novelist of Urdu (Muhammad Begum)". *Perspective* (Karachi) 3 (June 1970), pp. 59-60.

3437　**Rahman, Munibur**
"Political novels in Urdu". *Contributions to Asian Studies* 6 (1975), pp. 140-53.

3438　**Rajan, P.K.**
The growth of the novel in India, 1950-1980. New Delhi: Abhinav Publications, 1989. 152p.

3439　**Russell, Ralph**
"The development of the modern novel in Urdu". In: *The novel in India.* Ed. T.W. Clark. London: George Allen and Unwin Ltd., 1970, pp. 102-141.

3440　— • "The rise of the modern novel in Urdu". *New Orient* 7, 2 (April 1968), pp. 33-39.

3441　**Suhrawardy, S.A.B.**
Critical survey of the development of the Urdu novel and short story. London: Longmans, 1945. 316p.

3442　**Zaman, Mukhtar**
"The Urdu novel". *Pakistan Quarterly* 15, 4 (Spring 1968), pp. 82-88.

3443　**Zeno**
"The resurrection of the Urdu novel". *The Herald* (Karachi), June 1983, pp. 84-87.

SHORT STORIES

3444　**Ahmad, Jalaluddin**
"The Urdu short story in Pakistan". *Pakistan Quarterly* 2, 2 (Spring 1952), pp. 44-47, 60.

3445　**Alvi, Husain Musheer**
"The new Urdu short story". *New Generation* (Lucknow) 2 (1967), pp. 78-82.

3446　**Anderson, David D.**
"New insight in the Pakistani short story". *University College Quarterly* (East Lansing, Michigan) 12, 3, pp. 3-40.

3447　**Azam, Ikram**
Plays and stories. Rawalpindi: Nairang-e-Khayal Publications, 1985. 247p.

3448　**Azim, Anwar**
"Contemporary Urdu short story". *Indian Literature* 19, 6 (November-December 1976), pp. 7-22.

3449　**Coppola, Carlo**
"The Angare group: the enfants terribles of Urdu literature". *Annual of Urdu Studies* 1 (1981), pp. 57-69.

3450 Hashmi, Nasiruddin
"Muslim women story writers of India and Pakistan". *Islamic Review* 39, 1 (1951), pp. 32-36.
Brief discussion of twenty-two female Muslim writers.

3451 Husain, Intizar
"Emotions run riot". *Frontier Post* (Lahore) (August 1990).
Reprinted in *The Daily Jang* (London) (15-16 September 1990).
Review of Shabana Mahmud's *Angare ek jaiza*.

3452 Iyengar, K.R. Srinivasa
"Contemporary Indian short story". *Indian Literature* 13, 3 (1970), pp. 36-44.
Discusses Urdu with reference to Rajinder Singh Bedi's work.

3453 Khan, Khalique A.
"Urdu short stories". *Perspective* 4, 4 (October 1970), pp. 87-90.

3454 Khullar, K.K.
"Fasana in Urdu". *Thought* 23, 10 (6 March 1971), pp. 13-16.

3455 — • "The 'Fasana' in Urdu". Letter to the Editor. *Thought* 23, 18 (1 May 1971), p. 12.

3456 Kumar, Sukrita Paul
"The cognition of the self: a critical review of some post independence Hindi and Urdu short stories". In: *Comparative literature: theory and practice*. Ed. Amiya Dev and Sisir Kumar Das. New Delhi: Allied Publishers, 1988.

3457 Mahmud, Shabana
"*Angare*: Urdu literature and the founding of the Progressive Writers Association". *Modern Asian Studies* (in press, 1992).
Abridged English version of the Introduction to the *Angare ek jaiza*.

3458 Mehdi, Baqar
"Twenty years of the Urdu short story". *Indian Literature* 19, 6 (November-December 1976), pp. 23-50.

3459 Moazzam, Anwar
"Modern Urdu short story". *India Writing Today* 2, 2 (April-June 1968), pp. 65-70.

3460 Narang, Gopi Chand
"Major trends in the Urdu short story". *Indian Literature* 16, 1-2 (January-June 1973), pp. 113-132.

3461 Oesterheld, Christina
The concept of the hero in the contemporary Indian Urdu short story. Heidelberg: South Asia Institute (in press, 1992).

3462 Paul, Joginder
"The contemporary Urdu short story". *Indian Writing Today* 5, 2 (April-June 1971), pp. 82-89.

3463 Ramlal
"New Urdu short story". *Contemporary Indian Literature* 6, 5 (May 1966), pp. 18-20.

3464 Said, Taj
"Urdu story writers of Peshawar". *Scintilla* 4 (April 1963), pp. 82-84.

3465 "Twenty years of the Urdu short story". *Indian Literature* 19, 6 (November-December 1976).

DRAMA

Individual Authors

BIBLIOGRAPHY

3466   **Khaliq, Muhammad**
An annotated bibliography of Hindi and Urdu dramas. New Delhi: Idarah-i Talim-o-Taraqqi, Jamiah-i Milliyah-i Isamiya, 1959. 61p.

3467   **Mehta, C.C.**
Bibliography of stageable plays in India languages. Pt 1. New Delhi, 1963. 292p.
Covering Gujarati, Hindi, Kashmiri, Marathi, Punjabi, Sanskrit, Telegu, and Urdu languages.

AGHA HASAN "AMANAT"

TRANSLATION

3468   *Die Indarsabha des Amanat. Neuindisches Singspiel in lithographischem Original text mit Übersetzung und Erklärungen sowie einer Einleitung über das hindustanische Drama,* von Friedrich Rosen. 2 pts. Leipzig: F.A. Brockhaus, 1892.

STUDIES

3469   **Hill, Brad Sabin**
Indra Sabha: an Urdu fairy-tale in Hebrew character transcription. London: Valmadonna Trust Library, 1993. [in preparation].
Includes a facsimile of the lithograph and the illustrated manuscript (Calcutta, 1880 and 1887).

3470   **Zaidi, Mujahid Husain**
"Indar sabha of Amanat in the context of Lucknow culture: the first Urdu drama". In: *Proceedings of the 7th European Conference on Modern South Asian Studies (London, July 1981).*

MUINUDDIN, KHWAJA

STUDY

3471   **Enayatullah, Anwar**
"Khwaja Moinuddin: a great play-wright". *Perspective* 5, 6 (December 1971), pp. 39-44.

TAJ, IMTIYAZ ALI

TRANSLATION

3472   "Anarkali: an historical drama".   Trans. S. Amjad Ali.   *Pakistan Quarterly* 17, 3 (Autumn 1970), pp. 90-91; 17, 4 (Winter 1970), pp. 123-127.
Select excerpts only.

STUDIES

3473   **Iftikhar, M.**
"Syed Imtiaz Ali Taj". *Pakistan Review* 19, 6 (June 1971), pp. 36-37.
Also in: *Pakistan Review* 18, 6 (June 1970), pp. 6-8.

3474   **Qadir, A.**
"Syed Imtiaz Ali Taj: a pioneer in modern Urdu drama".   *Perspective* 4, 10 (April 1971), pp. 35-37.

DRAMA

History and Criticism

3475 **Abdul Qadir, Shaikh**
"Literature and drama; Urdu". In: *Modern India and the west; a study of the interaction of their civilizations.* Ed. L.S. O'Malley. London: Oxford University Press, 1941, pp. 522-534.

3476 **Ali, Abdullah Yusuf**
"The modern Hindustani drama". *Essays by diverse hands* 35 (London, 1917), pp. 79-99.

3477 **Enayetullah, Anwar**
"Theatre in Pakistan". *Pakistan Quarterly* 12, 4 (Autumn 1964), pp. 54-59.

3478 **Garcin de Tassy, Joseph Héliodore Sagesse Vertu**
Analyse d'un monologue dramatique indien [entitled *Duwazdah mansah*]. Paris, 1850. 23p. Also in: *Journal Asiatique* 4, 16 (1850), pp. 310-.

3479 **Hasan, Mohammed**
"Contemporary Urdu drama". In: *Drama in modern India.* Ed. K.R. Srinivasa Iyenger. Bombay, 1961, pp. 143-147.

3480 **Marek, Jan**
"The impact of Islamic culture on Urdu drama". *Die Welt des Islams* 23-24 (1984), pp. 117-28.

3481 **Mohyeddin, Zia**
"The Urdu theatre". *Pakistan Quarterly* 7, 4 (Winter 1957), pp. 30-35.

3482 **Qureshi, A.**
"Origin and evolution of Urdu drama". *Pakistan Review* 8 (January 1960), p. 15.

3483 **Rizvi, Syed Masood Hasan**
"Urdu drama and our stage". *Indian Literature* 3, 1-2 (October 1959-March 1960), pp. 138-140.

3484 **Shaida, Rajendra Nath**
"Urdu drama". In: *Indian Drama.* 1956, pp. 114-120.

3485 **Suvorova, Anna**
U istokov novoindiiskoĭ drami. Moscow: Nauka, 1985.

3486 — • *V poiskakh teatra.* Moscow: Nauka, 1988.

3487 **Tahir, Naeem**
"The theatre in Pakistan". *Pakistan Quarterly* 17, 3-4 (Autumn-Winter 1970), pp. 45-66.

3488 **Zahir, Sajjad**
"Urdu drama". *Indian Literature* 1, 2 (April-September 1958), pp. 139-144.

DASTAN

Individual Authors

AMIR HAMZAH

TRANSLATION

3489 *The Amir Hamza. An oriental novel ...* Trans. from the Hindustani version of the Persian original by Sheikh Sajjad Hosain. Calcutta: Globe Printing Works, 1892. Pt. 1.

STUDY

3490 **Pritchett, Frances W.**
The romance tradition in Urdu adventures from the dastan of Amir Hamzah. New York: Columbia University Press, 1991.

AZIZUDDIN AHMAD

TRANSLATION

3491 *The fruit of honesty.* Mirzapur: Legal Rembrancer Press, 1887. 148p.

BAGH O BAHAR

TRANSLATIONS

3492 *The Bagh o Bahar.* Trans. Bawa Chhajju Singh. Lahore: Rai Sahib Munshi Gulab Singh and Sons, 1904. 166p.

3493 *Bagh o Bahar.* Trans. Duncan Forbes. London, 1859. 135, 124p.
Includes Urdu text in roman characters; complete glossary.

3494 *Bagh o Bahar; consisting of the adventures of the four dervesh, and of the King Azad Bakht, in the Hindustani language by Mir Amman of Dihli.* Trans. Duncan Forbes. London: Wm. H. Allen and Co., 1859.
Includes Hindustani text in Roman characters and a vocabulary of words occuring in the text.

3495 *Bagh o Bahar, a translation into the Hindoostanee tongue of the celebrated Persian tale entitled "Aissa Chuhar Durwesh",* by Meer Ummun, under the superintendence of J. Gilchrist. Calcutta, 1804.

[Another ed.] Delhi; 1876.

3496　*The Bagh o Bahar; or, The garden and the spring: being the adventures of King Azad Bakht and the four derweshes: literally translated from the Urdu of Mir Amman of Dihli.* With copious notes and an introductory preface by Edward B. Eastwick. Hertford: Stephen Austin, 1852.

3497　*Bagh o Bahar: le jardin et le printemps. Pöeme hindoustani traduit en français.* Trans. from the Urdu version of Mir Amman by Garcin de Tassy. Paris, 1878.

3498　*The Bagh o Bahar* ... Trans. W. Quentin. Calcutta: Baptist Mission Press, 1901. 190p.

3499　*The Bagh o Bahar. For the examination of military officers and others by the higher and lower standards.* 2nd ed. Calcutta, 1902. 379p.

3500　*Bagh o Bahar; in the Hindustani language by Mir Amman of Dihli, ...* London, 1859.
Hindustani in Roman characters. Includes a vocabulary compiled by Duncan Forbes of all the words occuring in the work.

3501　*Bagh o Bahar* ... Ed. M. Williams. London, 1859.
Hindustani in Roman characters with notes, and an introductory chapter on the use of the Roman character in Oriental languages.

3502　*The chahar darbes; being the story of the four monks.* Trans. Basudeba Tripathee. Calcutta, 1900. 178p.

3503　*Selections from the Bagh o Bahar ... A new edition, with each word written in the Roman character immediately under the corresponding word in the Urdu, with a literal English translation at side of each page ...* Trans. J.F. Baness. Calcutta: W. Newman and Co., 1877. 249p.
Accompanied by a perfect key to pronunciation.

3504　*Selections from the Prem Sagar and Bagh o Bahar. For the examination of Military Officers by the Higher standard.* Trans. Adalat Khan. Calcutta, 1881. 399p.
First published 1877.

3505　*The stories of the Bagh o Bahar. Being an abstract from the original text.* Trans. Edith F. Parry. London: Wm. H. Allen and Co., 1890.

3506　*The tale of the four durwesh, ...* Translated from the Hindustani version of Mir Amman by Lewis Ferdinand Smith. Calcutta: Oriental Lithographic Press, 1813. 295p.

[Another ed.] with notes by the translator and appendix containing four letters by the same on Asiatic manners and customs. Madras: Carnatic Library Press, 1825. 248p.

3507　*The tale of the four durwesh.* Trans. Lewis Ferdinand Smith. Ed. Katherine Diehl. Calcutta: Oxford and IBH Publishers and Co., 1970. 313p.

STUDIES

3508　**Inayatullah, Shaikh**
"Amman, Mir".　In: *Encyclopaedia of Islam* 1 (1960), pp. 430.

3509　**Ranking, George Spiers Alexander**
Annotated glossary to the Bagh o Bahar ...　Calcutta: Thacker, Spink and Co., 1902.　2 pts.

HUSAIN, ZAKIR

TRANSLATIONS

3510　*Abu Khan's goat and other stories*.　Trans. Radhey Mohan.　New Delhi: Indian Publications, 1974.　40p.
A publication sponsored by Dr Zakir Husain Educational and Cultural Foundation, New Delhi.

3511　*Fables and stories*.　Trans. Radhey Mohan.　New Delhi: Indian Publications, 1974. 39p.

3512　*The tortoise and the hare*.　Trans. Khushwant Singh.　New Delhi: National Book Trust, 1970.　41p.

STUDIES

3513　**Ahluwalia, B.K.**
Zakhir Husain: a study.　New Delhi: Sterling Publishers, 1971.　127p.

3514　**Mohan, Radhey**
Dr. Zakir Husain as I saw him.　New Delhi: Indian Publications, 1974.　215p.
Includes memorial essays by many contributors and excerpts from Dr. Zakir Husain's own writing.

3515　**Mujeeb, Muhammad**
Dr. Zakir Husain; a biography.　New Delhi: National Book Trust, 1972.　248p.

3516　**Noorani, A.G.**
President Zakhir Husain: a quest for excellence.　Bombay: Popular Prakashan, 1967.　128p.

3517　**Trivedi, H.N.**
Dr. Zakir Husain; a special issue in his memory.　Bombay: Industrial Advertisers, 1970. 102p.

3518　**Zahir, Sajjad**
"Dr. Zakir Husain".　*Contemporary Indian Literature* 9, 4 (April 1969), pp. 5-6.

IKHWANU-S-SAFA

TRANSLATIONS

3519 *An English translation of Akhwa-noos-safa.* Trans. from the Hindustani version of Ikram Ali by Moonshee Syed Hoosain. Madras: Military Male Orphan Asylum Press, 1855. 104p.

3520 *Ikhwanu-s-safa; or Brothers of purity.* Trans. from the Hindustani version of Ikram Ali by John Platts. London: Wm. H. Allen and Co., 1869.

3521 *Ikhwanu-s-safa; or Brothers of purity.* Trans. from the Hindustani by J. Dowson. London, Edinburgh [printed], 1869.

3522 *The Ikhwan-oos-suffa.* Trans. from the Hindustani version by Thomas Philip Manuel. Calcutta: D'Rozario and Co., 1860. 42p.
Includes a vocabulary of the difficult words and phrases occuring in the text.

3523 *The Ikhwan-us-suffa.* Trans. from Ikram Ali's Hindustani version of the Arabic tales by Joseph Wall. Lucknow, Reprinted at the Newul Kishore Press, 1889.

3524 *Les Animaux, extrait de Tuhfat Ikwan Ussafa (Cadeau des frères de la pureté),* traduit d'après la version hindoustanie par M. Garcin de Tassy. Paris, 1864. 118p.

STUDY

3525 **Manuel, Thomas Philip**
A complete vocabulary to the Ikhwan-oos-suffa; with etymological illustrations of ... difficult words. Calcutta, 1862. 23p.

IZZAT ALLAH, BENGALI

TRANSLATIONS

3526 *Abrégé du roman hindoustani intitulé la Rose de Bakawali.* Trans. Garcin de Tassy. Extrait du Nouveau *Journal Asiatique.* Paris, 1835. 193, 388p.

3527 *Gul-e Bakavali.* Trans. R.P. Anderson. Delhi, 1851.

3528 *Gul-e Bakawuli.* Trans. Thomas Philip Manuel. Allahabad: National Press, 1901. 136p.
Translated into English prose and verse, with a vocabulary.

3529 *Gul-e Bakawoli.* 2nd ed. Trans. Bawa Chhajju Singh. Lahore, 1895. 130p.

3530 *The rose of Bakawali.* In: *A group of eastern romances and stories.* Ed. W.A. Clouston. 1889.
An English version compiled from Garcin de Tassy's French abridgement and Thomas Philip Manuel's English translation of Nihal Chand's Hindustani version of the Persian original of Izzat Allah.

STUDY

3531 **Garcin de Tassy, Joseph Héliodore Sagesse Vertu**
"La doctrine de l'amour ou Taj-ulmulk et Bakawali, roman de philosophie religieuse par Nihal Chand de Delhi, traduit de l'hindoustani par M. Garcin de Tassy". *Revue de l'Orient,* Paris, 1858.

KHWUSH-DIL

TRANSLATION

3532 *The adventures of a sepoy. Kissah i sipahi-zadah.* Trans. M.L. Dube. Agra: Rashid Press, 1892. 24p.

MIR AMMAN - see entries under the title BAGH O BAHAR

NAKHSHABI

TRANSLATIONS

3533 *The tota kahani; or tales of a parrot.* Trans. from Saiyid Haidar Bakhsh's Hindustani version of Muhammad Qasim's Persian abridgement of Nakhshabi's *Tuti nama* by George Small. London, 1875. 240p.

3534 *The tota kahani; or tales of a parrot.* Trans. Duncan Forbes. London: Wm. H. Allen and Co., 1852. 146p.
Includes Urdu text with full glossary.

TAHSIN AL-DIN

TRANSLATIONS

3535 *Kama-rupa and Kama-latha.* *A most interesting and captivating Indian love-tale.*
Calcutta, 1889. 73p.
An abridged English version of the Hindustani *Kissah i Kamrup o Kala* of Tahsin al-Din.

3536 *Les aventures de Kamprus.* *Qissah-i Kamrup o Kala.* Texte hindoustani [and
vocabulary] romanisé d'après l'édition de M. Garcin de Tassy, par M. l'abbé Bertrand.
Paris, Versailles [printed], 1859.

DASTAN

History and Criticism

3537 Ahmad, Aziz
"Hikaya. Urdu". In: *Encyclopaedia of Islam* 3 (1971), pp. 375-376.

3538 Clouston, William Alexander
A group of eastern romances and stories from the Urdu, Persian and Tamil. Trans. Edward Rehatsek, et al. Glasgow, privately printed, 1889. 586p.

3539 Crooke, William
The popular religion and folkore of northern India. 2nd. ed. Delhi: Munshiram Manoharlal, 1896. 2 vols.

3540 Dekhtyar, A.
Problemi poetiki dastanov urdu. Moscow, 1979.

3541 Hansen, Kathryn
"Urdu folklore and the qissa". *Annual of Urdu Studies* 7 (1990), pp. 111-116.
Review of Frances W. Pritchett's *Marvelous encounters: folk romance in Urdu and Hindi.*

3542 Islam, Mazharul
A history of folktale collections in India, Pakistan and Bangladesh. 2nd enl. ed.
Calcutta: Panchali, 1982. 260p.
Revision of the author's Ph.D. thesis, Indiana University, 1963.
Bibliography: pp. 218-246.

3543 Pritchett, Frances W.
"The dastan revival: an overview". *Annual of Urdu Studies* 7 (1990).

3544 — • "Kaukab's magic powers: strategies for 'Dastan' translation". *Annual of Urdu Studies* 6 (1987), pp. 55-67.
Includes an episode from *Tilism-e Hosruba*, with the original Urdu text.

3545 — • *Marvelous encounters: folk romance in Urdu and Hindi.* New Delhi: Manohar, 1985; USA: Riverdale, 1985. 220p.

INDEX OF AUTHORS

Brohi, A.K. 1929.
Brown, Charles Philip. 235, 286, 288, 746.
Brown, Douglas. 3099.
Browne, Edward G. 39, 1830.
Bruecke, Ernst Wilhelm. 443.
Bryant, Kenneth. 2352.
Brzezinski, Jan. 2875.
Buddruss, Georg. 444.
Bukhari, Suhail 445.
Bukhari, Syed Abdul Wahab. 2567.
Bukhsh, Salauddin Khuda. 1066, 1593.
Bunsi Dhar. 844.
Burnell, A.C. 230.
Burney, Sheila. 1775-1776.
Burney, S.M.H. 1963.
Busher, R.C. 903.
Butalia, Subhadra. 3227.
Butt, Nisar Aziz. 3434.
Butter, R.A. 1917.
Bürgel, J.C. 1930-1931.
Bürgel, Christoph. 1303, 2188.
Bykova, E.M. 505.
Cabaton, A. 26.
Cachia P. 1725.
Calcutta National Library. 89.
Calcutta University Library. 38.
Cambridge University Library. 39-40.
Campbell, Sir George. 547.
Campbell, William Rose. 261.
Campbell, G.L. 720.
Cantiracekaran T. 51.
Carmichael-Smyth, W. 98, 277-278, 329, 849.
Case, Margaret H. 7, 1274.
Catchpole, H. 904.
Chaghtai, Dr Abdullah. 1932.
Chaghtai, Mohammad Ikram. 164.
Chagla, Ahmed G. 1932, 2522.
Chakbast, Braj Narain. 2568.
Chalmurzaev, T. Ch. 446-447.
Chand, Attar. 1594-1595.
Chand, Lala Faqir. 240, 292.
Chand, Nihal. 3521-3522.
Chandar, Krishan. 2322, 2861, 3387, 3398, 3400, 3402, 3404.
Chandola, Anoop. 905, 3228.
Chandra, P. Agrawal. 3369.
Chandra, Sena. 262, 747.

Chandra, Sudhir. 3229.
Chandrasekharan, T. 52.
Chapman, Francis Robert Henry. 263, 748, 906-908.
Chaterjee, Nibaran, Chandra. 909, 1735, 1743.
Chatterji, Nandalal. 448-452.
Chatterji, Suniti Kumar. 329, 453-456, 1067.
Chattopadhyaya, N. 457.
Chaudhary, Mukhtar. 2433.
Chaudhry, Nazir Ahmad. 458.
Chawdhury, Kabir. 1933.
Chawla, Harcharan. 3385, 3404.
Cheema, Pervaiz Iqbal. 8.
Chelyshev, Y. 1596, 3230.
Chhanu Lal Gupta. 291, 610.
Chishti, Syeda Naseem. 2300, 2879, 3165, 3306.
Chitambar, J.R. 161.
Chittenden, John Franks. 249.
Chohan, Zahur Husain. 885.
Chopra, Hira Lall. 1934-1935.
Chowdhury, A.K. 749.
Christopher, C.B. 1936.
Chughtal, Ismat. 2513, 2886, 3382, 3404, 3415.
Clark, T.W. 459.
Clavel, L.S. 1937.
Clifford, William. 3088, 3189, 3211, 3401
Clouston, William Alexander. 3530, 3538.
Codrington, O. 76.
Cohen, Derek M. 2348-2350.
Comrie, Bernard. 551.
Contractor, Minocher K. 460.
Coppola, Carlo. 9, 462, 1068, 1238-1240, 1375, 1417, 1442, 1786, 1788, 2315, 2323, 2426, 2428, 2444, 2447, 2449, 2679, 2880, 2887, 3085, 3092, 3231-3232, 3449.
Court, M. Henry. 1763, 2641.
Courtois, Atwill. 750-751.
Cox, Edward Thomas. 250.
Craven, Thomas. 99-105, 161.
'Critic'. 1597.
Crooke, William. 230, 3538.
Cummings, Thomas Fulton. 463, 910.
Cyprian, Eric. 3002-3003.
Daabla, Basheer A. 3011.
Dabir. 2532.
Dacca University Library. 41.

Mathur, Ramesh. 2719, 2801, 2838, 2849, 3049, 3065, 3096, 3110, 3400.

Mathur, Vijay. 2497.

Matthews, David J. 591, 1153, 2418, 2547, 3015.

Mavi, Baldev Singh. 966

May, Lini S. 2084-2085.

Mazhar. 2547.

M.C. 3111.

M.C. Singh. 592.

McCarthy, Edward. 2086.

McLeod, Alan. 1118.

Meera Ji. 2531, 2549.

Mehal, Muhammad Nazir. 1665-1666.

Mehdi, Baqar. 593, 2310, 2539, 3458.

Mehren, August Ferdinand Michael. 62.

Mehta, C.C. 3467.

Meile, P. 594.

Memon, Muhammad Umar. 1154, 1489, 1625, 1648, 1697, 2087, 2110, 2483, 2632, 2749, 2770, 2901, 2905, 2914-2916, 2918-2921, 2924, 2930, 2932-2938, 2944, 2947-2948, 2953, 2963, 2982, 3036-3037, 3040-3042, 3076, 3131-3133, 3172, 3299, 3371-3372, 3409.

Menon, K.P.S. 2088.

Metcalf, Barbara Daly. 1159, 1228-1230.

Metzemaekers L.A.V.M. 2088.

Meyerovitch, E. 1816, 2089.

Milton, Daniel L. 3088, 3189, 3211, 3401.

Minai, I.A.

Minault, Gail. 595, 1231, 1750, 2489, 2675.

Mir Amman. 2009, 2011.

Mir Hasan. 2527, 2532, 2556.

Mir, Mir Taqi. 2526-2527, 2532, 2547, 2642.

Mir, Safdar. See Zeno.

Mirza, A. Jan. 967.

Mirza, Agha Iqbal. 2758, 2765, 2767, 2807, 2853, 3146, 3284, 3363, 3402.

Mirza, Baldev. 2548.

Mirza, Izhar. 1198.

Mirza, Muhammad Wahid. 2296-2297.

Misra, Mathuraprasada. 125, 818.

Misra, Satya Deo. 1536, 1667.

Misra, Shiv Kumar. 3250.

Missionary Language Board of West

Pakistan. 968.

Mitchel, D. 378.

Mitra, S.C. 302.

Mittal, Gopal. 596, 1155, 2273, 2316.

Moazzam, Anwar. 3459.

Mobbs, Michael C. 597.

Moghni, A. 1668.

Mohammad, Shan. 3020.

Mohan, Indar. 1466.

Mohan, Krishna. 2533.

Mohan, Radhey. 3510-3511, 3514.

Mohan Singh. 2090, 2593.

Mohanty, Jatindra Mohan. 12.

Mohi, S.A. 2394.

Mohiddin, S. Khader. 598.

Mohsin, Mahommad. 1024.

Mohyeddin, K. 599, 969, 1156.

Mohyeddin, Zia. 3481.

Moin, Mumtaz. 3023.

Moin, Shakir. 1098.

Moizuddin, Mohammad. 600.

Molholt, Garrett G. 601.

Molteno, Marian 602, 961, 970.

Momin, Muhammad Khan. 2526-2527, 2532, 2547.

Monier-Williams, Monier. 365-367, 819-820.

Mookerji, M.M. 821-822.

Morgenstierne, Georg. 603.

Morisy, John. 604-605.

Morris, H.E.A. 328.

Morris, J. 180, 303-304.

Mouat, Frederic John. 253.

Mufti, Masud. 3393, 3402.

Mufti, Mumtaz. 3380, 3389, 3392, 3404.

Mughal, Amin. 1324.

Muhamed, Sayed. 606.

Muhammad Abdulghani Sayyid. 823.

Muhammad Ali. 824.

Muhammad Asad Ali. 825.

Muhammad, Hasan Ibn Mushtati Husain. 826.

Muhammad Salih, Mirza. 368.

Muhammad, Shan. 3020, 3024.

Muhammaduddin. 827.

Muhar, P.S. 2091.

Muizuddin, Mohammad. 2092.

Mujahid, Sharif. 2093.

Mujeeb, Muhammad. 607, 1157, 1561, 1669-1671, 3318, 3515.

O'Malley, L.S. 3475.
Oakley, E. Sherman. 977.
Obeyesekere, Ranjini. 3252.
Oesterheld, Christina. 2552, 2925, 2966, 2968, 2985, 3170-3171, 3309, 3329-3331 3461.
Ohala, Manjari. 620.
Olphen, Herman Van. 621.
Orainui, Syed Akhtar Ahmad. 1164.
Ouseley, William. 68.
Pahwa, Thakardass. 978-980.
Painter, T.A. 285.
Pakistan American Culture Centre. 1685.
Pakistan Conference of Linguists. 623.
Pakistan-German Forum. 2124.
Pakistan Writer's Guild. 2553.
Paliwal, D.P. 3266.
Palladin, A.A. 2545.
Palmer, Edward Henry. 58, 369.
Pandey, B.N. 1249.
Pandey, D.P. 2846.
Pandey, Geetanjah. 3253-3255.
Pandharipande, Rajeshwari. 624-626.
Pangal, Abdul Majeed. 1211.
Panwahr, Maherunissa. 1014-1015.
Parker, Nevil. 1468.
Parks, Hedley Charles. 981.
Parnwell, Eric Charles. 185.
Parry, Edith F. 3505.
Parry, Shedden Chalmers St. George Cole. 273.
Parvez, Sallahuddin. 1269.
Pashi, Kumar. 2328, 2533, 2548, 2555, 2599.
Pattanayak, D.P. 91.
Patterson, Maureen, L.P. 14.
Paul, Harendra Chandra. 1686-1687.
Paul, Joginder. 3164, 3404, 3462.
Paul, Krishna. 3157-3158, 3160.
Paul, Stephen C. 186-187.
Paulinus, a Sancto Bartholomaeo. 69.
Pavie, Théodore Marie. 506, 831.
Pearson, J.D. 4, 15, 70.
Peer, Mohammad. 627.
Pegors, Mark. 2802.
Pelikan, Heike, 370, 628.
Penman, Dorothy. 919-920.
Pershad, R. 371.
Pertold, O. 629.

Pertsch, Wilhelm. 71.
Petievich, Carla R. 1255-1256, 2352.
Pezzoni, *Monsignore*. 372.
Philips, H.L. 274.
Phillips, Arthur Noel. 305.
Phillips, A.S. 729.
Phillot, Dougas Craven. 188, 306, 982-988, 2423.
Pickthall, Marmaduke. 630.
Pieterse, Liberius. 228.
Pilaszewicz, Stanislaw. 447.
Pirzada, S.A.A. 2125.
Platts, John Thompson. 126, 190-192, 340, 373, 762.
Playfair, G. 252.
Plunkett, George Tindall. 832.
Poleman, I.H. 72.
Pollock, W. 989.
Polomé, Edgar C. 561, 621.
Pomerantceva, L.M. 175, 199.
Pořizka, Vincenc. 631, 990.
Poulos, Steven M. 2884, 2996, 2998.
Powers, Janet M. 2713, 3293, 3367.
Prabhudasa Dasa. 307.
Prakash, Surendar. 3404, 3409, 3410.
Prasad, Kali. 60.
Prasad, Kashi. 991.
Prasad, M. 308.
Prasad, Nawal Kishore. 632.
Pray, Bruce Raymond. 375, 633-635, 3290.
Prem Chand, Dhanpat Rai Srivastavan. 1165, 3256, 3357, 3382, 3404.
Preussische Staatsbibliothek, Berlin. 73.
Price, William. 368, 376.
Prigarina, N.I. 1166-1167, 1688, 2128.
Pritam, Amrita. 2455.
Pritchet, Francis W. 16, 74, 1168, 1488, 2283, 2357, 2631, 2640, 2694, 2698, 2939, 2987, 3258, 3490, 3541, 3543-3545.
Prithvi-Chand. 992.
Prochnow, J.D. 377.
Pulatova Sh. 1752.
Puri, K.C. 194.
Pyami, Zafar. 2664.
Pybus. 636.
Qadeer, Sufi Abdul. 1568.
Qadir, A. 637-638, 3474.
Qadir, C.A. 1689.
Qadir, Qazi A. 2129.